FORGING DIASPORIC CITIZENSHIP

FORGING DIASPORIC CITIZENSHIP
Narratives from German-Born Turkish *Ausländer*

Gül Çalışkan

UBCPress · Vancouver · Toronto

© UBC Press 2023

All rights reserved. No part of this publication may be reproduced, stored in a retrieval system, or transmitted, in any form or by any means, without prior written permission of the publisher, or, in Canada, in the case of photocopying or other reprographic copying, a licence from Access Copyright, www.accesscopyright.ca.

32 31 30 29 28 27 26 25 24 23   5 4 3 2 1

Printed in Canada on FSC-certified ancient-forest-free paper (100% post-consumer recycled) that is processed chlorine- and acid-free.

Library and Archives Canada Cataloguing in Publication

Title: Forging diasporic citizenship : narratives from German-born Turkish
 Ausländer / Gül Çalışkan.
Names: Çalişkan, Gül, author.
Description: Includes bibliographical references and index.
Identifiers: Canadiana (print) 20220261946 | Canadiana (ebook) 20220261962 |
 ISBN 9780774866118 (hardcover) | ISBN 9780774866125 (paperback) |
 ISBN 9780774866132 (PDF) | ISBN 9780774866149 (EPUB)
Subjects: LCSH: Turks – Germany – Berlin – Ethnic identity. | LCSH: Turks –
 Germany – Berlin – Social conditions. | LCSH: Citizenship – Germany – Berlin.
Classification: LCC DD867.5.T87 C35 2022 | DDC 305.894/35043 – dc23

Canadä

UBC Press gratefully acknowledges the financial support for our publishing program of the Government of Canada (through the Canada Book Fund), the Canada Council for the Arts, and the British Columbia Arts Council.

This book has been published with the help of a grant from the Canadian Federation for the Humanities and Social Sciences, through the Awards to Scholarly Publications Program, using funds provided by the Social Sciences and Humanities Research Council of Canada.

Printed and bound in Canada by Friesens
Set in Futura and Warnock by Artegraphica Design Co.
Copy editor: Robyn So
Proofreader and indexer: Marnie Lamb

UBC Press
The University of British Columbia
2029 West Mall
Vancouver, BC V6T 1Z2
www.ubcpress.ca

I dedicate this book
to my parents,
Muharrem Çalışkan and Şemsi Çalışkan,
and
to my grandparents
Döndü Pınarbaşı, Satılmış Pınarbaşı
Elif Çalışkan, and Halil Çalışkan

Bu kitabı
annem Şemsi Çalışkan,
babam Muharrem Çalışkan
ve
anneannem Döndü Pınarbaşı,
dedem Satılmış Pınarbaşı,
babannem Elif Çalışkan
ve dedem Halil Çalışkan'a adıyorum

Contents

Foreword / ix
ENGIN ISIN

Acknowledgments / xii

Introduction / 3

1 The Model: Being and Belonging Together / 32

2 Constituting Germans and Outsiders / 49

3 Hostility–Hospitality: Accommodating the Ausländer / 85

4 Homesickness–Homelessness: Negotiating
Displacement / 147

5 Borderlands / 198

6 Forging Diasporic Citizenship / 224

Conclusion: Becoming a Chameleon / 279

Notes / 291

References / 294

Index / 316

Foreword

ENGIN ISIN

This book is an invitation to think about diasporicity – both as an irrepressible multiplicity and as a restless movement of people – and the kinds of problems in difference, identity, and belonging to which it gives rise. This invitation – perhaps unintentionally, but certainly irresistibly – draws one into a deep history of the planetary movement of peoples. Where does one start? Does one start one hundred thousand years ago when humans moved out of Africa? Or sixty thousand years ago when humans moved beyond Mesopotamia? Or ten thousand years ago with the first agrarian settlements? Or five thousand years ago with the emergence of organized polities (cities, states, and empires)? Or three thousand years ago with the origins of citizenship as an institution of domination and emancipation? Or one thousand years ago with the emergence of autonomous European cities and urban citizenship? Or five hundred years ago with the European colonization of the planet earth through which settlers conquered, dispossessed, and displaced indigenous peoples? Or two hundred years ago when earth itself was commodified by the restless movement of capital and peoples by extractivism and exploitation? Each moment is a vantage point from which to understand how humans treated peoples in movement, invented bondage, citizenship, kingship, lordship, polity, and slavery with which to govern themselves and others. Each moment is also an expression of how these governing institutions distributed peoples across various positions of domination and emancipation.

The planetary movement of peoples that began two hundred years ago is probably the moment in which we are now both witnesses and agents. This moment involved the conquest of the state by the nation and the eventual partitioning and settling of the planet earth into two hundred such nation-states – each with its own imaginary origin, illusionary unity, and sovereignty imperative. Although we do not know if this moment is more urgent, intense, or massive than any other, it would appear fateful to us as both witnesses and agents.

This pioneering book itself bears witness to a scene that began about sixty years ago with the arrival of Turkish workers in postwar Germany. Although its protagonists are Germans and German-born Turkish *Ausländer* and it examines how their relationship shifted and changed over the years, the book invites us to understand how nation-states governed internal outsiders. It diagnoses a significant failure in this regard but documents possible signs of a new relationship signified as diasporic citizenship.

The book eschews multicultural, multi-layered, differentiated, or cosmopolitan "models" associated with diasporic citizenship while insisting that it is a conceptual and political project of diasporic citizens themselves. It presents a sustained and impassioned effort for understanding the lived experiences of diasporic citizens from the vantage point of their everyday struggles as singularly multiple beings. The book maps these struggles against a complex space of encounters between insiders and outsiders ranging from hostility to hospitality and from homelessness to homesickness. The speaking subjects are positioned in this space of encounters, implicated in strategies and technologies of power, and perform as outsiders demanding to be insiders – but differently. Can this claim work?

This book makes two original interventions. The first intervention is that diasporic citizenship is not a normative or positive model, or a type of citizenship. Rather, it is a performative citizenship brought into being by people who are caught within the sovereignty imperative (us and them) and the categorical imperative (outsiders and insiders) with which nation-states govern pluralities. This is where the author appears at the scene as both a spectator and a protagonist. As a spectator, the author casts a critical eye on the details of the scene where insiders and outsiders shift their positions. As a protagonist, the author herself performs diasporic citizenship: multiply situated, multiply constituted, affectionate, impassioned, and affirmative.

The other intervention is that although diasporic citizenship is documented through German-Ausländer relationships, this book reveals a broader commitment to all those peoples in movement who are caught in

Foreword

relations of domination-emancipation. So, while we are firmly and tightly focused on one national context, we are also simultaneously thinking about many other peoples who are caught in their movements by the sovereign imperative condemning them to various forms of domination and its categorical imperative.

These two interventions bring the reader into a special relationship with subjects whose claims to diasporic citizenship are not merely documented. They enter a dialogue with the author as both a spectator and a protagonist. Throughout the book, diasporic citizens are interlocutors for the author, and indeed for the readers. They ask troubling questions about being outsiders, wanting to be insiders, yet demanding that traversing outside and inside must be performed together (by us and them) and differently (as insiders and outsiders). The readers, the author, and diasporic citizens enter a dialogue to work out what kinds of relationship can be envisaged and inculcated to move beyond sovereign and categorical imperatives, allowing us to embrace this collective moment.

Acknowledgments

Ayla, our now eighteen-year-old daughter, was a little over a year old. I would leave her at home to go to the library, and she would cry: "Anne, don't go dissertation." *Dissertation*, one of her first words, represented that terrible place I went, leaving her behind. My endless comings and goings between Ayla and dissertation have long been concluded, and that place has been transformed into a career for me at St. Thomas University, where my daughter, Ayla, just started a Bachelor of Arts degree as this book is being published. Life has a strange way of coming full circle.

The old family photo in this book's cover art is (left to right, back to front) of my parents, Muharrem and Şemsi; my aunt Hatice; little brother Tunç; my grandmother Elif; and me. The photo was taken in mid-70s, coincidentally around the time that *Gastarbeiter* (guest workers) family unification was at its height in Germany. My family members were not guest workers, but this image could represent any guest-worker family: a typical working-class family of several generations in one household. My grandmother Döndü's handmade rug and my aunt Yeter's lacework have become part of the artwork that represents my extended family. Several images from my passport and visa have also made their way to the cover, representing my fieldwork. This cover art represents both all guest-worker families of the 1970s and my own extended family, which has had such an impact on who I have become. I am grateful for my dear friend Angela Aujla,

Acknowledgments xiii

who contributed the cover art with so much love and sensitivity, and who named the image *Aile, Sevgi, ve Birliktelik* (Family, Love, and Togetherness).

Writing this book has been a cornerstone of my academic journey. It was a journey that started with the belief and encouragement of my parents, Şemsi and Muharrem Çalışkan, who instilled in me a sense of social justice long before I could articulate what that meant, from back in the days when the photo was taken. My little brother Tunç has always been my biggest cheerleader during my journey from Ankara to Fredericton, and the many places in between. Without the unconditional love and life-long support of these people, this journey would have been impossible.

It was not easy to have lost three grandparents, Döndü Pınarbaşı, Satılmış Pınarbaşı, and Elif Çalışkan, along the way. I could not visit them during their last days, nor attend their funerals. But I felt their love always with me, before and after they were gone. A sudden loss during the process was my cousin Can Demir, my always-present green light. I hope they forgive me for not being with them while their journeys on earth ended.

More recently it has been the unwavering love and encouragement of my partner for life Lyle Davidson and that of our daughter Ayla Davidson, which has helped me to enjoy research and writing so much, despite academia's high-pressure demands. Lyle and Ayla have remained my unconditional sanctuary to whom I go back when I need to recharge, even during the times when I take them for granted. I owe ineffable thanks to them both for making so many adjustments to their lives for me.

My deepest thanks go to all the Berliners who shared their stories, experiences, and perspectives. I am thankful to them for their valuable time, honesty, and their enthusiasm for my project; for offering their friendship and making me feel at home during my fieldwork; and for providing expert advice, support, and contacts. Learning about their remarkable accomplishments inspired me more than they can ever know. Whether they agree with all of the interpretations outlined here or not, I want to assure them that I have tried to understand and evoke their lives with care, sensitivity, and thoughtfulness.

During the analysis of the 2003 fieldwork, I received feedback and encouragement from many people. I am truly grateful for the intellectual support and professional guidance of Engin F. Isin. His insistence on excellence inspired me to stretch beyond the limits of my imagination. Ratiba Hadj-Moussa has been a star mentor and friend, whose tactful dedication inspired me to believe in good, committed academic work. Anna Agatangelou offered incisive, constructive critiques that enhanced this project. Sedef Arat-Koç, Michael Nijavan, and Lily Cho graciously gave it a detailed reading that I very much appreciate.

My special appreciation goes to the Center for German and European Studies at York University for providing me with academic and financial support to conduct the initial fieldwork. Mark Webber has mentored me with respect and solidarity. Jeff Peck shaped my research and guided me through it in every way possible. I could not have completed this research without the material support of The German Academic Exchange Service (the DAAD) in 2003 and that of St. Thomas University in 2016.

I am grateful for the support of my colleagues at York University and St. Thomas University. I appreciate the contributions from those communities of scholars – for their insights, intellectual stimulation, and frank criticism that shaped my thinking. I will name only a few of them here. Peter Landstreet, Alan Simmons, and Luin Goldring provided helpful comments and questions that gave me new lenses for considering this book's focus. I received valuable support from the Office of Research Services at St. Thomas University and want to mention two people there, in particular: Michael Dawson offered valuable suggestions on the process of the book proposal, and Peter Toner arranged an in-depth conversation podcast during the final stages of the book.

I am eternally indebted to Janet Webber for her generosity in reading my drafts with me. Her dining table, where we read my drafted chapters, was a sanctuary where my ideas could become well- crafted artifacts. I also want to thank my dear friend Kylie Bergfalk for reading the manuscript and providing thoughtful feedback during the final stages of the 2016 research.

I am eternally indebted to Janine Muller, who provided comradeship throughout this long-lasting research. Her friendship and support kept me going more than she can ever realize. Finding and connecting with Debbie and Will van den Hoonaard and with Janes Ryan has been a most special gift. Our weekly coffee dates have been occasions for mentorship, friendship, and kindness. I also want to mention Tia Dafnos. Our long walks and chats inspired deep reflection. Tia's presence in my life has kept my soul nourished and given me confidence. I am also thankful to my dear friends Şebnem Oğuz, Lina Sunseri, and Karen Roberts, who in different ways offered invaluable emotional support during the writing process.

My eternal gratitude also goes to my friends in Berlin, Neriman Kurt, and Therese Walther – for their friendship; for our discussions over breakfast, coffee, and dinner; and for their excellent advice and insights.

Acknowledgments   xv

I want to thank my research assistants, Hande Gür and Kyle Reissner, for their thorough work during the 2016 research. I would also like to acknowledge my students at St. Thomas University for their enthusiasm whenever I incorporated discussions from this research into their classrooms.

I also would like to thank Brian Griffith for his enthusiasm and the meticulous professionalism he demonstrated while proofreading several publications coming out of this project, as well as several variations of this manuscript. I turned to an editor and gained a friend. Douglas Vipond also helped in copy-editing various drafts of this book with care, generosity, and passion.

Reviewers Ayhan Kaya, of Istanbul Bilgi University, and Oliver Schmidtke, of the University of Victoria, have provided generous and constructive feedback that made a vital impact on the final product.

Megan Brand, production editor with UBC Press, has been the single most important anchor behind the production of this book. Megan made the process absolutely stress free for me after I encountered a major health crisis during the summer of 2021. Since then, she worked with me at my pace, giving my health needs a priority while keeping the project going. She was always there to be my reference, guide, and more. I am forever grateful to her for treating me with utmost care, generosity, and passion, even when I missed many production deadlines.

James MacNavin, senior editor with UBC Press, had a profound impact on the application and revision processes. Thanks also to Robyn So, copy editor; Marnie Lamb, proofreader and indexer; and Gabi Proctor, cover designer, for their attention to detail.

I would also like to acknowledge many other friends and supporters, who are unnamed here, whose positive energy gave me the strength to push forward even when I had self-doubts. Indeed, I had a whole community of supporters to make this work a reality. Even with all this support and encouragement, I remain solely responsible for any errors in this publication.

FORGING DIASPORIC CITIZENSHIP

Introduction

This is the struggle of the people who don't fit or belong neatly.
— Leyla, in 2003

I wish the people who are in their twenties now wouldn't feel the need to say: "Oh, you were born in Türkiye, ha?" or "Is your family also Turkish?" I mean, I wish it wouldn't matter whether they are Turkish or not. I wish this were the case, but I have a feeling it is not.
— Arzu, in 2016

Regulating labour migration is becoming harder and harder in a globalized world. The reaction to the inability to control the movement of labour is a nationalist one. The Castle of Europe is collapsing now. We don't know where this is going.
— Alp, in 2016

After 9/11, there was a curiosity about understanding Islam and the diversity of Muslims. At the same time, there was a critique of US foreign policy ... Theo van Gogh's murder [by Mohammed Bouyeri] in 2004, in Holland, was the turning point. Until then, the Ausländer were Palestinian, Turk, Kurdish, Albanian, and Iranian. On that day, the Ausländer had become Muslims. *The people from Türkiye are now under the roof of the broad* Muslim *category.*
— Erkan, in 2016

The twentieth and twenty-first centuries have been an age of unprecedented mass migrations from non-Western to Western nations, cutting across not only national borders, but also social lines of ethnicity, language, class, and religion. These movements reflect shifts in the global economy, in labour markets, and in the flashpoints of international conflict. The uprooted and transplanted lives of immigrants challenge a range of traditional boundaries. They introduce new forms of belonging and affiliation within Western society. These migrants typically seek both to establish themselves economically and to become full members of their communities. They often aspire to political membership as citizens, but their ties transcend the nation. Especially in larger cities, this unsettling development of diversified citizenship promises to alter the nature of society.

In our existing political systems, diasporic groups commonly articulate their aspirations as claims to group-differentiated citizenship. One image of such citizenship is *multicultural* citizenship (Holton 2013; Kymlicka 1995). Political sociologist Christian Joppke (2002, 245) describes this as "a mechanism to accommodate ethnic, national and other minorities in theory" through coexistence under a common system of social norms. Another image is *cultural* citizenship, which is concerned with "the maintenance and development of cultural lineage via education, custom, language, and religion, and the positive acknowledgement of difference in and by the mainstream" (Miller 2002, 231). A third image is *differentiated* citizenship, which is commonly presented as a politics of difference that rejects traditional inclusion and envisions a political accommodation of differing social systems for each cultural community (Young 2000). A fourth image is *multi-layered* citizenship (Yuval-Davis 1997, 2006, 2013, 171), which involves recognizing individuals' membership in "more than one community and polity – local, ethnic, national, state and cross/supra-state." However, all of these concepts of citizenship share a common limitation. They all presume that intercommunity relations are matters of binary oppositions between inherently different groups of people. Although each of these concepts tries to be inclusive, their visions for citizenship all imply some kind of hierarchy among groups.

The border-crossing people pose many challenges to modern understandings of citizenship, including the various ideas of group-differentiated citizenship. These people challenge the dominant discourses of identity, difference, and belonging – in which the factor of culture (and a particular way of understanding it) is given priority and the functions of power in determining priorities are masked. With the spread of migrant and settler

Introduction

communities across many nations, the Western idea of the homogeneous ethnic nation, and of the citizen as grounded in that identity, has become untenable (if it ever was tenable). The subjects who are driving this point home are diasporic subjects, especially those who were born in the country their ancestors migrated to – they are the ones who do not fit or belong neatly.

German-born Turkish Berliners exemplify many migrant populations who, having crossed a frontier, have entered the realm of diasporicity, or the condition of not fitting and belonging neatly. Being born and growing up as "Others" in Germany locates them in a social margin where the concepts of "us" and "the Other" are called into question. In the Western world's increasingly diverse cities, daily encounters between different people convey messages about their historical roots, their experiences of displacement and Otherness, and the problematic legacy of citizenship. Although they are obliged to define themselves by their Otherness, it is their relatedness to German society that seems to transgress traditional concepts of German (and Turkish) identity and citizenship.

The quotes given above express how not fitting or belonging neatly is an ongoing challenge for these German-born, Turkish-background people and how precarious their place in society can be. Although they may have lived in Germany all their lives, they often find themselves re-labelled as the quintessential Others and treated accordingly. The terms of their membership in society can suddenly change. As they combine German birth and upbringing with "foreign roots," these people are especially likely to challenge traditional assumptions about Germanness. They are living proof that political life now transcends the limits of citizenship in a nation. For them, social belonging is something greater than conformity with a particular cultural or national standard. These transcultural people illustrate the growing need for a new vocabulary to describe political subjectivity. When we look at their experiences, acts, and practices, we can discern the types of language they are forging, as their diasporic subjectivity offers a different type of citizenship.

The quotes that start this chapter also reflect the forces that are forging a new condition of citizenship. This is a condition I call *diasporicity*. Diasporicity involves both a quality of not fitting in neatly and an awareness that comes from a transnational, transborder perspective. Diasporicity is the condition for cultivating a new kind of citizenship that is unsettling our traditional understanding of political membership. This kind of citizenship is a creative response, a mode of critique, and a form of transgression among people whose ties transcend nationality. It is a citizenship of diasporicity – *diasporic citizenship*. Diasporic citizens are engaged in a meaning-making process. They seek to claim full political membership despite and because of diasporicity. Their presence unsettles any type of political membership that presumes a binary opposition between communities. Clearly, diasporic citizenship is a citizenship of Otherness. But how does it reconcile difference and belonging? How does diasporic citizenship express itself in political life?

In this book, I propose a map of everyday social encounters as narrated by German-born Turkish-background Ausländer (i.e., foreigners, outsiders). This map suggests a tension between people's experiences of displacement and the politics of their accommodation. Exploring this world of tension, I reflect on the questions these people raise. To theorize diasporic citizenship, I conduct a narrative inquiry to analyze people's narratives about their social encounters and life experiences. I examine the dynamics of German-born Turkish Berliners' acts and practices as they make claims to citizenship, express the ways they are rooted, and seek to achieve recognition.

This book is a product of story gathering, undertaken with the assumption that stories are political. The people who trusted me with their stories are central in this book. Their stories, however, are woven into themes and informed by a series of conceptual frameworks. Among the main conceptual frameworks that have shaped my research are scholar of Chicana cultural, feminist, and queer theories Gloria Anzaldúa's seminal book *Borderlands* ([1987] 2007); feminist writer and independent scholar Sara Ahmed's theorizing of "strange encounters" (2000); historical and political sociologist and leading name in citizenship studies Engin F. Isin's insights concerning "being and becoming political" (2002a) and performing "acts of citizenship" (2008); and Asian North American and Canadian literary scholar of postcolonial, diaspora, and cultural studies Lily Cho's writings on diasporic citizenship (2007a, 2007b). Other scholars who shed light on my analysis include German studies professor Jeff Peck, whose work explores the complex and ambiguous relationship between German and Jewish culture (1992); political scientist Ruth Mandel (1989, 1990, 2008); anthropologist Uli Linke (1999, 2011); and German studies and comparative literature scholar Azade Seyhan (2000, 2001), whose works explore the relations between Germany and its populations of Ausländer. Finally, political scientist Rita Dhamoon's framework of "meaning-making and identity/difference politics" (2009) greatly contributes to this work's theoretical underpinning.

Then and Now: From "We Belong Here" to "You Could Never Be from Here"

For the initial phase of research for this book, I lived in Berlin for eleven months, in 2002 and 2003, and used a *snowball* method as a recruitment technique, in which I asked the research participants to assist me in identifying other potential subjects. I met with about one hundred Turkish Berliners. Of these, I focused on the forty-seven participants who were born and raised in Germany. These participants have a diversity of cultural, economic, and social backgrounds, with a range of educational levels and political outlooks. I also included people with different gender identities and sexual orientations. My meetings with them combined the features of structured and unstructured interview, and followed a particular method of narrative inquiry (Çalışkan 2015, 2018).

Next, after over a decade of intellectual engagement with the topics of diasporicity and of Germany's relationship with its others, I felt a growing urgency to assess what had changed for the research participants, how they had changed themselves, and whether or how they were creating a more vibrant future for themselves. During the summer and fall of 2016, I conducted video interviews via Skype with twelve of the earlier participants who had been highly informative in my first research effort.[1]

Naturally, there have been many changes in these participants' lives. Most of them got married, and many became parents. Some were less active in social justice issues than before. Also, the participants' stories in 2016 illustrated significant changes in German society. In general, Germany has grown much more diverse than it was in 2003. However, a discursive shift has occurred, from labelling Turkish Germans as Ausländer to calling them "Muslim." This change in how the outsider is constructed mirrors a global change in social and political attitudes – toward greater insularity and desire for exclusion of others. In line with this shift, the participants have found that their encounters with Germans involve increasingly explicit encounters with forms of racism as they negotiate their everyday personal and professional lives. In response, the participants have evolved a stronger, more persistent, and sophisticated social consciousness of diasporicity.

These changes in the German context are strongly connected to global realities. Since 9/11, it has grown increasingly common for Western populist leaders to promote a sense of constant emergency, fear, and suspicion of Muslims in general, and of Muslim immigrants in particular. To justify subjecting visible minorities to targeted policing, certain media outlets, far-right political figures, and populist movement leaders argue that growing threats require greater security measures and stronger social cohesion. In particular, some political leaders have introduced laws to restrict Muslim head coverings and have developed policies for rooting out terrorism. The demands for such measures have encouraged popular attitudes of homonationalism (Haritaworn 2010). For example, in 2004, the French parliament adopted a law prohibiting headscarves in public schools. In 2010, another French law prohibited burkas and other face-covering veils in public spaces. In July 2016, the mayor of Cannes banned the *burkini* on public beaches. These fear-driven policies have indiscriminate effects on whole communities of people who are collectively labelled as threats to society. In Germany, various populations have been lumped together and collectively targeted for extra scrutiny. Both Turks and Arabs have been reidentified as *Muslims* and associated with a globalized entity of *Islam.*

Although Muslim immigrants are not new to Germany or to Europe, the issue of whether Islam can belong in Europe has become much more prominent than when I last spoke with the participants. The global discourse of hatred and fear rooted in 9/11 has become a full-fledged debate among both politicians and ordinary citizens. By 2016, the rise of Islamoracism all over Europe had become a major concern of my participants. Fatma, a social worker, says that the nature of racism has changed: "People have started being Islamophobic openly and without hesitation. But it is a global change too. It is not only in Germany. France is not any different, England is not any different. In Italy, it is the same. And I think it is not toward one race or ethnicity – it is toward religion, I think."

All of this may seem new. Perhaps the globalization of social issues is new, but the response reflects patterns of the past. Alp, a doctoral student of social anthropology, argues that if we want to understand what is happening in Germany, then we need to understand it in relation to the history of colonialism and contemporary globalization: "We can understand anti-Muslim and Islamoracist discourses better if we locate it in European colonial context. This is what we are facing now. This is a result of globalization." Emine Aslan, an anti-racism activist, says (in a media interview) that "Germany has only recently started speaking about its own colonial history There is still no collective memory around German colonialism and how this affects us now" (Sharma 2018, para. 35).

In 2003, the participants described an opening toward non-European cultures. Shortly after 9/11, people wanted to learn about Islam. By 2016, this had changed. As Fatma explains: "They wanted to understand Islam. We had a few projects, like connecting with the mosque, and both foreigners

Introduction 9

and Germans were trying to understand each other. But eventually, they started realizing that Islam is different. All the changes in the world I was telling you about happened. There is now clear fear toward Islam. Now, it is like there is a war between the religions." LGBTI+ activist Erkan's response was similar.[2] When I asked about the interest in understanding the diversity within Islam, he said: "Nope, it is finished. We understood that they are all one and the same!"

In 2003, the participants seemed optimistic. They spoke about how they felt part of Germany, how they were changing what being German means, and how Germany had to accept that. But by 2016, while still claiming Germanness in new ways, they showed a sobered mixture of hope and pessimism. I asked Erkan about the feeling among *Türkiyelis* (people from Türkiye), and his response encapsulated a profound change: "You could never be from here. This is very clear I think." There was a certainty in his voice. It was not pessimism, but an it-is-what-it-is kind of resignation. Erkan discussed his profound disappointment with German feminists and the LGBTI+ community for helping to label Germans of Muslim background as enemies of Western freedoms.

At the same time, these new Germans have continued to push boundaries, to claim that they are part of Germany, and to assert that Germany must reinvent itself to include them. For Alp, this is the main difficulty Germany faces today. Tunç, a devout Muslim and a youth worker, puts it this way:

> There is a new normal in Germany. Children and grandchildren of immigrants are at an equal level with white Germans' children and grandchildren now. But this change is not accepted by white Germans. They have worries and fears. They have to give up the superiorities they have taken for granted. They have to share the resources with Black and brown people and with immigrant children. So [white Germans] are seeking superiority in ethnic roots.

Many of the participants explain the necessity of solidarity-building among the Others of Germany. Alp speaks about the need for building spaces of resistance in collaboration with other racialized groups. They speak of alliances for a different kind of politics, beyond the politics of delimited identity.

This book tells a story of evolving, globalized diasporic communities. The actual experience of my participants demonstrates how the practice of diasporic citizenship is changing what it means to belong in society. The trends I document help to illuminate the emerging realities of diasporic populations everywhere, but these realities can only be grasped in the details of particular people's lives, at particular times and places.

Background of the Case Study

In Germany's past, the right to citizenship was based on *jus sanguinis* (the citizenship of the parents) and not on *jus soli* (the place of birth). Therefore, many foreign-born residents, despite their long residence and work experience, and despite fulfilling their duties such as paying taxes in Germany for many years, were still legally treated as *foreigners*. With a change in the citizenship laws in 2000, the German-born children of foreign-born residents began to automatically receive German citizenship, subject to certain conditions. Residents who had been legally living in Germany for eight years also became eligible to apply for citizenship, on the condition that they demonstrate a good command of the German language, have no criminal record, show economic self-reliance (i.e., they must not be receiving any unemployment or social assistance benefits), and agree to renounce any previous citizenship in another country.

Several of the challenges associated with modern German identity arise, at least in part, from the particularities of the country's recent history. These difficulties include the legacy of the Nazi regime, the postwar repatriation of ethnic Germans from other nations, the Cold War division of Germany into two supposedly hostile states, and the subsequent reunification of these estranged countries. Due to these unusual historical conditions, Germany itself is an example of social and cultural diversity. Many people who are considered German actually regard themselves as displaced people. Berlin has a particular place in this history, as this city was itself physically divided into capitalist and communist zones for decades and then reunited. For this reason, Berliners have experienced an unsettling of citizenship and nationality, which has made their city a socially complex space where many cultures meet and sometimes collide. Therefore, Berlin is "a vibrant sociological site for observing the dynamics of belonging and citizenship within the context of a changing Germany" (Çalışkan 2014, 3).

This once divided and then reunited city is a truly diasporic space. Berlin is Germany's largest city and the second largest in the EU, with 3.77 million people in 2019. It is also one of the most socially diverse cities in Europe. In 2019, over 20.6 percent of the people were Ausländer (foreigners) and 14.4 percent were *Deutsche mit Migrationshintergrund* (German residents with

Introduction 11

immigrant background), who originated from nearly two hundred different countries (Amt für Statistik Berlin-Brandenburg 2020). Thus, Berliners' experience of citizenship and nationality is unsettling. Any examination of this situation must work through the residents' often traumatic, conflicted, and multi-referential experiences.

In the 1960s, people from Türkiye began coming to Germany as guest workers. Since then, they have become a permanent part of Germany and the country's largest minority group. In 2020, ethnic Turks made up 2.76 million of Germany's 21.9 million people of migrant backgrounds (Bundeszentrale für politische Bildung 2021). However, despite their sixty-year history in Germany, Turkish-German people are still defined ethnically, socially, and, until recently, legally as others. The common term for such others is Ausländer, which simply means foreigners. This term may seem to indicate a common non-German identity for all *other people*. However, as political scientist of ethnic and migrant relations in Europe Ayhan Kaya (2012), Mandel (1989), and sociologist Antoine Pécoud (2002) have shown, the Turkish population is itself highly diverse – politically, economically, professionally, religiously, and culturally.

The diversity within Germany's Turkish community has raised a fascinating series of challenges and opportunities regarding the future of German identity and citizenship. As I have argued elsewhere: "Traditional understandings of Germanness, of Germany, and of its nationhood are encountering claims for recognition, both from its Ausländer and from other challenges arising from Germany's own history. Germans increasingly question rigid definitions of nationality, and many of them object to defensive reactions against ethnic diversity" (Çalışkan 2014, 4).

Many other researchers have written about the issues of nationhood, citizenship, exclusion, and cultural politics in the German context. For example, Linke's research (1999, 2011) investigates the aberrant conditions of modernity and global capitalism, and considers how national sovereignties produce borders, subjects, and militarized geographies based on images of Otherness and difference. Linke explores the politics of gender, race, sexuality, and space, and the specific forms of violence (physical, symbolic, judicial) that accompany or sustain the nation-building project.

Kaya's work (2011, 2012) more specifically focuses on how German Turks affiliate themselves with their countries of destination and of origin. Their features of transnational mobility, dual loyalty, and trans-ethnic orientation combine to both challenge and supersede the framework of national citizenship. German Turks constitute a transnational community, which makes it imperative that the existing institutions of citizenship (in both Germany and Türkiye) respond to their experiences and go beyond the framework of dual citizenship. The German Turks' practices of citizenship transcend national borders, but they must comply with the political, economic, legal, and cultural structures in their countries of settlement. They also need to actively engage in the process of political participation, despite the rising sentiment of Islamophobia (Kaya, 2011). The research participants have directly experienced the political and cultural issues that Linke and Kaya examine. The participants' creative responses involve exploring new forms of belonging for a different kind of society.

As the participants in my Berlin research project are Turkish-background adults who were born and grew up in Germany, I refer to them as *German-born Turkish Ausländer*. I emphasize *German-born*, because the fact that they were born in Germany is vital to understanding the challenges they bring to German identity. The term *Germans* traditionally described individuals or groups who were regarded as *ethnic* Germans. In the official statistics, the category of *German* represents people without an immigrant background, or people with two parents of German ancestry. This word, however, does not represent all people who view themselves as German; nor does it include people with a German forebear who came to Germany after 1945, such as the *Aussiedler* ("members of the German people," as defined in the 1953 Federal Law on Expellees, who lived in specified areas east of Germany) or the *Spätaussiedler* (people of German roots who migrated from the former Soviet Union and were born before 1993) (Groenendijk 1997; Takle 2011).

The participants in my study often refer to themselves with the Turkish word *yabancı*, even though they were born in Germany. *Yabancı* has the same basic meaning in Turkish as *Ausländer* (with an ä) in German – foreigner, from outside, or stranger. "Der Ausländer" is singular in nominative form, while *die Ausländer* is plural nominative. This term is generally used in its plural form in the German context. The participants also refer themselves in the plural Turkish form (*yabancılar*). Throughout the book, I use *the Ausländer* without definite articles *der* and *die*, to mean foreigners, outsiders. As my interviews are conducted in Turkish, the participants refer to both themselves and people of other immigrant groups as *yabancılar*. They rarely use *Ausländer*. Yet I use the word *Ausländer* rather than *yabancılar*, because the participants' Ausländerness is prior to their self-definition as yabancı. The term *Ausländer* represents how German society defines them. In modern Germany, this word is an important marker of social identity that shapes most aspects of people's lives.

These group designations, even when used in arguments to support social justice for minorities, can be ambiguous, homogenizing, exclusionary, or overinclusive. Using such designations can seem to reinforce the very social divisions that a writer wants to question. However, I have decided to use these designations because they play significant roles in the dominant discourses of political and social life. These labels of identity are widely used in everyday speech, in the media, and in literature. To examine the complex problems and opportunities embedded in these labels, and to deal with the difficulties involved in undoing their problematic associations, we need to name the labels under discussion.

Conceptual Framework

Multiculturalism

In response to conflictual narratives and continued border crossings, various modern discourses on multiculturalism and pluralism have emerged and matured. Such discourses have applied metaphors such as *melting pot* and *cultural mosaic* for speaking of tolerance, difference, and a shift toward accepting heterogeneous rather than homogeneous national populations. Several Western nations have officially recognized a multicultural understanding of citizenship in response to the aspirations of their diasporic populations. Germany, however, has not adopted such a policy, and the Ausländer of Germany have not experienced the type of multicultural citizenship that is promoted in, for instance, Canada.

Why discuss multiculturalism when the term and policy do not apply in Germany? I do so because comparing ways of accommodating the outsider (Ausländer or immigrant) is crucial for understanding diasporic citizenship. Also, a critical comparison between my German Turkish participants' sense of diasporicity and the policies of multiculturalism reveals that multiculturalism's vision of how outsiders and insiders belong together is profoundly different from what my participants actually experience. Understanding these people's experiences is significant for analyzing the kinds of politics that German-born Turkish Ausländer articulate. In discussing multiculturalism, I refer to liberal multiculturalism, as described in works by political philosophers Will Kymlicka (1995, 2007) or Charles Taylor (1994).

Multiculturalism promises a break from past demands for cultural assimilation and instead proposes to celebrate both diversity and unity simultaneously. According to Kymlicka (1995, 2007) and Taylor (1994), multiculturalism in an expression of the desire to renounce historical practices of discrimination, exclusion, and misrecognition, and to do so in the name of liberal justice and egalitarianism. My questioning of Taylor's and Kymlicka's arguments does not imply endorsement for the ways they have been critiqued in the German discourse on multiculturalism. Instead, I propose that diasporic citizenship differs fundamentally from multiculturalism. These two responses to diversity differ in how they treat issues of power and in how they respond to hybridity among social groups and the encounters between them. Despite the fact that multiculturalism is not officially embraced in Germany, this approach resembles the prevailing German discourse regarding Ausländer and the kinds of hospitality extended to them.

Rita Dhamoon (2009) helps to clarify how theories of multiculturalism conceal issues of power through their various conceptions of culture and diversity. She explains that liberal multiculturalism frames the politics of citizenship as predominantly a politics of culture, thereby mainstreaming the issues of diversity. As a result, the concept of multiculturalism fails to offer a rigorous framework for analyzing the issues of power that surround identity and belonging. Promoters of multiculturalism tend to ignore the politics of diasporicity that German-born Turkish Ausländer articulate through their acts and practices of diasporic citizenship, which involve disrupting and confronting issues of power. For Dhamoon, conventional multicultural analysis masks the practices of domination, oppression, and marginalization between social groups. Such analysis also masks the practices of resistance undertaken by people who are marked as multicultural others, despite being officially included within the rubric of cultural diversity. Actually, Western immigrants commonly make human rights a major focus of their activism, but they typically do so as concerned individuals who cooperate with a variety of social movements.

Dhamoon (2009) suggests that by glossing over the issues of social difference, multiculturalism fails to directly confront the histories and ongoing problems of white privilege, racial domination, class exploitation, marginalization, and discriminatory immigration policies. In that case, analyzing the experiences of Ausländer as a matter of multicultural citizenship may result in simply redefining Germanness, by marking diasporic people as multicultural subjects of the German state. Viewing the Ausländer experience through the lens of multiculturalism tends to obscure unresolved

Introduction 15

issues. Multiculturalism cannot serve as a tool for recognizing how the histories of domination continue to shape the interactions between Ausländer and Germans today.

Multicultural citizenship emphasizes culture as the defining feature of ethnic and national minorities, and then it fosters a multicultural politics focused on claiming rights for these cultural identities. Multiculturalism suggests the coexistence of well-defined, unchanging, homogeneous cultures within one national space. However, as sociologist John Porter (1965) argues, the various cultures are never equal within this framework of cultural diversity. Instead, they are arranged in a hierarchy, with a mainstream culture being superior to the rest. Dhamoon (2009) argues that by narrowly conceiving and overly determining the role of culture, multicultural theory disguises the process of how, why, and by whom certain values are determined to be superior, how these dominant values are resisted, and how the state regulates various modalities of difference.

Even though the word *diversity* may describe a multiplicity of identities, and the affirmation of diversity may signal a well-intentioned stance against prejudice, the multiculturalist understanding of identity has been extensively criticized. As Sara Ahmed (2007, 235) explains, the acceptance of diversity has become a way of treating difference as an abstract concept, or as an essence that exists in the bodies or cultures of others. Literary theorist and author Walter Benn Michaels (2006) observes that the enthusiastic celebration of difference masks and even contributes to neglect concerning the vast and growing economic divisions within societies that celebrate multiculturalism. Diversity offers a false vision of social justice – one that conveniently costs us nothing, while treating culture as a resource owned by individuals, groups, and the state.

In this understanding of cultural diversity, the term *social group* is also problematic. As multicultural citizenship is based on group-differentiated rights, the groups themselves (as defined along ethnic and religious lines) are portrayed as essentially homogeneous groups, between which certain kinds of coexistence and dialogue are desired. Multiculturalism accepts the notion of group-differentiated rights, but it often overlooks the histories of diverse subgroups within ethnic communities.

The context of multiculturalism has also served to promote *multicultural hybridity*, by which groups are treated as "one–other" combinations, such as German Turkish. In such constructions, ethnic and cultural differences are set in contrast to each other. In this kind of multiculturalism, hybridity cannot really be treated as something new, because it is always just a hyphenated combination of pre-existing identities. Therefore, the hyphenated hybridity of multiculturalism cannot inform the language of diasporic encounters or serve as a site of resistance, because it masks the political potential of diasporic hybridity. In actuality, diasporic hybridity involves an active process of subversion, translation, and transformation. By masking the spaces of hybridity, multiculturalism ignores diasporic experiences that involve critical disruption and the confrontation of binary oppositions.

In Germany, it has grown increasingly common to argue that multiculturalism has gone too far, and that it has caused rather than prevented a breakdown of social order and security. However, as Dhamoon (2009, 9) argues, multiculturalism cannot take us far enough. Multiculturalism invites us to imagine that national polity already accepts heterogeneity, so that the actual systems of inequality can be ignored. I argue that the politics of diasporic citizenship involves exposing how these systems of inequality are produced and how they function through the power relations that appear in the everyday social interactions and practices of diasporic subjects. I call these interactions *diasporic encounters.*

In my approach to examining difference, I analyze the content of actual social encounters. I argue that in learning from encounters we can and should go beyond political theorist Bhikhu Parekh's (2005,19) notion of "a democratic dialogue" between various communities or systems of values. We need a more direct understanding of how different cultural groups actually interact. Supposedly, democratic dialogue is the foundation of multicultural accommodation. However, focusing on the actual experience of diasporic encounters is something far different from trying to conduct an intercultural dialogue. Diasporic encounters are tools for revealing, disrupting, and confronting the power relations behind various claims regarding accommodation and interculturality.

Diaspora Studies and Citizenship Studies
According to writer and editor Bibi Bakare-Yusuf (2008), the condition of diasporicity concerns lived experiences and practices that have been rooted in a place, then uprooted and replanted in another place. Diasporic subjects have to be reoriented and remobilized afresh in each new location. Their awareness reflects the social, cultural, and political conditions that emerge from being uprooted and re-routed. In my analysis, diasporicity is a form of awareness that has two significant functions: it unties the intimate relations between culture and Otherness, and it bridges the tension between diaspora and citizenship.

Introduction   17

Diasporicity involves a capacity to see the multiplicity of power relations between citizens and diasporic subjects by looking through the surface of everyday encounters. This kind of awareness involves crossing over lines of identity to see things from several perspectives at once. Diasporicity allows an instant sensing of social situations without conscious deliberation. It involves a sharp awareness that emerges from ongoing dis-positioning and re-positioning in the borderlands between social worlds. Diasporic awareness is a kind of borderland sensitivity. As Anzaldúa explains in *Borderlands* ([1987] 2007, 61): "The one possessing this sensitivity is excruciatingly alive in the world ... Those who are pounced on the most have it the strongest – the females, the homosexuals of all races, the dark-skinned, the outcast, the persecuted, the marginalized, the foreign." Anzaldúa is not referring specifically to German-born Turkish Ausländer, but many of these Ausländer have all of these identities at once. This is why Leyla, a German-born Turkish resident of Berlin, says: "This is the struggle of the people who don't fit or belong neatly."

Both diaspora studies and citizenship studies theorize the political subject as emerging from a complex interplay of relations between people, communities, and nations. Both fields of study involve a critique of binary oppositions, such as colonizer/colonized, West/East (Braziel and Mannur 2003; Tölölyan 1996), and citizen/outsider (Isin 2002a; Isin and Turner 2002; Kaya 2012). Some studies (Isin 2002a, 2002b) criticize both binary opposition and the logic of exclusion. Other studies explore specific ethnic, racial, religious, and regional collectivities and examine the rights and obligations these groups have toward the multiple polities they engage with (Laguerre 2016; Lowe 2003). Contemporary debates in citizenship studies and diaspora studies have successfully challenged traditional assumptions of homogeneity, stability, and fixity in national identity. Yet so far, any interactions between these two fields have been limited, and few critical works have attempted to bring them together. A collaboration between these fields of study has the potential to capture an especially important pattern of relations, because such collaboration can juxtapose *citizenship* with *diasporicity*.

Diaspora studies aim to interrogate "contemporary forms of movement, displacement and dislocation" (Braziel and Mannur 2003, 3). This interrogation involves rethinking concepts of nationhood and national identity through a discourse on postnationalization, denationalization, and decoloniality. At the heart of contemporary citizenship studies is a concern for the process of responding to the rights claims made by various marginalized groups. In such studies, the question of what it means to be a modern citizen follows directly from the question of what constitutes a modern nation. However, the question of citizenship depends on the nation's collective identity only if we assume that the nation is the only valid site of citizenship. How does citizenship change if we assume the diaspora as the site of citizenship?

Diasporic Citizenship

The concept of diasporic citizenship suggests decoupling the notion of citizenship from the nation-state. In the social sciences, the idea of diasporic citizenship has been used to articulate other forms of civic belonging that transcend state boundaries. For political scientist Kim Rygiel (2003, 3): "Diasporic citizenship refers to the multiple and simultaneous participation in citizenship practices within and across nation-state borders." Professor of global studies Michel Laguerre (2016) explains that diasporic citizenship is demonstrated by the ways that Haitian communities in the US have built a civil society that could not thrive within Haiti itself.

Current use of the term *diasporic citizenship* treats diasporic belonging as an extension of the citizenship practices related to the nation-state. This use of the term offers a number of possibilities for thinking about transnational forms of identity and belonging. As sociologist Saskia Sassen (2002) would argue, diasporic citizenship is a pluralization of citizenship: it is denational, postnational, neonational, and transnational. It recognizes both the significance and the inadequacy of the national. Cho (2007a, 2007b) seeks to theorize diasporic citizenship by arguing for an uneasy relationship between diaspora and citizenship. Even so, she defines diasporic citizenship as a kind of group-differentiated citizenship that is similar to multicultural citizenship. She suggests that "in order for there to be equality among citizens, there has to be some forgetting of difference" (Cho 2007a, 105). Also, "the question ... is how ... we can fully embrace the differential forms of citizenship, that the nation engenders" (Cho 2007a, 96).

Cho is right to say that diaspora and citizenship do not fit together easily. Diasporas emerge as displaced collectivities, whereas citizenship is grounded in notions of individual autonomy. The diaspora exists uneasily alongside the nation, and citizenship emerges within the nation. The notion of diaspora challenges the amnesia that nationality and citizenship require, and it introduces a broader dimension of social memory. This inherent tension and dissonance between diaspora and citizenship presents a potentially productive opportunity for thinking through the differential histories

Introduction 19

of dislocation that citizenship involves and for moving toward an articulation of everyday diasporic politics.

I explore diasporic citizenship as a means of embracing our contradictions and possibilities, but I wish to modify the current use of the concept. What makes my understanding of diasporic citizenship different from other concepts of citizenship (such as multicultural citizenship or group-differentiated citizenship) is that I analyze it through the lived experience, perspective, and awareness (i.e., diasporicity) of transnational people. I argue that diasporic citizenship emerges during everyday encounters, in which the *mis-fits* between diaspora and citizenship are negotiated. In these encounters, the focus shifts from cultural difference to power difference. The acts and practices of diasporic citizenship untie the bonds between culture and identity and the bonds between nation and citizen. These acts and practices are not captured by the myth of homogeneity, and they are not (yet) articulated in the literature of diasporic citizenship.

On many levels, citizenship seems indispensable – unquestionably right and good. But acts and practices of diasporicity have the potential to *oppose* citizenship. Diasporicity involves a certain skepticism about citizenship, even when diasporic people embrace it. Diasporants seek relationship but on their own terms of hybridity, heterogeneity, and flexibility. They want the fullness of civic citizenship, but they are resistant and defiant toward pressure to delimit their identities. The relationship between diasporicity and citizenship is close but complicated; it reveals the multiplicity of power axes.

While acknowledging the indispensability of citizenship, I articulate diasporic citizenship in terms of a politics of belonging that go beyond the limited scope of multicultural interpretations, representative democracy, or liberal citizenship. I argue that through investigating the expressions of diasporicity, we can re-examine the politics of dislocation and accommodation. We can see the citizenship of diasporicity as a tension-prone, problematic relation between cultures. This tension allows us to acknowledge diasporicity as a unique basis for rights claims, as it relocates citizenship from the domain of nationality to the domain of diasporicity. I also locate diasporicity beyond the domain of culture. Indeed, my interpretation of diasporic citizenship questions whether the concept of group-differentiated citizenship is helpful at all.

Both citizenship and diaspora remind us that nations are made, not born, and that they are made in crucially inequitable ways. This awareness raises questions regarding the relationship between citizenship and nation. Such questions are apparent in the many contemporary forms of resistance that are led by outsiders, immigrants, First Nations, and others who are deemed threats to the status quo. Diasporicity is cultivated in the productive tensions between these diverse movements of resistance and the assumptions of Eurocentrism. The need for understanding such tensions is urgent.

I am seeking to analyze how enactments of diasporicity respond to contemporary social reality and to unbundle the package of national citizenship. Diasporicity challenges the limits of nationality but does not directly oppose it. It is informed by national borders, but considers other forms of belonging as well, whether they are based on ethnicity, class, race, religion, gender, or sexual orientation. Diasporicity does not exclude or replace nationality. Rather, diasporicity is both national and transnational.

Diasporicity, Culture, and Power

In her theory of identity and difference in politics, Rita Dhamoon (2009) argues that it is necessary to analyze the tensions between identity and belonging without assuming the primacy of culture or, conversely, without dismissing culture. Instead, she suggests that we need to situate specific cultural practices in their relevant relations of power. This discussion requires a more critical reflection on why and how culture gives meaning to, or gains meaning from, the many sites of social difference.

Like in Dhamoon's approach, my theorizing of diasporicity involves viewing culture as changeable and multidimensional, rather than treating it as an object with essential traits. The concept of diasporicity allows us to consider how cultural meanings change and to approach culture as just one dimension in the politics of citizenship. In that context, we can view society with a critical eye, noting how and why one mode of difference gains specific meaning in relation to others. In this perspective, no one dimension of identity is treated as the primary, defining feature. Instead of choosing culture, gender, class, race, or sexuality as the central organizing concepts, all of these systems of identification are viewed as integral to one another. Culture is no longer prioritized as the definitive axis of difference.

In conceptualizing diasporicity, I understand culture critically – in relation to the ways that difference and belonging are shaped through experiences of social struggle or social bonding. Naturally, these relationships and interactions involve issues of relative power. Diasporic people may find themselves regarded as powerless strangers in environments that belong to others. In defining themselves as members of the surrounding society, they must renegotiate the terms of power, both in relation to the structures of

Introduction 21

society and in terms of their relations with colleagues and neighbours. Diasporicity is concerned with how power functions in the experiences of diasporants and, in this case, the experiences of German-born, Turkish-background Ausländer.

Rita Dhamoon (2009, 10) explains power in Foucauldian terms, "as a relation and as a capacity that is spread throughout the socio-political body, rather than as something that is possessed or held by a sovereign subject or the state." As philosopher and political activist Michel Foucault (1980, 158) argues: "Power is quite different from and more complicated, dense and pervasive than a set of laws and a state apparatus." Consequently, the acts and practices of diasporicity analyzed here reveal how power actually works, not only through citizenship, which is closely connected with how the German state accommodates German-born Turkish Ausländer, but also through other social structures as they are encountered daily.

Foucault (1995, 194) suggests that "we must cease once and for all to describe the effects of power in negative terms: it 'excludes,' it 'represses,' it 'censors,' it 'abstracts,' it 'masks,' it 'conceals.' In fact, power produces: it produces reality, it produces domains of objects and rituals of truth." In my exploration of everyday encounters, I use the perspective of diasporicity to interrogate the functions of power and how they are justified. I explore Ausländer as a historically generated category and a kind of subjectivity, but also as a term whose meaning is subject to change and challenge. I explore how members of a particular diasporic community negotiate their own forms of citizenship. Power is a force that can be both creative and oppressive. I explore how power creates Ausländer and how the Ausländer themselves are wielders of power. They are both controlled by power and exercise it through their daily interactions with others.

Everyday social encounters reveal how power provides occasions for resistance to marginalization. Such encounters involve socio-political entities performing as subjects who interact with power. Instead of seeking to eliminate power, Ausländer seek to disrupt and redirect power in their human relations. They contest the discourse of power that generates favouring or reprimanding for specific understandings of Germanness or Ausländerness, or of other categories of difference that lead to social hierarchies.

In my view, diasporicity is not some new ideology for directing or managing people's lives. It is a kind of critical perspective that exposes and disrupts the ways that categories of difference manifest themselves. In fact, responding to these categories is what creates the diasporic citizen. Diasporicity is a creative response to being identified as a diasporic subject.

Identity and belonging in this context are both claimed and renounced. These things are treated as fluid but also as things that "can never be erased" (Dhamoon 2009, 12). Identity and belonging are contestable but not always sources of contestation.

This account of diasporicity is not an attempt to determine the categories of difference that the term *Ausländer* carries but is, rather, an exploration of how and why these categories are constructed and maintained, and their resultant effects. I examine how material and structural inequalities are integral to the construction of very particular understandings of Ausländerness. As Dhamoon (2009, 13) writes, discourse "shapes the actual lived experiences of people, [and] social structures shape discourse. Given this, radical social change on the level of discourse effects social change on the material level and vice versa." For example, the articulation of Germanness is premised on racialized, gendered, class-based, and heteronormative meanings, which are formed as contrasts with Ausländerness. According to these constructed meanings, some kinds of Ausländer are less desirable than others. Such meanings affect people's legal status, job opportunities, family relationships, and where they can live.

In analyzing the axis between hostility and hospitality toward "foreigners," I aim to go beyond treating this relationship as a binary interaction. Instead, my proposed model (of hostility/hospitality) involves an interrogation of how power works in building the perceived differences of Ausländer and how such meanings are created. First, I examine how formations of social differences are conditional and then show how alternative meanings for these differences are possible. By examining the acts and practices of diasporic citizenship, I show how messages of hostility and hospitality are laden with connotations of power in everyday social encounters. In studying such encounters, I seek not to smooth over differences but to confront them directly. My analysis thus contributes to an understanding of Ausländerness as something that evolves – "how it is made, how it changes, and how it is operationalized in various penalizing and privileging ways" (Dhamoon 2009, 13).

I argue that the acts and practices of diasporicity serve to demystify how subjects and identities are formed. These practices represent people's searches for alternative understandings of identity, difference, and belonging, which are inherently political. In this sense, diasporic citizenship is "a *mode of critique* that illuminates possibilities for political change" (Dhamoon 2009, 13; emphasis in original). As Ausländer identify and examine the mechanisms that produce their Otherness, they become activists, transformed from being mere objects who are marked as different. The practices

Introduction 23

of diasporicity interrupt the labelling and the norms or values behind the labels. These practices point to a potential for understanding and experiencing difference, identity, and belonging in new or renegotiated ways.

Although my account of diasporicity aims to disrupt the politics of culture, it also acknowledges the reality of culture. As Dhamoon (2009, 16) states, the existing culture "is individually, collectively, and legally important" in people's lives. Culture is especially salient when its claims are tied up with notions of nationhood, community, home(land), and displacement. Such notions clearly apply for Turkish Ausländer in general, and for the study's participants in particular. Their reports of hostile encounters, rooted in systems of fear and hatred, reveal that they understand culture as both a vital place of belonging and a resource for resistance. In Germany, culture is relevant to the Ausländer, because their citizenship status and the ongoing practices of their social exclusion are clearly related to the cultural context.

However, precisely because of the ways that Germanness and Ausländerness have been constructed, the historical context of German nation-building is the place where an analysis of culture needs to start. In Germany, this context has long involved exclusion and marginalization. The process of nation-building has involved constructing a delimited collective identity. German national identity has been premised, at least partly, on the attempted eradication, exclusion, and suppression of the Other. This attempted exclusion has applied to Ausländer, their ways of life, and even their physical presence. As the German nation has been (and still is) defined by ethnocentric norms, many Germans feel that the very existence of the nation-state is challenged by the Ausländer.

Diasporicity provides both a critique and a reconceptualization of how the politics of citizenship can operate. This reconceptualization has the potential to open up theoretical and political considerations that have been closed off by assumptions regarding multiculturalism and especially by considerations related to the constitution of power. Therefore, the alternative perspective of diasporicity radically repositions the analytical focus away from culture and toward the processes of meaning-making. My analysis demonstrates that this conceptual shift has the potential to expand, interrogate, and complicate the study of identity, difference, and belonging in our social and political lives.

The *Culture* of Accommodation
Understanding culture as a fixed identity seems to serve two main purposes. It gives legitimacy to the defence of culture as a valuable commodity, and it

reinforces the idea that cultures are entities whose boundaries can be defined and defended. For political scientist Patchen Markell (2003, 171), culture is both an object (that individuals can have) and a background of choice (for a way of life). To be denied access to one's culture or to be prohibited from acting in accordance with it are forms of injustice. According to Taylor (1994) and Kymlicka (1989, 1995), we deserve recognition of our culture-based differences, because such recognition enables self-realization. Culture provides a multigenerational collective resource for identity formation. These observations seem to affirm cultural boundaries as a human right, and such affirmation seems to free liberalism and citizenship from the legacy of exclusion. In affirming differences between cultural groups, the liberal state seems to stand above prejudice. However, the role of political interests in defining cultural groups remains unexamined (Hall 1997).

As Rita Dhamoon (2009, 47) argues, viewing culture as a solid entity ignores the differences within a culture among its members. This view solidifies a binary oppositional distinction between *modern* and *traditional*, and between us and them. Paradoxically, by accommodating the Other through hospitable encounters, the dominant members of society maintain their self-image of being in control, yet tolerant and accommodating. In such encounters, a regulated boundary remains between the Other and the norm.

This notion of relations between cultures simultaneously obscures the similarities between different groups and overlooks the ethnic, national, and linguistic differences within groups. It privileges certain kinds of differences over other kinds, and it overdetermines the bounds of group identity. At best, this understanding only partially captures the complexity of politics surrounding identity, difference, and belonging. At worst, this understanding mislabels, obscures, or erases the multiple dimensions of people's social relations.

As political scientist Anne Phillips (2007, 21) suggests: "When culture becomes the catch-all explanation for everything that goes awry in non-Western societies or minority cultural groups, while remaining an invisible force elsewhere, something has gone wrong with the use of the term." So the hospitable overemphasis on culture promotes a unidimensional analysis of difference that contributes to what social psychologist Valerie Purdie-Vaughns and psychologist Richard Eibach (2008, 377) call "intersectional invisibility." In this kind of simplified analysis, the interactions among different categories such as gender, race, ethnicity, religion, and sexuality become hidden. Similarly, scholar of law and critical race theory Kimberlé Crenshaw's critique (1991) of single-issue frameworks shows the problems

Introduction

of oversimplification that arise when struggle within one category is isolated from or prioritized over struggle in other categories, thereby producing a tension between culture-based forms of identification and other aspects of identity. In that case, the tension between different aspects of identity may appear irreconcilable, as seen in the tensions created between Ausländer's sexual orientations and their culture.

Philosophers Seyla Benhabib (2002) and James Tully (1995, 2002) attempt to expand the boundaries of the cultural centre to include Others who were previously excluded. They do this by reconceptualizing culture as a mode of identity and practice that is constantly changing, that is meaningful for different people in different ways, and that is situated within relations of power. These authors regard culture not as a passive and de-racialized identity, but as something constituted, experienced, and changed through the exercise of social influence. They treat culture not as an object of difference, but as an intersubjective, contested site in which differences are constituted and transformed. All of these insights are helpful, but Benhabib and Tully continue to assign primacy to one dimension of difference (culture) and to underestimate how discourses on culture can constitute regulatory paradigms. Although we cannot abandon the relevance of culture, we cannot make culture so central that other forms of difference are ignored.

In practice, our understandings of what culture means are diverse, constantly shifting, and contested. As Dhamoon (2009, 29) explains: "Cultures do not possess people, but people actually create, enact, and iterate cultural practices, symbols and differences." Sociologist, cultural theorist, and political activist Stuart Hall (1990, 226; emphasis in original) adds that cultural identity is "not an essence but a *positioning*." Professor of literature, public intellectual, and a founder of postcolonial studies Edward Said (1978) reminds us that viewing the East and West as two opposite cultures, monolithic and homogeneous, is a classic Orientalist gesture. A diasporic culture challenges such perspectives, as such culture is always remade in the context of differing nations and cultures. When people move, their identities, perspectives, and definitions change. That sort of change involves a negotiation of different positions – subjectively, politically, and publicly.

Grounds of Accommodation and Displacement

In the various theories of accommodation, culture becomes an umbrella term to describe specified ethnic, national, religious, or linguistic groups whose members are assumed to share a common identity. However, as political scientist Barbara Arneil (2007, 51–58) notes, culture has been interpreted in numerous ways – as civilization (as opposed to nature), as constructed and relative, as a contested terrain, as an object made up of incommensurable entities (as in current discourses on the cultural wars of religion versus secularism), and as a fluid category that goes beyond ethnic and national differences to include categories of colour, sexual orientation, and disability.

Traditionally, the dominant norms within a given culture were assumed to be central for everyone in the group. In that view, preserving the particular practices of the culture became a shared responsibility. Everyone belonged to one culture or another and could not move between cultures, although they could enjoy other cultures. In these perspectives, it is assumed that national identities are pre-given. Such assumptions ignore the ways that cultural identities emerge from the political production of differences, and the way the very notion of culture-as-nationality changes with ongoing shifts in government, emigration, and loyalty. Theories of preset cultural identity also assume that other kinds of identity, such as sexuality, class, race, and gender, are also products of culture. In general, the claims of culture are often separated from and prioritized over other claims. Cultural claims erase some aspects of difference altogether in the interests of social cohesion, as defined through a unified cultural identity.

As Dhamoon (2009, 25) explains, when culture is treated as a given fact of identity or as a pre-existing entity with a fixed set of characteristics, the differences between groups of people seem permanent and absolute. Cultural difference becomes the site of trouble that must be remedied. When the differences between people become problems, it is assumed that these differences should be regulated to preserve social cohesion and achieve accommodation. In the German context, for example, culture serves to define those who are viewed as incompatible with Germany's liberal values of tolerance and equality. Cultural qualities are treated as the explanation for social relations, and these qualities are understood as coherent essences that differentiate *them* from *us*. Intense public scrutiny of specified Ausländer cultures further legitimizes regulation of people marked as being too different in their Ausländerness. Specific cultural identities become the prevailing focus. In that case, the political contexts from which these modes and degrees of difference are generated remain underanalyzed.

Methodology: Politics of Narrating Everyday Encounters

Through everyday social encounters, people's complex understandings of social identity and belonging find expression. Such encounters may involve

Introduction 27

spontaneous interactions that open ephemeral ruptures in people's perceptions of social reality. The effects of such encounters may be fleeting, but over time they can form patterns that subtly shift the context of social life. By examining the social encounters of Turkish Berliners (through their own narratives), we can see how their lives are conditioned by social relations far larger than their immediate encounters. Their narratives about their encounters are purposeful, and designed for effect on their listeners. Therefore, narration itself can be a political act.[3]

As sociologist Francesca Polletta (2006, 34) states: "Stories are more than strategic devices ... We tell stories to persuade but also to make sense of the unfamiliar. Stories assimilate confusing events into familiar frameworks while recognizing that things are no longer as they were and we are no longer who we were." Furthermore, as sociologists James Holstein and Jaber Gubrium (2012, 33) point out: "Multiple voices can be heard in any single speaker's voice." This observation suggests that stories can carry not just people's personal experiences, but also the shared experiences of others. Through a conversation with one person, we can understand the intersectionality of various issues and discover opportunities for marginalized groups to be heard. Collecting such stories can catalyze change in the ways a community sees itself.

In studying diasporic acts and practices, I am concerned more about how people experience the challenges and successes of their lives, and less about the objective, technical truth of their observations. As Holstein and Gubrium (2012, 41) note: "[Stories] are non-specialized. If technical accounts depend on expertise, stories, in my observation, depend on imagination." In essence, stories are about experiences rather than concrete studied truths. Therefore, collecting stories creates an interconnecting web that can help a researcher discover the themes and issues surrounding a research question, rather than seeking to define a decisive causation. Polletta (2006, 34) argues that "stories contain rather than resolve ambiguity." They also have the power to rally people around what they share. Polletta often references the Black civil rights movement: each protester's story was unique, but they all involved shared experiences of oppression and struggle. Activists tell stories to build community. As political scientist Frederick Mayer (2014) shows, stories have an incredible capacity to inspire collective action. As stories are at the centre of mobilizing socio-political beings, it is vital to learn about diasporic citizenship by gathering stories.

The first step in narrative analysis is to allow room for people to relate their lived experiences. The particularities of personal narratives tend to contradict any assumptions that people represent compartmentalized singular or even binary identities. Noting the particularities of their narratives leads toward a larger picture of belonging that includes a fluid multiplicity of identities.

Narrative analysis allows us to examine the complexities of interaction in at least three ways. First, rather than treating all members of a social group as equally dominant or equally subordinate, narrative analysis enables the perception of differences within and between social categories. A critical examination of such narratives exposes how discursive messages operate through multiple forms of relative dominance.

Second, narratives expose the relational processes of Othering. They can show what is at stake in producing an undifferentiated category of Otherness and thereby masking a multiplicity of political effects. Narratives expose the ways in which dominance is made manifest; they reveal the interactive systems of normativity and the multiplicity of differences. As Dhamoon (2009, 141) puts it, an analysis of narratives can reveal how the "meanings (or standards) of Otherness" serve to "re-entrench specific sets of interactive norms" that privilege certain qualities, be they whiteness, masculinity, capitalism, or heteronormativity. This form of analysis attends to the conditions by which dominant meanings are organized and upheld.

Third, narrative analysis exposes the interrelatedness of different issues. In my analysis of my participants' accounts, it becomes evident that various social hierarchies are deeply interrelated, such that it is not possible to undo one particular mode of subordination without addressing them all (Fellows and Razack 1994, 1998). For example, as Dhamoon (2009, 141) argues, racist systems of meaning-making intrinsically involve other processes of domination, such as sexism and class privilege. Noting this does not imply that, for example, "gender or class are reducible to race, whereby race-thinking is [just] another name for all other modalities of difference." Instead, social differences are ontologically variable in their characters and effects. We cannot organize all social issues around only one or two forms of oppression, nor can we claim that one form of dominance is universally more significant than another.

Furthermore, focusing on the relationships between interactive processes allows us to examine social differences without entering a debate over which groups are most oppressed. Such competition tends to focus on "gaining the attention and political support of dominant groups as [oppressed groups try to] pursue policy remedies, leaving the overall system of stratification unchanged" (Hancock 2007, 68). Therefore, as Dhamoon

Introduction   29

(2009, 142) notes, the overall system of stratification has to be confronted so that the habitual process of "privileging and penalizing representations of difference" can be dismantled.

In using narrative analysis in a study of diasporicity, we cannot assume that all Othered subjects will "automatically be allies or, conversely, that they are inevitably different" (Dhamoon 2006, 142). For Dhamoon (142), narrative analysis serves as an account of meaning-making, which provides "a way to detect potential political alliances without assuming either that all struggles are fundamentally similar," or presuming that all Othered subjects are sisters and brothers. Of course, many commonalities exist among subjects who fall into any particular category of Otherness (race, ethnicity, gender, sexuality), as we see in the case of German-born, Turkish-background Berliners. In many cases, these various Othered people may desire some form of community and solidarity. However, their narratives still indicate great individuality. Understanding their particular narratives involves learning to respect both people's personal differences and the relationships between their struggles.

The socio-political struggles that diasporic people's narratives describe do not end with any official recognition of a minority by the state, or with an assignment of differentiated rights, or with any radicalized practices of inclusion. Instead, the changes that these Othered people long for arise through their own actions, as they themselves disrupt the ways that representations of difference are maintained.

The everyday encounters that arise in narratives can be analyzed in three ways. The first is to examine the processes that differentiate dominant subjects as the *norms*, and the subordinate subjects as the *Others*. In this approach, we need to look at how differentiated people relate to existing discourses about inclusion and exclusion. We need to listen to people's own accounts of how the general categories of *Otherness* are produced and how the varied meanings of these categories affect their lives. Second, we can study "how self-directed and externally imposed meanings are produced" (Dhamoon 2009, 14) in social life at the individual, intergroup, and intragroup levels. By examining how these interactions play out through the discourses of belonging and Othering, we can see how differences are regulated through dominant norms or challenged by participants who are marked as others. Third, we can take account of the relational processes within dominant discourses. We can look at the gradations of inclusion, exclusion, and belonging, noting the degrees and forms of penalty or privilege. This type of analysis allows us to explore relational differences in the context of "mapping out confrontations." In summary, a narrative analysis of everyday encounters seeks to account for interrelated social processes that include a) differentiation in general (rather than just the singular objects of difference), b) the ways that the meanings of differentiation are made operational (by the state or by members of society), and c) the interrelated processes of confrontation that contest differences among social groups (cf. Dhamoon 2009, 14–15).

Chapter Synopses

Chapter 1 develops the theoretical model anchored in the key term diasporicity, in relation to social tensions involving two axes of discourse. The first axis is the politics of accommodation for foreigners, as effected through the discourses of hostility and hospitality. The second axis is the politics of displacement, as effected through the discourses of homelessness and homesickness.

Chapter 2 examines the process of creating Germanness and outsiderness. This chapter offers a brief account of how the German nation was created and the significant role played by Ausländer (foreigners) in the process. It then turns to the politics and interpretations of the Turkish Ausländer experiences since these people began arriving in the 1960s. This account follows their careers as *Gastarbeiter* (guest workers), their lives in the period from the end of recruitment until the end of the Cold War era, and the significance of the wall for all Berliners. It discusses the racist attacks that have occurred since unification and the citizenship debates of the late 1990s and 2000s. It also considers the impact of Islamoracism since the early 2000s.

Chapter 3 analyzes the context of accommodation in greater detail, showing the graded degrees of inclusion granted to German-born Turkish Berliners, although they remain located as outside Germanness. This chapter examines everyday discourses in which the participants are judged by their skin colour, gender, or styles of clothing such as headscarves. I examine the discourses of ignorance by which Ausländer are (mis)recognized. Although German discourse about the Ausländer swings from hostility to hospitality, an underlying externalizing question is constantly posed: "Woher kommst du?" ("Where do you come from?").

Chapter 4 analyzes the diasporic experience of displacement in greater detail. It considers how the participants articulate the contradictions of being German-born Turkish Ausländer. I explain their experience as an ongoing negotiation of homesickness and homelessness. This chapter explores

Introduction 31

the complex and contradictory meanings of having a homeland, and the connections that Ausländer have with that land. Their experience of displacement enables the participants to identify social distinctions or ruptures at both subjective and societal levels. In that process, the whole notion of Germanness is opened for re-examination.

Chapter 5 investigates how Ausländer experience the struggle for identity and belonging as a subjective conflict. Some participants describe how they have sought to bring their Turkishness and Germanness together as a whole, while others have come to realize that they do not have to choose any combination of these two identities. They have the option of not choosing, because identity is multidimensional and ever-changing.

Chapter 6 concludes the account by exploring the notion of diasporic citizenship in greater depth. The participants show how their daily social encounters open ruptures with cultural expectations, thereby challenging prescribed roles and practices. Moreover, by interrogating the practices of exclusion, the participants change themselves. They come to understand their complex condition as a new type of citizenship. This chapter summarizes the social, cultural, and political characteristics of such diasporic citizenship, and it offers a broader understanding of what citizenship means in an increasingly multinational, multi-ethnic Western society.

The concluding chapter presents a review of the various ways this book contributes to studies on citizenship and diaspora. It reassesses the ways that communities of struggle can learn from diasporic citizens. Finally, it summarizes the reasons why Germany needs to redefine citizenship beyond the realm of the nation-state.

1 The Model
Being and Belonging Together

Meine Heimat trage ich in meinen Schuhen.
(I carry my homeland in my shoes.)
– Ela, 2003

The German citizens and the (Turkish) Ausländer dwell together in Germany's cities, and by belonging together they constitute each other. This belonging is a political relationship as much as a historical, cultural, or social one. Their complex relationship emerges in the everydayness of social encounters; the ways they interact serve to define and maintain both Germanness and Ausländerness. However, the dominant version of history treats this relationship as a matter of accommodation. In that context, the identities and differences of Ausländer and Germans are defined as characteristics essential to these groups, rather than as evolving sets of practices for dwelling and comporting together. As this relationship between cultures has been treated as simply a matter of accommodation, it seems that the only options are either conformity to German culture or social separation. As neither option is fully achievable, the Ausländer have remained long-term residents who are nonetheless excluded from German society at large, and whose citizenship status is precarious. Previously, it was assumed that these people would eventually go home. However, once they had settled, founded families, and started raising their children, nothing short of expulsion was likely to make them return to their ancestors' country. In that case, there has to be more to living together than accommodating the Ausländer to Germanness, and the Ausländer's ways of negotiating their belonging are important for shaping the future.

FIGURE 1

Map of belonging together

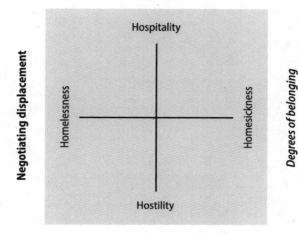

The spectrum of identity creation from almost-German to enemy alien

I propose a map of how the relationships between Ausländer and German people are worked out in everyday encounters. This map suggests how these encounters happen in a tension between displacement, proximation, and estrangement along the crossroads of two axes (see Figure 1).

The vertical axis represents the spectrum of relations between Germans and Ausländer, ranging from hospitality to hostility. This axis suggests how the identities are created and maintained through enactments of accommodation. This tension concerns the degree to which Ausländer (in general) and German-born Turkish Ausländer (in particular) can approach being German within the discourses of accommodation, identity, and difference. Such accommodation ranges from appropriation of the Ausländer as almost-German to their utter estrangement from Germanness, to even being regarded as enemy aliens who should be expelled to protect national cohesion. These relations arise from the ways in which belonging together is constructed and from the process of attributing characteristics to the Ausländer, both historically and during the course of everyday encounters.

The horizontal axis depicts the range of Ausländer's feelings and claims regarding their own belonging. Varying degrees of homelessness and homesickness indicate where the participants stand in negotiating their connections or estrangements. This axis reflects the characteristics of the diasporic home as flexible, contradictory, fluid, and multiple.

Accommodating Ausländer: Between Hostility and Hospitality

The historically constructed ideologies behind the politics of accommodation are reflected in people's everyday exchanges and interactions. These exchanges express discursive messages of hostility or hospitality, which serve to maintain Germanness and non-Germanness while regulating people's ways of living together.

My analysis suggests that despite the over sixty-year history of Turks living in German cities, the lives of Turks in Germany are generally seen as separate from the history, culture, politics, and social life of those cities. The Turks have become Others within, who are called on to conform to the ways of Germans. Accommodating Ausländer involves attributing certain characteristics to them. In this process, the power that Germans enjoy in this relationship is typically concealed or unconsciously assumed, and therefore it goes unquestioned. Although images of the self and the Other are both constructed over time through experience, they are commonly taken for granted as the given context that governs social relations. Therefore, it is not the physical conditions of being an immigrant, guest worker, or Ausländer that create the participants' Otherness. Otherness is an imagined construct of what it means to be Ausländer or German. The resulting politics of proximation and estrangement regulate forms of togetherness but generally overlook the mutual dependency between German citizens and Turkish others. Therefore, this form of politics seems to erase the complexity of identities, differences, and possibilities for belonging together.

The hostility-hospitality axis represents my analysis of the relationship between dominant and outsider groups. This relationship reflects the complex history of interaction between German identity and citizenship, as well as Germany's efforts to regulate and accommodate its Ausländer. These historically constructed relations are maintained daily through dominant discourses on race, skin colour, class, religion, and sexuality. The discourse of accommodation can involve ignorance, fear, or hatred toward the Other, and such discourse tends to maintain a homogeneous, blood-based German identity. Although Germans and Ausländer have dwelt together for decades, their identities have been commonly defined as mutually exclusive, socially, culturally, and politically. In recent decades, the assumption of incompatibility between cultures has been renewed through discourses regarding a *clash of two civilizations* – Christian European on the one hand, Muslim on the Other.

In Chapter 3, I discuss how the participants' bodies are marked as different, and how such differences are enacted in ways that allow or force the subjects to keep their distance. These encounters involve strategies for dealing with people whose bodies are viewed as strange or dangerous among the different groups who have to live together. Such strategies ensure that certain spaces are demarcated as the recognized citizens' domains, and certain lives are valued over others. Some bodies are more recognizable as alien. Although this complicated hierarchy was formed historically over decades, it is maintained on a daily basis.

One pole of the hostility-hospitality axis represents reluctance to recognize Ausländer as part of Germany. In the more extreme versions of hostility, Ausländer are treated as unalterably *alien* enemies or security threats. The other pole, hospitality, appears in public displays of strong support for making migrants part of German society. Hospitable encounters involve friendly, generous interactions between Ausländer and Germans. Policies on the pole of hospitality aim to enable the Ausländer to regularize their status and naturalize their membership in German society.

Negotiating Displacement: Between Homelessness and Homesickness

The horizontal axis represents the participants' subjective negotiations of belonging and displacement, which range from strong, direct, positive connections with the homeland to weak, indirect, or negative relations to any home.

One pole of this dimension represents affiliations characterized by statements of *homesickness*. Here, the diasporic subjects are so emotionally attached to their ancestral homeland that they can hardly stand being away from it. The other pole, *homelessness*, represents weak attachment to any place – a feeling of belonging nowhere.

Having some sense of connection with a prior home is necessary for a diasporic identity (Clifford 1994). However, this kind of belonging involves negotiation among multiple dimensions: the relationship with a homeland, the level of participation and inclusion in German society, the relations with other identities or affiliations, and the differences that mark those affiliations. Diasporas reach across multiple borders, including but not limited to national ones. As anthropologist Jonathan Boyarin and historian of religion

Daniel Boyarin (2002, 23) note, by "focusing on diasporic spread across national borders, we unwittingly reinforce the prejudice toward thinking of those borders as the 'real' power divides, the ones that really count." Other kinds of borders – race, class, ethnicity, religion, gender, sexuality – mark the dislocations of diasporic communities as much as those of the nation-state.

In these various negotiations, home can have several meanings. As Sara Ahmed (2000, 77) explains: "Home is ... not a particular place that one simply inhabits, but more than one place; there are too many homes to allow place to secure the roots or routes of one's journey between homes." The story of home grows complicated and multi-layered. For Ahmed (78): "The narrative of leaving home produces too many homes and hence no Home, too many places in which memories attach themselves."

German-born Ausländer fluctuate between experiences of homelessness and homesickness. In their negotiations of belonging, they reconsider what it means to be at home, and how place relates to their sense of identity. Whether they feel homesick or homeless, a sense of displacement remains. Homesickness in diasporic politics emphasizes a common history and memory – an imaginative unity of origin. It makes diasporic identity a *being,* "a collective and integral whole" (Safran 1991, 83–84). It is this exclusivist homesickness that keeps the Turkish language alive among Turks who were born and raised in Germany, and which incidentally enabled me to conduct all my interviews in Turkish. Homesickness can become a tool for politics, as a kind of strategic essentialism. However, homesickness also makes diasporants feel like outsiders in their own city. Through homesickness, Turkish guest workers and their descendants have made strong connections with Türkiye. Homesickness grounds being Ausländer as a condition of resistance, as constructed in terms of binary oppositions. Through being constructed as the Other and by resisting being constructed as such, the exclusivist, self-contained being moves toward homelessness.

As much as they are defined by homesickness, diasporic experiences also challenge the ideologies of homesickness – just as they challenge the ways that the ideologies of modern citizenship define people. For many German-born Turkish Ausländer, neither Germany nor Türkiye feels like home. Chapter 5 explores these tensions as *borderlands.* Through the push and pull between homelessness and homesickness, diasporic people redefine their identities. While negotiating their experiences of displacement and belonging, they challenge the meaning of identity. Despite being born and raised in Germany, some of them still feel a sense of displacement, as they continue to carry a living memory of the homeland. Homesickness is expressed by vacationing in the homeland, commonly for a few weeks every year. In addition, connecting with "my own people" in Germany involves a sense of identity that is rooted in essentialism. Such a self-definition leads Ausländer to remain reactive in the discourse of accommodation.

In the back-and-forth dialectic between homelessness and homesickness, the participants question their connections with both the homeland and Germany. When they claim they are from Germany, they confront and redefine Germanness as including themselves. The Berlin neighbourhood of Kreuzberg has become a particular focal point in this struggle to redefine homesickness and homelessness. Here, the discourses of hostility and hospitality are challenged. The participants typically feel that living in Kreuzberg is a privilege. Here, they feel both estrangement from Germany and ownership of a familiar locality within Germany. Such feelings of homelessness and homesickness are especially complicated for LGBTI+ people of Turkish background in Berlin, a theme that will appear repeatedly throughout the analysis.

Yet another way that diasporic people transform homelessness and homesickness is through the notion of *translocality*. As they challenge the meanings of home and of being accommodated, they renegotiate belonging from the borderlands they live in. Rather than choosing between identities, they find ways to stretch the boundaries, redefining their belonging as a *third* space.

In the contradictions of homelessness and homesickness, the everyday politics of diasporicity is inscribed both materially and imaginatively. On the one hand, diasporicity is the exclusivist place that homesickness longs for. On the other hand, it is a place to deconstruct the binary oppositions imposed by the dominant group. Diaspora is both a coherent, integral whole, and a fluid, multiple, hybrid set of particular identities. It is a mindspace of contradiction between rootedness and fragmentation; between being, becoming, and belonging. Here, diasporic subjects negotiate their sense of place and construct their identities. In the process, they transform themselves into political subjects.

Ways of Diasporic Belonging, Reception, and Confrontation

What defines the diasporic mindspace is displacement. When people cross a frontier, their ways of representing themselves, their cultural identity, and their political responsibilities all change. In other words, displacement transforms political values and citizenship practices. As sociologist and a pioneer of diaspora studies Avtar Brah (1996) and interdisciplinary scholar of history, literature, and anthropology James Clifford (1994) remind us, diasporas are historically contingent social formations, experienced variably from differing subject positions involving class, gender, religion, sexuality, and political orientation. Diasporic identity emerges through the contradictions of negotiating both displacement and accommodation. It challenges the nation-state's assumption of a homogeneous society, and it forges the potential to resist the dominant context.

Diasporic space is a shifting *political* environment. As geographer Steve Pile and anthropologist Michael Keith (1993, 221–22) describe it, political space is a social arena where people's sense of place is (re)negotiated and identities are (re)constructed. Therefore, I argue that the everyday politics of accommodating Ausländer are necessarily territorial. Such politics are conditioned by an incredibly complex network of places that are real, imaginary, and symbolic all at once. Political spaces of diasporic belonging emerge in the gaps between multiple identities. Diasporas, as defined through the contradictions of negotiating displacement and the politics of accommodation, are both non-places and multiple places. As social anthropologist Pnina Werbner (2000, 308) suggests, diasporas are "deterritorialized ... imagined communities ... [which] conceive of themselves, despite their dispersal, as sharing a collective past and common destiny, and hence also a simultaneity in time." The main questions are how diasporic subjects can exist alongside various nation-states with their fixed boundaries; how these people can challenge clearly defined categories of inclusion and exclusion; and how they can negotiate the participatory rights, duties, and loyalties of citizenship. These tensions can be conceived as an interplay between the two axes illustrated in Figure 2.

When the two dimensions of diasporic experience are combined as orthogonal axes, they map out four different types of diasporic spaces: first (upper left), a strong wish to be part of the host society, with a weak sense of belonging to the homeland; second (upper right), a strong attachment to the homeland, with hospitable encounters within the host society; third (lower right), strong attachment to the homeland with minimal adaptation to the host society; and fourth (lower left), a sense of exile from the homeland combined with isolation from the host society. The contradictions of homelessness and homesickness that arise from diasporic experiences generate a shift in the balance of power and, therefore, in the relations of hospitality–hostility. These tensions force a dialogue between the citizens of Western cities and diasporic people, as illustrated in Figure 2.

FIGURE 2

Spaces of belonging, reception, and confrontation

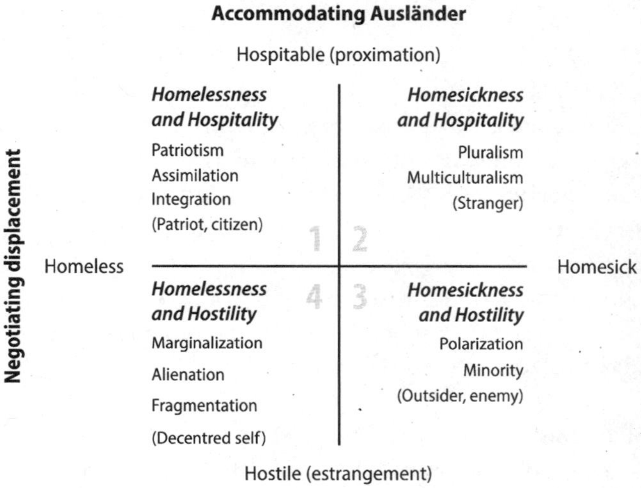

Accommodating Ausländer

Hospitable (proximation)

	Homelessness and Hospitality	*Homesickness and Hospitality*	
	Patriotism	Pluralism	
	Assimilation	Multiculturalism	
	Integration	(Stranger)	
	(Patriot, citizen)		
Homeless	*1*	*2*	Homesick
	Homelessness and Hostility	*Homesickness and Hostility*	
	4	*3*	
	Marginalization	Polarization	
	Alienation	Minority	
	Fragmentation	(Outsider, enemy)	
	(Decentred self)		

(left axis: Negotiating displacement)

Hostile (estrangement)

Different kinds of meaning-making processes can be mapped onto the four quadrants. Each quadrant represents a different way of claiming diasporic space. Even though some configurations take familiar forms – such as pluralism, multiculturalism, and the discourses of minorities – these forms are still part of diasporicity. Whether their political and social recognition is hospitable or hostile, and whether their sense of belonging involves homesickness or homelessness, their everyday encounters involve processes that influence the formation of both citizens (Germans) and strangers (Ausländer). Such processes involve relations of power and are, therefore, far from innocuous. They are not necessarily benign. Such processes trigger, to use Isin's (2002a, 33) words, "the formation of multiple, overlapping, and conflicting wills."

In the quadrants depicted in Figure 2, each dynamically formed position represents a boundary that is enacted in the midst of social encounters. The boundaries shaped by the various positions enable individuals to act as members of a group. Even when they are perceived to be acting as individuals, their affiliations inform their encounters. As sociologist Georg Simmel ([1908] 1971, 152) suggests, it is through the boundaries, proximities, or distances among the members of a group, or between groups, that their relationships are constituted.

Isin (2002a) argues that encounters among and between groups involve configurations that are physical, imaginary, symbolic, and geographical. Therefore, space becomes an object of contention in the struggle for domination and differentiation. Such struggle appears, for example, when the question: "Where do you come from?" is imposed on Ausländer, requiring that social boundaries be drawn. The same kind of struggle appears when Ausländer claim that they are Berliners. Therefore, in their encounters, both Germans and Ausländer constitute space as individuals and as groups. Space becomes an objective reality and a strategic property by which both Ausländer and German are constituted in the everyday world. This social space is not simply a passive background for the negotiations between displacement and accommodation for Ausländer. It is a *political* space, where processes and strategies of connecting or disrupting contend in establishing the boundaries of identity and belonging.

Quadrant 1: Homelessness and Hospitality

In this zone of diasporic relations, the prevailing sentiments emerge from the relation between a weak sense of belonging to the homeland and hospitable politics or enactments of belonging in Germany. The responses to this tension range from demands for assimilation to creative interaction. These kinds of encounters tend to promote a favourable relationship with Germanness. However, the Ausländer can never become full citizens; they can only become *almost* German. Prominent critical theorist in contemporary post-colonial studies Homi Bhabha (1994, 87; emphasis in original) defines this kind of accommodation as colonial mimicry, "the desire for a reformed, recognizable Other, *as a subject of a difference that is almost the same, but not quite.*" The diasporic sort-of Germans will never be fully or permanently German – not just because they may lack citizenship, but also because of their inherent racial, ethnic, cultural, or religious differences.

Assimilation (or integration) in its general, abstract sense means to increase similarity or likeness. The assimilation paradigm had its origins in the Chicago school of sociology during the 1920s. As the first institution to study ethnicity, this school emphasized the interactional stages of contact, accommodation, assimilation, and fusion. The process was claimed to begin with an initial stage of exposure to the values, norms, and culture of the host society. Gradually, the immigrants would transplant their pre-migration lives and construct their identity in a new society (Park and Miller 1921). After two to three generations, they would begin to lose the language, values, and

Being and Belonging Together   41

culture of their original homeland and increasingly assimilate into the host society. At this stage, they would no longer maintain their previous geographical or social boundaries (Gordon 1964; Thomas and Znaniecki 1927).

This notion of assimilation designates the direction of change rather than a degree of similarity. Assimilation in the sense of making similar can also describe state policies or programs that seek to assimilate people against their will. However, abundant historical and comparative evidence suggests that such interventionist policies rarely work. In fact, they are more likely to strengthen than erode differences, by provoking a reactive mobilization against assimilatory pressures, as witnessed in the Ausländer reactions to the immigration law requiring citizenship tests.

Integration, as the participants define it, involves transforming a sort-of German into a *new* German. In this view, being German means knowing the rules of the game, but it can also mean playing the game in a new way. Knowing German ways can be a means of changing the meaning of the culture and of creating innovative, hybrid lifestyles. New Germans master the German language. They are able to adapt to German customs and sometimes forget Turkish ones. They often have economic and personal successes. The existence of other Ausländer who are more foreign makes these people into new Germans by comparison. At times, it seems that the issues of citizenship and race do not matter, as the discursive space between native and Other collapses. In these cases, the interaction between German and Turk can be fluid; the boundaries between the two seem to move or even disappear.

In such configurations, Ausländer are generally expected to become part of German society – but *certain conditions apply*. Ausländer are expected to live like patriotic natives in their host society, but they are nevertheless still homeless. The Berlin integration model of education policies exemplified this expectation, as its aim was to assimilate immigrant children into monolingual German classes as quickly as possible. Another example is the way that skin colour functions in setting the parameters for being seen as German. Expectations regarding skin colour are such that Ausländer with light skin tones are invisible. If they are not *visibly* Ausländer, they do not disturb images of Germans or Ausländer. However, even though light-skinned Ausländer are welcomed differently from darker Ausländer, they are still Ausländer, and their separate identity is exposed in other ways.

Another example of this assimilation configuration is the way that some Ausländer become experts, exceptions, acquaintances, or perhaps model Ausländer. In these cases, assimilation seems to be given its due reward. Yet the

42   *The Model*

expectation of assimilation or integration is still based on a binary opposition between German and Ausländer. The Ausländer are met with hospitality but are expected to avoid or suppress any traits that reflect their homeland. The status of Ausländer, then, is almost that of a refugee or a stateless person whose best hope is to be accepted as a guest.

Quadrant 2: Homesickness and Hospitality

In navigating the configurations of homesickness and hospitality, Ausländer typically have a strong desire to be part of the host society. However, they also wish to maintain a myth of origin, which involves a strong sense of difference and therefore homesickness. In this tension of hopes and dreams, the Ausländer feel like strangers who are "near and far at the same time." They become *potential wanderers,* simultaneously attaching or belonging to a place and detaching themselves from that same place (Simmel [1908] 1971, 148). As Isin (2002a, 31) notes: "A tension arises because a drive toward identity has the effect of highlighting difference." The Ausländer become informants about and representatives of their culture. Also, the most obviously Turkish Ausländer become the ones who owe the most gratitude for what German society has given them. Thanks to Germany's hospitality, they can stay in the country and can live in their own neighbourhoods – without having to mix with Germans. The Bavarian model of education, based on the assumption that foreign workers come in and out of Germany in continual rotation, illustrates this configuration. Turkish cultural organizations, festivals, and ethnic associations typically belong in this quadrant. Thus, the Ausländer come to identify with Germany through discourses regarding "my own people." These Ausländer tend to keep speaking Turkish and claim a distinct Ausländer history in Germany.

Hospitable politics and enactments often go together with a strong sense of connection to the homeland. These sentiments are embodied in policies favouring pluralism and multiculturalism. Such policies promote tolerance in social interactions and allow boundaries of convenience to be drawn between groups. Minorities are permitted to maintain their differences within the hospitable spaces of the nation-state.

Hospitable accommodation can become the avenue for diasporic people to access goods and services in the dominant society. Sociologist Richard Day (2000, 9) refers to this process as "seductive integration," whereby dominant groups can award status to others, thereby creating a society where minorities want to integrate into the dominant norm. The minorities tend to cooperate because, as Dhamoon (2009, 8) points out, doing so improves their chances of political, economic, and social success. Policies that affirm homesickness with hospitable accommodation (such as multiculturalism) grant legitimacy to a governance that privileges some kinds of difference over others. The state has a role in deciding which groups deserve recognition, while monitoring those deemed most threatening, such as practising Muslims.

Arguments in favour of liberal immigration policies and multiculturalism are often expressed in terms of economic functionalism. As Seyhan (2000, para. 3) argues, the desire to transform Germany into a multicultural society is often expressed by highlighting economic benefits, such as the contributions made by foreign workers to social security, the growing number of businesses that provide jobs for native Germans, and the need for a young labour force to care for an aging German population. Yet these economic narratives fail "to account for the generation of intolerance, xenophobia, and ethnic violence."

The intermingling of hospitality and homesickness reminds us of the close linkage between the ideas of accommodation and democracy (Suárez and Coll 2005). For example, Parekh (2000, 341) claims that a "dialogically constituted multicultural" democracy is best suited to conduct the collective affairs of a multicultural society. Parekh therefore argues for intercultural dialogue. However, regardless of any emphasis on intercultural dialogue, group formation is primarily based on roots and the homeland. Both the dominant and submissive groups are expected to define themselves in essentialist ways.

The logic of hospitable accommodation is based on the notion that different types of minorities have fought for and gained different types of rights. This group-differentiated process is key in setting the terms of hospitable accommodation. A pluralistic ideology such as multiculturalism ("a liberal-democratic phenomenon," Kymlicka 1995, 2007) can become a problem for democracy, as it creates inequality among groups and their individual members. Group boundaries are necessary to define each group as homogeneous. However, the assumption of a homogeneous group ignores the heterogeneity in power-positioning within the group. The emotional sense of solidarity depends on a perceived community of feelings, but to be harmonious externally as well as internally, communities must provide not just a sense of belonging and wholeness for their members, but also genuine acceptance for their diversity.

Although the practices emerging from hospitable accommodation may enable inclusion and may democratize how Ausländer and Germans engage in political life, these practices do not fundamentally change the terms by which identities and differences are organized. In practice, the problems of dealing with the terms of identity are suspended until after rights and recognitions have been allocated.

Quadrant 3: Homesickness and Hostility

When social enactments and political policies are hostile and diasporic belonging is defined through a strong sense of homesickness, the diasporic subjects experience a distinct set of conditions. They experience a weak sense of participation in the daily life of the host society, while retaining a strong myth of origin and identification with the homeland. Antagonistic encounters with the host society involve conflict, competition, and tension. The diasporic subjects are then seen as potentially dangerous outsiders. Their response is to build islands for themselves in Germany, barricading themselves in their neighbourhoods and familiar routines. The term *unintegrated ethnic minorities* reflects such configurations.

The difference between hospitality and hostility tends to blur when members of the dominant group claim that they have, as Kymlicka (2007, 121) puts it, "gone beyond the call of duty, and in that sense have been generous, and indeed virtuous, in [accommodating minorities] ... They expect minorities to be suitably grateful for this generosity, and to acknowledge their good fortune in living in a country with such a tolerant and well-meaning majority."

When such attitudes are widely accepted, all types of diasporic people can be lumped together as minorities. Historically, these scattered groups, which share the quality of being unassimilated, have become the targets of racialized, xenophobic nationalist suspicion. As sociologist Louis Wirth (1945, 347–48) argues, most minorities are groups of people who often consider themselves objects of collective prejudice and unfairness. It is not their specific characteristics such as race or ethnicity that mark them as minorities, but the relationships between their groups and certain other groups in the societies they live in. In being identified as members of distinct minorities, these people commonly find themselves singled out and held in low esteem. They may receive differential and unequal treatment, ranging from casual contempt to ridicule, hatred, and violence from members of the majority population. Their degrees of social isolation commonly coincide with spatial segregation.

However, as Wirth (1945, 348–49) suggests, when members of such disadvantaged groups "become conscious of their deprivations" and start to consider themselves as citizens who have a just claim to recognition and equality, they can become potent political forces. To a significant degree, minority politics involves reaction against unjust treatment.

Remaining reactive, however, involves everyday struggles with antagonists. This defensive stance is intended to resist exploitation, appropriation, and the imposition of dominant norms. Such reactive responses may be popular among minority communities, even if they have only a marginal influence on the forms of domination (Scott 1986). As Foucault (1978) writes, resistance is sometimes a *reverse* discourse that seeks to undermine particular aims of normalization. The goal of everyday antagonistic resistance, according to both political scientist and anthropologist James Scott (1986) and Foucault (1978), is not to overthrow or transform a system of domination, but to survive within it for a while longer. The immediate aim is to endure to fight another day.

Many of my participants have experienced these kinds of pressure. They may be expected to show unconditional loyalty to Turkish identity and language, and such imposed loyalty can be expressed as a strong preference for communicating in Turkish. It can also involve a bias for defending people simply because they are Turkish, a minority, or foreign. The debates that Turkish community organizations engage in commonly concern how or how much Turks are alienated and the degrees to which they should demand the right to be different. Significantly, however, these sentiments are informed by dominant discourses of accommodation, such as considering Ausländer to be guest workers, whose rights should be commensurate with that role. Such discourses extend to contemporary state policies, and they echo German chancellor Angela Merkel's claim that although Germany has tried to accommodate foreigners, the immigrants have proved unwilling to assimilate, so that "multiculturalism has utterly failed" (Weaver 2010; Hall 2010).

Quadrant 4: Homelessness and Hostility

The configurations of homelessness and hostility arise when encounters tend toward antagonism, and the sense of belonging is weak. Diasporic subjects commonly face situations of exclusion or oppression in the host society, and they respond to experiences of alienation. In many cases, a sense of instability undermines their sense of belonging, both to the place they live and to the place *their people* came from. These migrants then commonly question their attachment to other diasporic subjects.

This configuration seemingly represents the worst-case scenario: the diasporic subject feels homeless and faces hostility from the surrounding world. In reality, however, the claims of diasporic citizenship are most strongly constructed in this situation. Diasporic awareness arises in conditions of alienation. Such awareness is characteristic of people who no longer strongly identify with their ethnic or cultural group as an essentialist entity and do not feel included in their host society. This kind of subjectivity is typically constituted via alienating discourses located outside the realms of socialization, association, or assimilation.

Configurations of homelessness and hostility may seem to promise only unbounded confrontation. An example is the situation faced by Turkish-background LGBTI+ people in Berlin. The Mehmet case, which is discussed in Chapter 3, is another such situation. Even though Mehmet had minimal knowledge of Türkiye or of Turkish, he was nevertheless labelled a Turkish rather than a German citizen and, therefore, deported. Another example is the treatment given to practising Muslim women who wear headscarves, both by Germans and by the secular Turkish state. Yet another case is the treatment of minority identities (e.g., Jewish, Arab, Kurdish) among the Turks of Germany. These people do not fit the definition of what the Turkish government itself considers Turkish, but in Germany they are still labelled as Turkish Ausländer, and they face discrimination for that reason. As these people are critical of Türkiye's majority, they are not accepted as insiders in their ancestral homeland. At the same time, they do not accept what Germans want them to be. Other examples include people born in small German towns, who grew up being considered as Turkish Others, but have so little exposure to Turkish culture that they cannot identify with the ethnic Turks they meet in Berlin or when visiting Türkiye. Such people often feel that they cannot be part of anything, and they question everything imposed on them.

In the sector of homelessness and hostility, the forms of resistance that people engage in are similar to those conceptualized by Foucault (1978) and Scott (1986). Such limited resistance does not require significant change, and it raises no serious challenge to the system. Still, people who experience both homelessness and hostility tend to challenge expectations about where they belong and who they should be. Sometimes they try to change the system, and sometimes they just try to survive it.

For those who experience homelessness and hostility, the tensions of diasporicity may suggest a realization that multiplicity, flexibility, and heterogeneity are the primary conditions of their lives. From this position, these subjects articulate their politics and explore self-created roles as diasporic citizens. A diasporic citizen embodies a very particular type of awareness, which emerges from the distinct conditions of diasporicity. Such critical awareness leads diasporic people to challenge both the politics of identity and the kinds of belonging imposed on them. When they actively challenge these politics of belonging, their inner struggles play out in the·ways they choose to live and interact with others.

In seeking to confront hostility and homelessness, diasporic citizens operate differently from those who embrace a group-differentiated vision of citizenship. Whereas group-defined people view citizenship as a path to assimilation, diasporic citizens raise challenges to the very definition of citizenship. Their forms of solidarity are different as well. For diasporic activists, solidarity is conditional. It means organizing to claim certain rights while retaining the right to be critically nonconformist. Rather than expecting undying loyalty to any one group, such activists question how each person can determine their own unique place in the social system.

Conclusion: A Two-Axis System

Although immigrants are often the subjects of study in social science, their interactions between displacement and accommodation remain underanalyzed in mainstream political theory. Mapping diasporic confrontations through the axes of hostility–hospitality and homesickness–homelessness is an especially valuable exercise, because it shows how identity, difference, and belonging are constituted relationally. To understand diasporic citizens, we must look beyond any single set of interactions between Ausländer and Germans. We also need to examine the interactions that occur between various additional forms of Othering. We need to look at how the discourses of racism, nationalism, and heteronormativity relate to discourses that produce more relational differences among people (such as the discourses of LGBTI+ or Arab Turks). By mapping the axes of displacement and accommodation as experienced by Ausländer, we can better examine the complex variations in how diasporic people relate. We can observe how they go about re-deciding their relations in new situations.

These individuals typically question their society's categories of class, race, gender, religion, ethnicity, or sexuality. Their own hybridity demonstrates how all of these identities are choices rather than given realities. Such people can take a number of different subject positions: Turkish, German, Muslim, queer, woman (Howarth and Stavrakakis 2000, 13). Diasporic people have the flexibility to move between several possible identities, claiming all of them. The fluidity of their constantly changing criteria of identity makes their affiliations hard to track.

The essential difference between diasporic citizenship and other forms of citizenship (such as group-based or multicultural citizenship) is the way in which diasporicity informs social interactions. However, the Ausländer's struggle involves more than deliberate argument against the citizenship privileges that Germans maintain. Drawing on philosopher Shannon Sullivan (2006), I view the participants as engaging in a more indirect form of debate. In challenging the roles and identities expected of them, they confound expectations by acting outside them. Through their everyday social interactions, the participants question and thereby reveal how categories of belonging or exclusion are produced. They become political – because it is political whenever "the naturalness of the dominant virtues is called into question and their arbitrariness revealed" (Isin 2002a, 275). I therefore argue for the emancipatory potential in diasporic awareness, because "difference could be embraced ... not as an objective in itself, but rather as a point of departure and a method for transforming repressive and anti-democratic social circumstances" (Yuval-Davis, in Sandoval 2000, xi).

Such diasporic awareness can provide "a series of methods for creating social movements and identities that are capable of speaking to, against, and through, power" (Angela Davis, in Sandoval 2000, xii). These characteristics of diasporicity highlight the participants' identities as matters of positioning, allowing various layers of narrative to breathe. Yet there is always the danger that diasporic identities can be pushed back into the fixed monolithic identities that societies traditionally expect.

Ever since the guest workers arrived in Germany, they have had to negotiate among several layers of narratives. My participants narrate their past and present experiences of marginalization within the various social spheres they inhabit. Such paradoxical marginalization may happen, for example, while looking for a house to rent or applying for a job. By doing ordinary things, as simple as speaking German, or not so ordinary things that are perceived as anything but, such as openly living a life that challenges heteronormativity, these diasporic subjects show their capacity to be several kinds of person at once. They protest against the ways that Germans label Turks, while dealing with the pressure to conform with Turkish stereotypes. Paradoxical experiences lead them to confront the ways they are linked to or separated from others. As the everyday politics of their social encounters intertwine with solidarity and activism, diasporic subjects become diasporic citizens.

2 Constituting Germans and Outsiders

Wir erwarteten Arbeitskräfte, und es kamen Menschen.
(We expected workers; what came were people.)
   – Max Frisch (cited in Wengeler 1995, 720)

Playwright and novelist Max Frisch's statement summarizes Germany's complex relation with its immigrants: seeing them as solely a labour force, rather than as people, as they gradually became part of Germany. This evolving relation to Others is commonly viewed as a new, modern-age challenge. Germans tend to forget that similar attitudes have shaped their nation's relations with migrant populations since the First Reich (also known as the Holy Roman Empire) between the ninth and the nineteenth centuries (Dale 1999; Özcan 2004; Şen 2003).

The relations between German identity and citizenship, and Germany's relations with its Ausländer, are complex and interlocking and have two significant characteristics. First, the idea of German citizenship derives from the country's long history as one nation split into many countries, where the sense of being weak and divided generated a desire for unification. Second, German citizenship has been defined to exclude non-German immigrants, who were seen as a temporary labour force, as outsiders to German identity.

Tracing the evolution of these interlocking relationships requires a deeper historical analysis, and such analysis is outside of the scope of this book. However, this chapter provides a short synopsis of the main events of recent history, which forms the contextual framework for the rest of the book. This synopsis is vital for recognizing the limits of viewing the Ausländer as a labour force only, and it helps us consider how Ausländer have become agents for re-articulating German citizenship. This chapter focuses mainly on the experience of Turkish Ausländer since Germany's postwar division. It shows a series of specific modifications in the ways that Turkish Ausländer belong in Germany and explains how those shifts have altered the essential principles for defining who is German. Through several profound social transformations, Germans have sought to redefine themselves by contrast with designated outsiders. These discursive shifts in German politics and attitudes toward Others have shaped the lives and the self-understandings of German-born Turkish Ausländer.

Creating Germanness

Following Germany's defeat in the Second World War, the Allied powers divided the country into four military occupation zones: French in the southwest, British in the northwest, Americans in the south, and Soviets in the east. The three Western zones were amalgamated as a German state on May 23, 1949, when the *Grundgesetz*, the founding constitution of the Federal Republic of Germany (FRG), was promulgated. Following elections in August, the first federal government was formed by Konrad Adenauer, of the *Christlich Demokratische Union* (Christian Democratic Union, or CDU). In the Soviet occupation zone, the Socialist Unity Party called a series of people's congresses in 1948 and 1949. Under Soviet direction, a constitution was drafted on May 30, 1949, and adopted on October 7, when the German Democratic Republic (GDR) was formally proclaimed (Coy 2011; Dale 1999; Turner 1992).

Soon after the war, Berlin became the seat of the Allied Control Council, which was intended to govern Germany as a whole until the conclusion of a peace settlement. In 1948, however, the Soviets withdrew from participating in the quadripartite administration of Germany and installed a communist regime in East Berlin. From then until Germany's reunification, the Western Allies continued to exercise supreme authority in their sectors through the Allied Kommandatura. However, to the degree compatible with Berlin's special status, they turned over management of the city's affairs to the West Berlin Senate and House of Representatives, which were governing bodies established by constitutional process and chosen by free elections. The Allies and German authorities in the FRG and West Berlin never recognized the communist regime in East Berlin or the East German authority there (Smith 1969). This establishment of two German states both reflected and intensified Cold War tensions. East German territory

Constituting Germans and Outsiders 51

surrounded West Berlin, and the GDR proclaimed East Berlin as its capital. Meanwhile, the West German government provisionally established itself in Bonn (Coy 2011; Turner 1992).

The FRG's *Grundgesetz* of 1949 adopted the ethnicity-based citizenship law of 1913. It did this as a way to keep the "German question" open and to allow for the repatriation of East Germans and of Germans who had relocated to Eastern Europe before and during the war. The Grundgesetz, which defined Germany by its 1937 borders, declared a unified Germany as its ultimate goal, with the pragmatic injunctions that the FRG act as the core of the future Germany and that this state speak for *all* Germans. Political economist Gareth Dale (1999, 134) argues that with the loss of German land and population in the East, granting citizenship according to birthplace would have appeared as a national humiliation. Instead, a "law of return" extended the claim of the German state to all "ethnic Germans" in the East. As Dale (1999, 128) continues:

Germany was refounded as a culturally and linguistically defined *Volksgemeinschaft*, with citizenship determined by ancestral "blood," a definition that still holds in ... "modern" Germany [not only legally but also ideologically and culturally] ... This legal-cultural apparatus of differential racialization served to divide immigrants into different groups, branding some as "foreign."

The FRG's post–Second World War immigration history is characterized by the nature of its parallel flows: ethnic Germans returning from abroad and foreigners with no German ancestry also entering the country. At different times, the immigration laws made the distinction between these two kinds of immigrants less or more important, especially in terms of the privileges granted to ethnic Germans. The *Vertriebene* (the expelled ones) were either German nationals who had lived in areas intermittently under German jurisdiction prior to 1937, or ethnic Germans from Eastern Europe. Furthermore, between 1945 and the construction of the Berlin Wall in 1961, about 3.8 million Germans moved from East to West Germany (Özcan 2004). Given the recent past of the Nazi regime and the postwar division into two hostile states, the question of German national identity was particularly vexed. Economic needs, coupled with the political past and inherited identity politics, determined official attitudes toward recent immigrants with no German ancestry.

Recruitment of Gastarbeiter (Guest Workers)

In West Germany, the *Wirtschaftswunder* (economic miracle) of the 1950s required a steady supply of labour. The first foreign workers, who were mostly ethnic kin from the east, began to enable the FRG's economic growth starting in 1953 (Wengeler 1995). Heavy inflows of immigrants with no German ancestry began in the second half of the 1950s, as the FRG became one of the most important destination countries for immigrants (Özcan 2004). In the late 1950s, the demand for labour in the FRG reached a peak. This demand could not be satisfied from the domestic labour market, despite the large numbers of refugees who crossed the border from the GDR at that time. Then, in 1961, the GDR built the Berlin Wall to prevent people from leaving the country, cutting off this source of labour.

An important component of labour migrants to the FRG were people categorized as international migrant workers participating in institutionalized worker exchanges (Çağlar and Soysal 2003). The first bilateral recruitment agreement, or *Anwerbeabkommen*, was signed with Italy in 1955. This agreement was followed by a series of others: with Spain and Greece in 1960, with Portugal in 1964, and with Yugoslavia in 1968 (Özcan 2004). In 1960, the number of foreigners in Germany already stood at 686,000, or 1.2 percent of the total West German population, with Italy providing the highest number of workers (Özcan 2004).

In 1961, negotiations began between the Turkish Ministry of Employment and the Labour Recruitment and Employment Office, and a *Deutsche Verbindungsstelle* (German Communication Office) unofficially opened in İstanbul. The Bilateral Recruitment Agreement was signed and implemented in September of 1961, and by the end of that year, seven thousand Turkish workers were living in West Germany (Abadan-Unat 2002, 43).

Under the rotation principle, migrants entered the FRG for one to two years and were then required to return home and make room for other guest workers. This system brought several million workers, mostly men from southern European countries, usually on contracts to do heavy, unpleasant tasks in the construction, metal, or automotive industries (Dale 1999). The policy allowed employers to recruit from a comparatively low-paid and flexible external reserve army of labour. The state assumed the tasks of enforcing the annual deportation of foreign workers and of regulating the immigrants' conditions of work and life (Dale 1999, 119–20).

This labour policy had a double purpose: preventing settlement and allowing German industries the largest possible number of foreign workers but preventing their settlement. The first workers of the 1955 recruitment

Constituting Germans and Outsiders

were called *Fremdarbeiter* (foreign workers), a term that resembled *Zwangsarbeiter* (the name used for the forced labourers conscripted during the Third Reich). The FRG replaced this term in 1960–61, due to its association with Nazi policy (Özcan 2004). As the migrants were supposed to be temporary visitors only, they were now euphemistically called Gastarbeiter (guest workers), which was believed to have no negative connotations (Wengeler 1995). However, as Dale (1999, 118) argues, the term *guest workers* clearly expressed the "stratagem of permitting the import of sufficient workers to meet demand, while preventing their settlement." According to the Interior Ministry, preventing the workers' settlement "was the only means to repeatedly impress upon both foreign workers and the local German population that [they] ... were merely aliens whose presence was tolerated and that their permanent settlement ... was out of the question." The official policy was that no integration was intended, and guest workers had to leave the country after their contracts of employment expired. Dale argues that this system promoted xenophobia and nationalism among Germans. As documentary photographers John Berger and Jean Mohr (1975, 140) explain: "The presence of immigrant workers, seen as intrinsically inferior and therefore occupying an inferior position in society, confirms the principle that a social hierarchy ... is justified and inevitable."

Most social science writing on migration during the 1960s reflected the official policies regarding the temporary labour force and the discourse on the migrants' so-called natural backwardness. Sociological and economic narratives such as that by sociologist and political scientist Nermin Abadan-Unat (1976) emphasized labour market demands, by which the surplus of workers in sending countries matched labour shortages in host countries. Meanwhile, anthropological narratives by scholars such as social psychologist Ali Gitmez (1979, 1983) followed the paths of peasants-turned-workers from their villages to their workers' quarters in the urban centres of the West. These writings facilitated the construction of the "inferior" guest worker. The usual image of the Turk was of a solitary male Gastarbeiter, completely separated from German society, invited to Germany to help maintain the German *Wirtschaftswunder*. His societal role was limited to his economic function. The presence of the Gastarbeiter represented Germany's economic success and the *Gastfreundlichkeit* (hospitality) of the German nation. This situation continued until the oil crisis of 1973.

Meanwhile, the tensions between East and West Germany culminated in the construction of the Berlin Wall (between East and West Berlin, and around West Berlin) by the GDR on August 13, 1961, followed by the tank standoff at Checkpoint Charlie in October. West Berlin was now part of the FRG, with a unique legal status, while East Berlin was a part of the GDR. West Berlin became a city surrounded by walls. It was possible for Westerners to pass from one part of the city to the other only through strictly controlled checkpoints. For most Easterners, travel to West Berlin or the FRG was no longer possible. It was not until 1971 that a four-power agreement guaranteed access across the GDR to West Berliners and ended the potential for harassment or closure of the routes (Berlin.de, n.d.).

When the Berlin Wall ruptured the city in 1961, the wall closed off the influx of émigrés, or *Aussiedler* (ethnic Germans from Eastern Europe), and of German migrants from the GDR. It was clear that this would cause labour shortages in some areas. As attracting workers from East Berlin and other parts of the GDR was no longer possible, the FRG intensified its recruitment of temporary workers from other countries.

Berlin's first temporary workers were Turkish. In 1964, a group of Turkish women arrived in Berlin with renewable one-year contracts (Özcan 2004; Ashkenazi 1990; Çağlar 1995). These workers entered the radically changed political landscape of divided Germany. Berlin was the place where the symbols and technologies of two ideologies clashed. The temporary workers were swept up in the repercussions of the German boundary conflict; they would become participants – even catalysts – in the remaking of Germany's national landscape (Mandel 2008, 27–28).

Throughout its twenty-eight years of existence, the Berlin Wall became supersaturated with meaning. Inscribed on it was a politics that signalled practices of exclusion, together with a severing of the city's localized identities. Mandel (2008, 29) writes that for many Berliners, the wall was not merely an abstract symbol of division, "but the visible inscription of a wound to be alternately ignored or confronted daily." Many Turkish Berliners, including my interviewees Tunç, Güler, and Ayşe, who were teenagers during the 1980s, lived "just next to the wall." For Güler, inside the wall was familiar; beyond it was a dark, forbidden region. Ayşe says: "The wall was a barrier but created security at the same time." In Tunç's words: "You don't see it as a wall; you lean your back on the wall and feel strong. Nothing can come in. The wall would protect me. At the corner, your life continues."

In the late 1960s, the demand for foreign workers declined as the FRG entered a period of economic recession, and workers faced unemployment for the first time since the war. During the recession in 1966–67, xenophobic feelings increased. "Germans" started to fear for their jobs and increasingly blamed guest workers for their economic woes. However, the economic

Constituting Germans and Outsiders 55

crisis was one factor affecting public attitudes. Another factor was the shifting identity of the temporary worker population. By the early 1970s, Türkiye had replaced Italy as the most important source of foreign workers. In 1971, Türkiye accounted for 23 percent of all foreign workers, with 652,800 Turkish people living in Germany. By 1973, the year the FRG instituted an *Anwerbestopp* (an official end of foreign-worker recruitment), Germany had 910,500 Turkish guest workers (Özcan 2004; Şen and Goldberg 1994, 15). Of the 14 million guest workers, 11 million had returned to their home countries. Yet high levels of immigration persisted due to family reunification. With the backing of European human rights laws in the 1970s and 1980s, husbands, wives, and children of the workers moved to Germany (Özcan 2004). Turkish Gastarbeiter in Berlin were able to bring their families, settling in low-rent areas along the Berlin Wall, especially in Kreuzberg, Wedding, and Tiergarten.

Naming these residents – who obviously could no longer be considered guest workers – became a new public issue. In 1970, a German TV network, Westdeutscher Rundfunk, held a contest to find a word with less negative connotations, which would give a better image for so-called guest workers and their arriving families. The winning term was *Ausländische Arbeitnehmer* (foreign coworkers). Other proposed words included *Arbeitsplatzräuber* (job stealer), *Kameltreiber* (camel driver), *Gaukler* (entertainer), and *Parasiten* (parasite), which clearly expressed widely held German attitudes (Wengeler 1995). The term *Ausländische Arbeitnehmer* itself defined Turks as alien people and reduced their role in German society to that of a labour force. No longer guests, they were now "foreign coworkers."

In the public domain, discussion arose concerning how these residents were being treated, not in a welcoming way but as servant-like workers. By the mid-1970s, discourses on the Turks of Germany began to appear in the media, literature, and the political arena. These discourses commonly represented Turks as racial and cultural outsiders, too foreign to have their own voice. German works of fiction of the 1970s and the early 1980s used stereotypical Turkish characters to comment on their poor working conditions or to criticize German society for exploiting them economically.

By 1973, the number of foreign residents reached 4 million, and the share of the FRG's total population was 6.7 percent. Some 2.6 million of these non-Germans were employed. However, while the number of foreigners stayed consistent throughout the 1980s (between 4 and 4.5 million), the labour force participation of immigrants decreased. Nevertheless, a large proportion of the earlier guest workers had already acquired long-term or

56   *Constituting Germans and Outsiders*

permanent residence permits. With the rotation model a distant memory, it was clear that many foreigners were now planning to stay longer, even permanently (Özcan 2004).

In public discourse during the 1980s, the term *Gastarbeiter* was increasingly replaced by Ausländer (foreigner) or, simply, *Türken,* referring to the largest group. For its part, the government began to wrestle with the still-rising number of foreigners. With the realization that these residents were not temporary, the problem was increasingly defined as a lack of cultural integration by foreigners, especially Turks, into mainstream society (House 1997; Nonneman 1997). This narrative gave birth to the *Ausländerproblem* (foreigner problem), a concept that reflected negative public attitudes and focused on the difficulty of cultural integration as the main issue. The lifestyles and religions of the Ausländer were increasingly characterized as "Oriental," which made these people's cultural nonconformity even more offensive. Jokes about Turks grew common in everyday discourse (Toelken 1985).

Starting in the 1980s, Turkish Ausländer became the main targets for xenophobia in the FRG. This tendency became extreme in unified Germany after 1990, as marked by the 1991 and 1993 arson attacks in Mölln and Solingen. Folklorist Alan Dundes, ethnologist Thomas Hauschild (1983), and folklorist Barre Toelken (1985) examined the roots of these tendencies by analyzing jokes told about Turkish workers in the 1980s. These included so-called Auschwitz jokes, in which "Jews and Turks are treated in the same joke" (Dundes and Hauschild 1983, 255). Here are several jokes that have been analyzed in various works, plus a few that I collected from the participants:

> *What is the difference between a white line and a Turk?*
> You cannot drive over the white line. (Abadan-Unat 2002, 263)
> *What do you call a black thing perched on a tree?*
> A Turk after a forest fire. (Abadan-Unat 2002, 263)
> *A Turk and a Jew fall from a house. Who falls down faster?*
> The Turk is shit, the Jew is ashes, so the Turk lands first. (Dundes and Hauschild 1983, 255)
> *A train full of Turks leaves İstanbul – and comes to Frankfurt empty. Why?*
> Because it went via Auschwitz, that's why. (Albrecht 1982, 220)
> *Did you see the latest microwave oven?*
> It has room for an entire Turkish family! (Abadan-Unat 2002, 263)
> *When you burn a Turk what is left behind?*

> A set of Mercedes keys. (Mesut, interview)
> *What is a garbage can under a traffic lamp called?*
> A Turkish disco. (Yıldız and Aynur, interview)
> *What is the Turkish version of "Alice in Wonderland"?*
> "Fatma in ALDI" [the cheapest grocery store in Germany].
> (Arda, interview)

Jokes told about the members of a particular group may offer a socially sanctioned outlet for the expression of aggression toward that group. In playing with words and exaggerated images, these jokes go beyond sarcasm and convey a desire to destroy: "Jokes are always an important barometer of the attitudes of a group" (Dundes and Hauschild 1983, 250). According to social scientist Richard Albrecht (1982), such jokes reflect fantasies of the extreme right wing in Germany. Many scholars, however, argue that these feelings and opinions are much more mainstream. For example, social scientist Christian Habbe (1983) analyzes expressions used in the letters that voters send to politicians, and he observes similar hatred. Abadan-Unat (2002) argues that these tendencies are rooted in Germany's Nazi past and its ideologies. In other words, xenophobia and hatred toward Turks cannot be explained solely as the result of the tensions of unification or the increasing numbers of asylum seekers in the 1990s.

Another response to the Ausländerproblem came from a group of German professors who circulated the *Heidelberger Manifest* (Heidelberg Manifesto) in March 1982. This manifesto argued that Germans were beginning to feel foreign in their own land, neighbourhoods, and workplaces. The text asserted that there are fundamental differences in peoples' genetic makeups and traditions. It discussed the potential eugenic disaster that would result from the integration of non-Germans into German society. The manifesto expressed concern for the education of German children in classes dominated by "illiterate foreigners." The children of migrant workers who spoke non-German languages were depicted as an intrusive Muslim peril. To bring "social and ecological relief" to Germany, the manifesto recommended offering development aid to the homelands of the Gastarbeiter. The writers of the manifesto sought to dissociate themselves from racism, ideological nationalism, and extremism of the left or right. But a vocal and angry public reaction to the document raised questions about its underlying agenda (GHDI 1982; Mandel 2008, 59–60). To this day, the manifesto is being circulated across the Internet (http://schutzbund.de). One of the more positive responses in this escalating debate was the introduction, in the early 1980s, of a *Tag des ausländischen Mitbürgers* (foreign citizen's day) (Teraoka 1997, 70).

Academic discourse on this issue has also changed. Compared with the literature on immigration of the 1970s (which focused primarily on labour struggles, class structures, and the plight of workers), the social science literature of the 1980s testified to the permanence and the personhood of the "guests who stayed here for good" (Çağlar and Soysal 2003, 6). Aspiring to a better understanding of migration, numerous social scientists considered the anthropological trials of moving and settling. In addition, this new discourse increasingly differentiated its subjects (the migrants) along gender, ethnic, and religious lines. The researchers have viewed migrants as women, as Turks, Kurds, Alevis, and others – not simply as categories in statistical tables, but as legitimate topics of inquiry in their own right (Çağlar and Soysal 2004, 6–7). We can observe a turning in the literature toward recognition of the Gastarbeiter as persons, with culture, personality, and feelings.

During the two decades following the end of labour recruitment (in 1973), foreigners in Europe were solidly integrated into many of the existing legal, political, economic, and social structures of their host countries (Soysal Nuhoğlu 1994). As social anthropologists Ayşe Çağlar and Levent Soysal (2003, 6) note, foreigners were counted as formal categories of Germany's population in the national and European statistics. Foreigners attained rights and privileges that were previously reserved for national citizens. Minorities became extensively involved in public life through associational activity, union membership, party politics, and artistic or literary production. At the same time, they fit into the existing patterns of income inequity, social differentiation, and ethnic or racial discrimination. In short, foreigners became subjects in a complex terrain of exclusions and inclusions, contention and accommodation, disenfranchisement and membership.

This period of the 1980s and 1990s saw numerous attempts to express the material and social realities of life for Turkish members of German society through social science studies, literary works, and the media. The portrayals of Turks and other foreigner groups expanded beyond stories of the struggling guest worker and grew more representative of the variety of non-Germans living in Germany. Such works started to explore the experience of the second-generation *ausländische Mitbürger* (foreign fellow citizen) who grew up in Germany. Some of these discourses dealt with the everyday racism that Turkish residents and other non-Germans encountered.

Constituting Germans and Outsiders

Here, the Turk was not a silent figure. Situations were not presented second-hand, but as first-hand encounters in which non-Germans addressed issues such as their motivations for seeking asylum. In the 1980s, representing the life of the "Turkish foreigner" became less a matter of understanding personal narratives or searches for identity and more about experiencing the despair and hardship of the foreigner. In many cases, the aim was to shock or cajole the German population into tolerance and respect for human rights.

This general trend in official attitudes started to appear in educational policies, which were implemented differently by different states, in variations of two main models: Berlin's integration model and Bavaria's rotation model. Because my participants were born and educated in Germany, the effects of these education policies appear prominently in their narratives.

Schooling for Guest Workers' Children

The first serious discussion about Ausländer children and their education began after the guest-worker program ended, as their children began to appear in classrooms due to family reunification (Shafer 1983, 29). By 1976, these children constituted about 9 percent of the West German school population (*Bulletin* 1976; Coburn-Staege 1979). In 1980, one out of every four children in the primary schools of West Berlin was an Ausländer (Shafer 1983, 30).

The Conference of Education Ministers had developed a policy in 1964 that involved a dual approach to Ausländer children. The policy aimed to enable 1) the children's integration into West German life, and 2) their eventual return to their home countries. In response to the economic recession of 1967–68 and the resultant constraints on further immigration, the second of these strategies was emphasized. The children were offered an education similar to what they might receive in their homeland. German was taught as a foreign language, often by teachers from Türkiye or other countries. By 1976, the Conference had agreed that whenever Ausländer children of any single ethnicity constituted more than one-fifth of a class, a separate section for these children could be established (Shafer 1983, 33–34; *Times* (London) 1971; Shafer 1983, 37–39; *Bulletin* 1976, 179).

As noted earlier, Berlin (in 1971) and Bavaria (in 1973) adopted different educational policies for guest-worker children. Berlin's approach was an *integration* model for assimilating immigrant children into monolingual German classes as rapidly as possible (Pfaff 1984, 271; Rist 1978, 25). Bavaria adopted a *rotation* model, on the assumption that guest workers (and therefore their children) would eventually leave the country (Rist 1978). Therefore, the Berlin model strove for the full integration of foreign children and their absorption into German society, and the Bavarian model stressed the immigrants' transiency and ethnicity. However, neither of these systems acknowledged the legitimacy of the diverse and heterogeneous society emerging in Germany. Both systems failed to respond to the fact that there were now thousands of foreign-worker families who wished to accommodate themselves to the country on a long-term basis, but also wished to honour their own cultural heritage. This contrast between goals created a profound disjuncture between the children's homes and their schools as the primary agents of their socialization (Rist 1978, 53).

In these educational programs, the separation of Ausländer children from German children has been justified as a better way of teaching the Ausländer to speak German and to *integrate* them more fully. However, in the participants' experiences, these practices have only further perpetuated the students' ethnic separation. Güler, a social worker, was in Grade 2 when she first experienced the classes for foreign children. As her grades were high, she was moved to attend *regular* German class with four other Turkish girls: "When they separated the classes, I thought ... my place is in that other class. Just because I am not there, it doesn't change that I am a foreigner child ... In the other class, I had my friends; I had bonds with them. I belonged there."

The question with this system is how much Güler, and the others who were "successful" in the German school system, could accomplish in transforming their own Ausländerness, if there were still separate classrooms for most other Ausländer children. In practice, being able to attend a regular class did not move Güler any closer to Germanness. When she was with German children and not in a special (Turkish primary-language) classroom, she remained an outsider socially – still an Ausländer child. Neither academic nor social integration had been achieved. In Berlin and in industrial cities such as Mannheim, many inner-city classrooms contained only foreign students, and others contained 60 to 70 percent foreigners (Shafer 1983, 40).

Schooling is the core of cultural reproduction through which existing disadvantages and inequalities are passed down from one generation to the next (Bourdieu 1973, 1986). Education can be acquired as a kind of capital and exchanged or converted into other forms of capital. So schooling plays a crucial part in determining the roles of Ausländer in German society. The participants experienced German education as a stratified system in which they received training suited to their Ausländer status. Such schooling

Constituting Germans and Outsiders

practices have institutionalized that status as outside of Germanness. The school program is structured to prepare Ausländer children for functions assigned to them *for* and *in* German society. Limiting their access to equal schooling means that Ausländer children will always have less education and less cultural capital than the *real* Germans, thereby cementing their Ausländer status as perpetual outsiders.

The widespread separation of Ausländer students into classes taught in their home languages has contributed to the gulf separating them from native students. The resulting academic disadvantage adds to the social, psychological, and economic barriers that Ausländer children face. According to a report issued in 1980 (Council of Europe 1980, 13), more than 50 percent of Ausländer children did not achieve the *Hauptschulabsschluss* (the school-leaving qualification). Of those attending *Berufsschule* (part-time vocational education), 50 percent did not complete their schooling, and only 4 percent of Turkish children were attending either the Realschule or the Gymnasium (secondary schools). Ausländer children were on the periphery of any classroom until they become fluent in German. In terms of social integration, a study in the Ruhr (Coburn-Staege 1979) indicated that more immigrant children wanted to play with German children than the other way around. As the children of Ausländer workers lagged behind their West German cohorts, they were mistakenly considered less able than West German youth (Shafer 1983, 42–43). This negative estimate of the minority students' abilities appeared to be corroborated when they commonly failed to qualify for apprenticeships on leaving school.

The German education system shows a strong tendency to reproduce social inequality (Söhn and Özcan 2006). None of its programs serve the educational needs of children who grow up as both German and Turkish, because Turkish children find themselves in unfavourable positions throughout the process of schooling. Furthermore, the educational policies work to undercut the trend toward an ethnically pluralistic society. The assumptions behind these policies reinforce unrealistic perceptions regarding the social reality in which guest-worker children grow up (Rist 1978, 54).

Although the proportion of Ausländer children and adolescents (including those born in Germany) has been rising since the 1960s, appropriate and consistent linguistic, educational, and social policies have failed to evolve (Rist 1978; Pfaff 1984; Uçar 1990). Germany has not recognized or legitimatized its new reality as a culturally pluralistic society. Yet despite the fact that many Ausländer children have attended Turkish classes or classes for foreigner children – and being repeatedly told that their role in German society remains that of their guest-worker parents and grandparents – my investigations show that many Ausländer students have used the education system to their advantage. In part, this finding reflects the fact that while collecting data, I did not focus on those who failed in this system. My focus was on activists and therefore on those who succeeded. Most of my participants, despite the difficulties they might have faced in the education system, have at least a post-secondary degree. Nevertheless, they report that the education system has created barriers for them. In many cases, it steered them toward ghettoization as working-class Ausländer. Most of the participants, regardless of how much education they have, reflect on the institutionalized disadvantages they faced in the schooling system and how that experience has affected them in significant ways.

This discussion of German education focuses on the research participants' experiences of the system as they grew up during the 1980s and 1990s. Since that time, the school system has remained a prominent topic of debate in the literature and the media, both in and beyond Berlin. In general, the contemporary literature supports the arguments presented here. For example, a study by ethnologist Werner Schiffauer (2004) concludes that the broad question of multicultural acceptance remains controversial among German educators and students. Immigrant populations of Turks and others (who are often still called guest workers) face significant obstacles to obtaining German citizenship, regardless of their participation in society or their access to the education system. Indeed, Schiffauer concludes that Germany's primarily ethnic definition of citizenship remains closed to the acceptance of immigrant populations, and this presumption affects the immigrants' access to education.

Unification, Das Volk

In 1989, the chant "*Wir sind das Volk!*" (We are the people!) was increasingly heard at the *Montagdemonstrationen* (Monday Demonstrations) in the GDR. This slogan was addressed to the single-party government of the GDR, and it usually signalled a call for the unification of Germany. The fall of the Berlin Wall in November 1989, the subsequent German unification, and the absorption of the GDR into the FRG less than a year later occurred at breakneck speed (Peck 1992). Berlin's special status as a separate area under four-power control and West Berlin's isolation 176 kilometres inside the GDR ended with the Final Settlement Treaty between West and East Germany. Under the terms of that treaty, Berlin became the capital of a unified Germany.

Constituting Germans and Outsiders 63

Unification brought out a number of contradictions regarding German identity, citizenship, and relations with the foreign resident population. The idea of *das deutsche Volk* (literally "German people," but also implying a national soul with a tie to the land) came under revision in a number of ways. The first new challenge lay in creating a homogenous people from a heterogeneous German population. Since unification, the notion of separate *Ossie* (Eastern) and *Wessie* (Western) identities, despite their common ethnic heritage, has been a recurring cultural and political theme. Politically, German legislators throughout the postwar era have consistently maintained the ideology of citizenship by jus sanguinis. However, the changing demographics in Germany, the cultural misunderstandings of unification, and the continued immigration of ethnic Germans have all raised questions about the viability of an ethnic German nation (Dale 1999, 114). Heterogeneous groups of immigrants have also challenged the notion of a birth-defined German identity.

All of these challenges have caused increasing tension, anxiety, and even violence, which have affected Germany's foreigners more than any other social group. Changing geopolitics and various crises within continental Europe have led to dramatic increases in the numbers of people seeking asylum in Germany. Beginning in 1989, large numbers of political refugees from Eastern Europe (*Asylbewerber*), ethnic German immigrants (*Spätaussiedler*), and East German immigrants (called *Übersiedler* until 1990) taxed the bureaucracy of the once-welcoming German government (Özcan 2004).

With the end of travel restrictions from the former Eastern Bloc countries, 3 million ethnic Germans moved to Germany between 1988 and 2003. Compared with other immigrants, these *Spätaussiedler* enjoyed certain privileges – including access to language training, employment, and welfare – in order to foster their integration into German society and its labour market. Nevertheless, Spätaussiedler, especially those who arrived in Germany in the mid-1990s, faced problems with economic and social integration. Unlike the East Germans or the repatriated Germans of the 1950s, these Germans were often second-generation Eastern Europeans. Many of them were not familiar with German culture or the German language and, therefore, were perhaps not as *German* as the already resident non-German groups (Peck, Ash, and Lemke 1997, 82). Still, in most statistical analyses, Spätaussiedler have been collapsed into the categories of native-born Germans (Özcan 2004). Also, the Bundestag (Parliament) has upheld the idea of an ethnically homogeneous Germany by continuing to support the immigration of ethnic Germans from Eastern Europe, although new yearly quotas reduced their numbers entering Germany after 1995 (Peck, Ash, and Lemke 1997, 82).

Due to the large numbers of Spätaussiedler entering Germany, numerous public debates, government documents, and newspaper articles have expressed concern over the costs of hosting these newcomers. As mentioned previously, the various sorts of *Aussiedler* (ethnic Germans) have been entitled to a wider range of economic supports than other immigrants because of their ethnic status (Peck, Ash, and Lemke 1997, 82). Some Germans have questioned whether their country can handle so many new immigrants, or whether ethnic Germans from Eastern Europe should still be considered German. Did they deserve citizenship simply based on the concept of *das Volk*? Although this concept of citizenship is enshrined in the German constitution of 1949, there are signs that the notion of a *völkisch* German identity is under revision.

In response to these issues, Germany once again introduced temporary labour agreements, bringing in a parallel flow of non-German immigrants. This time, the geographic focus was exclusively on countries of Central and Eastern Europe, including Yugoslavia (1988), Hungary (1989), and Poland (1990) (Özcan 2004). The sending countries were chosen partly out of pragmatism (so as to guide inevitable migration into legal channels) and partly for gaining geopolitical and long-term economic benefits (Martin 2006; Özcan 2004). These programs included the project-tied (or posted workers) program, along with the seasonal worker, trainee (Gastarbeiter), border commuter, and green card programs (Martin 2006, 18–22).

How did all these economic and political changes affect the Turkish immigrants of Germany? One effect was to stimulate a wave of racist and xenophobic violence by Germans. In these years of political and economic upheaval, the increasing presence of Ausländer in Germany provided a scapegoat on which to blame the problems of unification. Peck (1992, 75) says that "racism and xenophobia accompanied and in some cases was encouraged by the nationalist fervour of some Germans for their new-found unity and national identity." These feelings were reinforced by Germany's already-established economic power, large population, capacity for growth, and strong national image:

> Once upon a time, never upon a time.
> A long time ago, there was a city.
> It had a beautiful wall.
> This wall was the post that the world was fixed to.

Since it has been pulled out, the world is shaking.
In its very foundations, the parts rub together, it is crumbling.
Neighbours turn into murderers.
Streets turn into trenches.
Houses turn into gas chambers.
I have been pronouncing the name of the city softly since then.
My longing has been travelling without a ticket since then.
"How could he set fire to the house which he had been to so many times?"
Erkan Temiz asked.
"Why do they do this?" ...
As if there was an explanation.
As if the consequences became more bearable because of an explanation.

         – Kemal Kurt, *Not an Oriental (Fairy) Tale*

At present, the physical remnants of the Berlin Wall are hard to find; it has been almost completely dismantled during the past two decades. However, the mentalities that created the wall and kept it up for nearly three decades have been slower to change. Some of the Berliners I interviewed in 2003 still referred to East Berlin and East Germany. It was clearly unrealistic to expect that with the fall of the wall, the social barriers would also fall away. The demise of communism took away the concrete line that separated the two Germanys, but an invisible wall remained for years, separating political, economic, and social mentalities.

Historian Kelly Hignett (2011) writes that many people feel that the speedy disappearance of the wall has tended to eliminate opportunities for coming to terms with the past in East Berlin. The growth of *Ostalgie* (nostalgia for East Germany) in recent years has led to suggestions that although the wall may have been physically removed, a less tangible barrier remains – a *Mauer im Kopf* (a wall in the mind). Hignett adds that in a 2011 poll about lingering divisions between Eastern and Western Germans, 83 percent of those surveyed said they thought there was still an "invisible wall" running through the country. These enduring divisions appear to be fuelled primarily by post-communist disappointment, economic insecurity, and political stereotyping (with East Germans accusing West Germans of arrogance, and some former *Wessies* viewing *Ossies* as backward). Ali explains:

For Ausländer too, Berlin was still mentally divided when I came there in 2003. What has that meant in the context of everyday encounters among Berliners?

Maybe West Berlin has always been a special place. They were coming from West Germany: women, artists, ethnic minorities, homosexuals. When you compared it with West Germany, it was different and alternative. It was a middle-class city. Today, it is an ordinary city, not different from Hamburg or Munich.

For Ayşe, then seventeen, "the wall collapsed all of a sudden." Tunç, then eighteen, refers to the first encounters between East Germans and Turkish Ausländer that were most dramatic in Berlin: "The Easterners came to get their 100 euro, welcome money, to the banks at Kotti [city centre of Kreuzberg] ... We came face to face for the first time! ... We were looking at each other. We were dark. And it seemed like we owned the space."

Güler, then eighteen, explains that the Ausländer found themselves vastly affected by the opening of the wall and the anxiety over "what is going to happen to immigrants when there is one big Germany?" That was the beginning of "new tensions, anxieties, and violence for which they were ready targets" (Mandel 2008, 31). Soon after the Berlin Wall collapsed, on November 9, 1989, many immigrants in Germany began to feel uncomfortable, as the call that had toppled the communist dictatorship – "We are the people" – changed into "We are one people" (Weber 1995). The call for unification moved to quickly include all Germans in a reshaped political structure, but it also left many others out. Peck (1992, 75) writes:

While some of these peoples have found a home, even a new German "Heimat" (homeland), others are homeless. The united Germany has not made room in its house for the black, brown, and yellow people (7.2 percent of the population) who live there ... The impact of race on the definition of who is foreign, who is German emerged again as a central issue in German life.

Once the euphoria settled, the Ausländer became the ones who paid most for the consequences of unification. During the next decade, *Ausländerproblem* was again the popular code word for countless issues (Özcan 2004). The mainstream media of the 1990s was focused on naming the aspects of the Turks' ethnicity and culture that separated them from the German population – in the interest of helping to analyze Germany's issues. The word *Überfremdung* (implying foreign domination or foreign invasion) was applied to the children and grandchildren of guest workers, most of whom

Constituting Germans and Outsiders 67

were born in Germany and wished to claim membership in German society (Mandel 2008).

During this time, issues concerning foreigners, and especially asylum seekers, were fiercely debated in Germany. A flood of articles on *Ausländerkriminalität* (foreigner criminality) fingered the Turkish and Vietnamese minorities as primary offenders. The Christian Democratic Union (CDU) party and the tabloid newspaper *Bild Zeitung* led calls for limiting the populations of these ethnic groups. These discourses set off a wave of fear and xenophobia, resulting in sometimes lethal violence against foreigners and asylum seekers (Özcan 2004), especially those from southern Europe and Türkiye and from other continents. Incidents of violence rose dramatically, especially in the eastern regions of the new Germany. Beginning in 1991–92, the period of seemingly peaceful Turkish/German coexistence (with its problematic goal of "integration") was shattered by racist anger, precipitated by the political and economic unrest following unification (Peck 1992, 75). Sisters Sevgi, a stay-at-home parent, and Birgül, a kindergarten teacher, who were then twenty-one and eighteen respectively, express their feeling that *"duvar üstümüze düştü* (the wall fell on us)." Notably, Mandel (2008) reports that the participants in her study used that same expression.

In 1992, the revision of Germany's once-liberal asylum law helped cement the perception that foreigners were the cause of the violence. Many terms expressing negative attitudes toward foreigners grew common as people started dying in racist attacks: "Foreigners/Turks/Kanaks out"; "Germany is for Germans"; "Stop Foreigners"; *"Überfremdung"*; "social time bomb"; "social explosion" (Wengeler 1995). The trends in the media and in the official federal responses to the violence helped to establish the perception of foreigners in Germany as *ein Problem* (a problem) – instead of the lack of citizenship, integration, or equality being *die Probleme* (the problems). The *Frankfurter Allgemeine Zeitung* (Frankfurt General Newspaper) printed headlines such as *Dämme gegen Asylanten-Springflut* (Dams against the swelling tide of asylum seekers). Only a few arguments were raised against these discourses. For example, in 1991, the German Parliament's Commissioner for Foreigners, Cornelia Schmalz-Jacobsen, pointed out that the term *Ausländerkriminalität* was not a neutral word, because nobody spoke of *Deutschenkriminalität* (German criminality) (Wengeler 1995).

Throughout the 1990s, Turkish and other minority populations became the targets of extremist neo-Nazi youth groups who called for the elimination of "parasites" feeding on the German welfare system (Mandel 2008,

53). In September 1991, a neo-Nazi attack in Hoyerswerda, a small city in Saxony, forced the evacuation of an asylum-seekers' hostel. During the three-day riot in Rostock-Lichtenhagen, in August 1992, several thousand people surrounded a high-rise building and watched approvingly as militants threw Molotov cocktails. The Vietnamese inhabitants barely managed to survive by fleeing to the roof of the building. In November 1992, arson perpetrated by right-wing youth in Mölln killed three Turks. On May 28, 1993, four neo-Nazis set fire to the house of a Turkish family in Solingen. This attack was the most severe case of anti-foreigner violence in Germany at the time: three girls and two women died, and fourteen other family members were injured. One week later, in Frankfurt, an arson attack on a house with thirty-four foreigners was detected early, and nobody died. A case of arson in an asylum-seekers' hostel in Lübeck killed ten in 1996. That crime was never solved. In all, 135 foreigners died in attacks by neo-Nazis from German unification through 2010 (Bundeszentrale für politische Bildung 2016, 2018).

The media reporting these attacks helped to solidify stereotypes of the Turkish guest workers as the most visible group of foreigners in Germany. During the early 1990s, the terms *Turk* and *Ausländer* became synonymous in public discourse. To their German defenders, these attacks on Ausländer illustrated the need for tolerance and social awareness (Peck 1992, 75). However, the upsurge in violence led to heated public and parliamentary debate, in which the word *Ausländerproblem* was used to describe any area of tension between "foreign" groups and Germans, whether it was the large number of asylum seekers, the poor integration of Muslim women into German society, or the repatriation of ethnic Germans from Poland and Czechoslovakia. In short, all foreigner groups were fused together by the media and government, as Germans searched for reasons (or justifications) for the hatred directed at these groups.

The official reactions to these events involved both denunciation of *Fremdenhass* (xenophobia) and confirmation that the difficulties were indeed caused by the large number of foreigners in Germany. In its official statements, the federal government reinforced the notion that the former guest workers and other foreigners did not belong. Discussions of racist violence were lumped together with discussions of the Ausländerproblem, implying that the problem lay with the criminality of foreigners rather than the racism of many Germans.

Such violence caused great anxiety both within Germany and abroad. Many people feared that the moral fabric of German democracy might be too brittle to withstand the hurricanes of German unification and the surge

Constituting Germans and Outsiders 69

of migration following the breakdown of communist societies. The international image of Germany grew contradictory. On the one hand, there were almost daily reports of burning refugee camps and racist violence against immigrants, and electoral support for right-wing parties reached a new high (Özdemir, in Weber 1995). On the other hand, there were powerful signs of social solidarity, as millions came into the streets in candlelight demonstrations against the violence. In December 1992, large demonstrations against xenophobia took place all over Germany, with over 700,000 participants. This positive sign of spontaneous political activism was organized by sending out just one fax, which was then distributed to other groups. According to former member of European Parliament Cem Özdemir (cited in Weber 1995), the silent majority's message was that they would no longer tolerate political violence toward foreigners. As one official response, several neo-Nazi groups were outlawed by the end of 1992. However, two days before the Solingen attack, on May 26, 1993, the German Bundestag resolved (with a two-thirds majority) to change the *Grundgesetz* (constitution), limiting the number of asylum seekers.

During the 1990s, a number of public campaigns rose *against* xenophobia. One of them featured the slogan "*In 178 Ländern der Erde sind wir Deutschen selbst Ausländer*" (In 178 countries of the earth we Germans are ourselves foreigners). Another campaign was called "*Mein Freund ist Ausländer*" (My friend is a foreigner) (Wengeler 1995). These responses to the attacks on foreigners illustrate the inflation of terminology on both sides of the political spectrum – *ausländerfreundlich* (friendly to foreigners) on the left, *ausländerfeindlich* (hostile to foreigners) on the right. Such terms allowed the left to take the moral high ground but also to continue objectifying foreigners as Others. Neither left nor right put the term *foreigner* itself into question.

Many academic works from this period are also problematic, as most are based on unexamined definitions of Germanness and non-Germanness. For example, German linguistics and cultural studies professor Martin Wengeler (1995) sees the discourses of integration and lack of tolerance as problematic, but not the definition of Germanness. He continues to rearticulate a binary opposition, even while demanding a more neutral language and a *Sprachliche Therapie gegen Ausländerhass* (linguistic therapy against foreigner hate). Wengeler demands that the word *Ausländer* does not have negative connotations but fails to problematize the concept of Ausländer or to propose other terms. Peck (1992, 77–78) feels that these responses and terms of identification make it "impossible for foreigners to individualize an identity based on criteria of their own choice, to construct an identity that can accommodate both what they once were and are now."

After the racist attacks began to lessen in 1993 and 1994, articles and reports on Turks started to focus on subjects besides *Ausländerkriminalität* and the repression of Muslim women. Discussions about the Turks' search for a dual national and ethnic identity, their cultural and religious practices, and their cultural contributions to Germany grew increasingly common during the mid-1990s. In such discussions, the Turks of Germany became characters in their own right, with feelings, opinions, and motivations – not just victims held up as examples of injustice and intolerance. In general, these representations were more positive, or at least more personal, than past discussions of guest workers or Ausländer.

During the first half of the 2000s, however, the states around Berlin gained notoriety for a frightening rate of anti-immigrant, xenophobic, racist violence – even though immigrants and minorities were underrepresented there compared to the western states. That wave of violence also ebbed, but in April 2006, the media reported two brutal attacks: one on an Ethiopian-born engineer in the eastern city of Potsdam, the other on a state lawmaker of Turkish descent in eastern Berlin. Also, government reports quantified a rise in right-wing violence during the years after 2000 (Longman 2006; Smee 2006).

When nine people died, all of Turkish descent, and sixty others were injured in a fire in an apartment in the southwestern city of Ludwigshafen on February 3, 2008, this event was at first reported as another hate crime. Later, it was found to have been an accident. Clearly, German newspapers viewed this tragedy in light of the xenophobic attacks of recent years. Most newspapers praised the transparency of the ensuing police investigation (Bax 2008; *Der Spiegel* 2008). The left-leaning *Die Tageszeitung* (cited in *Der Spiegel* 2008, para. 7) wrote:

> This impression has its roots in the 1990s, when a murderous arson attack in the city of Solingen was met with ignorance and then indiscretion by political authorities. The racist motives behind the attack, predated by xenophobic assaults in Mölln, Rostock, and Cottbus, were later downplayed. Chancellor Helmut Kohl then declined to offer his condolences to the victims' relatives. This severely damaged German-Turkish relations. Now the German side has the opportunity to regain the Turks' trust.

The waves of xenophobia and violence had effects on the study's participants. A new layer of social division was added to their memories of living

Constituting Germans and Outsiders

in a divided city: "For us, it was as if the wall moved about one hundred metres back. You use the nice parks over there. Maybe you go to a soccer field. But you don't go any further" (Tunç); "I feel comfortable in the places where there are Turks or anywhere which is multicultural" (Ayşe). For many participants, eastern Berlin continued to feel like a zone of hostility toward Ausländer:

> My friends, my work, my family, and the places I go in the evenings are all in West Berlin. It doesn't mean East Berlin is a distant place to me emotionally ... I haven't gone to the outskirts of West Berlin before, like Spandau ... The same for East Berliners. The West doesn't give much to them. Their lives are in East Berlin.
>
> – Ali

During my interviews in 2016, I asked if the West Berlin/East Berlin divide still exists. Leyla said: "That division doesn't exist any longer. There is one Berlin. We do not have an invisible wall any longer." Maybe the invisible wall metaphor no longer suggests the exclusion of Ausländer, but for all of Germany that divide seems deeper than ever.

In November 2011, two suicides after a failed bank robbery were one of the biggest scandals in postwar German history. The two dead men and a woman had lived underground for thirteen years. They were part of the *National-Sozialistischer Untergrund* (NSU), a neo-Nazi group. Between 2000 and 2006, they murdered nine migrant small entrepreneurs in various German towns as well as a female police officer, and they were responsible for three bomb attacks and about fifteen bank hold-ups. These murders were called "doner murders" (as in doner kebab), and the police called their investigation team "Bosphorus." It was eventually revealed that some branches of the state apparatus, including the *Bundesamt für Verfassungsschutz* (the Federal Office for the Protection of the Constitution), police force, politicians, and media had systematically obstructed the search for the murderers, destroying the evidence as it emerged. Witnesses had disappeared or mysteriously died. The series of events created mistrust among people toward police and the justice system (Wildcat 2014).

Post-Wall Citizenship Debates

By the end of the 1990s, the rights of Turks of Germany were strongly entrenched in a legal sense, but they were still far from equal to the rights of full citizens. Social and medical benefits were extended to foreigners with an *Aufenthaltsberechtigung* (right to reside), but the right to vote or be elected to national public office was withheld from these *Mitbürger* (fellow citizens). Although the requirements for naturalization have since been altered, the process of legal integration remains difficult. Few Turks have become citizens, partly because Germany's citizenship law makes it hard for any foreigner to do so. Even those born and living in Germany have no automatic right to become citizens. In addition, dual citizenship is not allowed for adults. Many Turkish residents are reluctant to take a German passport because they retain family and property ties to their Turkish homeland (Wyatt 1998).

The Christian Social Union (CSU – the right-wing Bavarian party that was part of the ruling coalition in the late 1990s) declared that Germany was not a country of immigration, and it should be kept ethnically exclusive, despite the 2 million Turks living and working in Germany. The Bavarian election campaigns of September 1998 saw harsh anti-foreigner rhetoric. The ruling party put up posters urging people to vote for the CSU if they wished to limit the numbers of foreigners in Germany. Most people in the CSU did not consider themselves supporters of the far right, yet the rhetoric of extremism became an accepted part of this election campaign, thanks to the party in power at both the local and national levels (Wyatt 1998).

Fortunately, many people rejected extremist rhetoric. When Gerhard Schroeder was elected chancellor in September 1998, his Social Democratic–Green coalition government pledged to end the anomaly in German citizenship law and to normalize the situation for long-standing and German-born Turkish residents. The favoured solution was to permit dual citizenship for Turks (Persky 1999).

Two months later, in November, the famous Mehmet story broke (Gebauer 2001). A fourteen-year-old youth of Turkish descent, known by the pseudonym "Mehmet," was threatened with deportation after a crime spree in Munich. Despite being born in Germany, Mehmet was not a German citizen. Therefore, Bavarian officials applied for a court order to deport Mehmet to Türkiye, a country he had never visited, with a language he did not speak (Persky 1999). Cem Özdemir (2003), the German Bundestag's first parliamentary representative of Turkish descent, argued that Mehmet belonged in Germany, not Türkiye. It was Germany, not wherever his parents came from, that should be responsible for a child born in the country (Wyatt 1998). Nevertheless, the "Mehmet factor" took its toll on efforts to reform Germany's citizenship law (Persky 1999).

Constituting Germans and Outsiders 73

On April 1, 1999, the German parliament passed a law allowing limited dual citizenship – the first major citizenship reform since 1913 (Persky 1999). The children born to foreigners in Germany were entitled to German citizenship, regardless of their own or their parents' origins, provided that one parent had been a legal resident for at least eight years. However, the German conservative opposition refused to accept dual citizenship for adults. Therefore, dual citizenship was available only to children, and the children had to decide in which country they wanted citizenship by age twenty-three. Migrants who had been living in Germany for eight years (this used to be ten years) were entitled to apply for citizenship. However, they were required to have a good knowledge of German, to not be receiving unemployment or social benefits, and to have no criminal record. The Turkish Ausländer were upset by this new law, because they had hoped for dual citizenship as promised by the Social Democratic (SPD) government (Persky 1999; Şen 2003).

Until recently, the dual citizenship law posed a problem for young migrants. They had to choose one citizenship or the other when they turned twenty-three, and if they desired to maintain a foreign citizenship, the application had to be made by age twenty-one. Persons acquiring German citizenship by birth (without a German parent) automatically lost their German citizenship at age twenty-three if they had not successfully applied to retain it (Farahat and Hailbronner 2020). Still, the demographic effects of the new citizenship law soon became visible. In 2000, there were 41,300 children born of parents with non-German citizenship who became German by birth. In 2001, there were 38,600 more. Without the new law, they would have appeared among the statistics for the foreign population (Green 2003; Özcan 2004).

The debates surrounding the 1999 amendment of the German citizenship law (and other such debates across Europe) have revolved around differing notions of integration. Those supporting restrictive citizenship laws have upheld a communitarian idea of political community. This communitarian model emphasizes loyalty to the state rather than to individual rights. Its notion of equality for insiders requires a boundary marker around the nation. This position serves "as a sort of modern surrogate for a former ethnic nationalism" (Gerdes, Faist, and Rieple 2007, 69), and it provides a comfortable home for racist practices. In some countries, such as Holland (de Hart 2007) and France, liberal dual citizenship laws have been overturned. Naturalization has been redefined as the end result of the process of social integration. Citizenship has become a reward for conformity rather than a right. In Sweden, by contrast, toleration of de facto dual citizenship has eventually led to a full acceptance of that principle (Gerdes, Faist, and Rieple 2007; Faist 2007).

In August 2000, Germany introduced a green card system, yet another form of guest-worker program, to help satisfy the demand for highly qualified information technology experts. This was a sign that things had not changed. In contrast to the American green card, which allows for permanent residency, the German version limited residency to five years. This system was built on Germany's long tradition of recruiting foreign workers, but even so, this turn toward a more organized and focused recruitment of highly skilled labour marked a watershed. This change, coupled with a demographic shift toward a more elderly population and a continuing low total fertility rate (1.4 per 100,000 in 2004), led to broader discussions concerning a formal immigration policy. Supporters for new legislation pointed to demographic deficits and growing shortages of qualified personnel. Opponents countered by citing a persistently high unemployment rate, which in 2000 stood at 9 percent of the total working population but 16 percent for foreigners. Opponents also questioned German society's capacity to integrate more foreigners. Both groups, however, agreed on the need to improve the integration of foreign residents, especially those from former recruitment countries (Özcan 2004).

In 2000, the Federal Ministry of the Interior and Home Affairs (Das Bundesministerium des Innern und für Heimat) appointed an Independent Commission on Migration to Germany that would work out proposals for a new immigration and integration policy. In 2001, this commission presented a report titled *Structuring Immigration, Fostering Integration*. In response to well-known demographic developments such as increasing life expectancy, low birth rates, and a shrinking workforce due to an aging population, the commission argued for initiating a controlled immigration program for foreigners whose characteristics seemed favourable for integration into both the labour market and overall society. The report proposed a point system for selecting twenty thousand immigrants a year, based on criteria of education, age, and language skills (Independent Commission on Migration to Germany 2001). Germany officially became an *Einwanderungsland* (land of immigrants) in 2000. In practice, however, the immigrants accepted under this program were still considered Others, and legal changes that would grant them equal rights have not materialized (DOMiD n.d.).

According to the the Federal Government Commissioner (*Die Bundesausländerbeauftragte*) (2022) and social scientist Veysel Özcan (2004), the number of legally resident foreigners in 2003 was 7.3 million, or 8.9 percent of the total population. Citizens of the former guest-worker countries continued to form the largest share, including 1.9 million holders of Turkish citizenship, of whom 654,000 were born in Germany. The 575,000 Turks who had been naturalized since 1972 were not counted in the statistics of the foreign population. Other foreign residents included 1,050,000 from the former Yugoslavia, 600,000 Italians, 355,000 Greeks, 325,000 Poles, and 190,000 Austrians. About 25 percent of the total foreign population originated from countries of the European Union (EU), and an additional 55 percent came from other European countries such as Norway, Switzerland, Russia, Ukraine, and Hungary. Overall, 80 percent of the foreigners came from Europe, and only about 12 percent were Asians.[1]

A new *Einwanderungsgesetz* (immigration law) was discussed by the parliament and became effective on January 1, 2005. The title of the *Ausländerbeauftragte der Bundesregierung* (Parliament Commissioner for Foreigners) was changed to *Beauftragter der Bundesregierung für Migration, Flüchtlinge und Integration* (Federal Government Commissioner for Migration, Refugees, and Integration). The new law introduced two new conditions. First, it made integration of migrants a federal problem. Now integration was defined as a process involving a set of requirements for newcomers, such as language proficiency. Second, the old rights and exceptions given to people with German ancestry were eliminated. Still, people from the EU could live like German citizens in Germany.

To control discrimination and racism, the EU introduced Council Directive 2000/43/EC. However, Germany did not apply this directive in national law until the *Allgemeine Gleichbehandlungsgesetz* (AGG, or General Act on Equal Treatment) came into force in August 2006. Its purpose was "to prevent or to stop discrimination on the grounds of race or ethnic origin, gender, religion or belief, disability, age or sexual orientation" (Federal Anti-Discrimination Agency 2009, 4). This new law aimed to govern "the claims and legal consequences in the case of discrimination, both in the field of work and also for the sphere of civil law" (Federal Anti-Discrimination Agency 2006, para. 3). The law mostly focused on the employer-employee relationship, with a set of guidelines for both parties to follow regarding acts of discrimination.

From Erkan's perspective, Germany has been unsuccessful in implementing the AGG: "We are going to celebrate the tenth-year anniversary in August, this year [2016]. No one feels the need to make any changes ... Germany's attitude was always like, 'We don't have discrimination in our country, so we don't need this law.'" Erkan says that in practice, "[The law] is not enforced. If an organization has discrimination in its structure or daily functioning, it is not necessarily punished. This demonstrates that the law is so insignificant."

According to an Open Society Institute (2010) report, *Muslims in Europe: A Report on 11 EU Cities*, the unemployment rate of Turkish nationals in Germany is twice the national average. Some 28 percent of Turks report discrimination during job searches, and 23 percent claim they encounter discrimination at work. As discussed earlier, children born in Germany to immigrant parents are not automatically granted citizenship, and although they may apply for and be granted citizenship, Mandel (2008) shows that society as a whole commonly considers them non-Germans. Around the time that the anti-discrimination law came into effect, citizenship tests began to emerge. Different provinces or states have imposed different requirements for citizenship, such as certain levels of language skill.

Ausländer Has Become Muslim: From Van Gogh to Sarrazin

When I was in Berlin in 2003, the 9/11 attacks were still fresh in people's memories, and Germans had considerable curiosity about Islam and Muslims. At the same time, many people were critical of US foreign policy. A new dialogue between different traditions seemed possible. However, this attitude shifted after Theo van Gogh created the ten-minute short film *Submission*, telling the stories of four abused Muslim women in a visually shocking way. This film would probably have had a limited impact on public opinion, but on November 2, 2004, Van Gogh was murdered by a Muslim named Mohammed Bouyeri. This murder in Holland was the turning point. As previously mentioned, Erkan explains that "until then, the Ausländer were Palestinian, Turk, Kurdish, Albanian, and Iranian. On that day, the Ausländer had become 'Muslims.' The people from Türkiye are now under the roof of the broad 'Muslim' category."

On October 17, 2010, at her conservative CDU party's joint meeting with the CSU, German chancellor Angela Merkel declared that her country's attempts to build a postwar multicultural society had "utterly failed": "At the beginning of the '60s, our country called the foreign workers to come to Germany, and now they live in our country. We kidded ourselves a while, we said: 'They won't stay, sometime they will be gone.' But this isn't reality" (Weaver 2010; Hall 2010). She claimed that those from different backgrounds had failed to live happily side-by-side with native Germans.

Constituting Germans and Outsiders 77

The statements from this meeting emphasized a commitment "to a dominant German culture, and opposed to a multicultural one." Multiculturalism was declared "dead" (Weaver 2010; Hall 2010). Merkel's comment followed weeks of anguished debate sparked by the huge popularity of an anti-immigrant book by Thilo Sarrazin (Boston 2010). Other European leaders soon joined Merkel in declaring that multiculturalism had failed in their countries.

A study by the Friedrich Ebert Foundation indicated that by 2010, more than a third of residents (34.3 percent of 2,411 people surveyed) believed that Germany's 16 million immigrants, or people with foreign origins, came mostly for the social benefits. About the same number (35.6 percent) thought Germany was being "overrun by foreigners," and more than one in ten called for a "fuehrer" to run the country "with a strong hand" (Weaver 2010; Hall 2010). On both the political and popular levels, public discourse around foreigners spanned the range from hospitality to open hostility. The 2016 results of a University of Leipzig study showed increasing hostility to non-Germans in response to similar questions (AFP/The Local 2016).

Thilo Sarrazin, a former Berlin minister and member of the Executive Board of the Deutsche Bundesbank (until September of 2010), was described by Erkan (in 2016) as "really a social democrat and not at all rightwing." But in 2010, Sarrazin published his book *Deutschland schafft sich ab* (Germany Is Abolishing Itself). This book criticizes the failure of Germany's postwar immigration policy and weighs the costs and benefits of multiculturalism. Sarrazin argues against further immigration by drawing links between lower-class heritage and a lack of intelligence. In summary, he maintains that "Muslims in Germany generally have worse levels of education than ethnic Germans and that intelligence is largely hereditary" (Spiegel International 2011). He also claims that the influx of immigrants from Türkiye, the Middle East, and Africa is watering down German culture and warns about the "creeping Islamization" of Germany (Boston 2010). The book was widely taken as an attack on all Ausländer, and especially on all Muslims. Sarrazin (2016) has reiterated his arguments on a blog post.

In January 2011, Sarrazin appeared on the BBC's *World Have Your Say* program (BBC 2011). He argued that discrimination was not a problem for Muslims, and that Muslims have inherently inferior intellect. A Turkish-background journalist who wears a headscarf called in to tell her experience of being insulted in public because of her religious identity. Sarrazin replied:

I want you to integrate ... If you wear the headscarf it's your own choice, but if you wear the headscarf you should not be surprised if you are regarded by your environment as something separate. Those who wear the headscarf in Germany separate themselves on their own account from the mainstream of society, of their own choice. It is your own choice to wear a headscarf and to live in Germany. (Volkery 2011)

The first edition of Sarrazin's book sold out within a matter of days. As of May 2011, over 1.5 million copies had been sold. In the thirteenth edition, Sarrazin added a foreword commenting on the nationwide debate his book had sparked. Although the book had a racist, discriminatory, and nationalist message that targeted Muslims, Turks, and Arabs, it was received positively among vast numbers of white Germans. I asked the participants what the book's success revealed about Germany:

Even people who never read anything bought the book. It had become a symbol and gave framework for anti-immigrant and Islamoracist discourses.

– Ayla

This was evidence that racism and discrimination is not just at the margins, but rather at the core of this society. Racism and discrimination are mainstream ... No one objected to the kind of racism he was spreading, and elites, politicians, journalists were okay with him spreading it. It was followed by PEGIDA [*Patriotische Europäer gegen die Islamisierung des Abendlandes* (Patriotic Europeans Against the Islamization of the West)] movement and the emergence of AfD [*Alternative für Deutschland* (Alternative for Germany)].

– Alp

People used to think that the racist segment of society in Germany is only a small portion of the population, those who are not educated and who are unemployed. The success of this book, PEGIDA, AfD showed that it is actually not a small portion of society who are attracted to these ideas. AfD got 30 percent support, and 15 percent in Berlin ... People used to say there would never be a person like Hitler ever again, but this [book] showed that the middle class and intellectuals are racists too.

– Selim

Constituting Germans and Outsiders

This book's success showed that Germany has a big racism problem. Many people asked: "How could that be?" Maybe it was news to many Germans, but immigrants had already been experiencing racism in their everyday lives for decades. Sarrazin's book just expressed it in public. It became a tool of fear and hatred in politics, dividing people at the intersection between race and religion.

Eurocentrism and Islamoracism

Following Merkel's statement on multiculturalism, the British prime minister David Cameron also declared that his country's policy of multiculturalism had hindered Muslims' integration into British society and therefore had failed to prevent the radicalization of Muslims. Similarly, in 2011, French president Nicolas Sarkozy, Australia's ex–prime minister John Howard, and Spanish ex-premier Jose Maria Aznar also declared that multicultural policies had prevented the integration of immigrants.

In 2012, Sarkozy threatened to pull France out of the EU's visa-free Schengen Area, while simultaneously supporting the economic austerity treaty in the name of "European cohesion" (*First Post* 2012). British officials backed a proposal to double the time that a foreign spouse was required to spend in the country before being granted residential rights. They argued that this change would promote "community cohesion." The then–home secretary Theresa May announced radical changes to immigration policy in June 2012:

> If they want to establish their family life in the UK, rather than overseas, then their spouse or partner must have a genuine attachment to the UK, be able to speak English, and integrate into our society, and they must not be a burden on the taxpayer. Families should be able to manage their own lives. If a British citizen or a person settled here cannot support their foreign spouse or partner they cannot expect the taxpayer to do it for them. (quoted in Travis 2012)

The impact of these changes was felt immediately, as thousands of British expats around the world were prevented from going home (Fabb 2013).

In July 2016, the mayor of Cannes, David Lisnard, banned the burkini, a type of swimsuit that covers the whole body apart from the face, hands, and feet. He called these swimsuits "the uniform of extremist Islamism." The ban was adopted in fifteen other French towns in response to safety concerns following terrorist attacks in the country. Geneva adopted the ban, claiming that "wearing burkinis is against social cohesion and integration" (*Le News* 2016). On August 26, the French State Council reversed this ban, but the mayor of Cogolin declared his intention to ignore the ruling (Boyle 2016). Likewise, in August 2016, German interior minister Thomas de Maizière stated that the country intended to ban full-face veils as a means of promoting national security and social cohesion (McKenzie 2016). In the same month, regional interior ministers of Chancellor Merkel's CDU and her CSU allies presented a declaration on tougher security measures by introducing greater surveillance and increased police presence in public areas.

Various political and religious figures, such as mayors Sadiq Khan, of London, and Anne Hidalgo, of Paris, and Bishop Nunzio Galantino have denounced these restrictions on clothing. French education minister Najat Vallaud-Belkacem (Patel 2016; Chrisafis 2016; Goulard 2016) considered them a violation of personal liberties and "a threat to social and national cohesion." French studies lecturer Fraser McQueen (2016) criticized the ban on burkinis for disregarding their potential to *promote* societal coexistence, by giving women following Muslim dress code access to the same spaces as other women. The JAN Trust, a non-profit organization based in London, called the burkini ban a form of state-sponsored Islamophobia, which only served to weaken communal interconnection (JAN Trust 2016).

Opinion polls in 2016 showed division along religious lines. A survey conducted by the French daily *Le Figaro* involved a sample of around one thousand people in France and one thousand in Germany. The survey found that 47 percent of French people and 43 percent of Germans felt that the Muslim community posed a "threat to national identity." Almost two-thirds of the poll's respondents in France and just under half in Germany said that Islam had become too "influential and visible" (RFI 2016). Another study, by Infratest dimap (revealed in May 2016) found that 60 percent of Germans believe that Islam "does not belong in Germany" (Brady 2016).

Right-wing parties have made electoral gains in a growing number of European countries (Aisch, Pearce, and Rousseau 2016). According to the populist discourses of these parties, contemporary globalization presents serious challenges to modernity, democracy, and Western civilization (Kaya 2018). Such claims have encouraged a surge of neo-racism and Islamophobia, promoted through the tropes of fear and "unbridled hatred" (Soloveitchik 2016) from reactionary populists. These discourses reveal a crisis in which the legacies of European colonialism are exerting new influence on the current social order and on modern forms of knowledge (Çalışkan and Preston 2017).

The language of fear and hatred reflects a failure of previous attempts to understand the human experience of living in a globalizing society. This language reduces the world's vast social diversity to a polarized confrontation between West and East. Fear and hatred are reflections of a crisis in which Western society is losing its political, social, and cultural domination over the previously colonized others of the world. If this fearful reaction to an equalizing world prevails in Western society, it will signal an attempt to reverse globalization and to re-impose systems of cultural segregation and ranking (Diener and Hagen 2009).

These reassertions of traditional prejudice involve what may be called *habits of ignorance.* If these actions involve simple socially adopted habits rather than conscious choices, then discriminatory treatment of others can be portrayed as unintentional (see Giddens 1997, 582). Such habits perpetuate the forms of discrimination by which members of marginalized groups are denied the resources or rewards granted to members of dominant groups. Institutionalized habits of ignorance become "applied prejudice in which negative social definitions are translated into action and political policy" (Kinloch, cited in James 2003, 147). On a personal level, such habits are enacted as forms of avoidance or antagonism toward people who are different. For diasporic people, living with such systems of discrimination and marginalization presents many challenges, and reversing these patterns requires a difficult political process. The structure of exclusion itself becomes the issue, because it prevents more progressive options from being considered.

Times of Political and Discursive Uncertainties

German-born, Turkish-background individuals tend to be concerned with German politics, as their naturalization stems from being born and raised in Germany (Diehl and Blohm, in Sirkeci, Elçin, and Şeker 2015, 139). The immigrant politics of becoming German involve these people seeking social and economic rights and staving off discrimination (Ostergaard-Nielsen, in Sirkeci, Elçin, and Şeker 2015, 140). They grew up at a time when Germany's citizenship laws revolved around the principle of jus sanguinis (citizenship by "blood"), which regarded the nation "as if it were a 'biological inheritance rather than a cultural acquisition'" (Sassen, in Sirkeci, Elçin, and Şeker 2015, 143). They actively supported reforms to ensure that "non-citizen German-Turks can enjoy the same social and civil rights that a German would" (Sirkeci, Elçin, and Şeker 2015, 150). Then, they saw their rights come under growing threat.

According to Germany's *Statistisches Bundesamt* (Federal Statistical Office), by the end of 2014, some 8.2 million people holding only foreign citizenship were registered in the *Ausländerzentralregister* (AZR, Central Register of Foreigners) (Local Germany 2015). The recently earned right to freedom of movement for Romanians, Bulgarians, and Croatians (as EU members) – along with the recent refugee crises from nations such as Syria and Eritrea – helped to generate new surges in immigration over the last few years (Local Germany 2015). All these trends have further inflamed concerns over foreigners and national identity.

The Turkish Ausländer experience in Germany has concerned the trials and failures of "attempts to build a post-war multicultural society." But this experience has also forced many Germans to recognize that "there is no going back to old and simple social formations and traditions" (Özdemir, in Weber 1995). Merkel's position, and that of other leaders in Germany and Western Europe, shows the significance of these issues. As Erkan explains: "There is a weight on people that they can't shake off, from youngest to oldest. There is a certain unknowing ... Things are changing so very quickly, before people figure it all out."

The progressive segment of German society, which defends immigrant rights and stands against Islamoracist hatred, was very active during the first year that Syrian refugees arrived. Since then, this activism has declined. Fatma explains:

> I think part of it is that they see the social changes, and they are confused about what to support and what not to. When it comes to the community projects, voluntary activities, they are active; there are lots of initiatives, yes. When you ask them in private personal conversations, I feel that they are confused, and this fear affects them too ... The big question, "Where is Germany going?," is in people's minds. There is that political uncertainty ... I was going to start a project in Kreuzberg. It was cancelled two weeks before it was scheduled to begin. The project was about immigrant women's lives. So, there is that pause. Of course, at the same time, you have all these parallel experiences of racism. So we are living in uncertain times.

For Alp, the emerging discourse on post-migration is an indicator of an intergenerational transformation, as the children of one-time migrant workers

Constituting Germans and Outsiders 83

are now new Germans: "That Germany is now a post-migration society indicates that this generation of new Germans have successfully sought and found acceptance in society." Therefore, the recognition that Germany is a land of immigrants (*Einwanderungsland*) is only one aspect of the new Germany. Germany has to continuously redefine and reinvent itself. This is the main challenge it faces today.

Conclusion: The State of Ethnic Divisions

> There is a great divide and separation among Muslims. But for me, there is no need for this type of detail. It doesn't matter to me at all what kind of socks people wear, how they wear their hair, or whether they pray to Buddha. But if you want to control something, what do you do first? You put fear in people ... Then, you reach your goal.
>
> – Leyla, in 2016

In this chapter, I have argued that Germany has traditionally relied on ties of ethnicity and blood as the ultimate qualifiers of nationality and identity. In this view, Germanness is an inborn essence or an ideal nature, independent of and prior to the existence of Germany as a nation-state. This image has strongly shaped the policies of German citizenship and immigration. Germany has historically sought to regulate citizenship and unify all Germans, while importing workers but preventing them from settling. Dale (1999, 114) reminds us that reliance on the jus sanguinis principle for German citizenship has meant that naturalization in Germany is not a right but a privilege, which therefore remains difficult to obtain. The lack of access to citizenship and to political power has helped to entrench the cultural definition of Turks and other non-Germans as foreigners within German society. The concept of the German *Volk* as a homogeneous ethnic community maintains the Ausländer status of Turks and other non-Germans in Germany, as well as, more recently, the "Muslim Other" status of Turkish Germans. The construction of "Germanness," therefore, rests on the maintenance of immigrants as permanent Ausländer.

The way Germany treats its outsiders involves a question of how German identity and German citizenship are challenged by the nation's outsiders. Germans have been challenged to continually re-create both citizenship and Other-hood. The binary oppositional legacy of exclusion is the fundamental problem of modern citizenship in general, and German citizenship in particular. To date, the factors defining Germany's relations with its non-German population have changed very little and very slowly. Nevertheless, the recent proposals to grant German-born Turkish residents automatic citizenship and the growing debates over the nature of multiculturalism or the legal and cultural status of Turks and other non-German minorities indicate that the next major challenge to the definition of the German *Volk* has arrived. Unification brought a transitional phase of upheaval and social change to which the German people have yet to formulate an appropriate response. The official attitude gets more complicated with each political, economic, and social transformation, and as the Ausländer's experience of life in German society evolves. The main challenge now comes from the Ausländer themselves, especially those who were born and raised in Germany and are legally closest to being German citizens.

3

Hostility–Hospitality
Accommodating the Ausländer

They never say it to your face, but somehow it comes to you indirectly. You feel it.

> – Fatma, in 2003

But if you ask me whether I experience any nasty racism personally, not really. It is just a feeling when you walk on the streets outside. There is this noise that you hear from Germans that comes from their fear of foreigners.

> – Fatma, in 2016

Theories of accommodation concern questions of why or which cultures should be respected. The answers involve philosophical and moral justifications for tolerating or accommodating other cultures. Yet these answers usually do not address what changes are required of dominant groups, nor do they account for the powers and privileges assigned to some cultures. As Dhamoon (2009, 30–31) suggests, dominant cultures are presented as homogenized, stable norms, but they receive little analytical or critical attention. The politics of accommodation assigns histories of oppression or privilege to various groups, but the basis for assigning these roles typically remains unexamined. The research participants criticize this depoliticized (as opposed to apolitical) characterization of culture. They understand the legacy of the guest-worker program in terms of racism and classism rather than of culture. Although racism is perceived as having cultural dimensions, it is basically a product of economic, social, and political domination.

The ways of recognizing and accommodating German-born Turkish Ausländer are created and regulated through acts and practices that express a system of *proximation* and *estrangement*. In this system, Ausländer are framed by and contrasted with Germans. I locate this system on the axis of hospitality–hostility (Figures 1 and 2). The acts and practices involved serve to create and regulate the participants' sense of belonging in Germany or within a given social setting. The interactions range from friendly, generous, tolerant responses toward Ausländer (in which the Ausländer are given a measure of inclusion and acceptance *despite* their foreign qualities) to antagonistic, aggressive, alienating responses (in which Germans directly or indirectly reject relatedness with Ausländer). In some cases, the standards for these interactions are expressed formally, such as citizenship law. In other cases, the practices are institutionalized via government policies, administrative codes, or professional practices such as education policies. The patterns can also be institutionalized informally through social practices, such as renting or refusing to rent apartments to Ausländer. Some practices operate through official channels and institutions, others through untraceable networks of dissemination, such as casual jokes, rumours, graffiti, and informal conversations.

Whether its result is proximation or estrangement, the logic of exclusion leaves both Germans and Turkish Ausländer labelled as fixed, homogenized, and above all irreconcilable entities who share a territory. The colonial nature of such logic presupposes that the category of Ausländer existed prior to that of German, and that once Germanness was defined, it excluded these outsiders (even though the two categories overlap). Ausländer are identified by virtue of not being German. Likewise, German-born Turkish Ausländer find themselves recognized, in Sara Ahmed's (2000, 22; emphasis in original) words, as people "who are already figureable, *who have already taken shape,* in the everyday encounters." All this raises the question of how these predefined actors will interact day by day.

As in colonial discourse, the logic of exclusion presumes that Germans are the rightful citizens, who are virtuous, productive, fairly predictable, civilized beings (cf. Hall 2017). The Ausländer seem to represent something contrary, being dishonest, useless, strange, and more recently (as Ausländer have become the *Muslim* others), foreign-based deadly enemies. While Germanness is seen as a mode of living – a system of values, a pattern of adaptation, and a culture that is moral and rational – Ausländerness is commonly categorized roughly the way colonial subjects used to be, "as congenitally lazy, unreliable, aggressive, over-emotional, over-sexed, irrational, not well endowed intellectually and thus destined by nature to be forever low down on the scale of civilised societies" (Hall 2017, 104). These processes of categorizing involve respect conferred or withheld through

Accommodating the Ausländer

ethical judgment according to the perceived worth of the Other. All of this legitimizes the distinction between German and Ausländer, and it defines the Ausländer as less than full members of society. Through such logic, the dominant group decides what Ausländer lives are worth.

Certain preconceived ideas about Ausländer are essential for keeping the German-born Turkish Ausländer apart from Germanness and for preserving the privileges and advantages of Germanness for Germans. Both informal channels and official institutions have legitimized stereotyping, thereby preparing the ground for discrimination and marginalization in the interactions between Germans and Others. Even so, these stereotypes are spontaneous and ephemeral and, therefore, difficult to challenge.

Where a dominant context assumes, defines, and dispenses Ausländerness, varied forms of injustice result. However, as was detailed in Chapter 2, German identity and citizenship themselves are fraught with tensions and struggles, especially in Berlin. As it is precisely the differences between Germanness and Otherness that define German identity, Ausländerness forever serves to define Germanness. Although this dichotomy helps Germans to maintain their distinctive identity, it also forces Ausländer to assert their own belonging to Germany, thereby challenging the meaning of both Germanness and citizenship.

"Woher Kommst Du?" (Where Do You Come From?)

> I have only one answer for it: from my mother's belly, just like you came from yours.
>
> – Zehra

Historically, Germany has attempted to fit its residents into two main categories, Germans and non-Germans, and then further divide these groups into subcategories. This categorization ignores the complexity of conditions for both Germans and non-Germans, but it provides a context for people to continue living side-by-side without disturbing or challenging the status quo. The question "Woher kommst du?" (Where do you come from?) plays a very significant role in the formation and function of this categorical construction. This question is implied in the very term Ausländer.

As Ruth Mandel (2008, 56; emphasis in original) writes, "*Aus-länder* means from outside the country. It can mean simply 'foreigner,' particularly when counterpoised to *Inländer,* native." It can also mean "stranger" or "alien." Ausländer has become a standard term that represents both non-Germanness and Germanness as unproblematically identified entities. The standard Turkish term that my participants use for themselves is *yabancı kökenli* (foreigner origin). In the participants' lived experiences, Ausländer is the name for outsiders who are not permitted to participate in Germanness. Yabancı kökenli is the name for outsiders who have inherited the experience of being a foreign guest worker.

Ranking and Layering
Several of the participants discussed the social, cultural, and economic hierarchies found in German society. They argued that it is important to acknowledge the role of ranking, especially the way that only certain groups of non-Germans are ranked as Ausländer.

In an interview at a coffee shop in 2003, Leyla pointed out two women sitting at another table: "Look, these two are Germans; we, two dark-heads, are foreigners, speaking another language. Even if we were having a conversation in German, we are still foreigners. British, American, and French are not. Italian, Yugoslavian, Czechoslovakian, Arab, Roma are. Dark-head is." In this distinction between German and non-German, the rankings of race and guest-worker experience are intertwined. Both of these inherited conditions become synonymous with ethnicity where the term *Ausländer* is used to mean "the dark-headed ones." Dark-headed represents undesirability and innate backwardness, which the Ausländer will find impossible to change, even if they speak German well. Yıldız, a theatre student, explains: "The ones whose faces are different are the real foreigners. Never French or American – they are elite."

In 2016, Arzu, a writer, spoke about her multicultural neighbourhood, reflecting on the ranking of different foreigners in Germany:

In our neighbourhood, there are a lot of foreigners, but not a lot of Turks. You hear English at the cafés ... The guy who owns the café next to our place is from Australia. The company where my husband works is right across from our home, and they have people from sixty-seven different countries working there. So, they mostly speak English there. It is very multicultural, but not in the classic sense we would understand. When we say multicultural, what comes to mind is Blacks and Muslims maybe, but not this kind of multicultural ... When we say foreigner, it is not the kids whose moms came from Paris. Or it doesn't matter whether the kid who is from New York speaks German or not. It is not a problem that they don't speak

German. The ones who don't speak German and who create problems are always the Turkish kids.

It is apparent from these women's comments that they have experienced being a *real foreigner* in Germany, despite being born in Berlin. As a result, they have a critical perspective on the construct of Ausländer. Their experiences precipitate a process of critical reflection on how ranking people in a social hierarchy brings a series of social, economic, and political antagonisms into play. This sort of mental construct marks "some others as more outsiders than others" (Ahmed 2000, 25). Such ranking is justified through various kinds of rationales, such as ethnocentrism, Eurocentrism, and racism. Thus, the German/non-German distinction does more than differentiate Germans from others – it also designates a hierarchy of ethnicity, religion, race, and class.

Jeff Peck's analysis (Peck 1992; Peck, Ash, and Lemke 1997) shows many parallels with Leyla's, Yıldız's, and Arzu's accounts of popular attitudes toward the diverse Ausländer. Peck argues that the first category, Germans, is also divided into ranked subcategories. The owner of the house is a *real German*. Citizens of the former GDR are also Germans, who, as Peck explains, "were welcomed in the years after the Wall, until the collapse of the GDR, but have been disdained and resented, because of their financial drains. The resentment has spawned increasing awareness of distinctions of habitus, dress and language." Then there are the *ethnic Germans* who resemble the Germans physically, yet whose economic distress has rendered their integration problematic (Peck 1992, 79). Another group is the German Jews: "These almost Germans are ... indistinguishable from the Germans, except [for] their names" (Peck 1992, 79).[1] Thus, some Germans are more German than others.

Ethnocentrism also contributes to the belief that other people's ways of thinking and behaviour are aberrant and inferior (Cohen and Kennedy [2000] 2013). The ranking among residents of Germany presupposes a sense of ethnic superiority – a feeling that real Germans have modes of living and cultural values that are clearly superior to those of other groups. These modes of life constitute a standard against which all others are judged. Groups constructed as less German are denied access to resources available to those who seem more German.

Peck (1992, 79) explains that non-Germans fall into two main categories, namely noble foreigners and Ausländer:

The "Noble foreigners" are West Europeans ... and selected North Americans. While they may be called foreigners, they are not really Ausländer, since that word has a pejorative connotation and the German population treats them as equals ... The members of the European Community also have special privileges ... such as the rights to work and remain in the country without registration.

Behind the designation of noble foreigners lies Eurocentrism. Social anthropologist Roger Ballard (1996) argues that despite the many obvious cultural, historical, and political differences among Europeans, Eurocentrism holds that all Europeans share certain characteristics of race, language, and religion – which non-Europeans obviously lack.

The final group is the Ausländer, the real foreigners. In this category, we find Turks, other Mediterranean people, North Africans, *Südländer* (people from the south), Roma and Sinti (Gypsies), Indians, Pakistanis, Tamils, Black Africans, and Vietnamese from the former GDR: "They are the people with dark skins and hair ... considered greasy and dirty. Finer racial and ethnic distinctions are assumed by colour" (Peck 1992, 80). The Ausländer category is diversified with reference to various labels that carry complex social meanings of accommodation. These labels have economic implications, as most of them suggest types of workers, but the connotations go beyond economics. The immigrants who arrived under the recruitment programs of the 1950s and 1960s were variously referred to as *Fremdarbeiter* (foreign workers), *Gastarbeiter* (guest workers), *Ausländer* (foreigners), or *ausländischer Arbeitnehmer* (foreign workers). The *Ausländerbehörde* (Aliens' Bureau) oversaw all of them.

The discourse of hospitality has played a significant role in naming and ranking immigrants in Germany. As philosopher Jacques Derrida argues, hospitality, or the act of welcoming a guest to one's home, is an act that is imbued with particular dynamics of power (Derrida and Dufourmantelle 2000). The concept of hospitality involves welcoming immigrants according to their status, origins, and identities. The relation of each group to the German homeland, and where they are ranked between Germanness and non-Germanness, determines how they are recognized, what hospitality they receive, and how much access to resources they enjoy. Conditional hospitality makes the guest visible (Derrida and Dufourmantelle 2000). It shapes the non-Germans' lived experiences, guides their interactions with the dominant society, and shapes their relations with one another.

Accommodating the Ausländer

In the experience of the participants, such conditional hospitality treats German-born Turkish Ausländer as "perpetual arrivants" (Çalışkan 2014, 9). The members of the dominant society regulate places and roles of these Ausländer in Germany. Concerning this type of regulation, the question: "Where do you come from?" expresses the German's ever-present power to interrogate the intentions of German-born Ausländer. Sociologist Kristi Allain, social work professor Rory Crath, and myself (2020, 8) argue that such interrogations at a threshold, such as the entrance of the home where a conditional hospitality is extended, represent "a regulatory technique for imposing limits and maintaining the entitlements of whiteness." Being constantly asked "What is your name?"; "What are your intentions?"; "Where was your prior home?" (Derrida and Dufourmantelle 2000, 135) places the German-born Ausländer always on the threshold of a German home and of life in Germany. Such questioning designates them as perpetual arrivants. Conducting such interrogation marks the German as "the master of the house who lays down the laws of hospitality" (Derrida and Dufourmantelle 2000, 149).

These perpetual arrivants are not granted a collective name of their own choice or a distinctive personal identity; the host assigns the guest an identity. Thus, Germans often feel that they know who the Ausländer are before encountering them. Regardless of birthplace, they remain similar in name, identity, and origin. There would be no hospitality without this *exposure* to an *arrivant* – to someone who arrives before he or she can even be identified as a guest. "Where do you come from?" makes the labelling possible. It makes hospitality contingent on the answers, allows a series of conditional rules and responsibilities to be set, and secures ownership of the domain for the hosts, i.e., the Germans. In the 1960s, the term *Gastarbeiter* (guest workers) embodied this understanding of hospitality toward immigrants, who were seen as peasants-turned-workers. This label summed up the class- and race-inherited deficiencies that are still deemed to define German-born Turkish Ausländer.

As Mandel (2008) argues, guests are temporary, and are expected to return home. They are bound by the rules and regulations of the hosts, so they rarely feel at home in the foreign place they are visiting. These guests, however, are not casual arrivants but guest *workers* (Gastarbeiter). The term *Arbeiter* (worker) refers to their economic function, and this title values them solely in terms of their labour. Therefore, the difference between being an immigrant and a seasonal worker has been blurred. Such guest-worker programs, of course, are not unique to Germany (Shafer 1983, 46).

In addition to their guest-worker background, the place the diasporants are from is also a significant factor in defining their relation to Germanness. For the participants, the place their parents or grandparents came from suggests that they are still temporary residents. İrem, a sociology graduate student and a community youth teacher, points out how media representation functions to define Turkish Ausländer as coming from "rural parts of Türkiye." İrem argues: "The media show Eastern and Central Anatolia as backward, with poor living conditions; then, German people associate these [images] with the ones who live here." Such images of Türkiye, despite the complexity of that country's reality, become prima facie evidence of Ausländer's backwardness, which is treated as an inherited deficiency.

The names given to Ausländer define their places in German society, first as "workers" who (most of the time) do the unpleasant jobs that Germans won't. "Guest worker" also signifies class status. Dale (1999, 119–20) argues that the lower value of foreign labour can appear as a product of "natural" backwardness, rather than of economic disadvantage or institutionalized racism. Thus, the word *Gastarbeiter* serves as a living reminder to Germans of their own good fortune. The history of guest workers has significant discursive implications for the experiences of the participants. That history is mostly described as a tale of hardship and backwardness, in which class, race, ethnicity, and religion are the essential categories. In the course of the participants' telling these stories, various categories of identity appear, disappear, and reappear, often being used interchangeably.

In explaining Ausländerness, Yıldız describes a view of backwardness that presumes certain kinds of class-related behaviour: "Most of the Turkish people are coming from a lower class. They have many family problems. Unemployment is also a problem among Turkish youth, because of their unwillingness to work." In this view, the characteristic behaviours of Ausländer lead to the formation of an autonomous subculture, in which children are socialized into attitudes that perpetuate their inability to escape backwardness. This description has many similarities with anthropologist Oscar Lewis's explanation ([1963] 1998, 1966) of the "culture of poverty." According to this conventional but problematic view, the poor

> have a strong feeling of marginality, of helplessness, of dependency, of not belonging ... Along with this feeling of powerlessness is a widespread feeling of inferiority ... [They] have very little sense of history. They are a marginal people who know only their own troubles ... local conditions ... neighborhood,

and ... way of life. Usually, they have neither the knowledge, the vision nor the ideology to see the similarities between their problems and those of others like themselves, elsewhere in the world. (Lewis [1963] 1998, 7)

Such descriptions of Ausländer have little explanatory power.[2] Yet these accounts are still commonly repeated in social research concerning the Turkish Ausländer, who are portrayed as passive, submissive, ignorant, and content with the life they are forced to live.

Arzu describes how, in light of her family background, her "achievements" are considered extraordinary. "My [German] boyfriend ... says, 'Your parents came here and did a lot, succeeded in many things. So do you ... You succeeded in something really big.'" This discourse reoccurs in the lives of other participants, regardless of their education levels, language skills, or occupations. In acknowledging the Turkish contribution to the German economy, this discourse locates Turkish Ausländer as a class of workers, not as part of German society. The participants receive acknowledgment for their social, cultural, and economic achievements, but these accomplishments are judged in relation to their affiliations with the *backward group*. The boyfriend's admiration for Arzu and her parents' achievements in German society assumes their ongoing identity as people of a guest-worker background. Although Arzu can become a successful middle-class woman, her achievements seem to be a surprise. For the participants, their inerasable guest-worker history makes their achievements seem unusual. The expression of surprise can serve two functions. It can suggest that Arzu and her parents are not really part of German society, or it can present their achievements as something that challenges the meaning of Germanness. When the recognition of exceptionality serves as a tactic for ignoring the dynamism of change, it becomes an act of misrecognition that maintains the assumption of subordinate status.

The associations between backwardness and class behaviour can be overcome in time, but characteristics such as religion, ethnicity, race, and, especially, skin colour, seem to be permanent. The Turkish peasants-turned-workers have been identified with all these kinds of difference at once. A systemic mixing of religion, ethnicity, and colour therefore essentializes their marginality much more deeply than any one characteristic can do alone. The participants' stories show how this mixing of labels works. The belief that the essential features of Turkish Ausländer (class, religion, ethnicity, and race) are passed down from generation to generation seems to justify the continued marginalization of this backward group. Such a belief presents marginalization as a problem that the Ausländer create themselves.

The categories of identity that the participants described during the initial research in 2003 were still prominent in the follow-up interviews conducted over a decade later, except that the participants tended to more distinctly define non-European as a person outside the realm of Western society. This shift suggests a more race-based distinction for categorizing immigrants. Noble foreigners are still not considered Ausländer, nor are other Europeans such as Serbian or Italian workers, whom Germans generally like. These people's foods and their homelands are respected. Arabs and Turks, however, are Ausländer dark-heads. In this context, asking: "Where do you come from?" is crucial for maintaining these distinctions. As Leyla says: "Still, in the papers, when they report a crime, if the perpetrator is reported as a German of immigrant background, you can be assured that they are not talking about American Germans or English Germans. They are talking about 'black-headed.'"

Selim, an Alevi-Kurdish youth activist in 2002, a parent and business owner in 2016, argues that there has been a clear shift in the terms used for distinguishing Germans and non-Germans in terms of race. "Now we say 'Black.' Maybe we are not racially Black, but we know that Germans see us as Black. Even in Berlin, especially in the neighbourhoods that are predominantly white, we feel that we are Black." Clearly, the term *dark-headed* goes beyond describing visual darkness. It combines cultural, religious, racial, and class meanings, or even perhaps "mythic" (irrational) meanings, as in "the dark side."

Keeping Them Outside

The question: "Where do you come from?" perpetuates both the privilege of being German and the stereotypes of being Ausländer. The stereotypes then justify marginalization. Locating where they are from is a basic strategy for preventing German-born Ausländer from claiming to belong in Germany and therefore from becoming full partners in social interaction. Many of the participants' accounts of their exchanges with Germans illustrate this strategy. In some cases, it is simply an act of locating people as belonging elsewhere, even when they assert that they are from Berlin. In other cases, the question implies an insistence on their eventual return to Türkiye. The question may also imply a belief that the Ausländer's emotional connection

Accommodating the Ausländer

is to Türkiye rather than to Germany. In many cases, designations of outsiderness are insisted on repeatedly over the course of a single encounter. Güler refers to her experience in a social psychology course:

> The instructor said: "Everybody should introduce themselves including where they work and where they came from." I said to myself: "Okay, if I wasn't here, would she ask that question?" I emphasized strongly that I didn't come from anywhere; I was born and raised here. It was my parents who came from Türkiye. Maybe it was my groundless apprehension. But all the other German women came from different cities. Later, the instructor asked some specific questions to the individuals ... When it was my turn, she said: "Can you speak both languages?" The only question she could ask me was about my being a foreigner. She didn't want to know anything else.

The instructor invalidated Güler's belonging to Berlin by asking again: "[But] where do you come from?" – a question that was really about her ethnicity, culture, class, race. This question presumed a denial that Germany – where Güler had spent her whole life – had a primary role in who she was. The German instructor had to establish what sort of non-German she was and insist on locating her elsewhere. Although Güler repeatedly claimed her German identity, she remained Ausländer.

Ela, an assistant professor of Turkish language and literature, reports that "I still come across questions like 'Do you want to go back to Türkiye?' or 'When are you going back?' As long as this continues, I can't see myself as an equal individual. Never does a German ask another German, 'When are you leaving Germany?'" The question "When are you going back?" implies that Germany's initial condition for accepting Ausländer guest workers (the plan of sending them back) still holds. Being expected to go back seems to invalidate Ela's rights for equality with other members of German society. She is merely accommodated as a guest under the conditions of German hospitality.

The expectation of return is related to another common assumption – that foreigners must be homesick for their real country. Güler tells of receiving such presumptuous sympathy regarding her pregnancy. "Yesterday, in the obstetrician's office, the assistant asked my due date, and then she said, 'Then it's a pity that you won't be able to go to your homeland this summer.' Maybe she meant well. But I wanted to say, 'My homeland is here.' But I didn't." The assistant presumed to know Güler's emotional loyalties before asking anything about them. Güler was clearly identified as someone permanently alienated from her German homeland.

All these questions reflect the conditional hospitality and accommodation given to Turkish Ausländer, whose identity and character are simply assumed. These Ausländer may be deemed to pose a threat to Germans, possibly by questioning their right to sole ownership of their *Heimat* (homeland). The Germans' intrusive questions thus maintain a permanent distinction between Germans and non-Germans and indicate a clear hierarchy among non-Germans.

Another way of keeping the participants outside of Germanness is through the discourse about Ausländer as the children of guest workers. This discourse involves the widespread notion that the children of immigrants are *second generation*. The concept of the second generation suggests a homogeneous group, and this term is commonly used in social work studies. For example, the Board on Children and Families (1995) defines first- and second-generation immigrant children as the fastest-growing segment of the US population under age fifteen. In this literature, first-generation migrants are people who move, as adults, from one country to another, and second-generation migrants are their children, who were either young at the time of migration or were born in the country of arrival (Dion and Dion 2004). Similarly, sociologist Susanne Worbs (2003) describes second-generation migrants in Germany as the children of guest workers recruited from southern and southeastern European countries starting in the 1950s.

The notion of the second generation can be a useful descriptive tool that allows policy makers to make a distinction between this specific group and other children of their age bracket for the sake of developing policies to improve conditions for that particular segment of the population. However, second generation also implies that the cultures involved are two separate entities (Keyes 2006). Accordingly, studies of the second generation typically describe a process by which the children of immigrants live between two cultures: the homeland culture is something inherited and the receiving culture is something adopted. The result is a compromised, mutant cultural experience. For example, a whole section in anthropologist Steven Vertovec's *Migration* reader (2010) is dedicated to "the second generation," and it presents a host of studies focusing on this group with that framework – viewing the experiences of second-generation people in Western Europe as a tension between assimilation and exclusion.

In Germany, this kind of analysis commonly involves a misrecognition of Ausländer children. The misrecognition is twofold. First, the label "Ausländer children" implies that these young people are generational instalments of the immigrant group. Second, this way of recognizing them betrays expectations concerning the roles and rankings they should have, as well as the economic, social, and cultural resources (such as education) they deserve.

Critical linguist Martin Wengeler's (1995) analysis of German media describes how Ausländer children have been treated in public discourse. The arrival of Ausländer children in Germany during the 1970s was characterized in the media as a flood – a natural disaster. A wave of Ausländer children was seen as threatening German schools and kindergartens. The Council of German Chambers of Commerce warned of the Gastarbeiter inflow, predicting that by 1985, some 7 million foreigners would live in Germany. The children's arrival was even characterized as a Muslim counterattack or an invasion (Wengeler 1995). In almost all cases, Germany was seen as victimized by these children. Clearly, the media portrayed Germans as feeling oppressed by the families and children of guest workers. As the shocking and discomforting arrival of these families continued, the phrases "Gastarbeiter children" and "Ausländer children" emerged in public discourse.

The discourses of researchers or policy makers show how the dominant culture has used the notion of migrant generations to its advantage.[3] Various public discussions have focused on integration, particularly on that of Turkish women, children, and youths (Mueller 2006). Other investigations have considered the immigrant families' intergenerational relations, patriarchal structures, gender roles, and familial structures. Some of the main conclusions are that young Turkish women (who are reportedly not allowed freedom of movement to go out at night, to date, or to live alone) are forced into arranged marriages and in general are oppressed by the traditional patriarchal Turkish family. These discourses locate Turkish Ausländer as generational instalments, whose cultural deficiencies are passed down from one generation to the next. Individual observations, which can be accurate in particular cases, are turned into generalized portrayals that then serve to reinforce popular assumptions about Ausländer culture. For example, sociologist Claus Mueller (2006, 432–36) argues that the Turkish minority's lack of social and economic integration into German society reflects a systemic problem to which policy makers have not yet found a response. Mueller sees Turkish Ausländer as marginalized by the larger society, separated from the mainstream by their cultural and religious lifestyles. He concludes that a significant proportion of the Turkish minority is becoming a "parallel society," with its isolation reinforced by discrimination, restricted educational achievements, and low socio-economic status.

Alp, a social anthropology graduate student, explains how the perception that descendants of immigrants are a second- or third-generation people places them permanently in the category of Ausländer: "Let's say there are two brothers: one migrates to Germany, and the other stays in Türkiye. Both have children. The one in Türkiye is not an immigrant. Nobody calls his children second-generation and his grandchildren third-generation. But the children of the ones who migrate to Europe are considered as such." Alp argues that the term *second generation* involves imagining a homogeneous generation, as if all these children were essentially the same. This generalization fails to account for the heterogeneity of experiences and identities among immigrants. However, such a discourse has benefits for members of the dominant group, regardless of whether they embrace multiculturalism. At least four distinct benefits can be identified.

First, putting all children of immigrants into one category (the second generation) helps to justify treating them as a minority with an inherited problematic culture. Second, the discourse suggests a cultural politics of intergenerational struggle within immigrant families. Third, seeing people in generational instalments justifies their permanent status as outsiders who at best are in-between the country of their ancestors and their country of birth. Fourth, expectations regarding the second generation overlook the multiple ways in which the histories of exclusion and differentiation have traditionally placed particular immigrant groups in opposition to other members of their society. The discourse of the second generation therefore serves to maintain misrecognition, marginalization, and discrimination.

As discussed in Chapter 2, the Bavarian and Berlin models of education illustrate how the dominant society has exploited the notion of the second generation, to place Ausländer children outside of Germanness while tailoring their schooling to meet Germany's own needs. Most of the participants lived in Türkiye for part of their childhood and thus directly experienced such policies. Ayşe, who was born shortly after her parents arrived in Germany, talks of being "a suitcase child":

I am a suitcase child. I was in Germany until I was about six. Then I went to Türkiye ... to attend first and second grade there ... I adapted quickly and learned Turkish. I forgot the German language ... I came back for a year and went to school here ... Having to learn German again was difficult. I attended one of the Turkish classes. That made learning German even more difficult ... Then I went to Türkiye again. In a year, I was back here. These were not my decisions. Like a suitcase, others carried me from place to place. Suitcases don't move themselves ... I always felt connected to Türkiye. I wanted to go back. I always thought coming here wasn't my choice. My parents brought me here.

Like a suitcase, Ayşe served a particular function for her parents and for German society. Suitcases are only used as tools. They have no control over what they carry and have to carry the belongings of their owners. After joining their parents through family unification, many Gastarbeiter children (including those like Ayşe who were born in Germany) commonly moved between Türkiye and Germany. With their schooling split between the two countries, the suitcase children served to maintain a connection with the place to which their parents belonged. The suitcase-child model regards Ausländer children as conveniently portable and easily displaceable. However, these children have to work through the painful adjustments of moving between two places, neither of which is theirs, and eventually feeling compelled to choose between them.

In responding to these expectations, the education policies of both Germany and Türkiye have treated the children of guest workers as belonging to Türkiye. The suitcase children expediently carry the language, the culture, and the belongings of their guest-worker parents with them, representing a connection with the extended family and the homeland. For German society, the suitcase child is a symbol of Gastarbeiter temporality and a perpetual reminder that all Turks are only guests. While maintaining the temporality of Ausländer culture, suitcase children are also deemed to perpetuate their parents' deficient traits. To be a suitcase child is to be a product of preserved backwardness.

Similarly, within the German education system, Ausländer children are assumed to have a particular role to play for society. Arda and Selin talk about how their teachers perceive Ausländer and remind them of their place in German society. I met Arda through a special program that enables girls who could not finish high school to enter job training programs for nursing and doctors' assistants. She is one of the many I met who struggled with the German school system: "Germans think we can't succeed in anything; we should stay home and give birth. My teacher at junior high school always told me, 'Your place is behind the stove' ... She meant Turkish women can't do anything else but cooking." Selin, a doctor's assistant in her mid-twenties, gives a similar account: "The teacher told us that Germany does not need just educated people."

These comments from teachers are infused with negative notions of the natural backwardness of the Ausländer into which the second generation has been born. These examples show how Arda and Selin's place in German schools is defined in terms of the education level they need – or do *not* need – in order to serve German society. Their accounts indicate how everyday experiences at school are integral to institutionalized systems of marginalization and discrimination. This is how schools teach Ausländer children, starting from an early age, where they belong in German society.

Do second-generation subjects inevitably internalize the sense of being outsiders? Are there instances where they actually *resist* the messages and act as if they are insiders? Perhaps the term *suitcase children* is appropriate for describing the internalization of outsider status. The suitcase-child experience shows how both Germanness and Turkishness tend to become external to young people's experiences.

Children of Suitcase Children

The recurring experience of the German-born grandchildren generation is strongly connected to the schooling experiences of their German-born parents. They are the children of suitcase children. When I asked in follow-up interviews why the children of German-born Ausländer still have a disconnect to German society, Selim answered:

> The expectation was to get married young, to someone from Türkiye, and then have a family. Most people from my generation lived like that, maybe 80 to 90 percent. After finishing a college degree, most married and had children. There was no focus on building a better future in Germany or being part of Germany. We had older siblings who grew up in Türkiye with our grandparents or who moved back and forth between Türkiye and Germany. They had strong connections to their villages, their language, and to Türkiye. We felt proud; we didn't want to deny that we were Turkish. We were proud to be the children of immigrants, to be from Türkiye.

As discussed in Chapter 2, most German-born Ausländer were sent to schools with an expectation that they would study through middle school and then get a job. The expectations were very low for them. They grew up in Turkish classrooms, and the low expectations were passed down from generation to generation. The latest generation, however, has stronger connections with Germany, regardless of whether they look German.

Judging by Appearances

> You are a Turk. That means you are little; have black hair; macho if you are a man, and oppressed if you are a woman; and you have a conservative interpretation of religion.
>
> – Ali

In Ali's description of the Turk, the bodies of Turkish Ausländer are presented in terms of marginality, skin colour, oppressive gender relations, and traditionalist Islam. Their bodies are marked, acted on, inscribed, and constructed in ways that define them as a certain type of being (Foucault 1980). The aspects of Turkishness are ascribed to the physical and biological properties of the Turkish body – its colour, clothing, and behaviour indicate its social and cultural nature. The everyday acts and practices of ascribing meanings to these properties maintain the position that Turkish Ausländer hold in the ranking of Germanness, and they regulate the differences among Ausländer through norms set by the dominant culture. This judging by appearance raises questions of why or which cultures should be respected. That kind of judgment is a vital strategy in the colonial politics of accommodation.

Alles Getürkt (All Fake)

For most Germans, Turkishness is a unique instance of Oriental identity, combining ethnicity, race, religion, and history. However, for German-born Turkish Ausländer, the implications and meanings of Turkishness get further complicated. Turkishness is not external to these diasporic people, yet it is somehow detached from their bodily existence. It is a status ascribed not subjectively but from the outside: from the dominant German society and institutions, and from the Turkish state, Turkish Ausländer institutions, and other groups who constitute themselves through Turkishness. Whereas the dominant discourse defines Turkishness in a way that systematically preserves the superiority of Germanness, the Turkish communities in Berlin also treat Turkishness as more than a national identity. They commonly assert Turkishness as a mode of confrontation with Germanness, which takes the form of reaction as a defence mechanism. Between these various defined identities, the German-born Turkish Ausländer try to mark a new place for themselves and affirm new identities. To do this, they have to struggle against impositions from both of their communities.

Although the German-born Turkish Ausländer embody German traits of language, behaviour, habit, and lifestyle, the dominant discourses continue to ignore their possession of German properties. People commonly insist on recognizing them as Turkish Ausländer. Güler speaks of "incidents" and "little things" that reinforce this message: "About five years ago, we were looking for a place [to rent]. On the phone, they agreed to talk to us, but when they saw us ... they changed their minds. They said they do not rent their houses to foreigners." On the phone, only their language was evident – and it was German. There was nothing to indicate to the landlord that Güler and her husband were not German. When he saw them, however, he recognized their Turkishness, and the boundaries between German and Turkish identities were quickly redrawn.

Lifestyle and look can be fluid and flexible markers. Sometimes the markers are spatial. Sometimes the body itself is marked. The Ausländerness of the body may be obvious, marking it as Turkish, Italian, or Arab. But, as Yıldız says, the interpretation can change, "depending on where I am at the moment." In Kreuzberg, Turkishness seems more obvious, but in places with few Turkish people, the foreign body can be marked as coming from anywhere in the Mediterranean. As the body moves in the city space, what it represents can change. Lifestyles, attitudes, or bodily expressions that do not fit the Turkish image can be taken as indications of being German-like, or un-Turkish-like. Fatma refers to her colleagues' comments about her lifestyle: "If you look at me, I'm thirty, have a boyfriend, and live alone ... They cannot comprehend that. 'A Turkish girl doesn't behave like that' ... as if there is a certain book for Turkish girls about how they should behave."

The boundaries between Turkishness and Germanness can get blurred on a darker body as well, due to other markers such as facial piercings or a short hairstyle, as in Ayşe's case. Due to these features, her experience has been different from that of women with long dark hair. Ayşe's darkness signals her non-Germanness, but her style, attitude, and mastery of German prevent her from being located as typically Turkish. Her estrangement from Germanness and her proximation to it clash; her colour becomes the exception. She is seen as a different sort of a Turk.

Germans cannot easily locate the Turkish Ausländer who blur the boundaries of how Turkish and German bodies are supposed to look. But any such

Accommodating the Ausländer 103

passing-for-German or boundary-blurring lasts only until the Turkishness beneath is unveiled. These Ausländer become German-*like* (but not quite) or Turkish-*like* – but not quite. When these diasporants suggest, either verbally or by their style, that something is terribly wrong with the ways Turkishness is portrayed, they may be told, "You are not like other Turks, you're different" – implying that they don't need to be worried about defending themselves. Behind the assurance lies a belief that the typically Turkish is so well-defined that Fatma, Ayşe, and Yıldız (who live and look differently) cannot fit the frame of Turkishness. Even though they disturb conventional preconceptions, without which the mutual exclusion of Germanness and Turkishness would be impossible, somehow they remain Turkish. They are the exceptions who prove the rule. A German lifestyle or look may make them more accepted, but their acceptance remains conditional.

German-born Ausländer create suspicion when they claim German properties such as language, lifestyle, or behaviour. This suspicion has historically constructed, Orientalist, racist, and classist underpinnings:

> My professor jokingly said that my certificate must be *getürkt* [Turkish trickery] after I completed the seminar ... There is not an expression such as *gedeusched* or *geyugoslavisch*. He always sees me as Turkish. "We must support students like you," meaning Turkish and female. "While reading your work, I can't tell it is written by a Turk" ... He was shocked when he heard my English. He asked if my Turkish is as good ... It was not jealousy, but admiration, being surprised, thinking that it is too good to be true. There must be a trick, the belief that it is impossible Turks can be that smart. They never say, "You deserve it!"
>
> – İrem

Getürkt, which is still a common expression, implies deception. It means being successful but only by using dirty tricks. The term has historical connotations of a specific Orientalism concerning Turks. In "Alles getürkt," sociologist Margret Spohn (1993) examines the full range of Western images of the Turks since the early modern period. She argues that in every age, in the face of real or imagined threats, similar clichéd representations of the Turk as outsiders are recycled and lent renewed currency. İrem's professor's use of the term *getürkt* illustrates how these historical representations carry over into contemporary popular discourses.

Similarly, the participants refer to their experience of "never being good enough." Germans "always have doubts." The participants' Turkishness triggers doubt, regardless of their being born and raised in Germany, knowing its language, going to its schools, and participating in the same social and cultural activities. Even having German citizenship cannot eliminate the doubt. The connotations of Turkishness – being tricky, untrustworthy, furtive – render the participants suspect by association. Their loyalties and character are uncertain because they remain Turkish. It is the participants' obligation to prove that they can do what is required despite being Turkish. If they feel they have performed below the standard, they feel awful and embarrassed. As İrem explains: "It shouldn't be a big deal, but it is. A foreigner by origin can't make mistakes." The participants become perfectionists in this constant struggle. As Anzaldúa ([1987] 2007, 71) writes of the mestiza woman: "She has had to work twice as hard as others to meet the standards of the dominant culture which have, in part, become her standards."

Moreover, the participants are put in a position of constantly fighting such perceptions about being a Turk: "Am I really like this, or not?" (Ali). Ela talks about her "dreadfully tiring" search to discover how Turkish she is and where she belongs, as she looks at the Turkish communities in Berlin: "I attended seminars, reading groups, and political gatherings, discussing certain same predetermined and frozen issues ... 'Are we oppressed as Turks, do we let them do this to us? What should we do? What do we need to know?' ... I distanced myself from those who made being Turkish their jobs."

Ela recognizes that her obligation to Turkishness doubles whenever a group she is affiliated with also imposes Turkishness. Consequently, her affiliation with Germany – her birthplace – gets ignored. Implicitly or explicitly, Turks, family members, and Germans constantly expect German-born Turkish Ausländer to look for their *real* identity. They ask themselves if they are Turkish or German, where they belong. They feel obliged to evaluate themselves in relation to the Turkish attributes they are claimed to have: "Then, you realize you defend people only because they are Turkish, minority, or foreigner" (Ela). This pressure puts the participants in situations where they defend even things they do not like.

Through such imposed loyalty, Arzu's German life (as a journalist for a German newspaper) becomes a window for her Turkish friends as they look for examples of the injustices Turks face in Germany. Her friends and relatives want to hear that the paper treats her a certain way because she is Turkish. During a meeting with Turkish-background journalists working

Accommodating the Ausländer

with the German press (which was organized by one of the major Turkish associations), Arzu is asked questions such as "Do they always assign you certain news? Do they force you or expect you to do certain things?" These assumptions are defensive reactions to the Turkishness ascribed to Turkish communities, who see themselves as an oppressed minority. Arzu is expected to lose her critical outlook and avoid mentioning that imposed Turkishness does not accurately reflect the reality of her experiences.

The defensive version of Turkish identity develops a minority discourse, which challenges the dominant group by demanding the right to be different. Erkan claims that

> always the majority says to you that you are a Turk, or you are different, and you [must] accept that. You start thinking: "Being different and being a Turk is not a bad thing. It is normal." But because being Turkish and different is considered bad, you say as a spontaneous response, "But I'm like this, you should accept me like this." This is a dreadfully unnecessary struggle.

Still, the German-born Turkish Ausländer realize that they cannot define Turkishness as simply opposed to Germanness, since they themselves are also part of Germanness. They work at German workplaces, in the same jobs as Germans. They go to German schools, pay German taxes, have German citizenship. The more they are pushed to isolate themselves from the majority in German society, the more they come into conflict, because they are part of that society and cannot be cut off from it.

The way these expectations of Turkishness function disregards not only the participants' experiences within German society, but also the subminority experiences such as being Arab or Kurdish while dealing with imposed Turkishness. Turkishness also involves the Turkish state's self-definition as a homogeneous ethnic entity, whether or not its members are indeed ethnically Turkish. Even though İrem and Damla are Arabs, and Seda is Kurdish, Turkish identity becomes the only category available to them. As İrem explains: "We are democratic and secular. My parents are Atatürk's children. Their fathers did military service twice. They grew up with Atatürk's Turkishness. They always defend their Turkishness in Germany, in public."

İrem defines her roots through her family's role in the foundation of the Turkish state. She makes claims to being Turkish due to her family's loyalties to the principles of Atatürk, the founder of that state. This experience is reflected more controversially in Seda's expression of her Turkishness, despite her Kurdish identity:[4] "My parents are Kurdish. They don't speak Kurdish and neither do I ... They say they are Turkish ... [I will teach my children Turkish], because we are Turkish." Neither İrem nor Seda can eliminate Turkish identity from their experiences. However, this Turkish identity, given in Türkiye, is reimposed and insisted on in Germany. The attribution of Turkishness seems to erase their Arab, Kurdish, and German identities.

These sorts of attributed identities create constraints, whether they are imposed by the majority or maintained by Turkish communities themselves. Either way, the participants feel they are assigned an identity. Turkishness comes to mean all the attributes that separate them from Germans. No matter how little they know about or identify with the Turkishness attributed to them, no matter how much they object to such preconceived ideas, or how much more they relate to Germanness, they still feel obliged to *feel and act as a Turk*. In that sense, Turkishness is an obligation, a commitment, a loyalty. The participants are expected to behave in certain Turkish ways or to prove that Turks are not what Germans think they are. They feel responsible for Turkishness but limited to comparison and contrast within a binary oppositional framework. Defending Turkishness ensures constant exclusion at both the group and individual levels, and thus a continuation of binary opposition. When the participants' connections and affiliations with the German society at large are ignored, their relation to Turkishness becomes their primary means of being and belonging together, thereby limiting the space for confrontations.

The binary oppositions between Germanness and Turkishness, and between authentic and non-authentic Turkishness, both tend to mask differences formed through modes of racialization, gendering, class, sexuality, and religion. Turkishness becomes a wrapping that covers over many layers of difference. These prevailing interpretations present Turkishness and Germanness as if they were conceived outside the context of gendered, racialized, and class-based relations. They are pre-formed identities that serve to reinscribe dominant forms of nationalism and to mask various power inequities. Paradoxically, these interpretations tend to erase differences among Turks, but also among Germans. Each community tends to underrate how its members are shaped differently through their interactions between multiple modes of identification, beyond the scope of ethnicity, nationality, and linguistic difference.

Behind the Headscarf

> When they look at me, I want them to see me, not my headscarf, or not assume that they already know my life. A woman asked: "Are you planning on taking your headscarf off once you get married?" as if I were forced to wear it to hide from men, and once married, I would not have to anymore.
>
> – Emel

Emel's clothing, symbolized by her headscarf, becomes a vital part of both her material condition and the discursive construction of her condition. Her manner of dress is taken as central to her identity. As professor of cultural studies and sociology Meyda Yeğenoğlu describes (2002, 86) the Emel's headscarf as an essential item, conjoined with a Muslim woman's embodied subjectivity. Even though wearing a headscarf is her free choice, this fabric becomes a social construction because of what the headscarf represents and how it shapes her social encounters. Her choice of covering her head seems to become a non-choice, as it produces non-chosen experiences evoked by the stereotypes attached to the headscarf. As critical feminism and race studies scholar Sherene Razack (2008, 178) states, such intense preoccupation with the Muslim woman's body, and the veil in particular, is an indication that colonial relationships are resurging. Portraying the Muslim veil as an insistence on maintaining premodern practices justifies the discourses around how Germany (Europe) is under attack, which therefore justifies expression of anti-immigrant sentiments.

The notion of the body as a template on which social norms, practices, and values are inscribed can be extended to the discourses concerning the dangerous power of Muslimness. These discourses involve specific forms of gendered racialization that operate through the discourses of Eurocentrism and Orientalism, which sustain the marginalization of Turkish Ausländer as Muslim Others. Orientalism, as Edward Said (1978, 5–12) showed, is an Occidental perspective on the Orient in which European dominance (rather than the Orient itself) is created and sustained by a political, intellectual, and cultural agenda.

Although there is no direct correspondence between Islam as portrayed in common Western usage and the enormously varied lives of the participants, the headscarf evokes a stigmatization in which "the term 'Islam' becomes one simple thing, which is part fiction, part ideological label, and part minimal designation of a religion called Islam" (Said [1981] 1997, 1). Islam becomes an undifferentiated, monolithic whole, and the complex diversity of Muslim origins and lives is disregarded. As sociologist Alireza Asgharzadeh (2004, 130) writes, Islamoracism functions by representing Islam as a monolithic, fundamentalist religion rather than a diverse set of traditions. Some of those traditions serve as sources of spirituality; others as expressions of ethno-cultural identity, as markers of geography, oppositional ideologies, or official state ideologies. In the experiences of the participants (both male and female), the Islamic headscarf is a significant nexus of power (whether it is worn or not), through which Islam is defined as a polar opposite of Western civilization and is viewed with a special hostility and fear. Beyond being simply a symbol or garment, the headscarf becomes a site where the words *Muslim* and *Islam* become detached from their positive connotations of moral guidance, spirituality, or benign religiosity, and are re-created as an imagined identity suggesting violence, backwardness, and fundamentalism (see Baumgartl and Favell 1996).

The female participants in this research project describe how they are caught up in the rhetoric regarding how Muslim women should look and what that image represents (regardless of whether they personally wear a headscarf or not). Fatma explains: "According to Germans, Turkish women are shy and do not talk too much. They wear a headscarf. When they are my age, they must have four to five kids. They are close to their families and do whatever their husband asks them to do." Ayşe adds, "They are traditional and not open." These images combine images regarding gender (the oppressed, submissive woman who has no control over her own body), tradition (socialization in underdeveloped rural areas), or cultural background (Islam's backwardness). This combination of images defines these women as irrational, closed, threatening, archaic, and strangely foreign (Mandel 1990; Şenocak 2000). They are seen as silent victims unable to adapt without help to modern German society (Mandel 1989).

These stereotypes of Turkish woman and the significance of the headscarf cannot be separated from the image of how Turkish men treat Turkish women. In a workshop, a woman asked Güler if her husband is a typical Turkish man: "I reacted, 'What do you mean by typical Turkish man?' She explained, 'If he is macho, or doesn't help at home.' I responded, 'Just a little while ago, you were talking about your problems with your husband. I'm having similar problems as well ... Why do you think it is about where he came from?'"

This encounter exemplifies how Turkish women are seen as the embodiment of passivity and submission, while Turkish men embody aggression and danger. In the questions about how Güler's husband treats her, the problems of gender dynamics in marriage are detached from Güler's personal experiences and instead defined as essential to Turkish culture. The German woman also puts Güler in a defensive position, rather than framing the issue as a common problem they share as women. Thus, Güler becomes a central figure in an ideological justification for the superiority of Western culture. Progressive German culture is contrasted with the unchanging characteristics of gender relations in Turkish culture, and the German man (as an opposite of the backward Turkish man) is constructed as respectful, modern, and therefore superior. The German woman in Güler's story sees the gender dynamics in Güler's family that she does not wish to recognize in her own family. This view of Muslims, and the fear behind it, works to keep Germanness well-defined and distinct, while making patriarchy seem like a specifically Turkish problem.

By positioning Turkish women in opposition to German women, such discourses reconstruct the universal issues of gender inequality as if they were relevant only to Turkish culture and not to the personal issues between German men and German women. Instead of being used to create solidarity between women, this encounter is used to interrogate Güler about the oppression Turkish women face. When Güler tries to defend or explain herself, the process perpetuates existing relations and categories. Thus, the possibility of a feminist understanding between German and Turkish women is foreclosed.

The isolation of the Turkish man from German society is also maintained through calls for emancipating the Turkish woman from her backward Turkish man. Such judgment on the gender dynamics of Turkish Ausländerness leads to an institutionalized disrespect for Turkish men. Ayla, a social worker, shares her observation: "Nobody wants to work with young Turkish men ... They are full of anger and disappointment. When you gain their trust, you see how they are left alone."

Seeing the Turkish man in relation to the oppressed Turkish woman becomes a means for explaining the threat he represents to German society (and the general Muslim threat to the Western world). These explanations are part of the larger discourses that have justified general discrimination against Muslims (especially since 9/11), and, in extreme cases, have justified racist attacks. The post-unification racist attacks in Germany were excused by the extreme right on the grounds that Muslims presented a clear threat to Western civilization. Migrants and asylum seekers were represented as pioneers for a Muslim army of conquest. According to this theory, aggressive, domineering Turkish men have immigrated to establish bridgeheads for Islam in Europe, as part of an evil conspiracy to establish global Islamic rule (Werbner 2002, 121).

Although Islamophobia is not new, Dhamoon (2009, 132–37) points out that since 9/11 it has functioned to both justify the so-called war on terror and to regulate Muslim and Arab people (or those who appear to be Muslim) through discourses of nationalism and security. The discourses of the post-9/11 world, which are historically rooted in Orientalism, Islamophobia, and Eurocentric sexism, have taken on a new life through recent discourses on terrorism.

Seda, who has worn a headscarf since Grade 3, reports being verbally attacked on the subway: "Old German women make rude remarks about Muslim people, making sure that I hear them: 'I don't understand the headscarf in the modern age.' Some even accuse me [for September 11]: 'It is all your fault, you spiderweb head.'" It is not Seda that these Germans see but the stereotype of dangerous backwardness that her appearance represents to them. Thus, these discourses produce an expectation of Turkish Ausländer (both women and men) that they are by nature backward, culture-bound, non-secular, and perhaps a danger to the nation.

Fatma (who does not wear a headscarf) says, "My biggest fights with Germans are always when I'm with my mother," who does wear a headscarf:

> We got on the bus. A lady gave her seat to my mom. A German woman walked toward my mom. "You can get up. Why are you sitting? ... You are not working or anything, using our money" ... My mom wanted to get up. When I gave her a dirty look, Mom said, "That's okay. She is older, so she can sit." I said, "No, Mom, you stay where you are." I turned to the woman ... "She will remain seated" ... The woman said, "This is none of your business." I said, "Yes it is. She is my mom. Even if she weren't, she is a human being ... You cannot make her leave her seat." The German woman was shocked as she was not expecting I would be this woman's daughter.

In Fatma's mother, this German woman sees her own stereotype of the Turkish woman. Although she has never met this woman, she claims to *know exactly* what Fatma's mother is: lazy, unemployed, and on welfare. Fatma's mother's appearance embodies both the general public image of Muslim women and this German woman's mental associations with Ausländer-hood. In the German woman's eyes, Fatma and her mother do not belong together. Fatma's response, her German-style appearance, and her relation to a Muslim mother challenge what the German bus rider sees in Fatma. The political space for this encounter is thus split between the standardized image of Muslim women and the reality of their diversity.

"A headscarf," Ayla says, "is like a uniform." This uniform seems to designate a fundamentalist woman who is oppressed, abused, ignorant, old-fashioned – yet dangerous. Regardless of what other attributes the woman with a headscarf might have (such as being a business woman, an academic, or a political activist), her own subjectivity becomes invisible. Only what the headscarf signifies counts. Ünzile, an English literature student, complains that sometimes people on campus think she is a cleaner, as her clothing is plain and loose compared with other women who combine Western fashions with wearing a headscarf. Both sociologist Haideh Moghissi's (1999) and Yeğenoğlu's (2002) arguments support my conclusion that the representations of Turkish women as the symbol of a backward Türkiye render it not only possible, but also necessary to keep Turkish Ausländer and Germans separate. The Turkish Ausländer woman, as a woman of the Orient, becomes a signifier of cultural practices and religious customs that are interpreted as monstrous, invariably oppressive toward women. The barbarity of Türkiye and the Turkish Ausländer seem evident in the appearance of their women.

The act of unveiling the Muslim woman further perpetuates the meanings of the headscarf. Unveiling has two separate levels of meaning that become integral to the experiences of Turkish Ausländer women. The first level comes from the historical, government-decreed unveiling of Turkish women when the modern Republic of Türkiye was founded. Political anthropologist Mahiye Seçil Dağtaş (2007) discusses how Turkish modernity and hegemonic national citizenship have long been manifested in women's bodies and dress, both through an opposition to the veil or headscarf and through the relationship between secularization and Westernization. Dağtaş argues that women's emancipation was central in the process of state building. The second layer of meaning involves the German desire to unveil Turkish Ausländer women for the sake of integration in Germany. As many have argued, these discourses of modernization and integration mask the dominant depictions of Western superiority, and they reinforce sexist Eurocentric representations of Muslim women as victims of their oppressive culture. In this context, it has been widely assumed that only white men and Western modernity can save these women from Muslim men and the backwardness of Oriental tradition (Mohanty 2003; Razack 2005, 2008; Spivak 1993).

In the German context, unveiling the Oriental woman becomes a highly significant marker of integration into German society. Aziza A explains: "Even the music studio asked me to wear a black veil during an interview. 'You put it on first, and then throw it open, as though you are emancipating yourself.'" The studio manager was asking Aziza A, a rap singer, to manifest an image of a woman setting herself free from oppression. First, she is told to put on a black veil, then to throw it off, revealing herself as a rap singer. The rap-singing performance shows a further stage in Aziza A's emancipation, which makes the image of rejecting the veil seem that much more powerful. In this presentation, the veil seems to function as an essential part of Aziza A's body. For the media, her essentialized relation with the veil makes her music symbolize women's liberation from the traditions and cultures of the Orient. This construction makes Aziza A's more "alternative" than other rap music. Her act of singing becomes a revolution, even though she claims to "never see it as revolution." For the media, Aziza A's music represents how Germany can change a Muslim woman's life for the better, rather than how an Ausländer woman can express her own creative artistry. Aziza A explains that her studio manager wishes to impose his own message on her art: "Look, there are other people like her as well. The young people from different cultures can make it, thanks to being in Germany."

In the discourse of the German right, the headscarf represents proof of the Turks' fundamental inability to integrate. The headscarf is seen as backward and, most of all, un-German, but also as something integral to Turks and Turkish identity. The discourse of the left would have the headscarf symbolize Turkish practices of sexist, patriarchal domination of women. The headscarf thus represents the barrier that must be removed before successful Turkish assimilation into German society can be achieved.

These discourses echo the meaning that the headscarf assumed during the modernization process in Türkiye – as a symbol of how Türkiye and, therefore, Turkish people (including those in Germany) should see themselves. As women's emancipation was symbolized by removing the veil in the republican public space, it is no coincidence that several of the female participants who consider themselves secular express their desire for modernity through opposition to the traditional headscarf. Women who refuse to wear the headscarf are often highly critical of those who choose to wear it. Many modernist Ausländer women associate the headscarf with traditionalism, fundamentalism, and political Islam. They wish to differentiate themselves, and their own understandings of Muslimness, from the Islamist understanding. However, this choice is also an expression of concern about

Accommodating the Ausländer

the proper way of dressing as a Muslim woman. The manner of dress is still highly significant for how these women define their own Muslimness. They commonly mean to distinguish between Muslimness as a politicized act and as a private matter. As Ceyda, a self-identified secular Muslim woman, puts it, "I don't have to cover my head. I wear make-up. This doesn't indicate that I'm not a proper Muslim ... You don't need to show it ... I see myself as a good Muslim in my heart. It is a negotiation between me and Allah ... Nobody else can evaluate my Muslimness."

These women examine what the headscarf represents in society and then choose their own relation to this tradition in the privacy of their personal faith. They claim that their secular Muslimness is a more appropriate expression of faith than wearing an outward sign of their religion. Those who cover themselves are seen as bending to external pressure, or as making a public show of support for political Islam. Some women express suspicion toward the correlation between head covering and being a proper Muslim.

For Selin, the blackness of the veil symbolizes a backward past, which she hopes to leave behind: "I don't want to see black-veiled women. I don't accept negative attitudes toward Germans. We live in this country. Of course, we shouldn't forget where we came from, but we, as the young people who were born here, have to speak German without an accent ... if we want them to accept us." Selin suggests that the reason Germany does not accept Turks is closely linked to the gender images that headscarf-wearing women represent. She accepts a version of the Western construction regarding the lives of traditional Muslims in Germany. She accepts some German judgments on gender roles in the Turkish family and on Turkish reluctance to fully integrate with German society. She advises her fellow Ausländer to "speak German without an accent." Finally, she associates the veil with fanaticism and violence against Germans. Her comments reveal how the external gaze of Germans is implicated in her narrative and in the way she sees herself. Similarly, Yeşim talks about the headscarf's negative impact on Turks in Germany and on Türkiye's reputation: "Because of all these girls with the headscarf, German people think that all Turkish people are like them, and all Turkish women are backward. This is also why they do not accept us to the European Union. They think we are religious and not modern enough."

In this context, women wearing the headscarf become the primary negative image regarding Türkiye and of Turkish Ausländer (not only in Germany, but also across Europe). Islam is seen as becoming dangerous when it emerges from the private sphere of the home into the public sphere. Echoing this perspective, Yeliz, like Yeşim, Ceyda, and Selin, a self-identified secular

Muslim woman, argues that Islam is something personal between God and the individual, and it requires no intermediary agents or institutions. Accordingly, Islam should be practised voluntarily at home, as she and her mother do. It is Islamists who violate this rule, by claiming to be authorities over the public and *using* religion for their own political purposes. Political Islam represents loyalty to a collectivity other than the nation and, consequently, an alternative form of belonging in the public sphere. This alternative worries Ceyda, Yeliz, Yeşim, and Selin. For them, it is difficult to separate what wearing a headscarf means in Germany from what it represents for modern Türkiye and for secular Turkish identity. The headscarf becomes the public face of Islam, in opposition to what modern Türkiye has stood for.

For all of these various defenders of German, Turkish secular, or Islamic values, women remain the central objects of identity politics. Turkish wives and mothers have been the key agents in transplanting Turkish familial values, lifestyles, and children into German culture. The Islamic values and practices associated with traditional Muslim women have commonly collided with both German culture and secular modern Turkish values. In all of these contexts, the image of the traditionalist Muslim woman seems to demonstrate the need for eliminating the premodern social structures and values of Oriental cultures and for replacing them with modern practices that can produce the desired improvements in Turkish Muslim women's status.

In 2016, when I asked Ayten, a youth worker, how she is challenged by these various attitudes in her work, she replied as follows:

> Of course, it has effects. Not for Turks per se, but people who are close to Islam are more aware and conscious and careful. For example, the new generation, when they wear a headscarf, they are more aware of the implications and the responsibility they carry when they wear a headscarf. Because Turks and Arabs are assumed to be Muslim, these young women take the symbolism of the headscarf very seriously. Not only do they have their own fashion for headscarves ... they also have particular styles. They are very educated – university students. They are recreating these symbols and fashions as a reaction to the racism they experience.

The discourse surrounding and defining the multiple meanings of the headscarf reveals a complex set of markers. This discourse brings into focus a political, social, and gendered struggle for control over the conditions of its wearing. The encounters around the headscarf show how a

Accommodating the Ausländer 115

choice between cultural rights and gender equality rights is demanded when aspects of difference are conceptualized as oppositional, rather than relational, mutually constitutive, and co-implicative.

Skin Colour and Tone
Skin colour is another property to which meanings are ascribed in regulating the distinctions between Germans and Turkish Ausländer. Even though the Turkish population is diverse in skin colour, the dominant perception of Turkishness emphasizes the darker skin tone. The advantages that lighter skin (and the disadvantages of darker skin) give to German-born Turkish Ausländer are fundamental factors in the broader systems of discrimination.

No matter how German Arzu's lifestyle becomes, she looks and remains Turkish. Arzu grew up in a small German village. Her family attempted to fit in there, but they remained the different family. She talks about how her family's outlook has influenced her and her relations with Muslimness, Christianity, and religion in general. She was German in many aspects of her daily life, including familiarity with Christianity, as she attended a Catholic school, went to church every Tuesday morning, and knew many prayers in German. Still, she and her family were always "different and little." Arzu considers herself socially more German than Turkish, yet with her black hair and olive skin, Turkishness comes to her, even at the times she forgets about it: "When I said, 'I don't see myself as Turkish,' my colleague said, 'Of course you do! If someone looks at you without knowing your name, they would say, this short Turkish girl."'

Due to such daily explicit reminders of her Turkishness, Arzu catches herself asking how others will perceive her, even though this questioning initially comes from others: "When I sit with friends, I ask myself, 'Do they see me as different right now? Am I the only person who is different right now? All of them are Germans' ... Then I remember when I was going to school, what kids said on the school bus. 'Do they see me as different; do they see me as bad?"'

According to sociologist Margaret Hunter ([2005] 2013, 2), such self-interrogation contributes to the maintenance of white supremacy, which is predicated on the notion that "dark skin represents savagery, irrationality, ugliness, and inferiority. White skin, and thus whiteness itself, is defined by the opposite: civility, rationality, beauty, and superiority." In the world where Arzu grew up, Turkishness meant being recognizably different and probably dirty or smelly. She reflects on her self-consciousness: "I was biking to work, and I was thinking, 'Am I stinking? No, I showered. I changed my clothes."'

She says: "When I look at the mirror, I don't question whether I look Turkish or not, or how Turkish I am." But no matter how she identifies herself, she cannot avoid being different due to her skin tone. She remains a Turk.

Belma, who is a nurse; Funda, a drama student; and Arda, a high school student, have *naturally* blond hair with light skin. Their accounts of people's responses to their skin tones provide another perspective on how Turkishness is associated with darkness and what dark skin represents. Their blondness gives Belma, Funda, and Arda advantages that Arzu does not have. Yet even though their appearances fit the stereotype of Germanness, their experiences show how a binary opposition (and the racial hierarchy that comes with it) is maintained. In the end, they remain Turkish.

Funda refers to how Germans automatically talk to her in German. This continues in institutional settings, even in the Turkish consulate. They think she is German until she gives them her Turkish passport. In a public setting, where these blond Turks do not know anyone, their Turkishness is invisible. They can pass in public as Germans. In certain situations, they can keep it that way or make their Turkish identity visible as they choose. With the assumed superiority that blondness gives them, these participants can be flexible in their Turkishness. They can play with conceptions of skin colour, depending on the context, through their responses to the others' responses. They can correct people or not when they are mistaken for Germans.

Having the choice of keeping their Turkishness invisible, they can operate in the domain of Germanness. As Funda admits, when their Turkishness is invisible, they can "keep their distance" if they wish to avoid Turkish guys in Kreuzberg. However, as Belma notes, invisibility also means that in a German environment they hear "bad things about Turks." They can make their Turkishness visible to Turks in Kreuzberg by responding in Turkish, or to Germans by intervening in the negative talk they hear about Turks. For example, while embodying white privilege with her own light skin, Arda can confound Germans by showing them that Germans do not know "all about Turks." As she explains: "Germans too think that I'm German and don't believe I'm Turkish. I correct them all the time, though ... I feel proud to be a Turk ... Then they ask whether my father or mother is German; I say both of them are Turkish."

Even in contradicting the skin tone stereotype, Arda's skin colour remains a factor in how she is judged. Turks who do not fit the stereotype may seem invisible, but they can find themselves judged for not appearing as a Turk should. Maybe their character is deceitful. What happens when they are discovered? Funda refers to how the treatment she receives from an of-

Accommodating the Ausländer 117

ficial switches the moment her Turkishness is revealed: "I was applying for a job once. The woman thought that I was German at first, and she invited me inside. I put my Turkish passport on the table, then her face changed. 'Oh! Are you Turkish?' ... She somehow sent me outside, saying I have to wait some more. I was angry, but I couldn't say anything."

Sometimes their Turkishness is given away by their name, by not knowing a nuance in the German language, or by their passport. As soon as their Turkishness is revealed, something changes. The thought-to-be-German becomes German-*like*. Fatma says that even German citizenship holders are told, "A German passport doesn't make you German."

Belma is so blond that German patients can be surprised that she speaks Turkish so well and that she does not "look Turkish at all." Some patients cannot imagine that Belma can be both blond and Turkish, as this challenges their assumptions. However, just as Arzu cannot escape being Turkish, Belma cannot claim blondness as a Turkish property. Either way, the racial hierarchy remains intact.

Those who are light-skinned are also treated differently when encountering Turks, as they are often considered to represent the domain of Germanness. Such judgment can be negative, as in a case reported by Arda: "Me and my twin sister were eight or nine years old. Turkish teenaged guys bullied us on the street. They apologized when they found out that we were Turkish. Maybe they wanted to get back at Germans."

Likewise, Belma is often blamed in encounters with other Turks while doing her job in the dominant German environment, because she is invisible to Turks as well: "If Turkish patients can't speak German, they go to my other friend. She is dark. They don't hesitate to talk to her in Turkish right away. When they find out I'm Turkish, they might even get upset at me. They think I feel embarrassed being Turkish. Sometimes they blame me for not helping or pleasing them."

An internalized sense of lower self-worth and status associated with darker skin influences how the patients react to Belma. One might argue that they feel angry that Belma does not have to go through what they have to deal with. Such feeling is sometimes expressed in claims that lighter-skinned Ausländer are being deceptive. This suggestion can be stated in a seemingly positive way, as a compliment. Zeynep, a stay-at-home parent with two young kids, refers to the assumptions about skin colour she encounters when she and her husband are visiting Türkiye: "People jokingly ask my husband whether I am his German wife, and where his Turkish wife is."

Belma claims that even when her Turkishness is known, she is still treated differently because of her light skin colour. She realizes there is something seriously wrong with the way she is accepted, but the other Turkish nurse she works with is not. Belma feels terrible when "Germans treat the other Turkish nurse badly, sometimes like a dog ... I know that if I had dark hair, they would do the same to me." Belma claims that her chief doctor can accept her and see her as a Berliner, but as for the way the doctor treats her darker friend, "He hopes that she will go back." Belma's skin colour, combined with her lifestyle, seems to place her in opposition to her darker friend. Yet Belma's solidarity is with her friend: "We are here, and we won't go back anywhere."

Blond Ausländer have access to opportunities that dark Ausländer do not. Funda explains how her blondness has worked to her advantage in gaining cultural capital. She had difficulty registering in a high school in West Berlin because of her low grades, but she was able to get into a school in the East: "When I first went there, I didn't have many problems because I'm blond, but they rejected my best friend. They openly said they didn't want Turks."

Even after disclosing her Turkishness, a light-skinned Ausländer is viewed by other Turks and by Germans "as higher status, less racially conscious (and therefore less threatening), more respectable, and more assimilable than her darker-skinned counterparts" (Hunter [2005] 2013, 6). These perceptions give Funda a competitive edge in schools and job markets still tainted by racism. Therefore, the advantages that skin colour conveys make it a form of social capital. Funda and Belma both benefit from the social and material capital that helps them operate within the institutional structure of the dominant society. At the same time, this fact maintains the privileges of being German. White supremacy is maintained by the light-skinned Turk, reinforcing the privileges of whiteness.

Although lighter-skinned Turks have seemingly higher status, this status is not something they have earned; it is something they are given. The privilege does not belong to them, but to Germanness, which is strongly associated with being white and blond. The light skin colour of these Ausländer strengthens German privilege, not that of the participants. It functions almost as a disguise. These Turks remain outside of being German so that passing as German, or the privilege associated with their own blondness, serves the interest of Germans in maintaining white privilege. As the experiences of Belma, Arda, and Funda indicate, "The values associated with physical features set the stage for skin colour stratification" (Hunter [2005] 2013, 3).

The systems of meanings surrounding identity, belonging, and difference operate on at least two levels in terms of religion, ethnicity, race, and colour. The first level of discrimination concerns the meanings assigned to each category. The second level involves a hierarchical ranking within the categories, such as the degree of religiosity or skin tone. This is a hierarchy of habits and behaviours. These two levels of ranking can be distinct, but they are usually inextricably entwined. The degrees of identity, belonging, and difference of Turkish Ausländer are defined through this system and somehow serve to secure certain privileges for Germanness, even when the stereotypes clearly break down. Even if German-born Ausländer hold high-ranking government jobs, like Ayten's husband, they face comments like "You don't look like a German, but you speak perfect German." His rank in the administrative structure does not protect him from discriminatory assumptions.

"People of Colour"

Erkan and Alp point out that in recent years, people have increasingly used the term *people of colour*. This term is most often used among young activists and academics, but it is used in several different ways. In the German context, it is increasingly used to suggest a natural connection between diverse ethnic minority groups, and there are several reasons for this development. First, being an immigrant is growing less important, and racial discrimination is becoming more descriptive of what minority groups experience. Alp proposes that

> Germany has had a substantial Roma population for the last four hundred to five hundred years. The racism they experience has similarities to that experienced by other people of colour. They are not immigrants, but they are being treated as such. Or there are Black Germans: Afro-Deutsch. They have been living here for centuries as well. *Immigrant* does not cover their experiences. Polish or Russian immigrants are white. So, in other words, the category of the Other is fluid and changing.

The various racialized communities have both commonalities and differences. In the past, there was no common space for all the kinds of minority groups within Germany. The term people of colour reflects the search for a category that will include them all. Clearly, the racial, cultural, and generational differences among these minorities add to the difficulty of finding a common term and a basis for unity. Alliances have started to form between the people of different diasporas. This is a significant form of solidarity among diasporic people, which builds on the commonalities that racism constructs.

Preserving Privilege

> Germans don't have the urge to question their own identity ... Everything is natural and familiar to them. They determine the rules, the laws, and the norms, and enjoy the advantages of being the majority. They are always right ... "We are German. What does that mean?" is never discussed in Germany. Only if you are minority do you have an ethnic identity, a different gene ... In fact, however, Germanness is also an ethnic identity.
>
> – Erkan

Erkan notes the German privilege of not having to answer questions about who they are and where they come from in the same way that Ausländer do. This intangible privilege derives partly from a sense that Germans are the hosts and owners of the home. In everyday encounters, the privileges of being dominant operate as unstated assumptions – "unseen, invisible, even seemingly nonexistent" (Sullivan 2006, 1). These privileges provide the comfort of having social status as a natural right, without having to earn it or think about it. Such privilege is presumed to reflect an inborn identity that is self-evident, without any reference to the Other. This way of recognizing the native and the Other makes it seem natural to avoid becoming familiar with the Other. Therefore, for many members of the dominant group, it can seem as if only their own people really exist.

For the members of a majority group (in this case, ethnic Germans), exchanges and interactions with marginalized groups (such as German-born Ausländer) become situations of tension. Those who are used to feeling dominant may feel challenged. They may sense a need to assert their position and defend their role. Such defence requires a binary oppositional logic of exclusion, with compromises settled somewhere along the axis of hostility–hospitality. In interactions with others, it is generally assumed that Germanness and Turkishness have different essential characteristics, and these differences justify the higher ranking of Germanness. Such assumptions are either strengthened or challenged as people question whether they are justified. Examining the expressions of ranking that appear during encounters between Ausländer and Germans allows us to analyze how the

Accommodating the Ausländer

privileges and advantages of being dominant are guarded. Such analysis lets us see how dominance is maintained during everyday social encounters and how the Others can either perpetuate or challenge these privileges.

Preconceived Ideas and Habits of Ignorance

> You go to a government office. Let's say your outfit is European, and your German is perfect. As soon as you show your ID, the first impression you gave disappears, and you are instantly put into a category because of the Turkish image in their heads. Getting out of this image is impossible.
>
> – Ayla

Ayla notes how the stereotype a Turkish name evokes overrides her European appearance and German language skills, placing her in the presumably homogenous category of Turkish Ausländer. This image seems to make no allowance for individual variation, change, or choice. Even when Ayla looks just like a German, her Turkish name leads German officials to apply their preconceived ideas as if they were revealed truth.

Getting to know the individual, having the misconception challenged, or having an intimate connection with an Ausländer rarely makes any difference to Germans' beliefs about the correctness of their stereotypes. As Germans generally view the participants through the lens of a particular stereotype, they tend to overlook the realities they experience in knowing these people. Fatma explains of her colleagues, "They don't change their minds about Turkish women or culture, although we have been working together for five years." Stereotyping allows most Germans to keep their distance and keep the Ausländer outside of Germanness.

The process of recognition that Ayla and Fatma describe involves two seemingly contradictory yet codependent tactics. The first tactic is to simply accept preconceived ideas and stereotypes, with an assumption that the Ausländer are already well understood. The second tactic is to practice habits of ignorance, which involve treating Ausländer in the ways that other Germans do. This kind of unconscious imitation usually seems like a series of innocent mannerisms. As habits of ignorance are mostly unconscious, people can claim that no ill will is intended. Those who unthinkingly express widely shared prejudice feel innocent of personal malice, and they feel unjustly attacked if criticized for their behaviour. Therefore, confronting preconceived ideas often simply perpetuates the stereotypes. Both forms of behaviour tend to limit how well Germans can get to know Ausländer as individuals.

Dominant groups are in a position to choose the categories for defining others. Certain human characteristics are designated as particular to the Others, producing stereotypes that maintain an unbridgeable social distance. Although Germans see other members of their own group as individuals, they commonly view those of the out-group as an undifferentiated mass. When little or nothing is known about the individual – as in the case of the government official dealing with Ayla – then, as James ([2003] 2010, 143) explains, "stereotypes 'fill in' the missing information, thus providing an organized perception of the group" to which that person is assumed to belong. For example, Arzu published a book about the diverse Ausländer women in her life. But when Germans asked her about the book, they typically showed no interest in the particular individuals it describes. Instead, she got questions about her Turkish background, in general telling me in 2016:

> "What does your family say about you publishing your book? Is what you write real or fiction?" I would get only very few questions about the substance of the book. And then I would think, in the book I am talking about the women in my life, my mom, my aunt, my cousins, like maybe fifteen to twenty people. So in the book, they are telling their stories. Cannot we just read them without generalizing? Why does it have to become about Turkish society? These generalizations are like, "You have to remember and think about this all the time." But when we generalize, there is something always wrong, always missing.

I use the word *ignorance* to refer to an insistence on certain fixed assumptions about the Ausländer regardless of evidence to the contrary. This ignorance maintains stereotypical images of the Other and the negative connotations attached to these images. Through such ignorance, Ausländer remain problematic subjects, frozen, timeless, and lifeless, or *out-of-place* aliens who are, nevertheless, living among Germans. The combination of ignorance and stereotyping is necessary for Germans who wish to live alongside Ausländer while keeping Germanness as a property that belongs to themselves.

Everyday encounters – ranging from one-time interactions with total strangers to regular exchanges with coworkers, friends, or neighbours –

Accommodating the Ausländer

become venues for accommodating the Ausländer. In the course of such interactions, stereotypes typically inform the conversations that Germans have with minority people. The subtext becomes an examination of who the Ausländer should be and where they belong. Prejudgments raise barriers to recognizing the Germanness of Ausländer, and these assumptions impose expectations of Otherness that justify their marginalization, exclusion, and oppression. All of this occurs in spaces that Germans claim as their own, regardless of the Ausländer's social, cultural, or political affiliations with these same places (such as the cities they live in, the schools they attend, and the places they work). Marginalization restricts the Ausländer from claiming ownership of being German or belonging to Germany. The Ausländer are labelled as arrivants, and the Germans are designated as hosts.

These habitual assumptions serve to block dialogue that could challenge discrimination toward racial, class, religious, or ethnic groups. Such habits function below the surface of awareness, as if they were nonexistent. The invisibility of stereotyping makes it more effective, as privileges function best when they appear not to function at all. Still, those who are labelled as Others look for ways to challenge their labels, and those challenges play out in the everyday exchanges of social life.

"They Have to Get to Know Us": Acquaintances, Experts, and Exceptions

The Ausländer sometimes buy into the logic that they can make themselves known to Germans through simple explanation. They typically find, however, that identifying and challenging habits of ignorance is close to impossible. When a problem is perceived within the binary oppositional logic of exclusion, that problem appears in one of two ways. Either the Turkish Ausländer are unable to adapt to Germanness, or the Germans are unwilling to acknowledge and respect Ausländer. As long as these habits of interaction remain unconscious, the primary challenge for the participants is overcoming the stereotypes, for example, when several of the participants claim that Germans are incapable of truly to getting to know a Turk. Selin believes that "a German can understand a Turkish person *to a certain extent,* and this is a problem of acceptance ... and a lack of reciprocity." She feels that the Germans' attitudes make it impossible: "Things would have been different if they were friendly, sincere, and positive, and weren't ungrateful ... Germans never get close to us, or try to understand and accept us ... They consider us as a problem, whether it is our fault or not. If something is wrong, they blame it on us."

In my recent set of interviews, the participants refer to forms of conditional acceptance. For example, Arzu (2016) spoke about Turkish as a second language at her daughter's school:

> In preschools, you see these little children are learning Turkish and German; it is cute. But when they start elementary school, you don't see that many students are learning Turkish anymore at schools. Once they hit Grade 3, if there are Turkish students in the classrooms, German parents still want their children to change schools. They don't want their children to be exposed to the Turkish language. But you see, we have American, Greek, and French schools, and they are packed.

Even though Germans and Ausländer have the capacity to see each other as individuals, the encounters between them are shaped by how the privileges of being German are played out. Is getting to know the Ausländer possible if these visitors can never step over the threshold of the home? Does *gaining sensitivity* overcome preconceived social distance? The answers lie in exploring how powerful the preconceived ideas are, and how the logic of exclusion functions through these ideas. Clearly, the problem is deeper than a simple lack of knowledge about Ausländer. Simply getting to know them does not dismantle conditional hospitality, nor does it eliminate the hierarchy of German and non-German.

Aynur, a theatre student with olive skin signalling her Turkishness, feels that it is possible to overcome social distance with honest communication. She remembers her experience as a patient in a former East Berlin hospital:

> They had never known any Turkish person ... [The other patients asked questions:] If my family beats me, or forbids me doing many things, because I'm a girl? If my brother would be angry with me if he finds me sitting in a café with them? If he carries a gun? But at the end, they liked me. They said, For the first time, they told their problems to a Turkish person ... They didn't know that Turkish people are like this.

Aynur's account exemplifies how, when an Ausländer enters a place that is considered the domain of Germanness, she is questioned before she is let in. She has to answer whatever questions the Germans might have about Turks, regardless of whether those questions are relevant to her own experiences. Then, she has to prove that their preconceived ideas are not applicable to her. Most Germans evaluate her as a Turkish person rather than by her own personality. In the incident Aynur describes, she is made a representative of the Turkish Ausländer people. When she was in hospital, the German patients took positions as judges, assuming the authority to confer or withhold recognition (Oliver 2000). Throughout these interrogations, the Germans' own worth was never questioned. At best, Aynur felt she might contribute something of value to the Germans' awareness of others.

Funda, whose blondness allows her to blend in with ethnic Germans, felt that she succeeded in making such a contribution at a school she attended in the former East Berlin:

> I was happy with my teachers. They were supportive. My grades were good ... After Grade 10, when I received my grade report, they said it was great having me at this school, as a Turkish person. They had a Turkish student for the first time. I took Turkish culture to the school. They have learned a lot about us. It was a great feeling.

Funda, Selin, and Aynur all wanted (or needed) to believe that the problems of exclusion, discrimination, and prejudice were solvable with straightforward hard work and persuasive rational arguments. As Sullivan (2006, 18–19) describes this hope: "White people will gladly fill in the gaps in their knowledge and eliminate their racism. [However] This view of ignorance problematically softens the ugly realities of white dominance by presenting simultaneously a positive image of white people and ... an optimistic outlook on the prospects for eliminating racism."

In dealing with this issue, it is misleading to treat preconceived ideas as a lack of knowledge. It is the dominant group (Germans), not the Others, who benefit from the ignorance. Although the ignorance typically displayed by Germans appears to be an innocent oversight, it is actually a deliberate choice for maintaining privilege. We need to examine the participants' practical experiences regarding how habits of ignorance and stereotyping function together to retain distance and difference between Germans and Ausländer.

I draw a distinction between individual experiences and collective constructions of the Other. Funda is not wrong about her school experience – she probably did not feel any discrimination. However, Funda, Selin, and

Aynur clearly occupy specific positions in German society, and awareness of those assigned positions is central to the process of change that I attempt to describe. Awareness raises questions not only about the prejudices of the dominant group, but also about the responses of the Others. Awareness of the unstated basis for social ranking allows us to mediate between social worlds in a self-conscious way. If we are to understand how Funda, Selin, and Aynur see their reality, we need to go beyond simply describing discrimination. Their perspectives represent only part of the whole story, but they are previously ignored parts, and they render the entire picture much more complex.

The Germans' insistent *ignorance* and *insensitivity* regarding Ausländer constitute a strategy for maintaining privilege through discourses of proximation and estrangement. Ignorance and insensitivity serve to reinforce social ranking, racial dominance, and the privilege of being the hosts. They do this through manipulating the configurations of hostility and hospitality. Ayla talks about how difficult it is to deal with a combination of ignorance and insensitivity that persists without being openly expressed. Judgments may appear as positive comments. When Germans say how much they like Turks and Turkish food, or how they spend their holidays in Türkiye, Ayla reflects, "You can't easily challenge this." Well-protected ignorance can be expressed as curiosity, and Ausländer are then put in the position of explaining themselves or needing to teach the curious and ignorant ones. Many participants describe how they seek to prove themselves by being an exception or being an expert who can represent Turkishness to Germans. Some participants believe that if they explain themselves well, they can enable Germans to question their preconceived ideas. However, it is still typically assumed that the people to be explained are the Ausländer, whereas Germanness requires no explanation.

Yıldız's experience with her German friend's friends shows how Turk and German commonly find themselves placed in two irreconcilable categories, between which reciprocal relations seem impossible by definition:

> With Elke, we have known each other for over seven years ... When [her friends] first met me, I felt from their looks that they weren't comfortable with me ... They became open eventually; [I felt,] *I have become accepted.* Only then did they tell me they found it weird that Elke has had a Turkish friend for over seven years. They said that after getting to know me, they felt close enough to tell this to me.

Accommodating the Ausländer 127

Elke's friends eventually became comfortable enough to express to Yıldız their sense of distance between Turks and Germans. After Yıldız gained their trust, they finally admitted their judgment about friendships between these types of people. However, they showed this familiarity by expressing their sense of the distance between Germans and Turks, so it was just a reaffirmation of her Turkishness. She had become proximated, but only as a Turk. Then she felt that getting to know Elke's friends better had failed to remove the assumption of inborn difference.

The participants describe how, when talking with German friends and colleagues, they tend to become informants and experts on the aspects of Turkish life about which Germans "lack information." Seda, a teenager who wears a headscarf, explains how she is treated as a representative of Islam and that she has to answer all the questions her German friends might have. Her friends' ignorance is expressed as desire for relevant information. As Seda's headscarf seems to represent her expertise on Islam, she is presumed able to satisfy her friends' "extreme curiosity about the headscarf." She admits that she likes telling them "more about our religion," even though she feels that her knowledge is not "deep enough ... to give them accurate information." Still, her headscarf represents an essential part of the stereotype of the "Turkish woman." Seda therefore becomes the expert who needs to provide information to her friends, so she can disrupt their negative perceptions of Turks and Islam.

Arzu confronts her colleagues at the newspaper where she works when they treat her as an authority on the Turkish community of Berlin, an expert on Türkiye, and an adviser on how Germans should handle their relation with Turks:

> People call me if they want to write something about Turkish people. "If I write 'Turkish grocer,' is it racist?" No. "Then I'm writing okay?" They ask: "We're going to Antalya for our holiday – how is the weather there now?" How would I know? I'm not in Antalya right now. Go check on the Internet.[5]

Arzu becomes a guide for German journalists. Her assigned authority enables them not to think about their questions for themselves. Such behaviour allows the journalists not only to maintain their ignorance but also to locate Arzu in Türkiye and in Turkish culture, outside of Germanness and German culture.

When the space for communication is open, and Germans and Ausländer develop an ongoing relationship of work, study, or friendship, the Ausländer can prove stereotypes to be wrong and gain a proximity to being German. This proximation seemingly breaks down prejudices toward the individuals concerned. Yet in most cases, the individual Ausländer becomes accepted only as an exception, an anomaly, or an expert representative, and thus the stereotype is preserved. Approved proximation keeps the stereotypes in play and maintains the distance between Germanness and Turkishness.

The following incident illustrates how overcoming ignorance by filling in gaps in information can actually perpetuate the distance between Germans and Ausländer. This incident differs from most everyday encounters, because it involves interviews with Aziza A, a German musician born in Berlin in 1971 to Turkish immigrant parents. The interviews were covered in the public media:

> The interviews ... were not about my music, but my personal life ... "What percentage Turkish are you; how much of you is German? ... How do you get along with your parents? ... Did you run away from home? Does your father support your singing?" ... I questioned myself ... Am I Turkish or German? What am I? Should I be thinking about this? ... It took some time to realize what was going on.

This particular type of media representation had an effect on Aziza A's self-perception. She started questioning herself about her difference. Defending her actions and convincing the journalists that she has a "normal life" became a struggle for her. A journalist asked her for an interview in her home – to see it and the cultural symbols in it. Responding to this request of "just to look" and an assurance of "no harm is intended," Aziza A agreed "to show them my lifestyle is as normal as any German family's." She found herself taking on a mission to help this journalist overcome his ignorance by filling in the gaps in his knowledge regarding the lifestyle of an Ausländer. She attempted to prove to the media and, therefore, to the German public that she had a normal family life. However, as well-intentioned as the journalist was, he failed to notice anything that would seem non-Turkish or that did not fit his assumptions about Aziza A, her family, or what they represented. While expressing the wish to do no harm, the journalist proceeded to treat Aziza A and her family as objects, ignoring their subjectivity.

Accommodating the Ausländer 129

As this example illustrates, representations of the Other, including those carried by the public media, are rarely, if ever, natural, value-free, or innocent. Judgment is implicit in the way language is used, fossilized in word and image, and complicit in exclusionary practices.

What Does Ignorance Have to Do with It?
As Sullivan argues, white people in general are deeply unaware of how to live with their whiteness in ways that promote racial justice: "Even worse, their ignorance poses as knowledge, making it all the more insidious" (2014, 3). This sort of racial privilege perpetuates "seemingly invisible, often unconscious forms of white racism" (2014, 4). In the German context, this process proceeds in much more subtle ways, but with more harmful effects, as *race* has particularly difficult historical connotations.

In the dialogues I analyze here, the participants find themselves prejudged as Turks, as outsiders seeking membership in German society, or as needing recognition from the dominant Germans. In their dialogues, certain values are embraced and others are rejected. Individual interactions challenge German notions of the Turk, yet the stereotypes themselves – which have been socially, politically, culturally, and historically established – are seldom altered. Changing the social context of identity is difficult but not impossible.

The privileged status of ethnic Germans involves claiming sole possession of Germanness and of Germany, and most Germans involved in the encounters analyzed here are clearly reluctant to give up their sense of ownership. As Ayla reasons: "If there is a real wish, the effort comes with it ... What is the point of disturbing their comfort?" The real wish must operate at many levels: individual, political, social, institutional, and cultural. To act on it requires reconfiguring the rules of recognition, giving a place in the home to the arrivant, rewriting history, and questioning dominant ideologies.

Faces of Orientalisms and Racisms

We indeed always experienced racism ... With the refugee crisis, the fear-mongering has increased. AfD and PEGIDA have showed the true face of Germany. Increasing racism has revealed a neo-fascism in Germany. We immigrants knew this, but people were uninformed about racism in Germany.

– Selim, in 2016

In recent years, Germany has made an effort to redefine itself as a nation with a *Willkommenskultur* (a culture of welcome), an immigrant society, a country that accepts refugees, which is opening itself to the world. At the same time, a supranationalist discourse is showing itself in the increasing influence of racist movements such as PEGIDA, which is the acronym for *Patriotische Europäer gegen die Islamisierung des Abendlandes* (Patriotic Europeans Against the Islamization of the West), in the emergence of the AfD (the *Alternative für Deutschland*, which means Alternative for Germany), and in the popularity of Sarrazin's book. Ayhan Kaya and political scientist Ayşe Tecmen (2019) find that right-wing populist party leaders across Europe have increasingly relied on rhetoric regarding a clash of civilizations and Islamoracism. As sociologist Rogers Brubaker (2017, 1208) observes: "The growing civilizational preoccupation with Islam in European populisms has profoundly transformed the political semantics of self and other: the collective self is increasingly defined in broadly civilizational, not narrowly national terms."

On all levels, such discourse is changing from a focus on Ausländer to a focus on Muslims. One dramatic change is the prominence of Christianity as a signifier. Erkan discusses how this focus works:

If you always see the person as Muslim, you have to define yourself as Christian. We haven't had this in Germany, especially in former East Germany, with its socialist past, where religion was not important. But now we see in East Germany people are saying: "We are Christians, we should not let Muslim refugees in, and we should have Christian refugees from Syria come." When you look at Germany's history, this would be something you wouldn't have seen in Germany, of all countries.

Fatma explains why she thinks Islamoracism has increased in the past three years: "There is a tremendous amount of hatred toward Islam. It is growing exponentially ... It was hostility toward foreigners, and now it is hostility toward religion – toward Islam. Their fear is that Islam has increased in influence, and Christianity is in danger of destruction." Leyla also describes how concern over a clash between Christendom and Muslimness has grown more pronounced in recent years:

As far as I remember, Muslimness did not really have prominence. You were Turkish, you were Arab. It was talked about as such. Now, it doesn't matter if you are Turkish or Arab. Maybe this is to do with where the world is now. But I also think that at some level it was always there, that we were Muslim first, for them, but maybe we didn't see it. Turks were more "foreign" than Americans, Greeks, or French? Maybe religion was something that flowed between the lines always. But now, we see this very clearly. It is in our face.

When I asked what made this clear for her, Leyla continued: "It was the Syrian war. And that people came in here in huge numbers. When all these people mixed up with religion, politics, and war, what happened? Turks became like them too."

The University of Leipzig has carried out a study on racism in Germany at regular intervals since 2002, seeking to examine the extent of racist and authoritarian beliefs in German society. The results in 2016 revealed that "one in every ten Germans wants their country to be led by a 'Führer' who applies a firm hand for the common good. Eleven percent of respondents say that Jews have too much influence in society. Twelve percent think Germans are by nature superior to other people. Four in ten people think Muslims should be prohibited from immigrating to the country" (AFP/The Local 2016).

In *The Cultural Politics of Emotion,* Sara Ahmed (2004, 43) argues that the emotions of hate and fear as conveyed toward the Other involve a position that is deliberate. These emotions are experienced as expressions of "love to the nation." This concern for the nation, however, arises in response to a fear that the nation's identity is threatened by the very presence of the stranger. Ahmed argues: "Hate is not simply present as the emotion that explains the story (it is not a question of hate being at its root), but as that which is affected by the story, and as that which enables the story to be affective." Narratives of hate and fear create "a subject that is endangered by imagined others," whose presence is "imagined as a threat to the object of love." This kind of fear and hate toward the Ausländer has been articulated in very concrete ways, as the participants in this research explain from their own experiences.

AfD and PEGIDA: People with Small Fears Making Up the Rallies

We have AfD, *Alternative für Deutschland.* Although it has quickly become a fundamentally right-wing group, when it was first founded, its members were business people, lawyers. But now, they have neo-Nazis. They criticize and attack media. They have views similar to Trump's views. It is like: "The refugees should not bring their families; they should go back. We should force them to learn/speak German; if they don't, they should be punished." There used to be anti-foreigner rallies every Monday, organized by Protecting Germany and German Culture from Islam [PEGIDA].

– Arzu, in 2016

PEGIDA is a nationalist, anti-Islam, far-right political movement that was founded in 2014 (Rothwell 2016). The leaders of this movement have denounced Chancellor Merkel as a "traitor of the people," blaming her open-door policy toward asylum seekers as the cause of a national refugee crisis (Connolly 2015). In response to such accusations, Germany's domestic intelligence service reported that the incidence of far-right violence escalated in 2015 by 42 percent, to a total of 1,408 attacks (Deutsche Welle 2016; Rothwell 2016). These incidents included 75 arson attacks against refugee centres (Deutsche Welle 2016). Germany's interior ministry announced that at least 950 hate crimes were committed against Muslims or mosques during 2017 (Jones 2018). Leyla explains:

And now these right-wing people have started going out to the streets. They were there already, but now no one can hold them back. And now they have AfD to be their voice. I mean, this political party starts from this, this fear ... I watched it on TV the other day. How the party leader speaks. What he said was: "We are the voice of our people; you don't want to hear their voices. We are losing Germany. We feel like foreigners in our own country." This was there before too. It is not new. They are repeating themselves. None of this rhetoric is new.

September 2017 was the first time that the AfD party and the PEGIDA group were seen at the same public demonstration, with more than two thousand attendees in Dresden (Deutsche Welle 2017). Right-wing extremism has now infiltrated the mainstream political process, directly threatening the rights and roles of immigrant Germans.

When I asked what had changed since our last meeting in 2003, Ayten reported: "Really, there is not much big change, to tell you the truth. Well, actually, in the last four or five years; the hatred toward foreigners has increased at work and in personal life ... You hear people using racist words much more comfortably." Fear has become a part of everyday life, and the media play an important role. In 2016, Ayten reflected on how fear is spread:

Accommodating the Ausländer 133

When we say *fascists*, I am not really talking about the most extreme. These are people with small fears. I think what is different is that these people are the people with little worries. It is like fear inspired by the sight of four or five Turkish men hanging out. The "Would they do something to us?" kind of fear. It is not like radical fascism. They are really fringe. They were always there, and they are not the mainstream. But there is also that fascism grew with this fear ... You hear that: "We are happy with the foreigners we have here, [but] we don't want new ones."

Fatma notes that white Europeans now associate bearded brown people with terrorism. She narrates an incident, which was caused by an abandoned suitcase, that she witnessed while shopping with her son at Alexanderplatz. A few young brown men were standing around the suitcase, and then they disappeared. So the authorities emptied the square and the police came. Fatma took her son and left in panic, as the others did. She reflects on the incident:

I thought to myself that the social behaviour has changed. Foreigners, religion, and terror go together now, somehow ... People keep away from any place where there are a few brown men gathered or talking. People don't get on the subway car if there are a few bearded brown men in it. They change their route while walking on the street. I feel that this is becoming more and more prominent ... I even see it in myself: I change my way if I see a few brown men. I cross the street. Especially when I am with my son, or with the kids I work with, I feel I am more alert.

Fatma mentions her long-familiar German neighbour and how this neighbour tells stories about her experience with Turks. She sees Fatma's relatives as they visit and knows how close they are. But this neighbour easily distances herself from such familiarity, allowing herself to forget that she is also talking about Fatma's family when she complains, "Turks are very crowded; they are loud." Fatma reflects, "Then I realize how much my living close to her place bothers her." The complaint about Turks includes Fatma's family too. Fatma says she does not see these feelings as fascist or as rightwing extremism: "It is that woman's own feelings; she is talking about her extensive feelings of dislike toward Turks, while forgetting that I am Turkish as well."

Referring to this example and others, Fatma continues:

These are small everyday things. But at the same time, we also see big neo-Nazi rallies in the media. And I think, It is the kind of people, like my neighbour, who have these intense feelings of dislike toward foreigners who are the ones attending these rallies. Because the more visible the foreigner became in Germany and the more these fears increased, the more of these ordinary people started walking the streets to protest. They want to give a political response, to make it clear in this political climate that "we are here too." It is these people who are marching against immigrants.

The experience of these small fears and hostilities has become ubiquitous. It appears everywhere and is increasingly common. Even Fatma shares the fear, as in the case of the abandoned suitcase. What happens to Muslims in these situations? Leyla talks about how people become self-conscious and feel the need to explain themselves:

When Charlie [Hebdo] was murdered in France, I had a children's clothing store. I also sold second-hand clothing. One day, a young man came in – here, you can't tell Muslims and hipsters apart; they have the same kind of facial hair. He looked like a hipster, Muslim, I don't know. He said that he and his partners had just closed down their store and wondered whether I would be interested in buying the clothes they had. I don't know how I looked at him, but he said: "I am sorry. I didn't mean to scare you or disturb you. We don't support what happened to Charlie. Islam wouldn't support this. We are not related to those people." He felt the need to explain. I was kind of taken back. I said everything is fine, no problem. My parents are also Muslim. So that happens too. And I thought to myself, "Oh my ... "

Arzu talks about how she has been hoping and waiting for being Turkish "to become natural, so it does not become so important. The Turkishness will only remain in the names, and they are just like anyone." She hopes that it might be different for the new generation, but she says they seem to be worse off now (2016). For the next generation: "Maybe all we worked for and gained is lost now ... especially for men. Maybe suspicion toward them has increased, or perhaps their Muslimness became the forefront ... It has become an essential part of them all of a sudden." Young Muslim men are now so strongly suspected that many nightclubs refuse to admit them.

Erkan says: "Yes, it is impacting everyone, but differently. Some [Germans] feel more confident about their belonging in this society, while

Accommodating the Ausländer 135

others live in hesitance." The biggest negative impact is for the people who have been Othered. The rising suspicion of others affects their job searches or causes them to lose their jobs. Sometimes they cannot find housing. On the subway, the police search them and their belongings; at the borders, they are treated differently. It impacts women and men differently.

Citizenship Tests: Markers of Fear and Hatred

Citizenship tests have become primary examples of institutional and structural racism. In 2006, the conservative politician Heribert Rech (the interior minister of Baden-Württemberg) implemented a thirty-question citizenship test, applied exclusively to applicants who had a previous nationality from a Muslim country. This test was offered as a set of discussion guidelines to be used for determining these applicants' attitudes toward the German constitution and so-called Western values. The test also required suspected immigrants to give their views on democracy, terrorism, and the rights of women and gay people (Charles 2006). Supporters of the test claimed that people of migrant descent should not be granted German citizenship unless they demonstrate their adherence to certain "German" values. Some of the questions are as follows (Furlong 2006):

How do you view the statement that a woman should obey her husband, and that he can beat her if she doesn't?

You learn that people from your neighbourhood or from among friends or acquaintances have carried out or are planning a terrorist attack – what do you do?

Some people hold the Jews responsible for all the evil in the world, and even claim they were behind the attacks of September 11, 2001, in New York. What is your view of this claim?

Imagine that your son comes to you and declares that he's a homosexual and would like to live with another man. How do you react?

These questions are targeted for uncovering the applicants' assumed outlooks toward Islamic terrorism, anti-Semitism, and gender and sexual orientation rights. They interrogate the applicants' acceptance toward, for example, LGBTI+ individuals, while assuming that the acceptance of different sexual orientations is inherently German. As sociologist Ilgin Yorukoglu (2010, 424) notes, this problematic assumption ignores the LGBTI+ victims of the Nazi regime. It also overlooks the fact that Germany decriminalized "deviant" sexualities only in the late 1960s and that the age of consent was higher for male-male sexual activity than it was for heterosexual acts until 1994.

The proponents of the test suppose that "Muslim" people are a threat to cherished values of German society. A variety of social and political activists have defended the "Muslim test." The questions to be asked were not left to the discretion of the civil servants administering it but, rather, were set in advance by state authorities. This kind of requirement illustrates what is meant by institutionally and structurally required racism, as opposed to merely personal racism. The constitution says that no one can be stripped of German citizenship unwillingly. However, as Erkan explains,

> with this Muslim test, you were told that if you lie you might lose your German citizenship. Not for a day, not for two months, but forever. You have to be true in your answers. You are forever under surveillance. In twenty-five years, if you are seen to not show understanding of your gay son, you might lose your citizenship.

The courts ruled that this citizenship test violated a basic constitutional right – the first such violation since the Second World War. The test was therefore officially rejected but not before media coverage had cemented a popular view that the post-migrant population – to whom formal citizenship rights had just been extended – was unassimilable and unworthy of citizenship (Haritaworn 2010).

Homonationalism

> I remember being in Frankfurt and going to an LGBTI+ bookstore. I saw [Sarrazin's] book in the shop window. The bookstore owner said: "The Muslim youth in our neighbourhoods are also very homophobic, and we need to talk about this." And I said: "Okay, you can do whatever you want ... Are you aware that you are telling me, another queer person, that you don't want me?"
>
> – Erkan

The rise of homonationalism illustrates how even former or expected-to-be allies can end up on the hostility end of the hospitality–hostility axis. In 2016, Erkan claimed

Islamoracism is the main fellow-feeling [among LGBTI+ people] it seems: "Muslims are disgusting; let's join forces against them." Feminists, LGBTI+ activists, environmentalists, left-wing groups, liberals all joined the mainstream. As they found a new enemy, the foundation for unity [with migrants] disappeared. For example, if an LGBTI+ activist says we need the police to protect us, then it is over. LGBTI+ activists never criticize what the police are doing to immigrants, Blacks, Roma people, homeless people, or poor people, because the police protect LGBTI+. And that is the truth too. Sociologically speaking, once the hierarchies changed, the foundations for acting together also disappeared, and nothing has replaced it yet.

Sociologist Jin Haritaworn (2010, 71) explains that "in Germany, fundamentally racialized hate crime activism is the latest episode in a moral panic over 'homophobic migrants.'" Recently, the phrase "society as a whole" – which really means ethnic German society – has become a tool to mobilize a new popular cause in Germany: opposing "homophobic Muslims who cannot handle diversity" and who present a serious threat to it (Haritaworn 2010, 71). After several years of helping to generate this kind of moral panic in close collaboration with journalists, politicians, and academics, a number of influential gay organizations such as the Lesbian and Gay Federation Germany (LSVD) and the gay male attack hotline in Berlin (MANEO) are benefiting from their solidarity with Muslim-bashers. Therefore, LSVD activists have played a significant role in promoting the Muslim test. According to Haritaworn and Jen Petzen (2011, 57–58), the LSVD spokesman Alexander Zinn "welcome[d] the motion and call[ed] on the Berlin Senate to follow Baden-Württemberg's example ... He explained that the Muslim test inserted a new sexual citizen into a public [who was] busy inventing 'core values' and even traditions of gay friendliness."

When Judith Butler turned down the *Zivilcourage Prize* awarded by Berlin Pride in 2010, she explained:

Some of the organizers explicitly made racist statements or did not dissociate themselves from them. The host organizations refuse to understand anti-racist politics as an essential part of their work ... I must distance myself from this complicity with racism, including anti-Muslim racism ... If I were to accept an award for courage, I would have to pass this award on to those that really demonstrate courage. (quoted in Vail 2010)

138 *Hostility–Hospitality*

An organization called SUSPECT (which represents queer and trans migrants, Black people, people of colour, and their allies) applauded Butler's "bravery in openly critiquing the organizers' closeness to homonationalist organisations" (SUSPECT 2010). The organization issued this statement:

> In these times and by these means, LGBTI+ are recruited for nationalism and militarism. Currently, many European governments claim that LGBTI+ rights must be protected and the new hatred of immigrants is necessary to protect LGBTI+ people ... Therefore, we must say "no" to such a deal. To be able to say no under these circumstances is what I call courage. But who says no? And who experiences this racism? Who are the queers who really fight against such politics? (SUSPECT 2010)

The form of racism that Butler and SUSPECT oppose is a subtle racism, different from traditional "supremacist" racism. With a new set of alliances among social groups, the common everyday racism of ordinary local people has been changing, as Erkan argues, into politicized racism as a mainstream movement. Erkan makes these observations on the emerging homonationalist type of Islamoracism:

> The difference between Islamoracism and mainstream racism is that feminists and LGBTI+ groups are supporting it. If you are being racist in the name of asking for equality for women and LGBTI+, then it is not seen as racism ... So [Islamoracism] easily distances itself from the white supremacist type of racism, which wouldn't be supported in the mainstream. But it is different when one argues that "the majority of violence on the streets against LGBTI+ is by Muslims." This is a different argument altogether.

As LGBTI+ rights become connected to the nation – and are used as indicators of European values and superior "civilization," these rights concurrently have grown detached from their historical relation to politics of the left (Günkel and Pitcher 2008). As Yorukoglu (2010) argues, the positioning of LGBTI+ rights as a symbol of freedom has been used to justify the wars in Afghanistan and Iraq and to justify restrictive, racist immigration policies in *Westernized* nations. As a result, the discourses around "society as a whole" are being used to justify unequal legal and citizenship policies for certain populations. Haritaworn, a co-founding member of Inclusive Mosque Initiative; engineer Tamsila Tauqir; social economist

Accommodating the Ausländer 139

Esra Erdem (2008); critical diversity and community studies professor Jennifer Petzen (2009); and queer theorist Jasbir Puar (2007) document this trend.

Everyday Racism: The Political Is Leaking into the Private

When I first visited Berlin in 2003, many activist participants spoke about how the personal and subjective was political. In my recent visits, it seemed that this argument had shifted:

> I think it is just the opposite now. Now, what is political is leaking into the private. The racist discourses are so dominant now that it is not coming from the extreme right or the neo-Nazi or populist parties. It is in the society as a whole. Even if someone is not facing it everywhere and all the time, there is that consciousness and hesitancy we live with. It becomes internally personal; anyone becomes sensitive when they can face racism at any time. It is impossible that this would not impact people's lives, relations, thoughts, and emotions. It is so very dominant.

The following reports of encounters with hostility illustrate how the political has leaked into the private. Although making definitive conclusions is difficult, we can examine particular examples. Arzu's encounters with subtle hostility occur in a rather progressive environment:

> On the one hand, all my friends are very left, liberal, open-minded intellectuals, artists, musicians, theatre players. But when I think about the emotional stuff – like "Where do you send your children to school?" or "Do you mind having Turkish children in the class?" – when these topics come up, they still want their children to go to the school with fewer Turkish kids ... Even if they eat all these organic fruits, or define themselves as leftist or liberal, they still discriminate in this way ... I feel like there are only very few people who really feel that the foreigners who live here are a part of this country. But still, I am very hesitant to make any generalization.

Sara Ahmed's analysis of "emotions of fear and hate" is useful for understanding these narratives of Orientalism and racism. She argues that "the impossibility of reducing hate to a particular body allows hate to circulate in an economic sense, working to differentiate others from other others, a differentiation that is never 'over,' as it awaits others who have not yet arrived.

Such a discourse of 'waiting for the bogus' is what justifies the repetition of violence against the bodies of others in the name of protecting the nation" (Ahmed 2004, 47). In addition, she describes how repeating these narratives of difference serves to "create impressions of others as those who have invaded the space of the nation, threatening its existence" (46). For Ahmed, these emotions are not something that particular bodies evoke but emotions that circulate among bodies, both socially and materially, due to "the sticky relation between signs and bodies" (191).

Understanding Germany's Islamoracism

As Said (1978) notes, the currently popular Western depiction of Muslim people is not new. Orientalism has long been based on the ideology that there is a Christian world and a Muslim world, irreconcilable and in conflict. Following the collapse of the communist bloc and since 9/11, the traditional enmity toward the Muslim Other has resurfaced as a primary concern of Western leaders. As Çalışkan and sociology graduate student Kayla Preston (2017) explain, a thread of Orientalist thinking runs through Western history. A theme of fear and loathing, with demands for control over the Other, connects the advocates of colonialism from Balfour, Cromer, Huntington, and Lewis, to contemporary discourses in Germany such as those of Sarrazin, the AfD, and groups such as PEGIDA.

In his article "The Roots of Muslim Rage," Bernard Lewis (1990) seeks to explain why Muslims are antagonistic toward the West. He argues that Islam has never modernized and is incapable of understanding other civilizations. Lewis depicts the Muslim as absurdly angry with the innocent American public, which has done absolutely nothing to the Muslim people. He argues that the US should ignore Muslim hatred and maintain the peace. As Said (1998) points out, Lewis makes sweeping characterizations about the one billion Muslims living across the world, who have numerous different languages, traditions, and histories. Lewis's representation of Western civilization is just as simplistic. This depiction of Muslims as one giant mob, furiously angry with Western modernity, belittles and dehumanizes the Muslim Other. Lewis's portrait of Muslim depravity suggests that Western dominance and control over Muslims is an inescapable necessity.

Similarly, in "The Clash of Civilizations," Huntington (1993, 22), argues that "the great divisions among humankind and the dominating source of conflict will be cultural ... [and this struggle] will dominate global politics." His core vision is a constant confrontation between people of different traditions.

Accommodating the Ausländer

Said (1998) seeks to explain how harmful modern Orientalism has become. As the writings of Lewis and Huntington are widely seen as objective and scientific, they make traditional ethnocentric prejudice seem like fact-based realism – in the same way that *race science* made the Nazi war for survival of the fittest seem inevitable. "The angry Muslim" serves as a discursive basis for the politics of fear and hatred that shape global policy decisions, while at the same time fuelling resentment and violence toward Muslim people at the local level (Perry 2014). This kind of political realism is evident in the series of policies recently introduced in Europe that seek to promote social cohesion, as urged by sectarian writers such as Sarrazin.

Huntington, Lewis, Sarrazin, and many of Europe's contemporary politicians have sought to unite *their people* by arousing hostility toward assigned others. These ideologues draw on provocative theories that portray life as an ongoing battle for dominance. Their theories ignore the vast benefits of constructive interchange between people of many cultures over the course of world history. They ignore, as Said (1998, 3) explains, "the enormous advances in our concrete understanding and theoretical understanding of how cultures work. How they change, and how they can best be grasped or apprehended." Said (1998, 5) warns us against the polarizing urge to speak "in the name of large entities" such as the West or Islam. These simplistic generalizations, he argues, are manipulable abstractions that "collapse particular religions, races and ethnicities into ideologies."

This practice of interpreting cultures and peoples as homogeneous entities builds on the legacy of colonialism. The old French notion of Europe's civilizing mission presumed that some races and cultures have higher aims in life than others. As Said (1998, 5) explains: "This [presumption] gives the more powerful, the more developed, the more civilized ... the right to colonize others, not in the name of brute force, or plunder, both of which are standard components of the exercise, but in the name of a noble ideal." That ideal involves the politically sanctioned ranking of some social groups over others. For example, the economy of the modern Western world has been built on a foundation of force-backed colonization, expropriation of resources, removal of native populations, and slave labour. Germany's economy has also been built on the backs of subordinated or marginalized people such as the guest workers. That labour was based on relations of inferior-to-superior. And now, it is the demand for continued superiority in an ever-more ethnically integrated, multipolar world that brings many Germans to call for a "return to superiority."

Economists Naci Mocan and Christian Raschke (2016) show that fear and hatred toward racialized minorities in Germany tend to increase when perceived economic well-being is uncertain. Ironically, the same economy that is built on Ausländer's backs becomes the focus of perceived economic vulnerability. As Çalışkan and Preston (2017, 9) point out, when the descendants of Germany's guest workers ask for equal rights, it is taken as a threat to the status of others, those who traditionally enjoyed a superior rank cry, "This is my country." In calling for social cohesion, they argue that "we do not want to take on these immigrants any longer, it is failing." Their cry for cohesion against the "new German" Ausländer shows a crisis of nationalism: "As white people in Western society are increasingly called on to renounce their domination of others, they have commonly lashed out in self-defence or insisted that they have no such position of privilege."

One of the greatest crises of identity affecting countries such as Germany, France, Britain, and the US stems from the growing realization that "no culture or society is purely one thing" (Said 1998, 9). Sizable minorities, such as the Turks in Germany, challenge the idea that homogeneous societies are even possible. There are no insulated cultures – there never were. By attempting to separate people into the impermeable compartments of culture, Sarrazin and other like-minded contemporary writers pose a threat to culture's variety, diversity, complexity, and hybridity.

Diasporic citizens, including those who took part in this research, commonly argue that we should be pursuing a more integrative path. As they themselves have integrated the gifts of two or more cultures, they view the world's diverse cultures as making up one vast whole. The exact contours of that whole may be impossible for any one person to grasp, but diasporic people experience that unity as an emerging reality. Diasporants advocate for an expanded sense of community, understanding, sympathy, and hope. Their kind of mentality is already found in the many global movements that stress community and sharing rather than competition for dominance by any one race, gender, or class. Their vision of wholeness is the opposite of that proposed by politicians and ideologues like Sarrazin. As Said (1998, 10) argues: "Efforts to return the community of civilizations to a primitive stage of narcissistic struggle, [sic] need to be understood, not as descriptions about how in fact civilizations behave, but rather as incitements to wasteful conflict and unedifying chauvinism and that seems to be exactly what we don't need."

The idea that everything is clashing is a prescription for war. However, a world based on relations of mutual benefit is not just a possibility; it is a clear and present reality. As Said suggests, we have the ability to live with

Accommodating the Ausländer 143

those who are different from us in all kinds of ways and to be enriched by that interaction. Diasporic citizens are the models of such potential. They are already living it.

The current European populist reaction against Muslims appears to reflect the earlier nineteenth-century rise of anti-Semitism to meet "the Jewish threat." In debates on the "Jewish question," numerous political and religious leaders insisted that Judaism was the eternal enemy of Christianity. The accomplishments of Jewish business people, thinkers, and artists threatened to "contaminate" Christian society. The efforts of Jewish political activists seemed part of an anti-Christian conspiracy to upend the European social order. The nonconformity of Jews in terms of dress, circumcision, language, and religious teaching was treated as a peril to Christian civilization, much as Muslim traditions are treated today. Wertheim (2017, 267–68) finds a common theme: "The demand [is] for Jews or Muslims not to be who they really are – to compromise their inner selves." Wertheim examines the similarities among Jews and Muslims and provides two stories of well-known Muslim and Jewish individuals, Ayaan Hirsi Ali and Heinrich Heine, who assimilated to mainstream European culture rather than maintain their own backgrounds – the ultimate price for any minority.

British discourses on Islam have also influenced Jewish-Muslim relations, as the war on terror has been used as a political tool to instill fear among non-Muslim citizens. Anthropologists Yulia Egorova and Fiaz Ahmed (2017, 286) explain how the historical memories of anti-Semitism shape Jewish fears toward Muslims. Although many Muslims are highly educated people, they often fail to comprehend Jewish history. They usually associate Jews with Israel (particularly with the Israel-Palestine conflict), and they misinterpret Zionism. If the similarities between Jewish and Muslim experiences in the Western-dominated world were better understood, surely their views toward each other would become more positive (Egorova 2017, 286). At present, Muslims are far more identifiable than Jews in Europe. Most Jews have successfully assimilated to modern Western society, whereas most Muslims are still new to Western cultural norms. As Egorova and Ahmed (2017, 288) argue, the Muslims of the UK, who are "mostly recent immigrants, [are now] going through in the UK ... what Jewish people had experienced in the past ... Jews had already been forced to assimilate."

In general, Muslims view Jews as being "luckier," more "successful," and "further ahead" than themselves (Egorova and Ahmed 2017, 290, 294). Although European Jews have been treated as an enemy population in the past, they are now generally accepted in society. Muslims, however, are seen as an active security threat both to Jews and to other Europeans. In the wake of the 9/11, 7/7, and other terrorist attacks, even Muslims have started to doubt their future in Europe. Many have come to expect discrimination; some even wonder if a Muslim Holocaust is imminent (Egorova and Ahmed 2017, 295). Overall, there are many similarities between modern Muslims and prewar Jews in Europe, yet discrepancies abound between contemporary Jews and Muslims. It is clear that Muslims are the current reference of discrimination and racism in Europe, and even the former victims of such racism, the Jews, are often deeply wary of Muslim immigrants.

The discourses of accommodation are extensions of the discourses of exceptionalism, social cohesion, fear, and hatred. These discourses are not focused on confirming the truthfulness of their claims. Instead, the claims appeal to traditional hopes for status gained and fears for status lost. Ethnocentric Germans want to ensure the superiority of their own people and their own traditions. They want people of other cultures to remain subordinate, with their traditions accommodated to German standards. The accommodation axis represents a competitive model. The discourses of exceptionalism, which range from hospitality to hostility, actually tell us nothing about Muslim immigrants or Turks in Germany. However, they do tell us a great deal about how power-building works.

Conclusion: Ways of Relating with Ausländer
In this chapter, I have analyzed particular practices that locate Ausländer in separate and unequal relations with Germans (and with each other) along lines of gender, ethnicity, class, religion, and skin colour. I have illustrated how the discourses of hostility and hospitality serve to relationally mark some Ausländer as more or less threatening than others. Some Ausländer are preferable and others undesirable, with the superior status of one depending on the subordinate status of the other. The result is to deny the status of full partner to some partners in the interaction. We have explored how these interactive processes construct Ausländerness differently, yet in direct relation to norms that privilege the dominant subjects.

I have unpacked the variations in meanings that are assigned to Ausländer as they appear on the axis of hospitality–hostility. The relationally constituted differences and hierarchies within the categories of Germans and non-Germans render some Ausländer as German-like, or almost-German. However, Germans and Ausländer are also ranked among themselves, and the competitions for advantage seem to require a deeper, more unbridgeable division based on a broader ethnic identity. Therefore, the various ways of accommodating Ausländer are not simply expressions of free-floating cultural attitudes. They extend beyond culture, beyond a list of multiple differences, to an underlying politics of proximation and estrangement.

According to Sara Ahmed's analysis (2000, 3), strangers (such as Ausländer) have to be seen as aliens to gain recognition: "To be an alien in a particular nation, is to hesitate at a different border: the alien here is the one who does not belong in a nation space ... The technique for differentiating between citizens and aliens ... allows the familiar to be established as the familial." However, the stranger is not simply a person who does not belong. As Ahmed puts it: "Strangers are not simply those who are not known in the dwelling, but those who are, in their very proximity, already recognised as not belonging, as being out of place" (20). Therefore, Ausländer become Ausländer only in their proximity or nearness to spaces and places that are imagined as places without Ausländer. Acts and practices of hostility and hospitality are the characteristic ways of relating in these spaces where Ausländer are present but not deemed worthy to be present.

Examining everyday encounters shows us how this kind of social order is maintained by ordinary people. Through their common sayings, jokes, and judgments, local people uphold the privileges assigned to racial, gendered, Orientalist, and ethnocentric norms. These dominant interpretations of social difference produce relational distinctions among the various Ausländer. However, in relation to Germans, these views of social difference have an opposite effect, of collapsing the various political, geographic, social, economic, religious, and ethnic differences among Ausländer into one common, overarching identity. Such dominant lenses for viewing social relations are troubling, not simply because they sustain privilege, but also because they may be adopted by the less privileged, who then take on the same habits of ranking in a mirror image of the dominant.

My analysis shows how the changeability of Ausländerness supports both proximation and estrangement in the practices of hostility and hospitality. The participants do not feel at home in their country of birth, and they still stand out as Ausländer, even when they look and live like Germans. Even as the significant markers of German-versus–non-German status diminish, the distance between Ausländer and Germans does not automatically decrease. Although being and belonging together with Turkish Ausländer is unavoidable, Germanness is protected from the *outsiderinsiders* through special means of categorizing, defining, and recognizing them, as well as through devising structural and legal policies. The historically constructed politics of relations between Germans and Ausländer are evident in the participants' experiences. Through these practices and policies, the dominant discourses can deny the reality that minorities and majorities are historically fluid. The conventions maintain that the lives of Germans and Ausländer should be parallel, so the realities of how they intersect can be ignored.

The participants' encounters illustrate how a narrow categorization of the Ausländer overlooks the heterogeneity and dynamism of their lives, ignores their demands for access to varied choices, and erases the complexity of their identities. The participants' accounts demonstrate how the *unknowable* Ausländer fail to fit into fixed categories. Their accounts also illustrate how even known individual Ausländer are constructed as threats, or offensive deviants from German standards. The need for such distinctions and boundary lines requires that the participants must be recognized as German-like or as exceptions to the presumed rules. However, the actual human conditions of both Turks and Germans are heterogeneous and far too complex to be categorized neatly as an opposition between German and non-German ways of life.

The identities of both Germans and Others have always been changing and are anything but fixed and stable. For both Germanness and Turkishness, the instability of identity is an opportunity and a threat at the same time. In this ongoing struggle, German-born Turkish Ausländer challenge the limits of what it means to be German and to belong in Germany. They do this through their subjective inner struggles and their everyday acts or practices of social life, as they seek new forms of identity and a more inclusive diasporic citizenship.

Homesickness—Homelessness
Negotiating Displacement

> One must betray one's fatherland and go to another place to be at two places at the same time. Through such a change of place, one's own history becomes larger and more magical ... The search for identity is different in a foreign land than in one's homeland.
> – Emine Sevgi Özdamar (culturebase.net, 2001)

The author, director, and actress Özdamar describes the condition of displacement: it is like going to another place and then having the sense of being in two places at once. However, for German-born Ausländer, there is a sense of being forced to live without having any place at all. Germany is neither a place they have chosen to be, nor a home they can claim as their own. Migrating to Germany was their parents' or grandparents' choice, and being born in Germany does not entitle them to Germanness. Therefore, they experience a sense of being forced into separation from their ancestral homeland, yet alienated within Germany. Their perceptions and experiences of displacement, which involve leaving a homeland behind even though they were born in Germany, colour their negotiations of identity and belonging. They experience the perplexing predicament of simultaneous homelessness and homesickness.

German-born Ausländer use essentialized, anti-essentialized, or strategically essentialized ways of expressing what displacement means to them. Therefore, rather than questioning whether their connections with a homeland are natural or if they are socially constructed, I focus on analyzing the conditions in which their displacement is given positive or negative meanings. These people's negotiations of displacement involve both essentialized and variable representations of their identity, difference, and belonging.

Their reflections lead to what Butler calls a "double movement" (1993, 222). On the one hand, diasporic people invoke the notion of homeland; hence, they conditionally posit an identity. On the other hand, they entertain the notion of identity as a site of permanent political contestation. This double movement – an emotional and positional oscillation between homelessness and homesickness – leads them to criticize the socio-historical conditions in which representations of belonging are formed. A back-and-forth movement destabilizes the idea that a person's identity is ontologically either one thing or another. To counter the logic behind dominant conceptions of belonging, it is necessary to examine the contingency of people's foundations for belonging.

Inexplicable Connections to Homeland

> Immigration is a trauma. It is like coming out in the sense that when you come out [as a queer person], you open up to your family, and you start experiencing your identity. It can cause a collapse, and a big part of the mosaic either disappears or it can become a new piece in the mosaic.
>
> – Erkan

When comparing immigration with "coming out," Erkan puts displacement at the centre of both experiences. Displacement means leaving family, friends, home, city, and a familiar culture behind and moving to an unknown place. It involves losing "the comfort of the familiar and [of] being accepted" (Erkan) in one's own homeland. Political theorists David Howarth and Yannis Stavrakakis (2000) would agree: immigration means taking a risk, as the disruption might "cause a collapse" in one's sense of self. Migration and coming out are both forms of displacement that cause social ruptures in communal life. Something is gained but much is lost. The loss requires a reconstruction of memory as a way to bestow meaning and integrity on one's past. This reconstruction, however, does not necessarily imply a reactive nostalgia. By losing the comfort of the familiar, immigrants gain a chance to restructure themselves even as they experience ruptures and discontinuities. The loss of their old identities compels them to act and assert anew their subjectivity. At the same time, they cultivate a strong sensitivity to dislocation. As Azade Seyhan (2000, 2001) reminds us, cultivating such sensitivity is critical for meeting the ethical challenge of belonging in diaspora.

As most diasporic subjects intend to reside permanently in the country where they live, they are not casual visitors or travellers. However, their

Negotiating Displacement

sense of belonging includes experiences of displacement, dislocation, and relocation, which pass from generation to generation. German-born Turkish Ausländer cannot step outside their experience of being constantly located elsewhere. They can, however, interrogate this experience, call into question its naturalness and continuity, and so reinterpret it.

Over time, the disorienting experiences of diasporic people tend to accumulate. Their displacements are often layered with memories of previous migrations. The negotiations of these displacements bring memories into play. For many participants, their family histories become interwoven with contemporary experiences of displacement in Berlin. Their sense of being simultaneously connected and displaced manifests itself through two distinct yet related notions: *living memory* and *myth of return.*

Diasporicity emerges with the sense of being a minority, which typically follows migration. Steven Vertovec (2018) reminds us that migration involves the transference and reconstitution of both cultural patterns and social relations in a new setting. That reconstitution usually involves the migrants becoming minorities who are set apart by race, language, cultural tradition, and religion.

Living Memory

The German-born Turkish Ausländer's sense of displacement emerges not just from geographical dislocation, but also from the ways that past displacements continue to shape the present. These displacements require migrants to face the question: "Where do you come from?" This is not just a question of origin. It is asked like a sentry's challenge to an intruder. I have already discussed how Germans commonly use the question: "Where do you come from?" to map Ausländer onto a narrow cartography. For the German-born Ausländer, declaring that they are "from Berlin" is not a satisfactory answer, as they are categorized at first glance as foreigners. Therefore, a seemingly friendly question turns into a contested claim over ownership and belonging (Alsultany 2002). The facts of where they – or their parents or grandparents – came from stay with them forever. Their sense of connection with Türkiye and with their parents' cultural heritage is forged through specific practices and representations in everyday life, as is their sense of having a home in Berlin. I use sociologist Gilroy's (1993) concept of living memory to analyze how the diasporic past can live on in the present through gestures, habits, and desires.

Many participants express deep emotional connections with the places most relevant to their parents' and grandparents' lives. Their Turkishness becomes more than an ethnic identity or a matter of acknowledging where they came from. Their parents' immigration becomes their own experience of displacement. Tunç describes how his parents' migration experience continues to shape his sense of belonging: "The older I get, the better I realize how my parents affected me. The traditions, the respect are in my bones. When I am at the village, having talks with the people, it is wonderful ... If I have enough money, I will build a house there." Tunç feels a continuity of identity in relating to the place his family came from. His feeling of strong connection with the traditions and people in his parents' village is expressed as a desire to *return* and maybe even build a house in that village one day. Arzu also talks of feeling connected to Turkish culture: "Sometimes, I find myself watching Berlin's terrible Turkish [TV] channels and crying at the silly movies. When ... I listen to ... Turkish pop music, I feel myself more at home in my parents' place." Arzu has that feeling of connection that a movie or a song can carry. For her, however, this emotional connection is to the place where she grew up – her parents' house in Germany. Yıldız, likewise, has never lived in her ancestral village, but still she yearns "for the natural landscape of [that] village on the Black Sea." All these longings – Tunç's connection with his parents' village, Arzu's feelings evoked by Turkish music, and Yıldız's longing for a landscape she didn't grow up in – reflect a desire for the comfort of home. This feeling of connection gives the foreigner solace, happiness, and well-being.

Many of the participants connect their yearning for Türkiye to the ways their difference is perceived in Germany. They refer to a predicament in responding to questions over where they belong. Yıldız says:

> Since my childhood, I can never accept being here, as I always feel I'm a foreigner here, whether because of the friend of my German friend, the colour of my eyes, or my father's long, thick moustache. My name is different. My outlook is different. I say, okay, I do not want to be a foreigner. I'm German; I was born here, raised here. It is only my parents' language that I know, and this is my Turkishness.

Yıldız finds herself negotiating over what makes her German, attempting to see Turkish as simply her parents' language. She acknowledges that her connections with Turkish go beyond its being just a language that she learned at home. What connects Yıldız to Türkiye and makes her Turkish are the feelings and emotions that Turkish songs and poems evoke. For her, the Turkish language connotes security, love, self-respect, and comfort. It

Negotiating Displacement

reflects the values she identifies with. German-born Turkish Ausländer typically carry sentiments of anger, commitment, and yearning that are not really their own, but belong to someone older. They have yearnings for places they cannot name, longings for experiences or objects they cannot pin down. They yearn for a lost experience – the fulfillment of a homecoming (Cho 2007a).

This yearning connects them with others who share the same feelings. Their ties of memory represent an obscure miracle of connection, which binds generations and individuals. However, many German-born Turkish Ausländer also have actual personal connections with these places and experiences beyond any memories of their parents' displacements. Many of these Ausländer have directly experienced those Turkish places and relations, often in annual visits. For them, the connection is as real as their extended families and the places where they spend their vacations.

Memlekette İzin Yapmak (Vacationing in the Homeland)

Almost all of my participants spend most of their summer vacations in Türkiye. Most have family summer houses and business connections there. Beyond it being a vacation place, therefore, visiting Türkiye has a special meaning for them. In this pattern of life, Türkiye and Germany have distinct functions. Many participants strongly associate their belonging to Germany with having social rights and economic well-being, whereas their belonging to Türkiye is about feeling at home. Germany represents the place they work and live, and Türkiye is like a home – a place to go after work to rest and find comfort. Neither of these two places can replace the other. The meaning of homeland and the feelings that come with taking a vacation overlap. Türkiye is their *memleket* (homeland) but not necessarily the place they came from. Visiting Turkish relatives and spending time at Turkish holiday destinations are breaks from the everyday experience of Otherness in Germany.

Tunç explains his relationships with Germany and Türkiye by distinguishing how he lives in each place: "We are surrounded by concrete [in Berlin]. This is how we grow up. This is where we feel home in Germany, not in nature. We can't live in nature in Germany." Tunç explains the meaning of living in two places through a contrast between nature and an urban environment. His relationship with nature in Türkiye is strongly connected with vacationing, and this represents what Türkiye means for him. Using concrete as the symbol for life in Germany, Tunç argues that he can exist in Germany only in urban surroundings. He does not know how to relax in nature in Germany. In his expression of displacement, returning means re-connecting with nature, which comes with vacationing.

The feeling of comfort and the desire to escape from the everyday experiences of Otherness leads to the creation of a myth. The Turkish places that German-born Turks visit while vacationing are viewed as a kind of paradise. The local Turkish people they meet seem to represent all the best aspects of human nature. Many participants maintain that both the people they know in Türkiye and their Turkish neighbours in Berlin are "their own people."

"Benim İnsanım" (My Own People)

I'm a tourist there, yet it is my own familiar culture, people, and language, genuine heartfelt feelings ... You can get close right away ... I miss Türkiye, Turkish people, the dialogue with the waiter. I think our country is beautiful.

– Ceyda

When Ceyda describes the importance of the Turkish language, she reads Turkish values and a nurturing identity into all the everyday activities she considers Turkish, regarding these as reflections of her displacement. Her everyday interactions in Türkiye evoke heartfelt feelings of cultural affinity. Many other participants express similar sentiments. Funda feels that the bonds among people in Türkiye are ties of fraternity and sharing. For Selin, it is the feeling of "one big family" – of "calling a total stranger 'sister' or 'brother'." She explains that in Türkiye, "an old person could treat me as their granddaughter." Aynur says that every year she comes back from Türkiye crying. She is sad to leave. She feels that Turkish people are warmer and happier because they are not greedy. Imagining such cultural values – of treating one another as one big family, having unconditional compassion, and being satisfied with less – can evoke deep yearning for an idealized Türkiye. Selin reports longing for "the response we receive in Türkiye, to the heartfelt feeling that binds us there, as we don't get it here."

A similar connection is assumed to exist among Berlin's Turks. Selin's sense that the Turkish Ausländer of Berlin are "my own people" implies a feeling of equality and unconditional reciprocity. Among themselves, Ausländer are never asked, "Where do you come from?" A shared history and memory of being Ausländer creates an idealized connection among them, although this connection emerges largely from their common experiences with Germans.

Negotiating Displacement 153

In these images of communion among Turks and Turkish Germans, the sense of threat or challenge seems to be missing, partly because the imagined unity often fails to account for the differences among Ausländer. Arzu talks about how language conveys a sense of loyalty, solidarity, and belonging to an idealized *we* – and how such language reflects the imagined bonds of everyday life:

> Once, I called the credit card call centre about a mistake in my bill. The guy's name was Turkish. His Turkish was as bad as mine, yet he was forcing himself not to speak German since he knew my name [he also knew I am Turkish] ... We have that constant feeling. We need to signal each other: I am also like you.

In this exchange, to avoid using the German language represents loyalty to Turkishness. However, such a bond of solidarity is quite imaginary, as it fails to acknowledge or affirm the separate identities and experiences of the other Turks. When I spoke to Arzu in my later visit, the issue of bonding came up again as she asked, "Do we always need to find each other in Turkishness?" She recalled,

> I was at a birthday party the other day. My friend is German, her husband is from Israel, and they lived in New York, but now they live in Berlin ... My friend said: "Let me introduce you to my friend. He works at a Jewish museum; he is one of the architects working at the museum. His name is Bülent." I asked: "Why do you want to introduce us, while there are so many other people?" She said, "His parents are also from Türkiye." I could tell that neither one of us wanted to talk about where we came from or where our parents are from. But then, still ... in the end, we started talking about these issues. But at first we were like, "No, we are citizens of the world." It is like, not to hide it or anything, but will this always be binding us? ... That was the sense I had ... But then ... we found each other right there [in our connections to Türkiye].

The Turkish government also promotes Turkishness as a homogenizing project of the nation-state. In perpetuating a communal sense of we, it treats the diverse ethnicities and cultures of different Turkish Ausländer as private variations among people who share one overarching national identity in the public sphere. Many of the participants understand these meanings and values as marks of a greater culture and a common bond.

Many Ausländer like to imagine their connection with people in Türkiye or with other Turks in Berlin as a kind of true friendship. This relation seems to promise timeless intimacy – an unreasonably high expectation of other people. Of course, actually having such an emotional bond in any practical way is hardly thinkable. Also, claiming an imagined connection with people in both Türkiye and Berlin tends to overlook the fact that close relationships are always contingent, developing, and unfolding. The interpretation of Turks as friends, and of friends as second selves, tends to both idealize and totalize friendship between Turks in both Berlin and in Türkiye. This friendship becomes an impossible ideal – a reflection of oneself, but never a threat, a challenge, or a genuine other. The communal ideal also fails to take account of personal differences. Ignoring the differences and separateness of identities among friends is an important condition for the kind of solidarity the participants describe. However, as Lynch (2002, 101) puts it, this kind of idealized bond takes "the life out of friendship – while at the same time taking no account of the possibility of the death of friendship."

There is another way in which these values and connections to the homeland and to other Turks help to establish comfort and belonging. Such connections enable Turkish Ausländer to feel capable and secure in a bewildering social setting. In the participants' experiences, the dominant context of German identity and citizenship often excludes them through its laws or its racist attitudes, and the constant exposure to such exclusion can seem to define their lives. The Ausländer have an urge to respond by viewing Germans as outsiders to a Turkish reality. By distancing themselves from Germanness, perhaps they fill a need to feel some control or to regain a positive concept of themselves. Typically, the discourses among Ausländer do not have the same power to define social reality as the dominant discourses of German identity and citizenship. Ausländer discourses cannot set boundaries to exclude Germans, and they have little power to influence the dominant context.

Stuart Hall (1997) refers to such ongoing psycho-political struggles over boundaries and influence as the initial form of identity politics. This activity seeks to constitute some sort of defensive alliance against the practices of a racist society. People blocked from identifying with the majority need to find some other foundation on which to stand. That need is reflected in the way the participants argue over us-versus-them distinctions. It is also reflected in the way the same kinds of opposition function differently for dealing with the axis of hostility–hospitality from the way they deal with the axis of homelessness–homesickness.

Negotiating Displacement

For example, Güler insists that Germans are being biased when they think in us-versus-them terms toward Ausländer. However, she also feels that "I have the right to make an us-versus-them distinction" toward them, and it is not "oversensitive and judgmental" to do so. This sentiment is based on a claim that Ausländer deserve to have their hitherto under-acknowledged distinctiveness taken into account. This sense of *our* distinctiveness emerges from a collective experience of misrecognition and status subordination. The sense of common identity does not depend on any pre-given reality, but instead arises from a discursive process that constructs what *we* call reality. The insult, denigration, and subordination implied in the word *Ausländer* feels real to these people, and it is more than an issue of their individual, personal sensitivities. Their shared sentiment feels real, and it becomes part of their social reality precisely because expressing it reiterates an inferiorized collective experience.

Although major differences may exist between Ausländer groups and their individual members, it is sometimes advantageous for them to strategically essentialize themselves. They feel a need to assert their group identity in a simplified way, to achieve certain goals through their everyday acts and practices. Essentialism is the philosophical theory that groups of people (or races) have fundamental qualities, properties, or capabilities. Strategic essentialism is a variation on this idea, as it is adopted by oppressed groups. Although strategic essentialism also maintains that groups have essential attributes, it differs from true essentialism in two ways. First, the essential attributes are defined by the group members themselves, and not by a dominant external group. The group, therefore, has the power to decide which attributes are essential and which are not. Second, in strategic essentialism, the essential attributes are acknowledged to be a construct. The group paradoxically acknowledges that such attributes are *not* natural or intrinsic but are merely invoked when it is politically useful to do so. When used in this way, strategic essentialism can be a powerful political tool.

When German-born Ausländer enact their understandings of who they are and where they belong, they are also questioning the future. When articulated through their everyday social acts, their subjectivity raises the possibility of a future where their social recognition "will be a matter of rich and complex negotiation and not [a] result of some blind and official decree" (Radhakrishnan 2003, 129). Therefore, the participants can admit that the term *Ausländer* does not represent a natural or static category of identity but is a socially constructed status. This collective identity is situationally specific and adopted for political reasons. It is strategic in the sense that literary theorist and influential postcolonial intellectual Gayatri Chakravorty Spivak (1993) understands strategic essentialism. As interdisciplinary cultural studies scholar Lisa Lowe (2003, 151) explains: "Just as the articulation of identity depends on the existence of a horizon of differences, the articulation of differences dialectically depends on a socially constructed and practiced notion of identity." In other words, it is possible to utilize specific signifiers of Turkish Ausländerness as a racialized ethnic identity, and to do this for the purpose of contesting and disrupting the discourses that exclude these people as a group.

The Myth of Return

I was initially puzzled by the way that most of the participants insisted on "going back to Türkiye in the future," even though they were born in Germany. Their desire to live in Türkiye one day – just like their feelings of comfort during summer vacations – was real. I could see this as a significant example of the myth of return. As Cohen and Gold (1997, 376) explain: "Myth (usually a fantasy) and return (maybe a reality), connote a wishful fantasy, or belief, of immigrants that, in an unspecified date in the future, they will return permanently to their homeland." This belief "represent[s] a practical cognitive solution to a cognitive contradiction," namely, being identified with a homeland but living in a diaspora. This myth allows immigrants to simultaneously maintain their memberships in both the homeland and the diaspora.

On a societal level, the myth of return calls for maintaining tight links with fellow Turkish Ausländer, participating in ethnic organizations, and visiting the country of origin during holidays. On a personal level, the myth ranges from a general sense of homesickness to an "obsession with the need to return, to the point of affecting daily functioning ... [although it] may ease the emotional pain by promising a more harmonious existence in the future" (Cohen and Gold 1997, 375–76).

James Clifford (1994) argues that for the construction of a diasporic identity, it is necessary to have a sufficiently strong sense of connection with the prior home. Political scientist William Safran (1991) also suggests that the myth of the homeland is necessary for the continuity and ontological security of the diasporic individuals' identities. Diasporants never lose their narratives of homeland, exile, and return so long as they feel threatened (Mishra 1996). Yeliz talks about how the recent rise of hatred against Turks has changed her sense of comfort and safety in Germany and how she has started planning to live in Türkiye in the near future:

Negotiating Displacement 157

> I never wanted to leave Germany and live in Türkiye. I had been comfortable here. But lately, there has been serious hatred against foreigners ... These several incidents against foreigners, and knowing that this could never happen to me in Türkiye, made me change my mind ... It is not a constant fear, but it is always on my mind.

The fear is real, and it is combined with the desire to return to Türkiye. Both the exclusion and the imaginative unity that accompany collective memory are vital sources of belonging in the diaspora. As members of a diaspora feel that they belong elsewhere, they harbour dreams of returning to the homeland. Even though they question the homeland and may feel sure that they have left it for good, they keep the hope of returning alive.

Nevertheless, the participants also express the limits of their connection. Their critical awareness goes beyond acknowledging their Germanness and questioning the binary opposition of German versus Turkish. Their guest-worker history and class background play significant roles in limiting their connections to Türkiye and to Turkishness.

Alamancı: Where the Connection Ends

> We are *yabancı* [foreigners] here and *Alamancı* [German guest workers] there.
>
> – Selin

Many participants talk about how, when they are visiting Türkiye, the term *Alamancı* (referring to their economic function) is used to categorize them as a subordinate group. As Ayşe points out, "Alamancı still means 'working class,' 'peasant,' 'backward.'" This interpretation of their guest-worker history – peasants-turned-workers – is significant in explaining their experiences with the label Alamancı in Türkiye. For Selin, Alamancı and *Almanyalı* (from Germany) carry different connotations: "In Türkiye, when we go to a nightclub ... I feel Almanyalı. They cannot understand why we enjoy Western pop music. They also think we are there to show off our economic status, which makes us Alamancı." This distinction between Alamancı and Almanyalı implicates ethnocentrism in determining Turkishness within Türkiye. Both their class and their membership in the diaspora shape how the participants can relate to Türkiye and Turkishness and how they are perceived in Türkiye. Ela refers to her experience while teaching in Poland, in a program sponsored by Türkiye. She found herself considered less of a Turk than the members from Türkiye: "The program [in Poland] received a call from Türkiye asking why they had some Turks from Germany among the teachers."

When Seda and Belma talk about being identified as Alamancı in Türkiye, they both say that people immediately recognized that they were from Germany. Each of them protest, "I don't dress differently." They complain about Turkish shopkeepers: "They increased the prices." Aynur defines Alamancı by saying that "they came from Germany for their holidays to spend money, to rest, and to be a tourist."

Middle-class residents of Türkiye commonly depict Alamancı as backward. Their use of the term *Alamancı* reflects a sense of superiority to peasants-turned-workers. The term perpetuates hierarchies of a classist and nationalist logic. People in Türkiye use it to claim their own civility, middle-class respectability, and superiority – as the real owners of Turkishness and of Türkiye itself. The notion of civility merges with that of bourgeois sensibility in the perception that real Turks are culturally sophisticated people who know how to behave.

Alamancı refers not only to the migrants' peasant background. It also connotes individuals who have been corrupted by Western values in Germany. The Alamancı are, therefore, condemned for their "loose morals," while simultaneously envied for their Western success. Within the context of such an ambiguous label, Turks in Türkiye recognize that Germany has provided indentured labourers with the opportunity to become upwardly mobile. Consequently, they expect that Alamancı should be grateful to Germany for that opportunity, even as they are corrupted by Western culture.

Memleket Neresi? (Where Is Your Hometown?)

Memleket means both homeland and birthplace. It can also mean the place (country, region, city, or village) that one's ancestors came from. When displaced individuals connect with their homeland on a personal level, migration adds another layer, but it also blurs the line between past and present experiences. For example, Funda describes the cultural heterogeneity among Turks in Berlin who have migrated from different parts of Türkiye: "Sometimes, I wish I were born in Türkiye; other times, I think it is neat to know another language [German] and culture. If I were in Türkiye ... the people would be from the same city all the time. Here, I meet many ... from different parts of Türkiye: the Black Sea, the Aegean, the Mediterranean."

Funda's observation reminds us of the mythical side of *we-ness* for a diasporic group. Similarly, in Arda's account, the origins are layered: "In this

Negotiating Displacement 159

school, everybody asks, 'Where do you come from?' before they ask your name. I say 'I'm from İstanbul,' as my parents are from İstanbul ... Because they already know I live here ... they want to know where I came from in Türkiye." She talks about the conflicts among students who come from different parts of Türkiye. The multiple origins among Ausländer signal not only heterogeneity but also hierarchy, as secular people hold advantages over religious Muslims, and Turkish ethnicity has higher status than Kurdish. In their experiences, the idea of home has layered, textured, and often contradictory meanings for German-born Turkish Ausländer.

Many participants examine their relation with Turkishness by reclaiming cultural memory. In doing this, they call into question the homogeneity of Turkishness through a particular discourse I call *Türkiyelism*. Instead of locating themselves as Turkish beings, they refer to themselves (and other Turkish people) as *Türkiyeli* (from Türkiye). By saying "I am from Türkiye" rather than "I am Turkish," they redefine Turkish identity as belonging to a place as opposed to being a type of person. Türkiyelism highlights a geographic location (Türkiye) rather than an ethnicity or nationality (Turkishness). It also signals a new understanding of citizenship. Through this sort of discourse, these people reclaim a cultural memory, a place, and its history, but they also claim a new future for citizenship.

Erkan talks about his family's history of movement from Spain to Greece, Greece to İstanbul, then İstanbul to Frankfurt, and finally Frankfurt to Berlin. He also mentions his family's unspoken conversion from Judaism to Bektaşism (a particular type of Alevi Islam). He discovered all of this history only after becoming a young adult. Concerning the effects of this discovery, he says:

> My mother's family first came to Thessaloniki from Spain, and then to İstanbul. They came as Jewish. They spoke [a type of] Spanish in their house for five hundred years. It is called Ladino.[1] When I was little, when they didn't want us to understand them, they spoke this language. When we asked, they said they were speaking Greek, because they didn't want us to know we were Jewish. Then I had a Spanish boyfriend, and I studied Spanish for a while. Later, when I was in Türkiye, I could understand what they talked about. It was remarkable. I said, "This is Spanish."

Erkan says that finding out about these hidden displacements and conversions would have upset him if he had thought there was only one pole of identity, similarity, and continuity. As it is, he accepts that even single-family histories have multiple identities and displacements. In the axis of homesickness and homelessness, the poles operate not only in the present and the future but also in relation to the past.

Erkan explains why reclaiming the memory of displacement is significant: it is a family history of conversion from one hidden identity to another and the hiding of the change through language and through silence. Reclaiming memory for Erkan means acknowledging multiple sufferings in his family history in relation to homeland, language, and religion. When, after leaving Spain and Greece, Erkan's family settled in İstanbul, the family converted to Islam, and İstanbul became the original homeland for their newly transformed identity, thus covering over their guilt over giving up a previous identity. However, the transformed identity was silenced. Having been doubly silenced and "twice diasporized" (Hall 1995, 6), the family members then became guest workers when they migrated from İstanbul to Germany, making theirs an identity of multiple outsidership. Erkan says:

> Having learned about this background might have ... agitated everything I knew and was familiar with. I could have thought, "If I knew this when I was little, I would have been a different person." But I didn't think that ... I became more interested in the religious and societal aspects of it. I started researching the connections between Judaism and Alevism ... You realize how culture and identity are a construction and even a fiction. They don't want to talk about that issue. They destroy it every day. They pretend as if it doesn't exist. They hide it. So that maybe it is protected that way.

Political scientists Anna Agathangelou and L.H.M. Ling's (2009) notion of *worldism* is helpful for understanding how the multiple worlds that Erkan embodies afford him a different perspective on his experiences in Germany. The diasporic politics that emerge from his awareness of multiple worlds resonates with worldism. Erkan's discovery of multiple displacement made him realize how culture and identity are, as he aptly puts it, a "construction or even a fiction." This realization illustrates what Agathangelou and Ling (2009, 85) describe as "the various and contending ways of being, knowing, and relating that have been passed onto us from previous generations."

İrem talks about a different kind of silencing in her family. Her Arab identity is covered over in public but maintained in the privacy of her home and her small community:

Negotiating Displacement

My mother comes from a family who loves Atatürk, and my uncles are leftists from the sixties. My maternal uncle is a DSP [Democratic Left Party]
supporter, and my father is an HP [People's Party] delegate. Still, they are
not political when it comes to their Arab and Alevi identities. They put a lid
on their Alevi and Arab identities. They were afraid. There were massacres,
and their fathers were leaders but yet oppressed. With the republic, they felt
relieved ... In a strange way, their Arab identity continues, but they could
hide it at the same time ... My parents never lost Arab identity. We grew up
in three languages. My first language is Arabic ... Arabic has always been
present. I think it is because of our strong family structure we never felt
groundless.

As Erkan's and İrem's accounts suggest, the question of what defines a
national identity within and outside national borders can be posed within a
larger historical context, but it doesn't necessarily elicit a clear response.
These participants' cultural memories reflect how modern Turkish history
has been variously forgotten, rejected, and re-evaluated. As Azade Seyhan
(2000, 2001) argues, there are many experiences of Otherness in Türkiye today, including the Otherness of her own past. After the end of the Ottoman
Empire and Türkiye's victory in the war of independence, Atatürk founded a
secular republic of the frèe Turks. To re-member "a new nation from the
multi-ethnic, multi-religious, multilingual shards of an imperial mosaic,
[Atatürk] scripted a discourse of progress that entailed a radical transition
through a series of Westernizing reforms, from the *alaturka* [Turkish] to
the *alafranga* [French] way of life" (Seyhan 2000, para. 5, emphasis added).

To be recognized by the West, this new nation-state had to lay its recent
past to rest, put an end to the caliphate, and "erase all traces of Ottoman
Islamic culture from official memory ... The founding of the Turkish Republic conformed fully to the modernist [ideal] of newness. Choosing to be
a Turk was driven by a strong identification with the 'mother tongue'"
(Seyhan 2000, para. 5). However, much of the past was repressed. Social
anthropologist Bozkurt Güvenç (1993) feels that because of the repression
of Türkiye's cultural history, Turks today have difficulty understanding, accepting, or incorporating the diverse traditional identities of their heterogeneous society.

Next, numerous people of Türkiye's modernized state migrated to Europe. Seyhan (2000, para. 10) describes the effects on the migrants: "In mi-
grancy and exile, the resistance of linguistic and cultural heritages to those

162   *Homesickness–Homelessness*

of the national and dominant community is markedly lowered." In the midst of all these dislocations, the discrimination against Turks by Turks results from the clashing identities among *hemşehricilik,* or fellow countrymen. These tensions reveal the multi-ethnic and multicultural fabric of Turkishness. The various divisions, differing memories, and varied identities are all based on places of origin, ethnicity, and religion. Nevertheless, the various expressions of art and literature among diasporic people (and the emerging discourse of Türkiyelism) tend to give German-born Turkish Ausländer ways to re-imagine their past. For example, when Ayşe describes the historic Othering process, she integrates the notion of Türkiyeli into her analysis:

> Alamancı [German guest workers] refer to how *Türkiyeli Türkiyeliler* [Turks from Türkiye] see *Almanyalı Türkiyeliler* [Turks from Germany] ... I have experienced this with Türkiyeli Türkiyeliler in America. These people go to school in America with financial support from their parents. At first, I thought I could get along with them. They go to there to escape from Türkiye and Turkishness ... They see themselves different from the rest of the Turks in Türkiye ... as "white Turks."

Ayşe articulates class distinctions and deconstructs ethnicity within the binary opposition of Türkiyeli versus Almanyalı Türkiyeli. The notion of Türkiyeli (from Türkiye) challenges the meaning of Turkishness, as it looks to geographical origin rather than ethnicity for identity. The term Almanyalı (from Germany) also challenges Germanness as being an ethnic identity only. These notions suggest a new way of claiming Germanness and Turkishness through belonging to both Germany and Türkiye, making both countries and societies into sources of identity. By not saying "Turks from Türkiye," or "Turks from Germany," Ayşe takes the ethnicity from both identities and makes the genealogy of belonging into a multiplicity. Therefore, in her response to the label Alamancı, she questions belonging to either a nation-state or to a deconstructed ethnicity – participants Barış and İrem do this as well:

> I have a Kurdish, Turkish, and Armenian background. I'm a mixture. Calling myself Turkish is nonsense. I'm an immigrant from Türkiye.

> The terms are determinative. I try to use Türkiyeli rather than *Turk.* That means I don't want to be determined as Turkish ... I want to get used to

using Türkiyeli, because then I include different people. I don't see Türkiye as a nation-state. It is a multi-ethnic mosaic.

Accounts such as those of Erkan, İrem, Ayşe, and Barış illustrate creative ways of filling the gap between cultural recognition and translation. Especially in the experiences of German-born Turkish Ausländer, the conditions of cultural memory and diasporic citizenship defy all sense of uniformity.

Türkiyelism is a significant discourse for disputing Turkishness and negotiating for heterogeneity, multiplicity, and expanded cultural memory. This kind of identity demands recognition for the struggle of a minority within a minority. It challenges the authoritative voice of Turkishness and questions the meaning of being a Turk. The idea of being Turkish presumes that belonging to Türkiye is an unquestioned, omnipresent component of Turkishness. But Türkiyelism also challenges the claims of the nation-state. Such a critique of Turkification emerges from the tensions between memory (continuity) and amnesia (discontinuity). A Turkish memory dating from 1923 has been built over the multi-ethnic, multicultural, multi-religious memory of the Ottoman Empire. Türkiyelism reclaims the older heterogeneous background, reminding us that Türkiye itself is a diaspora. Seyhan (2000, para. 6) adds: "To make themselves the masters of memory and forgetting ... is the major preoccupation of groups that have historically dominated others. Therefore, reclaiming memory is an act of cultural assertion for those who have ... [surrendered] their right to national spaces and histories."

Within this context of migration history and its hidden identities, does "knowing" change one's perspective? Sunnis, who are a majority in Türkiye, are a minority among Muslims in Germany, and a minority-majority relationship between the Sunnis and Alevis, which is rooted in Türkiye, continues among the population of Turkish Ausländer. The remembering and reclaiming of all of this is not easy. As political scientist Benedict Anderson (1983, 204) observes: "All profound changes in consciousness bring with them characteristic amnesias. Out of such oblivions, in specific historical circumstances, spring narratives."

Through the lenses of the participants' recollections and interpretations, the specificities of experiences related to class, ethnicity, religion, and gender are often forgotten, silenced, or ignored. However, suppressed voices often resurface to remind us of an ethical imperative toward others. The political, social, and economic factions that have fractured the foundation of the modern Turkish Republic have multiplied among the Ausländer. İrem says

> When they ask me ... where I am going, if I say, "I'm going to *Cemevi*" or "I'm teaching an Alevi class," I get that look.[2] My identity splits again, there and then ... You struggle in both frontlines. You have an identity problem with the people you share a language with ... [and also] with the Germans.

Senior research analysist at EU External Affairs Heinz Kramer (1997) calls attention to the radicalization of ethnic and religious gaps between Turks, because of the free operation of separatist organizations and groups in Germany (which are likely to be banned in Türkiye), as well as the growing self-consciousness regarding linguistic, religious, and ethnic origins and identities. As he explains: "Political and social cleavages such as the left-right dichotomy, the secular-Islamist cleavage, the Sunni-Alevi differences, or the Turkish-Kurdish problem, are reproduced in Germany" (Kramer 1997, 16). When groups begin to remember their common pasts differently, old wounds are reopened, and clashes between various groups begin to emerge in the present. Those who considered themselves collectively as the Turks of Germany before the 1990s now identify as Kurds, Alevis, Sunnis, Assyrians, and the like. In the complicated web of history, memory, and responsibility, each new confrontation with an economic, political, or moral crisis can involve one group displacing another as the feared Other in the popular imagination.

Repeating (Diasporic) Experiences

Continuing immigration through taking marriage partners from Türkiye has contributed to the social experience of Turkish-background Berliners. People who were born and raised in Germany continue to seek out and marry partners from Türkiye. This pattern leads to a reoccurrence of the social experience of being newcomers. The challenges around German language proficiency are renewed, as learning German is not easy for an adult. Besides, more immediate challenges may require these new migrants to focus on their homes, families, and parenting. Therefore, for these newcomers, gaining the skills to adapt in German society still takes time. This difficulty is reflected in every aspect of social life in Berlin, and it shapes the basic conditions of Turkish-background Berliners' lives in diverse ways. Fatma describes the challenge of schooling for Turkish people with diverse levels of exposure to German:

Negotiating Displacement

> Let's say in Ilkay's class, if three kids are like mine, then seven of them will speak Turkish better than German. They are having problems with German communication. Some children are not open to the wider German culture. Or there are people like us, who have fully accepted that we are here. We live here, we are aging here, and we are having our children adapt to this culture, and we are more focused on German.

When I did my research in 2003, I was able to conduct all my interviews in Turkish, as my German was very basic. I asked the participants if I would be able to do my research in Turkish in 2016. Leyla answered:

> You definitely can. However, there is one thing. Now we see the young people are changing the German language. They are creating a new way of speaking it. For example, they omit articles. This might only be in Berlin; I am not sure. We still switch between German and Turkish a lot too. And the young people are also doing this a lot. They almost turn German into Turkish. Half of the sentence is Turkish and half is German. The verb is Turkish; the noun is German. The new generation's Turkish is not better than ours, but it is there. I don't know anyone who doesn't care about passing Turkish on to their children, no matter who they are.

This transformation of language reflects how diasporic citizenship is an object in motion and often rapid motion at that. Such transformation in language is connected to diasporic citizenship.

Arzu speaks about the Turkish-as-a-second-language classes offered in her daughter's school. As is traditionally done, the language teacher is hired through the Turkish consulate. The school invites parents to attend on Friday afternoons to see how the classes are going. Arzu describes her visit: "It is a very mixed age group. There are kids who don't know how to write, and there are older kids." This is partly due to the limited demand for Turkish at that school. With many children coming from other European countries and the US, the number of Turkish-background students is limited. In some homes, maybe one parent is Turkish. In some, Turkish is spoken, and in others it is not. It is difficult to create a shared lesson plan because of the students' varied levels of proficiency and exposure to Turkish language at home. The main issue for Arzu (2016), however, is the lesson style, which puts Turkish geography and history at the centre and language at the margins:

The teacher brought a map of Türkiye, and he was like, "Show me where your parents were born." Of course, none of these kids' parents were born in Türkiye; they are from here. Then he goes, "Where were your grandparents born?" ... To begin with, the kids my daughter's age wouldn't know a Berlin map, let alone Türkiye. What is it to them learning the provinces of Türkiye at a language course? ... And then he asks about April 23, Children's Day. He asks, "Who gave us April 23?" expecting the answer would be "Atatürk!" But the kids go "the teachers" or "God." What is April 23 to these kids?

These grand- or great-grandchildren of the guest workers do not have the historical or geographical connections to their ancestral homelands that their parents (the participants) do. Arzu continues

For them, these lessons are distanced from reality, and they cause no reaction and make no sense. The children need to learn that maybe Türkiye is on another continent and that they speak another language, and their language is like this ... I imagined it to be ... just a language class. Take all the burden off Atatürk and off whatever.

Here, we see an insistence of maintaining the legacy of Turkish identity politics. Such politics extend from the participants' experiences of schooling (with a curriculum based on what was taught in the classrooms of Türkiye) to the ways that transplanted identity politics emerge in Berlin's Turkish language classes. These classes are still treated as a means of creating Turkish citizens. In 2016, I asked Fatma if there is still a strong connection with the Turkish language:

It is not as strong as it was before in my social circle. Turkish parents are raising their children bilingual, but I think it is more German now than Turkish, even for the expression of feelings. They have more problems speaking Turkish than German ... Of course, the parents try to prevent the children from forgetting Turkish. If nothing else, you want your kid to be able to communicate with the family ... But the kid focuses on German language after a while.

Fatma indicated that her children are much closer to the German language, which supports Arzu's claims. For these young Berliners, Turkish is just another language.

Negotiating Displacement 167

As opposed to such enforced Turkish identity-creation through language classes, there is a much different and still relevant aspect to speaking Turkish: it remains a strong basis of common ground for these diasporic citizens. This reality has a lot to do with how these diasporic citizens are perceived in Germany.

Turkishness

> We are still not considered 100 percent German. We never will be. There is still Germanism.
>
> — Selim

A disconnect with German identity and Germany persists for Ausländer. Selim speaks about what such a disconnect means for his generation, the German-born children of the guest workers:

> Due to the dominance of Turkish and Türkiye in our lives, my generation experienced a disconnect with German identity and Germany. In school, we used the curriculum of the Turkish ministry of education. Due to education policies in Germany, my generation had a stronger connection with Türkiye. We consciously defined ourselves as foreigners. Our connection with Türkiye started with our families' connections with their villages in Türkiye, with our visits to Türkiye once a year every summer.

For Selim, this was not a nationalistic connection per se, but part of the network of social connections they have had for decades. The sense of being Turkish and belonging to Türkiye is still something instilled in the new generation, at least to a degree. The young people still carry these feelings with them. However, there is a shift in the kind of deep connection that the new generation feels toward Türkiye:

> Even though the new generations are much more integrated into German society, and though they have not experienced the kinds of difficulties we experienced growing up in Germany, they still feel they have deep connections to Türkiye ... When we look at the new generation, they don't have some of the same problems we had – they have good education, they have competence in German – but they are much more nationalist and religious than we ever were. It seems like my generation has been much more progressive. We have changed much more than the new generation.

Similarly, Ayla (2016) says:

> The majority of the youth claim that they are Turkish, and they are proud to be so. They are much more nationalist than my generation was. They proudly claim the flag, the Turkish identity ... But if you look, they only spend holidays in Türkiye; they have no lived experience in Türkiye. They don't really know much about Türkiye.

Selim argues that the young generation's connections are changing. This generation has had good education, and they have a more confident relation to German society, but they still feel a strong connection to their roots. One might argue that it is their families who encourage this connection and this conservatism. But Selim argues that it is also a reflection of the fact that Germanness still has its biological meanings. In response, Turkish identity is strongly connected to how "this feeling of being Othered and feeling like a foreigner was passed from my generation to the next."

The narratives of the participants reveal how the diasporic home is solid, flexible, and fluid all at once (Cohen 2018). As their ancestral past becomes a mythical home, memleket becomes the embodied *original home* in the imagination of German-born Turkish Ausländer. However, the focus of homesickness and homelessness is fuzzy. Young Ausländer find fragmentation and fictiveness in this fuzzy home. As British-American novelist and essayist of Indian descent Salman Rushdie (2018, 227) writes of India's diasporas: "We will, in short, create fictions, not actual cities or villages, but invisible ones, imaginary homelands, Indias of the mind."

This yearning to belong while at the same time negotiating displacement is a complex tension that distinguishes diasporicity from other forms of political awareness. In proposing a homelessness–homesickness axis, I seek to articulate the sense of belonging as an ongoing negotiation over how to capture the multiplicity, fluidity, and solid reality of a home in diaspora. Cultural studies scholar Jane Mummery's dichotomy of *at-homeness* and *not-at-homeness* (2018) portrays this tension as more like a set of alternative states. The framework seems to describe a static, ongoing tension. Such a framework has limited potential for examining diasporants as active agents who make their claims to belong while also making displacement an integral aspect of belonging. Therefore, I feel that the homelessness–homesickness axis is more helpful for capturing diasporicity as a particular form of social awareness.

Negotiating Displacement 169

Redefining Germanness

As noted previously, German society has been founded on a division between German and non-German, in which European identity is central. The Ausländer are constructed as distinct from and external to this normative core. Moreover, a highly stigmatized representation of Ausländerness circulates within this context. Even so, the Ausländer also seek to identify with Germanness, even though this affiliation involves different qualities, dynamics, and challenges for different people, and affiliation with Germanness does not have the same effects for every Ausländer. Therefore, analyzing the extent to which the research participants feel themselves to be part of German society is essential for understanding their patterns of belonging. After all, the participants are in the unique position of being both Ausländer and German-born, and their lives have been shaped in the heady dynamics of German society since unification.

"And the Wall Came Down"

> Germany is changing and it is difficult, because there is no inner dynamic for these changes. It was from outside, like the democratization of Germany in 1945. Others are coming and changing it from the outside ... Similarly, others are saying Germany is an immigration country ... [The change] will need time, and it needs to come from inside.
>
> – Şenocak, interview in 2003

A prominent German writer, Zafer Şenocak, refers to the significance of acknowledging that at the time the guest workers arrived, Germany was coping with serious wounds from the recent past. For Şenocak, understanding the Germanness of Turkish Ausländer is not possible without noting their connections with those conditions. The changes Şenocak describes happened through Germany's reunification, as symbolized by the fall of the Berlin Wall. Since then, Germany has been struggling to understand a minority that fits neither its idea of the German *Volk* nor shares political equality with the rest of the nation, yet is destined to become an integral part of the German population.

Many participants describe how Germany's unification led to confusion, re-evaluation, and change in their relationships with German society. Prior to reunification, they felt a stronger sense of solidarity among Turkish Germans and a greater sense of separation from anything German. At that time, Ela used to feel that "if they are Turkish, they are one of us; I should defend them." This sentiment is still common among many Turkish Berliners, because "finding collective similarities and differences is exciting and easy."

However, as noted earlier, being in absolute solidarity with other Turks to defend Turkishness has put the Turkish Ausländer in a reactive position. This position traditionally meant that Ausländer distanced themselves from any of Germany's historical and political realities that were not directly relevant to their own experiences. It also meant distancing themselves from the German aspects of their own lives. Taking this reactive position has prevented German-born Ausländer from creating discourses about their own realities and claiming Germanness as a birthright. Şenocak (2003) describes how German Turks reacted to reunification: "When the wall came down, it took a long time [for Turks in Germany] to start thinking and writing about it, as if it was an issue that the Germans had to think about among themselves. Although the people who lived here were also part of this issue, there was no participation, as if they were foreign to these issues."

Many other participants also talk about the unification of the two Germanys as a turning point for the Turkish Ausländer of Berlin. With the rush to incorporate and provide for all ethnic Germans in a newly reunified nation, foreign workers seemed unneeded, or even unwanted. They found themselves in a position to revaluate their lives in Germany. Ela refers to a general pause, followed by an awakening after the wall came down: "When the East/West opposition collapsed, the people suddenly lost their life goals ... Maybe we are trying to define an identity for ourselves."

As long as Berlin was divided, immigrants – including German-born Turkish Ausländer – saw themselves as guests. Several participants agree that today, the Turks in Berlin realize they are not guests any longer. Now, they have to make their own reception and their own roles in Germany. Erkan argues that this change is not due to any generational difference or to being born in Germany per se, but is a reflection of how unification has marked an important change in society:

> My grandmother came here first; if she were alive, she would have had the same concerns ... "Who am I? ... I am a human being, and I'm here. What does that mean? ... Where can this take me? Why?" This is everybody's concern since the mid-nineties ... Nobody was doing this in the eighties. Being Turk, Yugoslavian, or Arab meant they would go back when the time came. All the money they made was invested in Türkiye. Now ... they invest here ... They have businesses here.

Negotiating Displacement 171

In addition to this general reorientation, the participants refer to their changing personal perceptions regarding their existence in Germany since unification. A different kind of political activism has emerged following the racist attacks of the 1990s. The participants increasingly demand that Germans understand Ausländer as part of this society and not just as victims of social inequality. Diasporants are increasingly involved in political debates about the changing public perceptions of Ausländer and of their ways of belonging to the German nation. The question has changed from "When will I go back?" to "How do I belong here?" Although many of the same contradictions persist, the self-understandings of Ausländer have shifted.

Along with these historical changes, the facts of being born, raised, and still living in Germany have made a significant difference to how the participants claim their lives here. Tunç refers to a transformation in Oranienstrasse, the main street of Kreuzberg, which he attributes to the generational difference brought by Ausländer who were born in Berlin:

> Our youth create a culture: they open restaurants, buy houses, they now do what their fathers didn't do. They take responsibility. Our parents did not see it that way. Most of ... [their fathers] didn't know much about trade, business, or art when they arrived [in Germany] from their [Turkish] villages. They were thinking about their own villages.

Tunç sees such changes as responses to the post-unification racist attacks. He argues that in response to those threats, the Ausländer started to assert themselves differently.

The transformation of space has also had a significant impact on how the participants view their belonging and recognition in Germany. Berlin and its Kreuzberg neighbourhood are the two particular spaces that are symbolically and materially integral to how the participants experience their affiliation with German society. These places provide an example of how global changes inform life conditions and disrupt traditional understandings of binary oppositions such as East versus West. When Turkish Ausländer claim rights to the city where they were born and live, this claim challenges and redefines Germanness.

"I Am a Berliner"

To be a Berliner is a significant thing in Germany. Leftists, gender minorities, socialists, anti-militarists, immigrants, and other local Germans all take great pride in belonging to the city. Being a Berliner carries pride in the city's unique history. Berlin has shaped the forms of German national identity, including those of the Ausländer. Given its history of division, Berlin has been a space of both governing and resisting. It is, therefore, an excellent site for mapping struggles for recognition – in this case, for observing how German-born Ausländer have struggled to realize their claims to Germanness and Germany.

The participants describe the changes they have witnessed in Berlin's built environment. They speak of how material construction and deconstruction has served to enable or restrict, reveal or conceal the identities of Turkish Ausländer. In their accounts, the policies and practices of German identity, with all their paradoxes and dilemmas, are illuminated with dramatic clarity. Berlin is the primary place where Ausländer (especially those who were born and raised there) have increasingly negotiated their relations with Germany, thereby redefining Germanness.

For Aynur, being a Berliner does not require a certain ethnic or religious identity. By identifying as a Berliner, she challenges the notion of needing any other origin: "Berlin is part of my heritage." Being a Berliner provides its own origin, and she has built her life on that origin through her experience in the city. Leyla explains, with reference to the infamous Mehmet case: "They can send *back* a criminal ... [But for me,] there is no such place as 'back.' My roots are here ... I've never lived in Türkiye. The only place they can send me back to is Berlin."

Even though German-born Turkish Ausländer have difficulty being accepted as Germans, for many of them being from Berlin means feeling at home there. They define themselves as Berliners because they feel a strong sense of belonging created over the course of their lives and assume they have an unassailable birthright to the city.

Even so, many participants emphasize that they are not just ordinary Berliners or typical Turks from Türkiye, but members of a special group: the Turks of Berlin. For example, Fatma says: "If they ask me where I'm from, I say Berlin ... My family came from Türkiye, from Trabzon. I'm from Berlin." The seemingly automatic acknowledgment of where her parents came from while claiming they belong in Berlin shows that for Fatma, being a Turk always carries a memory of the guest-worker experience. Selin notes another layer of complexity, as she claims rights in Germany, despite being Turkish, but refuses to claim Germanness: "I'm a Berliner, but I'm a Turkish Berliner. I never feel myself as German." For her, to be a Berliner is to be part of German society and to belong in Berlin, but to be a Turkish Berliner is to resist assimilation. Turkish Berliners have built a diasporic community. They

Negotiating Displacement 173

maintain the history of displacement and the memory of guest workers, and their sense of identity transcends Germanness.

The claims that the participants make to Berlin challenge the conventional understanding of citizenship and alter the traditional connection between citizens, cities, and nation-states. Isin (2000, 9) argues that a citizen's identification with a city "does not contradict ... his identification with the nation. Rather, it becomes the foundation of the nation-state." However, the participants challenge the idea of a nation that sees them as foreigners and, therefore, the notion of a connection between citizens and their nations as objects of political allegiance. Diasporic citizens make this challenge by emphasizing their belonging and obligation to a city, namely Berlin. They claim Berlin as their own social milieu for local creativity.

One milieu of Berlin has special significance for the participants – Kreuzberg. To understand how the guest worker and German identities have been constituted, contested, and transformed, we need to consider how the participants include Kreuzberg in their negotiations of identity, rights, and belonging.

"Es ist ein Privileg in Kreuzberg zu leben" (Living in Kreuzberg Is a Privilege)

> Kreuzberg is so very hip right now. The rents are skyrocketing. The people who open companies here, coming from Cologne or Stuttgart, they want to live here. People from abroad buy property like crazy here. There has been a significant change. Of course, Kreuzberg is not Germany or Berlin. I still feel more comfortable here; it is more international. Kreuzberg is still the most lively place ... In Kreuzberg, some live side-by-side, some live with one another, but it is still very comfortable to live in.
>
> – Leyla

When I went to Kreuzberg for the first time, on an early Saturday morning in the summer, the scene I saw was striking. Almost everything was Turkish: the sounds, the smells, the names of the shops, and the people. It felt like Türkiye, but not quite. I was puzzled by the existence of Turkish shops – everything from florists and supermarkets to furniture stores. All the products were imported from Türkiye, so that Turks in Berlin could shop for Turkish things, even though local versions were readily available. The first interaction I observed was a Turkish restaurant owner offering Turkish tea to a group of hippies at the exit from the Kotti U-bahn (subway) station.

Their laughter, mingling with their conversation in German, reminded me that this was not Türkiye. It felt contradictory. It seemed to me as if what I could see, smell, and feel that day – and every time I was there – was not just a unique coexistence but a surreal magic. Aynur once said: "Everywhere else in the world sleeps at night, but in Kreuzberg, the lights never sleep."

Art curator and critic Hou Hanru (2006) writes: "Migrants turn their 'exile' into a process of engaging and negotiating with the urban/suburban spaces." The cultural and physical presence and the active involvement of Turkish Ausländer strongly influence the social and cultural structures of Berlin. Kreuzberg is the most visible sign of how the local population, with its patterns of public behaviour and social values, is being transformed to create a much more diverse and prosperous neighbourhood.

When I asked the participants to say what made them feel most comfortable about living in Germany, most of them mentioned Kreuzberg. Feelings of belonging were generated by enjoying the neighbourhood festivities, experiencing the variety of foods and music, meeting friends at cafés, shopping in Turkish-owned stores, or simply seeing people in the streets. Kreuzberg is an exceptional neighbourhood. It embodies the history of Germany, including its relations with immigrants. It is a space where unpredictable groups, identities, experiences, and political acts occur in close proximity. Among the various social groups such as other Ausländer who live in Kreuzberg, Turkish Ausländer have played a significant role.

For many Ausländer, living and interacting in Kreuzberg provides a comforting sense of belonging and ordinariness that connects their experiences of Türkiye, Germany, and Berlin. Just being in Kreuzberg conjures up a sense of familial and community belonging, which is comforting in a setting of vulnerability and exile. Many participants refer to the familiar places and routines of Kreuzberg as part of who they are. The environment reflects the lifestyles they have created over the years, and their social networks are wide and vibrant. Kreuzberg's residents and those who regularly spend time in the neighbourhood commonly know one another. Many participants have spent their whole lives in this familiar setting. For Tunç, a former gang member and now a social worker, graffiti artist, and filmmaker, Kreuzberg is not only a place of residence, but a gigantic extended family:

> The school I went to was just next to the wall. The area was old ... In the early eighties, I grew up in construction sites. It was ghetto-like. Parallel to that, the Autonomists were occupying these houses. The politicians

Negotiating Displacement 175

> decided to renovate these houses along the wall to prevent invasions ... Autonomists, Communists, Anarchists, Islamists all were mixed here ... Such an environment has had an important impact on me ... I observed the demonstrations, how they dressed, which art they engaged in. Oranienstrasse was like an art gallery. You could see people from every walk of life. Walking on this street was pretty cool as a child ... All these Turkish stars would come here ... The whole of Kreuzberg was like a playground for me.

Tunç loves Kreuzberg's combination of comfort, chaos, and contradiction. He likes the sense of "never feeling as a stranger here." For many participants, growing up in Kreuzberg meant participating in the neighbourhood's changes through the years. Its ambience and familiarity let them find the social networks to do anything. Tunç spent his teenage years in a youth centre in Kreuzberg, to which he returned as a social worker: "I've changed. I've grown up, got an education, but I haven't moved away. I've always stayed in the same place. Many people still don't understand that. We are here; we're part of it all."

In the years since they settled as guest workers in Kreuzberg, the Turkish Ausländer have transformed the area into a home where they feel comfortable and in control. The neighbourhood has become a space of belonging that incorporates familiar values, ideas, and norms of behaviour. Such values and dispositions are necessary, given that the Ausländer remain the Other.

Ayla claims it is true that "in Kreuzberg, you can spend all your life and have all your needs met without knowing one word of German." This is comforting for anyone who speaks Turkish and not German, but there is much more to the feeling of comfort that Kreuzberg offers. İrem says it is not just the comfort of communicating in Turkish (she is comfortable in both languages) – the real reason she prefers Kreuzberg is that she does not experience any status subordination there. She does not have to explain herself. She is ordinary.

All the research participants without exception talk about the feeling that Kreuzberg offers. Kreuzberg is not only an integral part of who they are, but also a place where they can be free of feeling like Ausländer. Leyla says that in Kreuzberg: "Nobody comments on how your eyes or eyebrow colour are different. An incredibly diverse population lives in Kreuzberg. The people don't walk around with nine question marks in their heads about which Turk you are ... It is a place where, where you came from doesn't matter."

Here, they exist as ordinary people. The status subordination they experience in German society at large is absent.

Aziza A (culturebase.net 2010), a well-known hip-hop artist, says: "The [people in Kreuzberg] ... accept one another, at least in practice. They are as different as chalk and cheese, but are somehow able to live with one another, whether punk or yuppie." Kreuzberg is a place where contradictions comfortably coexist. Experiences and social behaviours that normally do not fit together mix side-by-side. It is rich with different cultures. Neither my own experience of Kreuzberg, nor that of my participants, matches the "bad area" image that Kreuzberg has in the mainstream media. And although social workers confirm that there are many problems associated with Kreuzberg, most residents are happy to be there. Ayla says that "in all of its unattractiveness, all of its dilemmas, poverty, and hopelessness, people still live with one another, and peacefully." Alp says that "Kreuzberg is no Little İstanbul. Here is a space of everybody's utopia."

However, even utopia has its dilemmas. Hierarchy and power dynamics come into play. Everyday encounters with the Other in Kreuzberg do not necessarily promote cooperation. As geographers Jane Jacobs and Ruth Fincher (1998, 5) argue, cities are not so much communities as sites structured around the "being togetherness of strangers" – who are joined through uneven power relations. This reality has direct implications for the ways that justice gets instituted in urban space.

In general, the rhythms of everyday life in Kreuzberg do bring a certain tolerance and understanding. Yet such coexistence takes place within a particular temporal sphere and context. Spatial and temporal belonging together may provide Ausländer with an escape from the challenges of Otherness and the lower status they experience in other places, but it also offers a space for politics. In that sense, many participants say that they see themselves operating as citizens in the city through their social encounters in Kreuzberg. For Tunç, the sense of building relations is powerful: "On this street, the gangsters are on one side; the artists are on the other. For me, this is normal. When the artists [from outside] are with me, they have to be in contact with this world whether they like it or not."

Diversity offers a politics of identity and belonging that challenges the dominant discourse. To be part of the artist groups in Kreuzberg, an artist coming from outside has to develop an understanding of the parallel social worlds in these spaces of temporary belonging. Tunç explains how the parallel lives that are visible in Kreuzberg open up a space for freedom and for

Negotiating Displacement 177

making claims: "My stories always start and end here. The characters go elsewhere in the world but come back. Kreuzberg is the epicentre. I find this incredibly artistic." For Tunç, the competition of political ideologies is openly expressed on Oranienstrasse, be it through graffiti on the walls or talk in the cafés.

In the midst of its dilemmas and paradoxes, the participants feel that the practices and policies of categorizing Ausländer are created, questioned, and challenged in Kreuzberg. In everyday encounters, numerous elements come together in different formations. The kinds of communication and exchange that happen cut through categories of identity and belonging, as individuals and groups negotiate the terms of their interaction. This is what constitutes Kreuzberg's translocality.

During my visits in 2003, many participants spoke about the 2002 World Cup in soccer, in which Türkiye was very successful, finishing in third place. They said they felt strong, powerful, and positive about being Turkish at that time, and the usual strong distinction between Turks and Germans seemed temporarily transformed. Seda says:

> It was incredibly nice and crazy during the World Cup. We went to Ku'damm and danced. Everybody was supporting [the Turkish team]. There was a Nike ad: "Our dream is a Germany-Türkiye game." I have a big flag in my room. Before the World Cup, I didn't care for soccer, but this was a totally different experience for me. An article in the paper said Berlin is red and white. It was great to see all the papers were talking about Türkiye in that way.

The soccer team's success had nothing to do with the participants' daily efforts, but, as Selin says, it did "something much more effective than a Turkish politician could ever do." Soccer seemed to represent national success as a people: "They talked a lot about Türkiye. Being Turkish felt great" (Yeliz). It was not about the soccer itself, but about what it represented, what effect it had. Being talked about and getting acknowledged in positive terms went beyond uniting the Turks of Berlin. Even for those who do not care about soccer, it represented something amazing – feeling good about being visibly Turkish. For the first time, they felt a sense of public esteem that was comparable to being accepted like Germans. Being Turkish represented power.

The euphoria of Türkiye's World Cup success collided with another event that was important for some participants: the annual celebration of

CSD, the Christopher Street Day International Pride Parade. Ayda and Müge, two lesbian women, talked about how they felt that day. Ayda says:

> Two big celebrations on the same day! The way it turned out was interesting. The CSD crowd was concerned that Turkish people would not let them walk on Oranienstrasse. The big CSD parade was in Kufürstendamm [Ku'damm]. They moved the Turkish [soccer] people to Potsdamer Platz. But many people were still at Oranienstrasse. The CSD people were saying, "Türkiye!" Turkish people were answering back, "CSD!" An old woman was dancing with the CSD crowd. It was celebrating parallel lives. It was a special day in which I felt good about myself as a woman, lesbian, and Turk, all at once.

For Ayda and Müge, this experience added another layer to their feelings for Kreuzberg. Their queerness and Ausländerness were in peaceful coexistence. Even if it was only for a short time, it was empowering. This is how they experienced their multiple identities as almost flowing into each other. It was "a tale too good to be true" (Müge). In the long run, this incidental proximity did not change the everyday lives of Ausländer in Berlin or the dominant discourses that regulate German-Ausländer relationships. But it did show one thing: no matter how strictly drawn and protected they are, the boundaries that divide people into categories can dissolve.

I attended the CSD parade the following year. An extraordinary kind of joyful coexistence was evident. The parade started at Nollendorfplatz, the commercial centre of former West Berlin, and ended at Oranienstrasse. On the way, the major streets were closed to traffic. LGBTI+ people claimed their rights to the city by taking over a central space. A core group who continued to parade into Kreuzberg were met at the Kotbusser Torr with a big message reading *"Kreuzbergli Orientalar gey ve lesbiyenleri sevgiyle kucaklar"* (Kreuzberg's Orientals warmly welcome International gays and lesbians).

The celebration of CSD in Kreuzberg was an example of both claiming space and sharing experience. People who normally do not mix came together in the streets. The experience intensified the complexity of local social life. All aspects of this experience – the differences, complexity, and solidarity – offered resistance to dominant contexts. These diverse people, whose communities included multiple places, were sharing the same spaces for different purposes.

Translocality

> My parents worked, retired, and had their kids married. Now, they have money. They don't have any responsibilities here, so they want to make the best of their time. They are healthy enough; they don't want to stay in Berlin full time but want to be active. They go to Türkiye, and my father has family in Holland. They also visit them. And my sister got married and moved to Belgium. So we go visit her too.
>
> – Selin

Most of the participants talk about this kind of mobility that Selin and her family enjoy. Once guest workers become transnational, they add an interesting dimension to the meaning of translocal mobility. Many participants explain that their parents and grandparents spend six months in Berlin and the other six months in Türkiye. They live in both places, without having to choose between the two. In both countries, they have circles of relatives and friends. They have houses in different places, visit their villages, and go for holidays. They do not live in the same city or country as their children; they visit them. They have face-to-face and virtual relations with their multiple community affiliations.

Ausländer families have settled down and become translocal in the process – their migrations have not ended. Their ability to create spaces for themselves makes them immigrants of a new kind. Their experiences of translocality involve a multiplicity of migrations and different forms of movement, not simply the experience of crossing a border. Yet their experience is *not* one of constant displacement: of leaving where they lived, establishing something new, severing bonds with where they came from. They are not nomads, guests, or tourists. They go and then come back. In motion, multi-local, they are living their lives in more than one place.

Translocal experience reminds us that a diaspora is a result of the settlements and accommodations of a dispersed population (Anthias 1998; Gilroy 1993; Hall 1990; Kaya 2007). Diasporic subjects, in their movements, participate in the "global cultural flow" (Appadurai 1996) that involves the transportation of ethnicity, religion, race, class, gender, and sexual orientation, along with various discursive narratives and practical applications. These qualities are also translocal because they are singular local formations distributed within larger geographical, economic, and cultural formations. The movement of people from their home country to another situates them in a diaspora, whereas their ongoing border crossings place them as translocal and transnational.

Anthropologists Nina Schiller, Linda Basch, and Cristina Szanton-Blanc ([1992] 1998, 1) refer to the experience of this new migrant population as "transnationalism" and the people themselves as "transmigrants." Their networks, activities, and patterns of life encompass both host and home societies, cutting across national boundaries, bringing two or more societies into "a single social field." As migration and mobility produce new subject positions, Turkish-background Berliners develop and maintain multiple relations – familial, economic, social, organizational, religious, and political, which commonly span borders. Their space is not that of the nation but of the cosmopolitan city. They transform the local and the national to create new subjective experiences of place and belonging. A culture of circulation emerges among them through their mobility at different levels, both translocal and transnational.

Almanyalıyım (I Am from Germany)

Gül: Do you remember the first day that I met with you and your friends? I said my research was about Turkish-German women, and you became upset. Why?

Aygen: Because I am not German; I am Turkish. I am not German just because I was born and raised here ... I don't feel I belong to Germany ... Being German and being Turkish are two totally different things.

Gül: What do you think about the word *yabancı* [foreigner]?

Aygen: They are right. We are yabancı in the end. I find it wrong and ridiculous that people think getting a German passport enables them to become German ... To be German, your mother, your father, all your past, everything should be German ... If my parents and my grandparents are Turkish, I am Turkish as well. Just because a piece of paper indicates that I am German, that does not mean I can be German ... Everybody is human, but there are fundamental differences that separate us, such as culture, way of socialization, language, and religion. I feel closer to Arabs, for example, than to Germans.

When I interviewed her, Aygen was an eighteen-year-old high school student who enjoyed writing poetry and organizing her school newspaper. She

Negotiating Displacement

articulated a pronounced sense of binary opposition between being German and being Turkish. She understood that being German does not rest on mutable characteristics such as legal status, political loyalty, cultural knowledge, or language fluency. As Peck (1992) reminds us, Germanness is not generally perceived as an open or flexible category.

For many participants, the feelings of marginalization they experience in German society prevent them from fully identifying as German. Ela, a university lecturer from southern Germany, feels a particularly strong allegiance to Germany. Yet her interview is replete with references to the distinction between being an Ausländer and being a German. She says that belonging to Germany is difficult for her. Germans see her as an Ausländer because they define Germanness through blood. And the stereotypes they impose on her (even though she is German-born) are even more troublesome. Being German entails being treated as an equal individual. Therefore, Ela cannot see herself as ever being "an equal individual in this society." Similarly, Fatma says: "Having German citizenship status does not convey the feeling of 'being home' in Germany: it is in the details of everyday life."

It is striking that none of the participants, regardless of class, generation, or degree of integration, considers the prospect of becoming German to be desirable, realistic, or even imaginable. German-born Turks typically "feel that neither the colour of their passport nor the degree of their cultural and linguistic fluency will ensure respect or acceptance" (Klimt 1989, 69–70). They recognize that "only those immigrants [*Übersiedler* and *Aussiedler*] who are not legally considered foreigners [*Ausländer*] can call Germany home" (Peck 1992, 80).

The sense of being forever non-German is accentuated by the fact that issues of consequence to Turkish Ausländer are often missing from the political agenda. To illustrate, Selin refers to the 2001 celebrations of the fortieth year of the Turks' arrival in Germany – a celebration that occurred just after the racist attacks of the late 1990s. Explaining the celebration, Selin says that her estrangement is related to the "Germans' ungratefulness for what Turkish Ausländer have done for Germany." She thinks that feelings of estrangement have been shaped by issues of class and race. Selin explains:

> We grow up with Germans; we get to know them. Still, when we go somewhere like the hospital or government offices, the cleaning staff are still old Turkish women. They did everything for Germans. They gave their health and life. Germans are ungrateful. I have never heard them thanking us for

the things we have done for them. Last summer, there were celebrations of the Turks' fortieth year in Germany: [Chancellor] Schroeder mentioned this only through a letter, not even a speech. Maybe I did not experience extreme racism, but I always remember the families that were killed by fascist groups. Okay, I do not want them to be thankful to us, but they say that Turks are taking their jobs and using their education opportunities. They even blame Turkish young people for the increasing unemployment rate in Germany.

Many German-born Turkish Ausländer experience a sense of exclusion from mainstream German society. They may feel as though they live under a scrutinizing and stigmatizing gaze; there is a subtle feeling of recurrent ostracization. But despite all this, most of the time the participants view Germany as fluid and ambivalent. They associate being German solely with ethnic identity, but they also describe it in more complex terms. They view German society – particularly Berlin (and even more particularly Kreuzberg) – as a space for competing, contingent narratives of identity, belonging, and status. Many participants identify with Germany. Indeed, as far as knowing German ways is concerned, their investment in Germanness constitutes a fundamental link to German society.

Therefore, most participants convey a sense of simultaneous belonging and estrangement. What it means to be Turkish Ausländer and German is ever-shifting and relational. At times, the two statuses are constructed in either-or terms. At other times they converge – for example, when feeling proud to be from Berlin, when expressing appreciation for the socio-economic opportunities available in Germany, or when talking passionately about feelings for Kreuzberg. Then again, some say they feel they are from Germany only when they are away from it.

The notion of being German does not convey the participants' personal complexity. It fails to recognize their ability to speak fluent Turkish, to include their Turkish families, or to describe their relationships with other Turks in Berlin. The notion of Germanness omits the fact that many of them spend four to six weeks every summer in Türkiye. For them, being German translates as whiteness, loss of culture, and homogeneity of identity. Nevertheless, they also argue that when they do call themselves German, it is a way to sabotage the Ausländer/German dichotomy. Each time an Ausländer becomes legally or socially German, it changes the definition of these words. It also changes everyone else who refers to themselves as German. Because

Negotiating Displacement

of their ethnicity, race, and religion, most participants feel a need to articulate their belonging to Germany in new ways. They seek to claim a different kind of Germanness for themselves.

As one example, for Arzu, being German means "knowing the rules of everydayness." She defines belonging in Germany through her relations with her everyday environment:

> My boyfriend is German. The place I live is predominantly German. I feel good in a German environment, and I don't even think of it as a German environment. It is mine. When I think of home or homeland, I think of my parents' house with the garden in Swabia. I never have a yearning for Türkiye ... But sometimes, when I go to a Turkish family and see the typical furniture, or when they bring tea and *börek* [filled pastry], then I feel I belong here. I feel I belong to both very much. In a German setting, I feel better, as I can be more myself. I know the rules. When I visit a Turkish family, they offer food, and I say, "No, thank you." They still offer more, even though I don't want it. For a German family, the words "yes" and "no" have more explicit meanings. To a Turkish family, I cannot say a definite no. I like being able to communicate with such a definite "yes" and "no" in a German family.

For Ela also, knowing German ways is a means of changing the meaning of German culture. She means to take Germanness as a lifestyle rather than as an ethnic identity: "The life is easy for me here. I know the language and the culture. I know its ways. When I want something from someone, I know how to approach them. I know how I will prove myself. I know when to pull back."

German-born Ausländer master the language, adapt to German customs and culture, and sometimes forget, or never learn, Turkish customs. Many Ausländer have also achieved economic and personal successes. All these things make them German. As a result, German-born Ausländer challenge what being German means, while they resist considering themselves German in the conventional sense. Sometimes, the discursive space between Ausländer and Germans seems to collapse, and with it issues of citizenship and race. At other times, the participants feel indelibly classified as Ausländer.

Selin questions the meaning of remaining permanently in Germany and not being able to relate to Türkiye. She feels most German when Turks regard her as different. I asked Selin when it is she feels she's from Germany. She said: "When I'm in Türkiye, I suppose. When people complain how difficult life in Türkiye is ... No matter how difficult the life conditions are, you are in your own land. But here [in Germany], you have a yearning for ... your country in another land ... The people in Türkiye do not understand that."

The question "where do you come from?" is central to the way participants experience the tension between being Ausländer and German. Arzu says:

It hurts when [Turks] say, "You are German," because they say it looking down on you. It is like *"Almanlaşmışsınız"* [you have become like Germans]. *Almanlaşmak* [becoming like a German] is something negative for Turks. It means looking down on your own culture, becoming cold like [Germans], being egoistic like them. Almanlaşmak never means you feel good about yourself in this society. Or [it never means] you go with the same tempo as they go, or you made a good place for yourself in this society. It means you have taken on all the negative aspects of being German. It is like being placed on an extremely detailed scale.

In 2016, Selim told a similar story:

When asked, I say, "I am German" or "Turkish Germaner." But when they insist on asking: "Where are you *really* from?," I kind of make fun of it and say: "Are you asking my race?" I sometimes say I am a Turk from Asia, or I am a Bavarian Turk. As a teen, I hated to be Turkish, to be a foreigner, because I wanted to fit in. But not anymore. Of course, I am Turkish, and of course, I am a German Turk.

The German-born Ausländer's ability to move comfortably between Germanness and Turkishness creates suspicion on both sides. It does not sit well with the binary opposition of German and Ausländer. It is as if they are ambassadors and spies for the other. Their ability to belong to both creates tensions – the tensions of accepting changes in identity. Such tensions challenge both Turkishness and Germanness to become more flexible, to share characteristics considered as belonging to the other.

Shefali Milczarek-Desai, an advocate for marginalized populations and a legal scholar on sanctuary city issues, (2002, 134) argues that the question of how one understands home is "profoundly political." So, in declaring Germany as their homeland through the claim "Almanyalıyım [I am from Germany]" rather than "I am German," the participants define Germany in

Negotiating Displacement 185

a way that reflects their own multiple identities. In calling themselves Almanyalı [from Germany], they re-create what it means to be German. By insisting that all their identities are included in being Almanyalı, they refuse to view the different parts of themselves as contradictory. Not viewing the contradictions as contradictions destroys the categories that would have them choose among their many selves, which are, in reality, inseparable. They are learning how to live with their many identities, how to resist the categories that others would place them in.

Claiming German Citizenship

> We are citizens of this country, with or without the passport. We pay taxes and contribute to the economy of this country.
>
> – Fatma

By claiming German citizenship, many participants demand an official recognition of their right to be and belong in Germany. As İrem points out, this has practical value in everyday life. By having citizenship, many participants have in mind both a legal and social recognition. Leyla, for example, challenges the narrow meaning of citizenship. For her, claiming German citizenship means demanding more rights. She wants the option of dual citizenship: "Dual citizenship means more rights. [Germany] does not want you to have more rights." As Leyla describes what being a citizen of somewhere means, her claims to rights, values, and relationships overlap. For her, claiming citizenship in public involves forming, through everyday encounters, her loyalties and bonds to Berlin, the city she lives in. It doesn't mean patriotism for Germany, "but it means loving Berlin, having your everyday life here. Citizenship is about feeling comfortable. It is to do with love and heart; it is the place ... I don't see myself as a foreigner. Indeed, it is much more complex than people want it to be," Leyla says.

In addition to the right to participate in politics, citizenship includes other kinds of rights in the public sphere: civil, socio-economic, and cultural. Citizenship confers legal status, but it also involves moral and performative dimensions of belonging in a society. For the participants, however, having a German passport does not make them German; neither does it erase their Turkishness. Leyla explains: "I'm also a German. I have a German passport, but I don't accept myself as a German. I should, maybe. I can vote, I pay taxes, and my life is here; and as any German, I was born and grew up here, and I will die here." Erkan also feels unable to view himself as German in a conventional sense. He articulates German citizenship as a new way of being German, which he redefines as something beyond bloodlines. Like Leyla, he takes German citizenship as more than a set of political rights and obligations. It is about the everydayness of building his relationships within Germany; it is also about birthright.

Selin refers to the everyday burden of having a German passport with a Turkish name, which makes the German passport "just a paper": "A German passport ... does not make things easier. In the end, you have a Turkish name. Your colour is dark. You can't lose this." Nonetheless, there is something very powerful in having a German passport, as Ayşe explains. She says that she is a *Dilekçeli Alman* (contract German):

> *Dilekçeli Alman, Auftragdeutsche* is a political term. It refers to the legal procedure of becoming German. My Germanness is stronger than the Germans' Germanness. I can prove it by documents. I got my German identity by documenting it. I became German. Once, I was just Turkish. My fear has disappeared. I do not need a visa to travel. I have political rights such as voting.

Becoming a contract German is a specific type of political act that simultaneously claims truth, value, and rights. It means enjoying the fruits, despite the dominant group's resistance, of the fifty-year struggle for the right to Germanness.

Other participants choose to not to take on German citizenship, and they often see their choice as an act of resistance, a continuation of the struggle. Ayda is one of them:

> I decided not to become a German. The only thing I can claim my Turkish identity with is my Turkish passport. So I decided not to apply for German citizenship ... Whenever I want to travel, I have to get a visa. Everybody was saying that I should get a passport. I was protesting, "No! I don't want to forget how difficult it is to get a visa" ... When I travel somewhere with my girlfriend, at customs she gets into the line for Europeans, and I go to the line for non-Europeans. It was always important for me to show that.

Some participants seem to claim Germany as a possession, like property that belongs to them. Arzu says: "This country [Germany] is my country,

Negotiating Displacement

and I never let people treat me as if I'm a guest here." Others say that official membership in German society means that Germany belongs to them as much as they belong to it. Therefore, they challenge the values attached to identities in the context of binary oppositions. When Ayşe claims to be part of Germany, she assumes a place for herself in both the physical and social spaces of the nation. Yet by saying she is not a German, she makes a commitment to a third space, which starts with a suspicion of binaries. By critically resisting the categories of Turkishness and Germanness, she deconstructs both. She challenges what constitutes Germanness, thereby giving it new meaning. Claiming Germanness and Turkishness at the same time transforms the meanings of both.

"I Belong Here": Reclaiming Ausländerness and Challenging Integration

> We have already integrated. It has to be accepted. For me, integration is not dressing like them or behaving like them. They have to see our differences, and we have to meet on common ground. We already meet with each other. A woman with a headscarf and a German woman meet through children's education. Both face the same problem. They meet at the school, kindergarten, and daycare. It has to be accepted that we [Turks] have a big role in the flow of life in Germany. We have contributed to the economy. This is also a common point. We meet through the music. There are always meetings of different cultures, music, lifestyles. We meet at Karneval der Kulturen [carnival of cultures]. We share the entertainment there. Everybody should appreciate this sharing in everyday life. We have to make these meeting grounds more visible. The teachers, as educators, should show that.
>
> – Fatma

When the participants explain their understandings of integration, many insist that the Turkish Ausländer are already here and functioning. They use various terms to define their integration. Fatma describes herself with the derogatory term *Kanake*, which is used for immigrants and foreigners (according to Wikipedia, it means "wop"). She says, "I can call myself Kanake. But it is different when a German uses it." Originally, the term referred to Italian, Greek, and Spanish immigrants. Now, it more commonly refers to immigrants of Turkish, Arab, or Persian descent. The word originally derived from the New Caledonian (or *Kanaky*) word for human, *kanaka*. Much like the words *nigger* or *queer*, Kanake has been co-opted by some Turks and proudly used as a term of self-identification, although the vernacular use of the word may be declining. More commonly, the participants use "yabancı" as a self-identification. They play with the label. Even those who were born in Germany refer to themselves as foreigners. When Selin says she is a foreigner, she reclaims the diasporic class memory the term carries:

> Saying *"Ich bin eine Ausländerin"* means "I was born here, I speak your language well, and yet I'm not one of you." It is important to be able to say that I'm better than a German young person. My grandparents and parents have been treated badly and oppressed. How can I forget that? I would never say I'm German.

Selin emphasizes that her family members have built their lives here. Yet when referring to that memory, Selin is critical of the experience itself, holding her first-generation relatives responsible for their choices:

> They came here just to work, and they always thought they would go back. But when they started having their life here, they should have learned German. Take my parents. Their German is poor. When my father misunderstands and gives a wrong answer to a German, he puts himself in an awkward position. When I see that, it makes me upset and angry with the German. But it is also my father's responsibility; he could have taken a German course.

When participants confront the estrangement of being treated as a foreigner, they can resist by reclaiming the identity of a foreigner. In doing so, they demand that the guest workers' experience of displacement be acknowledged. They claim recognition for the hardship they have experienced, the trust and hope they have lost. They challenge the original meaning of the word *foreigner* in order to transform it.

Saying "I am a Turk in Berlin" involves a struggle for recognition. It is a matter of not hiding themselves – of working with and against the stereotypes imposed on them. Such self-identification challenges the discourses of integration. Most of the participants redefine integration in a way that differs from the dominant understanding. Many German-born Ausländer

Negotiating Displacement   189

regard integration as the ability to develop strategies for challenging the old ethnocentric ways of being German and belonging in Germany. "Even with that appearance," İrem says, pointing to a Muslim woman wearing a headscarf, "indeed we adapt; we are integrated." The dynamics of unification and of over fifty years' lived experience in Germany have already resulted in integration for the Turkish Ausländer.

The participants use overlapping terminology. They articulate their responses to "Where do you come from?" as new ways to reclaim integration. While critically evaluating traditional Germanness, they negotiate their rights to a new kind of Germanness. They claim their right to Germany by saying "Almanyalıyım" (I am from Germany), and claim their right to both Germany and to being Turkish by saying "*Almanyalı bir Türküm*" (I am a Turk from Germany). As for their right to the city, they say "*Berlinliyim*" (I am a Berliner). The right to both their country of origin and their city of residence is affirmed with "*Türkiyeli Berlinliyim*" (I am a Berliner from Türkiye). They may further claim the right to a particular district of the city with phrases like "*Elhamdulillah Kreuzbergliyim*" (thank God, I'm a Kreuzberger). For their right to German citizenship, they say, "*Ich bin ein Antragsdeutsche*" (I am a German on application). There is no agreement on terms for claiming belonging, but it is significant that such claims are being articulated in ways that suggest various aspects of new Germanness. Such claims of belonging mean that those who came as guests are neither going back nor conforming to a German mould. These claims open a space for being treated as equal members of society in Berlin, Germany, and Europe.

For Erkan, the diversity of claims is significant, because until the mid-1990s, immigrants were still saying, "I am going to go back." Now, they increasingly sound like Erkan: "I was born here, or I came here as a young kid. I live here and I'm going to die here. My children, my grandchildren were born here. They graduated from school here; they work here; they will die here." Starting from this claim, the participants demand certain rights: "I want to be treated as a German. My identity has to be seen as a real identity, not an incomplete identity. I am not sitting between two chairs but have the richness of the two" (Leyla). This mentality is now becoming accepted, as Erkan explained in 2003:

> So far, we have been seen as a defective culture; we were subjects of scientific research. In politics, the foreigners' law, crime, and abuse were the

main topics about foreigners ... They were not talked about in culture or national politics. Today, in all political parties except the CDU, they have representatives in the federal assembly ... [Their] presence in parties, associations, and businesses is becoming increasingly normal.[3]

In earlier years, Germans did not support this – and the immigrants did not demand it – but now things have changed. The way minorities name and identify themselves has become an important question that has led to important debates.

Claims of belonging have changed from "I'm going back" to "I belong here." Then, "I belong here" became "I demand rights here." The rights are both subjective and political. Subjectivity changed from having an "incomplete identity" or "sitting between two chairs" to "having the richness of two cultures." Ausländer changed from being objects of study to subjects who are changing (Aliens Act), society. Whereas the main political issue used to be *Ausländergesetz*, now diasporic subjects are becoming active in political parties, associations, and businesses, which in turn will affect German law. Obligations bring power. The emerging diasporicity is not a generational issue; it is an expression of the times and the stages of development that people are experiencing.

All this change involves controversial developments. In some places, Turkish Ausländer adapt well to German society; in other places, they do not. But what does adaptation mean? What kinds of adaptations are necessary? The debates are so new that the issues cannot yet be fully identified. Everyone seems to have a different idea or model in mind. Nevertheless, just thinking about these issues leads the participants to a critical position, as writer Zafer Şenocak explains in his interview with me:

Everyone understands integration differently. There is no consensus. It is vital to show that. My understanding of integration, for example, is individuals finding themselves where they live, where they are. This can be experienced everywhere, not only in Germany or in Türkiye. If they can build their world, this means they are integrated. But indeed, this is the antithesis of integration. Because the expectation for integration is that my old world must be destroyed and must disappear; another world is then presented, and people adapt to this other world. But it doesn't work that way. People have their inner worlds. When society accepts that, it will be a relief indeed. But it does not. Germany has such an inner dilemma. Generalization is not right, as there are different tendencies. People are different every-

Negotiating Displacement 191

where. But the difference is [that] heterogeneity disappears in these discourses, the heterogeneity of Turks and of Germans. This has to be opened up in scientific and literary works.

For many Ausländer, integration means knowing German ways and how society functions. They belong to Berlin because they know the ways of Berlin and of German society. Veli, a lawyer, points out the significance of understanding the legal and institutional systems of the society: "It is not just language; it is knowing all other systems and ways. If parents know how, where, and what to claim [i.e., their rights], and when they do claim, if they know the system, they will not feel excluded."

Neue Deutsche (New Germans)

Neue Deutsche, new Germans ... this is who we are. The second and third generations, who were born and raised here in German ... Not only Turks either, those with Polish and Russian backgrounds are all new Germans. Former East Germany has a substantial Vietnamese population. They are like us too ... In everyday parlance, it is more like "German of Turkish background," even in the news. In the past, they wouldn't use this definition. They would say "Turkish" or "Russian."

– Selim

The new Germans have become an integral part of social, political, and cultural life in Germany. They commonly refer to how hard their generation has worked to open up a path and how they have come a long way. Many participants talk about how this has changed in their lifetimes. Fatma explains:

For a while ... the police force was looking for candidates who can speak Turkish and the people who are familiar with Turkish culture. It was similar with TV channels, radios, media, press, etc. And when they hired people, speaking Turkish and knowing Turkish culture were assets. They wanted to increase the number of people with Turkish backgrounds. There is still that. When you turn on the TV, they don't want you to only see blond news anchors.

Arzu argues that being Turkish or Muslim no longer determines what you can do or what your place is in German society:

In the past, it was foreigners who would deal with foreigner issues. For example, in the paper, Muslims wrote about Muslims. Now, sometimes, I turn to the paper's science page, politics page, or economy section; I see a Turkish name; and the topic is like the life of whatever, butterflies.

Leyla says: "Now when you look at the TV shows, youth with Turkish backgrounds do not play stereotypical roles. We overcame that." Selim too reflects on the increasing visibility of people with foreign backgrounds in mainstream public arenas, pointing out that before the mid-1990s,

there were no main characters with Turkish backgrounds in the movies. Before, they would play a role that a Turkish person would stereotypically be suitable for – someone with a cleaning job or a foreigner. That has been changing now. There is an opening in Germany. Politically speaking, we have Cem Özdemir, the leader of the Greens. We wouldn't have imagined this ten or fifteen years ago.

In some fields, these new Germans are very prominent, such as in soccer. As Tunç points out: "We have three Turkish-background players on the German national team in soccer. Actually, it is a very diverse team, with Arab- and African-background players too."

In my research update, many participants compared their twenty-to-thirty-year-old selves with people of that age today. Fatima says:

They have more than we had. They are more free; they have more both economically and emotionally. We had to work for everything. I started earning money when I was fourteen or fifteen. I used to do cleaning jobs to buy something I wanted. It was a struggle for us, but I see from my niece and nephews, they, at twenty, thirty-five still live at home. They do not have any desire to move out.

Ayla feels: "Our generation was different. We were trying to figure out how to belong here." Yet Selim argues that younger German Turks are too complacent:

In my opinion, we are missing an opportunity in this great opening in German society ... This new generation has the opportunity to capture the change in German society. However, they are resistant to this change. They have the opportunity to contribute to change more substantially. They should

Negotiating Displacement   193

be self-confident and go-getters. And then, we can have an even bigger change in German society. However, there is almost a resistance to this change from the teens, the new generation – this clinging on to Turkishness.

I was singing at a bar. The next day was May 1, Labour Day. It was after midnight and I said: "Friends, it is after midnight, so happy Labour Day. My greetings to your parents and grandparents, for everything they have done." It was like they had no idea what I was talking about. The average age was about twenty to twenty-four. These people are young enough to be my kids. Then I thought to myself, "So, they would have no idea because their parents are my age."

I asked whether this new understanding of being German is changing in German society as a whole, as it is for the new generation with Turkish background. How could the participants explain why the new generation does not feel they belong? What were the sources of their resistance? Fatma answered, "The new generation is not feeling comfortable here either." I asked Fatma: "What kind of German will your son become? How will your son's identity be shaped, do you think?"

I think they will have a totally new personality and identity ... They will be new Germans. They will be their own unique persons ... Even though I was born and raised in Germany, I always felt like a foreigner in Germany. But I believe this is not the case for Ilkay ... He doesn't question whether he is German or not. I remember when I was a teenager, or even younger, I used to question where I belong. Am I from Berlin, or am I from Türkiye? I don't see Ilkay having this problem. Ilkay feels himself belonging here. He feels good about being and belonging here. For him, Türkiye is a place where his grandparents are from. It is a place he enjoys going; it is a place with people he loves. But Germany is his country, where he is from. When you ask him, "*Woher kommst du?* [Where do you come from?]" he would say, "Germany"; he would say he is German. But, if you ask me, I can't say that with the same certainty and comfort. I can't see that he will grow up to have that feeling. I think he won't have this feeling of not belonging to Germany.

The only problem he will have might be culture and religion. That is our problem now. For example, there was an issue around ham at school – we had that problem recently. We spoke about that at home with him. At home, we don't make it an issue. We don't eat a lot of meat, but we don't care if it is ham or beef either. At school, parents requested that the school

194   *Homesickness–Homelessness*

not give the children ham for lunch. We had to explain this at home to Ilkay. So we explained that it is because Muslims don't eat ham, just like vegans don't eat meat. That's how we explained it to him.

Parenting: Raising the New Germans

The parents among my participants all emphasize how they consciously invest in giving their children a sense of belonging that is not defined through strictly compartmentalized ethnic and cultural experiences. They want their children to feel the fluidity of being a diasporic citizen. They aim to raise their children as new Germans, yet ground them in where they came from. Selim explains that he doesn't want his son to put all his energy into figuring out who he is and where he belongs: "We try to raise our son neutrally ... Our hope is that he will never live the dilemma and questioning of Who am I? We want him to be self-confident so that he won't feel he has to belong in one group of people."

Parents feel that the significant difference between them and their children is that their children do not experience being strongly different. Despite their youth, these new Germans are clearly integrated into the culture in Berlin. Still, in terms of social relations, the parents admit there has not been much progress. Fatma says that the maintenance of foreignness now tends to come from other German-born Turkish-background Berliners, such as her son's teachers:

> My son, Ilkay, sees himself as a Berliner, not as a Turk ... But still, I feel he experiences this being foreigner. Most of his friends at school are Turkish, even though his classroom is diverse: Turkish, German, English, Spanish, etcetera. Because the majority are Turkish, [the teachers] still bring the Turkish culture to the centre. And I see that again at home with Ilkay. We start speaking about Turkish culture. We still feel the need to do so ... but he is much closer to German than Turkish. Since he was three or four, he has been speaking German. This demand for him to speak Turkish comes from teachers. He has started learning and speaking Turkish now.

What's in a Name?

When the parents of young children talk about dismantling the compartments of binary oppositional structures in the society, they often mention another important aspect: naming their children. Fatma and Leyla state:

Negotiating Displacement 195

Ilkay is going into Grade 4. He has already started questioning his name. I mean, he has two names: Ilkay Leon. Leon is French. The teachers keep asking: "Is your father French? How come you have two names?" He needs to explain sometimes. He asks me why he doesn't have a German name. It [being Other] still comes to him.

Did I tell you what my son's name is? It is Kolya Yunus Çetin. Kolya is a Russian name. It is Slav, and it comes from Nikolay. It means "the hero who brings freedom to his people." This is his first name.

Leyla and Fatma invested considerable effort in searching for non-German names. They want names that are international, yet recognizable among their community. Naming their children is a particular strategy that these women mobilize. First names are the foremost identifier of a person, and they connect an individual to culture and society. Generally, the first name identifies a person's ethnicity. One's first name also comes with emotional ties. As sociologist Birgit Becker (2009, 202) asserts, the material and economic costs of choosing names are low. However, the long-term social costs can be high, as certain names may leave individuals exposed to prejudice. Because Germanness is heavily grounded in ethnic identity, many parents such as Fatma and Leyla feel "obliged to choose nonethnic names to avoid discrimination" (Gerhards and Hans 2009, 1107). In Türkiye, too, parents are highly unlikely to give their children foreign first names. Some 82.5 percent of children receive names that are common only in Türkiye. But among German Turks, children who hold German citizenship are more likely to have a first name that is common in Germany (Becker 2009, 210, 212). Leyla explains:

As we talked about my son, I just thought of this: it is really upsetting that we've lived in Germany for decades, but they still cannot pronounce our names. Coming back to naming my son, I did not want to have letters of the Turkish alphabet with accents. I looked for a name that would not have the kind of letters that don't exist in the German alphabet ... I searched all over the Internet to find a name that they will pronounce correctly. Like my name is Leyla, only [five] letters ... And I receive letters and emails calling me "Sir/Mr." I have to correct them. I even got called "Ali."

Güler remembers:

> We were discussing this with my friends the other day, how we've started pronouncing our names like Germans pronounce them. We started accepting this. It is like: "Let's give up trying to correct people, and accept their pronunciation from the beginning. Make it easy for everyone." But that is not the point. I want my name to be pronounced as I pronounce it. This has to do with respect ... The other day, I called the bank. The person on the phone said, "This is Sakir. How may I help you?" It is really Çakır [CHAH-ker], not Sakir ... This is something that is also happening.

Several factors are related to whether Turkish immigrants adopt or avoid German names for their children. The parents' levels of education, their religion, inter-ethnic relationships, citizenship, friendships within the host country, and their child's gender – all these things affect the choice of names for Turkish immigrants.

Naming involves a range of significant practices for ethnic maintenance. Some Turkish-background Berliners give their children globally grounded, Turkish auditory-appropriate names, as Leyla did with Kolya, or Fatma did with Leon. Others Germanize the pronunciation of their traditionally Turkish names. Some teachers question their students about their non-Turkish names, as Fatma's son's teachers do. The parents may demand that Germans learn to correctly pronounce their children's Turkish first names. In all cases, these people are challenging the politics of acculturation. Going beyond the issue of *whether* they belong in Germany, the participants are exploring *how* they will belong – how will they shape their belonging in both Germany and Türkiye. Such choices involve inner struggle and social controversy. They involve taking a new standpoint in a new kind of community, which I call *the borderlands*.

The claims that German-born Turkish Ausländer make to Germanness serve to remind Germans (and Germany) that these guest-workers' children and grandchildren are integral to Germanness. Such claims are constant reminders that nativist accounts are fictitious. As these children negotiate their diasporic displacement, they demonstrate the fluidity, multiplicity, and heterogeneity of both Turkish and German identities.

Conclusion: Displacement Flows into Belonging

In this chapter, I have analyzed how German-born Turkish Ausländer negotiate their sense of displacement, belonging, and home. I show how their sense of belonging is discursively informed, socially practised, and historically situated in the contexts of Berlin, Germany, and Türkiye. In exploring

Negotiating Displacement 197

these ways of constructing a diasporic home, I show some of the complex ways that the participants' negotiations and social practices have evolved. I examine their tension between homesickness and homelessness. They have both complex and intangible connections to a homeland and a profound sense of claiming Germanness and Germany as their own.

German-born Turkish Ausländer are members of a contemporary diaspora whose narratives take shape in an emerging postcolonial society. Their narratives originate in, as Hall (2017, 143) would agree, the power relations between the "West and the rest." It is in a new postcolonial space that diasporic awareness leads from displacement toward a sense of belonging. Diasporic awareness evolves as "a sort of substitute for 'identity'" (Hall 2017, 144). The diasporic community is a kind of double inscription, of creolization and multiple belongings, despite being continually displaced. These negotiations of displacement that take place on the axis between homelessness and homesickness remind us that power relations in society are always complex, fluid, and interlinked. German-born Turkish Ausländer yearn for a home that is both a mythic place of true belonging in the diasporic imagination and a lived experience in a real locality (Brah 2018, 236). Negotiating this sense of displacement is "a process of multi-locationality across geographical, cultural, and physical boundaries" (Brah 2018, 237).

In the following chapter, I examine the way this ongoing negotiation is shaping the identities of German-born Turkish Ausländer. I show how diasporic awareness is emerging for people who live in a *borderland*. As a metaphorical and geographical space, the borderland is a site where diasporicity is activated, and the politics of diasporic citizenship finds its ground. Borderlands are specific places where German-born Turkish Ausländer cultivate their sense of belonging as diasporic citizens.

5 Borderlands

*I am not in-between, for I have lost my sense of direction. Often
I do not recognize the camps, and have to ask my way through.
Then I'm found out as someone who does not know his way.
Then I'm scrutinized, eyed, eavesdropped on, and suspected
until I leave again.*

— Şenocak (2000, 67)

Through their negotiations between homelessness and homesickness,
German-born Ausländer come to realize that they have more options
than merely choosing which place to call home. As their identity is multidimensional, evolving, and ever-changing, they also have the option *not*
to choose. Ayhan Kaya (2007, 483) refers to this tension among people
who seek "a separate space of their own." Chicana lesbian feminist Gloria
Anzaldúa ([1987] 2007, 25) characterizes this experience of straddling
multiple worlds as life on the *borderlands*. She presents the metaphor of
borderlands as a way to describe a type of hybridity that the participants
in Berlin also experience. A border represents a dividing line – "a vague and
undermined place created by the emotional residue of an unnatural boundary. It is a constant state of transition." The term *borderland* means more
than a geopolitical zone between countries. It also refers to any linguistic,
psychological, sexual, or spiritual boundary where the edges of two or more
ways of being mix, forming representations of hybrid identity.

In addition to identities, forms of belonging are also always mixed and
mixing. German-born Ausländer are a case in point. They embody opposite
qualities that come together to produce a borderland voice and perspective.
The multiplicity of their identities may signal a failure to build an integrated
identity (as understood in dominant discourses), but it still reflects their

Borderlands

actual socio-political realities, in which representations of difference go beyond being one thing or the other.

As the participants experience contradictions and tensions over their identity and belonging, they negotiate their responses at a subjective level. The notion of borderlands reflects their experience as they question the boundaries and limits of social worlds while affirming a state of in-betweenness. They practice an ongoing creative effort to examine meanings that have been naturalized in dominant German and Turkish discourses and are, therefore, seldom questioned in relation to each other. As Anzaldúa ([1987] 2007) would argue, life in the borderlands may seem to make diasporic people incomplete, but their experiences of ambiguity, complexity, and fluidity challenge the idea that a *pure* identity is superior to a hybrid one.

I use the term *borderlands* in referring to a dialogical space between two forms of identity: being and becoming, pure and hybrid. In his analysis of diasporic identities, postcolonial cultural theorist Stuart Hall (1990) argues that although identity offers a sense of unity and commonality, it is also a process of change that involves discontinuity and fluidity. Hall (1990, 224–25) writes:

> We should not, for a moment, underestimate or neglect the importance of the act of imaginative rediscovery which this conception of a rediscovered, essential identity entails ... We cannot speak for very long, with any exactness, about "one experience, one identity," without acknowledging its other side – the ruptures and discontinuities which constitute, precisely, [its] ... "uniqueness."

Rather than being eternally fixed in the past, the identities of German-born Turkish Ausländer are subject to continuous fluctuations of history, culture, and power. Their identities are shaped by dialogic negotiations concerning a homesickness that emphasizes similarity and a homelessness that emphasizes difference. The first negotiation concerns giving people some grounding. The second reminds people that what they share includes the experience of profound discontinuity. In the borderlands, people perceive themselves as shifting between various cultural, social, and political contexts. These contexts are constantly negotiated during the interactions of everyday life.

In this sense, the identities of borderland dwellers are not pre-existing realities but are communicative constructions. Identity arises at the unstable meeting point between lived experiences and the stories of history

200   *Borderlands*

and culture. The range of meanings and qualities that participants ascribe to themselves suggests the potential for a radical, transformative identity. From their hybrid experience, diasporic people create focal points for telling counter-stories, which redefine who they are and where they belong. Şenocak (2000, 72) explains that growing up simultaneously in two cultures is like being *twice a child* in the same lifetime.

Being Twice a Child: Negotiating Double Consciousness

> I was twice a child. Once in Turkish, once in German. As a Turkish child, I could not speak any German; as a German child, I could already speak Turkish. Thus, the Turkish child learned German. But the German child never had to learn Turkish ... The Turkish child is intimidated. He has met many strangers. He never became an adult ... The German child on the other hand had to think and die in order to grow up. Thus, I'm a child in Turkish and an adult in German ... Can this turn out well?
>
> – Şenocak (2000, 72)

Şenocak's narrative illustrates how German-born Turkish Ausländer grow up with two identities. Even though the identities live together, each brings different challenges, not to mention the challenges of coexistence. Being a Turkish Ausländer and a German at the same time causes these identities to intertwine, dialogue, and merge. Turkish and German identities transform each other, creating beings that have never existed before, linguistically, culturally, or ethnically. Şenocak articulates the process as dying as one subject and being born as another. This dynamic process is key to the challenge confronting German-born Ausländer.

At the core of being twice a child is a kind of experience that American Ghanaian sociologist, socialist, historian, civil rights activist, Pan-Africanist, author, writer, and editor W.E.B. DuBois ([1903] 2017) called *double consciousness*. This is an awareness of "belonging to more than one world, or being both 'here' and 'there', of thinking about 'there' from 'here' and vice versa, of being 'at home' – but never wholly – in both places; neither fundamentally the same, nor totally different" (Hall 2017, 140). This crucial property of diasporicity gets further nuanced and mobilized through engaging in the acts and practices of diasporic citizenship.

As they have an inner relationship with both Turkishness and Germanness (and experience the asymmetrical relations between them), many participants say they do not see themselves as living between worlds. Ela

Borderlands 201

explains: "A well-meaning German pedagogue says, 'It is a pity you are in-between two chairs, between two homelands. If I was in-between Türkiye and Germany, I would be in Romania, but I'm not!'" However, Ela does not feel that she moves between two languages, cultures, or ethnicities. Her experience is more complex than being two things at the same time or having to move between the two without being able to claim either.

Many participants say that their relations to Turkishness and Germanness are unclear and that this unclarity is discomforting. Belma talks about an everlasting sense of inconclusive negotiation for belonging and identity: "On the one hand, I believe I can combine the good things about Turkishness and Germanness. On the other hand, I feel like I'm lost. I do not know where I belong. I do not think we will ever know." Aynur feels lost and homeless, with "an intense constant yearning for here and there." Yet the tension between not belonging anywhere and belonging to both identities can be empowering.

Ayşe emphasizes space over ethnic identity when referring to personal affiliation. This emphasis transforms the essentialized sense of ethnicity and opens up a place for overcoming the burden of having to choose between two identities in binary opposition. Being in-between means the ability to travel between the two, "[but] it is not even travelling between the two, because both are in me."

When Fatma talks about who she is and where she belongs, she senses that "something is missing." In the end, however, she defines where she belongs through the city she lives in: "I am a Turkish person from Berlin ... I have chosen certain things that suit me in the Turkish and German cultures." Fatma's identity is an outcome of remembering and changing. It comes from creating a space where the boundaries of being Turkish and German are blurred. Both Germanness and Turkishness question each other's authority, challenging the hegemony of Germans and Ausländer alike. This questioning involves a struggle for recognition, a search for a different kind of belonging. But the German and Turkish sides never have equal power. One voice has the authority; the other is the voice of survival.

The most important German characteristic available to the German-born Ausländer is fluency in German. The capacity to belong to a nation is inherently linked to its language (Bhabha 1990, 1994). Not understanding the meaning of German speakers' words and gestures makes one a double outsider who is unable to understand either the linguistic or the cultural meanings exchanged by indigenous Germans. Fluency in German unlocks the mysteries of the nation. Clearly, the rewards of fluency are great, but language is not the only obstacle in the path to belonging. Fatma points to the ambiguous effects of language policies:

> German language classes are offered for Turkish staff at the school. I have always been against that. These people are here because it is a bilingual school, which means Turkish and German are the two official languages. This is why we have Turkish teachers. Recently, they have been saying, "The school staff either have to learn German or find another job" ... Learning should be encouraged ... The Germans don't always speak proper German either. The classes should have components of reading and writing comprehension, and they should be open to both Turkish and German teachers.

Fatma's concern about language courses at work reflects her concerns about exclusion. She claims that through the language courses, integration becomes exclusion.

Fluency in Turkish can also be a liability, because it makes it too easy for Turkish patients to not speak German. Belma, for example, is expected to isolate herself from the Turkish language at work: "[German doctors] don't like it when a Turkish patient calls and asks for a Turkish nurse. They get upset that these people still don't know German ... And they don't like us to be translators for the patients." Although the priority of the medical system should be the well-being of the patients, speaking both German and Turkish is held against Belma, even though it could lead to better care for Turkish-speaking patients.

The skills that were emphasized for the Turkish workers who entered Germany decades ago are not the skills that determine prosperity now. Language has replaced the strong back and the willingness to work long hours as the prime economic advantage. Integration into the work force, membership in the community of productivity, and belonging in Germany are all tied to linguistic ability.

The issue of whether one speaks Turkish or German can become a matter for confrontation. Speaking Turkish in public is a right Fatma claims, even though "Germans don't like that." She describes this kind of confrontation as it developed in a teacher-parent meeting:

> At a parents' meeting, most of the parents were Turkish. We were two teachers, me and a German teacher. We planned a bilingual meeting. So she did the talk in German and I did it in Turkish, as planned. After my opening

Borderlands

speech, the parents started asking questions in Turkish. The exchange in Turkish between me and the parents continued for about half an hour. Then I realized that it was not right, as there were two Germans in the room. I felt uncomfortable. They made some comments that we should go back to German. The reason the conversation turned to Turkish was because the parents didn't know German. They needed to ask and get answers in Turkish.

In this example, exclusion happens in an explicitly bilingual public space. But demands over language can also intrude into private affairs. Güler's neighbour feels free to interfere in Güler's private conversation with her husband:

The other day, I was going down the stairs with my husband, and we were talking in Turkish. A neighbour saw us and she said, "Hey, German is spoken here!" She said it with a smile. Ahmet said, "But this is our mother tongue we are speaking." She laughs. "I am just kidding!" We said, "We always hear these things. Enough already." She said, "Maybe we are jealous that you are bilingual."

These examples show an insistence on using German language – even for people who speak Turkish in private conversation. Many participants attribute this insistence to the dominant understanding of integration in German society. Yener, an LGBTI+ activist, says: "Integration is reduced to language. As if everyone who speaks German will be integrated, and the most important barrier is that Turkish is still dominant." Veli, also an LGBTI+ activist, feels that "where integration is concerned, the focus is always language ... They conclude that a person who can speak German is an integrated person. This simplistic suggestion is not a sufficient solution toward integration." Like many participants, Yener and Veli are critical of the general understanding that equates integration with speaking German. Kemal, a former graffiti artist and a youth counsellor who speaks fluent German, found that he needed a Turkish-speaking counsellor, because Turkish is the language of his emotions, whereas German is only his language of education and work. The participants feel strongly about retaining the Turkish language. They actively use it, even though it is a barrier to integrating into German society.

Katarina, a sociology graduate student, shares her observation regarding one form of resistance to speaking German:

In the mid-1980s, young Turkish people spoke perfect German with each other. It changed in the 1990s. They started speaking a hybrid language with a very strong accent. They all make the same mistakes. They develop a way of using German grammar in a wrong way, consciously. Is it a conscious choice? Why did this shift occur? I think this is significant. Maybe this is them saying, "If you don't let us belong, then we don't want to belong either."

Almost all of the participants refer to how they mix German and Turkish. Fatma says, "Mixing the two languages is easier than expressing myself with one." The term *Kanak Sprak* describes the German dialect used by Turks in Germany. Its name comes from the title of an eponymous book by Feridun Zaimoğlu (1995). *Kanake-talk* refers to the word *Kanake*, which was originally used as a pejorative but now has been reclaimed. Mixing languages in everyday speech has become part of diasporic politics. Philosopher Mikhail Bakhtin (1981) would say that such linguistic hybridity is a dialogic structure that can undermine authority, making room for the less powerful. It is a strategy for resistance and activism, especially for those caught between their indigenous language and the language of their colonizers. By mixing languages, participants can use German without privileging it. On the other hand, mixing means that monolingual Turks and Germans become observers only, and thus mixing is a tool for marginalization. The dynamic combination of different linguistic systems critically appropriates elements from the dominant culture to form a new mixed system. Kanak Sprak serves to destabilize the linguistic domination of German and Germans.

Culture and language are inseparable. Yıldız says that "German vocabulary is not sufficient for expressing feelings." If it is about feelings, it is Turkish. But if it is about politics or everyday life, German. Selin says that "German friends ... think we do it on purpose. It's just the way we talk; it comes naturally ... I listen to Turkish pop music. German music is not my style. Neither are German TV and shows."

Despite their identification with Turkish culture, the estrangement of German-born Ausländer repeats itself in Türkiye. Using mixed language in Türkiye is seen as being unable to speak "good Turkish" – a weakness. Speaking German in a Turkish encounter is also a weakness. Mixing is taken, by Turks, as showing off one's Germanness and rejecting Turkishness as inferior. Turkishness means speaking good Turkish, *without* mixing it with German (or any other language). Selin says that in the summer of 2002 when

Borderlands

she was in Türkiye, she wasn't able to participate in conversations: "I couldn't express myself and my thoughts. It was embarrassing." Aygen says, "In Türkiye, when they correct my Turkish, it hurts." In Türkiye, where being fluent in Turkish is desirable, being fluent in German is considered disloyal – a choice to become German. Mixing may be a conscious act of resistance in the German context, but in the Turkish, it becomes an issue of losing one's Turkishness. At some point, however, getting back to a single voice in either language becomes impossible.

As a form of hybridity, linguistic mixing creates a situation where the discourse of authority loses its univocal grip on meaning, and people find themselves open to the language of the Other. Mixing undoes the univocal nature of authoritative, colonial discourse. It signals the arrival of performative creativity. In acts of mixing, resistances happen discursively. Bhabha (1990) describes such mixed gestures as forms of mimicry or *sly civility*.

For postcolonial theorist Robert Young (1995, 22), the crucial moment of mixing comes when "one voice is able to unmask the other. This is the point where authoritative discourse is undone." Authoritative discourse understands itself as single-voiced, monologic. It annihilates the voice of the Other. Bakhtin (1981, 344) notes that a dominant language "is by its nature incapable of being double-voiced; ... [it] cannot enter into hybrid constructions." When authoritative discourse encounters itself as a hybrid, single-voiced authority is undermined.

The participants' narratives reveal the dynamics and fluidity in their modes of difference. They illustrate that, as Dhamoon explains (2009, 57; emphasis in original), "no identity is pure, for all criss-cross *in various degrees*." Thus, the representation of difference does not stand in contrast to a pure thing, as there is nothing that is pure. Some representations may be more constant or more conforming to a specific way of understanding difference. But these accepted ways are also constituted by intricate processes of interruption and mixture. The idea of crossing entrenched boundaries of difference is an important aspect of diasporic subjectivity.

The participants' accounts reveal that hybridity can produce not just negative feelings of ambiguity but also positive feelings of belonging. In addition to feeling good about combining Germanness and Turkishness, some participants play with other categories such as gender, sexual orientation, race, or religion. In their own social contexts and family histories, they describe their subjectivities by identifying the ways in which their physical appearances and historical experiences of displacement place them as Ausländer, erasing their Germanness. At the same time, they recall the cumulative impact of being Alamancı among Turks in Türkiye, of experiencing anti-German attitudes among other Turkish Ausländer in Berlin, and of facing racism among Germans. As previously discussed, these representations of difference are situated in the historical contexts for the formation of German identity, with its innate relations to immigration, the guest-worker program, ongoing racism, and classism in both Germany and Türkiye. The participants' experiences in Germany and Türkiye may seem to render their identity ambivalent, but hybridity does not necessarily produce an ambiguous form of identification. When two or more inscriptions of identity are grafted together, something new appears. With their narratives of borderlands, these diasporic subjects disrupt the idea that fixed categories of identity exist (such as male versus female; German versus Ausländer; homosexual versus heterosexual; white versus non-white). At the same time, the participants reveal that although their encounters with representations of difference are ambiguous, their choices regarding hybridity are commonly unambiguous expressions of their personal identities.

Third Space and Third Place

The other day, I asked a powerful question to myself ... "Where will I be buried? Berlin or Türkiye?" I said: "Neither here nor there, I should be buried elsewhere ... in another country that I have no relation or connection with whatsoever." I was born here, and I go to Türkiye only for holidays ... If you ask me where I would like to live, I would prefer here ... Yet, even though I do not know it well, I have an incredible yearning for Türkiye ... You accept both places ... I combine going back and forth between two countries with the "buried" issue ... You are neither from here nor from there. You had better go somewhere else, where you do not have any connections, and be from there.

– Yıldız

Many participants say that neither Germany, where they were born, nor Türkiye, where they are from, are theirs by choice. They were thrown into these spaces, but they can belong to neither; in both, they feel outsiders. Zehra, a hejabi woman and a shop owner in Kreuzberg, says, "We are neither from here nor from Türkiye. Our feet are not on the ground." I interviewed Yıldız and Aynur together. Yıldız talked about her need for something

Borderlands   207

to hold on to: "You aren't fully accepted and don't belong to any place; you aren't at home anywhere." When I asked if having a home is that important, she replied: "Having a home wouldn't be bad, of course! I can compare it with religion ... It is like clinging. You need to hold on to something. *Vatan* [homeland] is like that too. If they ask you where your *vatan* is, you can answer. But I can't."

Aynur disagreed: "No, I can say I'm Turkish," to which Yıldız replied, "But I can't insult the place I was born. I have such a dilemma." The problem Yıldız has with defining herself as Turkish involves excluding her life experience in Germany. She resolves the dilemma by thinking about going to a third country. Yıldız continued: "Maybe this is why I want to go to another country. There, at least, they will not see me as Alamancı or as I am considered, a foreigner in the place I was born. In that third country, I will be a foreigner, and it will be my choice."

For Damla, a theatre student, the third space is about *not* feeling like a foreigner. Seda sees the third space as a place where she can build her life the way she wants. For Belma, the third space functions as a dream: "There should be a state for the people in-between."

In-betweenness allows participants a possibility of creative restructuring, which draws selectively from two opposing categories of being Turkish and German. This approach draws on the real material worlds to create new alternatives as "creative recombinations" of realities (Soja 1996, 5–6). In the third space of in-betweenness, things that seem to be oppositional can work together to generate different kinds of knowledge, different discourses, and other forms of being and belonging.

A third space builds on many spaces: the multiple belongings to different places produce a continuously emerging space of hybridity. This is the self-renewal process of negotiations in borderlands. Therefore, the third space is a source of power in everyday life. As Bhabha (1994, 37) argues, the notion of the third space evokes the instability of signs and symbols, which presents a challenge to dominant conceptions regarding the "unity and fixity" of culture and language. If meanings and symbols have no fixed sense, if signs can be appropriated and resignified, then the dominant discourse is open to divergent but independently valid interpretations.

Arzu, Ayda, and Ela are not originally from Berlin. Their relations with Germanness and Turkishness are different from those of people who were born and grew up in the city. The first challenge for these women is their relation with Turkish identity. For Ayda, this challenge rose from her desire to become a proper Turk and Muslim in the small Turkish community of her German town. For Arzu, it was a struggle to figure out her family's difference from the rest of the residents in her German village. For Eda, it was trying to function through the hierarchy of Turkishness in Berlin. Their second challenge is that they are not accepted by the Turks of Berlin, which is the group they aspire to belong to, because of their out-group orientation. Therefore, they experience being marginalized by other Turks in a different way. Each woman highlights a different aspect of her negotiation of identity and belonging, and each describes how her negotiations differed in her hometown and in Berlin, where she arrived as young adult.

Ayda, a social worker and a self-identified lesbian, describes how not being "Turkish enough" has affected her search for belonging. In her hometown, she did not fit in well with the small Turkish community: "I was the Alamancı of the family, with my appearance, attitude, and clothing, and my [lack of fluency in] Turkish." Similarly, for Ayda, the dominant expectation was "becoming a proper Turk." Yet she was clearly different from the other Turks she knew – in her hometown, in her immediate and extended family, and in Türkiye. Ayda's struggle to overcome being "outside a little" included taking Turkish classes, attending a Koran school, and trying, as a child, to fit in as a Muslim by fasting. Nothing worked: "I took Turkish classes. The girls there wouldn't play with me because I looked German ... They attended Koran school, and their problems at school were different ... The neighbourhood we lived in was different. They lived in a Turkish neighbourhood."

Ayda wanted to become a proper Muslim but failed. At Koran school, after only a few classes, the teacher urged her to quit, because she was always questioning what they taught. Once, she wanted to fast with her father:

> My parents said I could, but only for half a day ... I was at my father's nephew's barbershop. Half a day passed, and I had a glass of water. I thought that I'm a child and, therefore, God would accept this ... But they started criticizing what I did. And then and there, again, my attempts to be a Turk went down the drain.

Ayda's desire to be a Turk led to an active search for belonging that eventually grew into political activism. She ran away from her parents' home: "I had to choose homelessness to find myself, and this is how I came to have a different political awareness." After coming to Berlin, Ayda stayed "a little outside" Turkish identity in general, and outside Berlin's Turkish-background

Borderlands   209

LGBTI+ community in particular. Referring to Ayşe, who is a significant
political activist in the LGBTI+ community, Ayda describes how Ayşe relates to the German lesbian community rather than to Berlin's Turkish-
background LGBTI+ people:

> Ayşe said one day, "Ayda, how can you live with nine German women?" It
> was normal for me ... I started thinking about what she said and recognizing
> the differences. There were lesbian meetings. I never saw myself on the
> other side, on the side of Turkish lesbians, or on the non-German side. I
> never thought they saw me as different. I did not see myself as among the
> ones who are non-German. In my culture, I was looked down on, but I
> never felt that when I was with Germans. Maybe that is because I never had
> shown my own culture.

The only Turkish people who Ayda now associates with are members
of the LGBTI+ community. She talks about her differences with these
people:

> I don't introduce myself as "My name is Ayda; I'm a lesbian Turk." I don't
> show this. But it is different for the ones who were born and raised in Berlin
> ... For me ... it is important, but there are more important things. For that
> reason, there is no consensus with them ... I don't have a Turkish circle,
> because Berlin Turkish women and people are different from the way I
> grew up ... The racism they face here, the problems they faced at schools
> feel foreign to me.

Ayda describes her different relation to language: "I came from Bremen.
I know ... [a Turk] from Bremen. I always see him with Germans. When
we see each other, we say '*Hallo*' [German], not '*Selam*' [hi, in Turkish].
Maybe this is also significant. Ayşe always says 'Selam'; I respond 'Hallo'. I
think the feeling is different ... Here, it is like there is a pressure."
She compares Berlin's Turks to those of her town:

> Bremen is different. I was fourteen when we went to eat doner for the first
> time. It was a Greek gyros place really. My mom took me there. But, as it
> was made with pork, we sat at the back so that nobody Turkish would see
> us ... The Turkish community isn't as big. Turks' and Germans' work mixed.
> From the beginning, they [Turks] started learning the language. Everybody

210   *Borderlands*

knows each other. There was a big Turkish association. We were close with German neighbours; here [Berlin], people don't know any Germans ... Even the women are different in Bremen. They would collect money and bring in singers and arrange field trips.

Ela, who came to Berlin as a teenager from a smaller German city, also talks about her view of Turks in Berlin: "The criteria are constantly changing on both sides. You have to work hard to keep up. You have to follow both Germany and Türkiye and the issues and concerns of Turks in Germany." She explains about the ranking among Turks in Berlin: those who just arrived, those who grew up here, those who were born here, and those who came as political refugees. She argues that the hierarchy among them is based on how well they know Türkiye and Turkish: "If someone doesn't have mastery of Turkish and a certain knowledge about Türkiye, then they cringe with embarrassment or are excluded. They might leave in order not to be embarrassed and looked down on. They keep their distance. I didn't want to leave or feel embarrassed."

Ela argues that the longer a Turkish person lives in Berlin and the better their Turkish is, the higher their ranking. As someone lacking in both attributes, Ela decided to make the Turkish language her career. She is now a professor of Turkish linguistics.

Standing in a third space can also mean literally going to a different geography – a third city, a third country. Living in a place that is not physically or socially related to Turkishness *or* Germanness gives a German-born Turkish Ausländer an experience different from what they have in Türkiye, Germany, Berlin, or Kreuzberg. In the third place, the inner struggle takes a different turn: "There was no one place I missed, but people, a view, or a tree ... I didn't miss any particular nation, or a country with certain borders ... Homeland wasn't an issue, because there was none. This is not a bad thing, by the way ... If someone can live without a homeland, then maybe it is not vital," Ela concludes.

Here, Ela explains how she questioned the notion of homeland during her stay in Poland, where she realized that she yearned for neither Germany nor Türkiye. A third place can be a way out for Ausländer who are searching to understand why and how they are different and where they belong. Arzu says of her six-month stay in England: "When they asked where I'm from, I always said, 'I am from Germany,' but 'I am Turkish.' My roommate asked if I was proud of being Turkish. 'Why are you telling everyone, emphasizing every time?'" However, Arzu just wanted to ward off the questions that would

Borderlands 211

follow any explanation of what she was. She worried that if she said, "I'm from Germany," people would say, "But your hair is such and such," or "But you don't look German."

Arzu found that in her encounters with English people, they did not really express doubts about her Germanness: "They weren't curious about my Turkishness. It would have been enough if I had said I was German." For the first time, during this stay in England, she realized that she was trying to be something she really was not. She did not feel herself as a Turk who happened to be from Germany. The question "Where do you come from?" did not have the same weight it had in Germany. Clearly, Germany and England are different in terms of their relations and history with their immigrants, as well as their understanding of citizenship.

Arzu talks about a similar encounter in Berlin, this time involving a journalist from Türkiye:

> He asked where I'm from. I said, "My grandparents live in Gaziantep [a city in southeast Türkiye]," as I was used to answering that way. He said, "I'm not asking that. Are you from Berlin?" I was surprised to get this reaction from someone from Türkiye. When Turks ask, "Where you are from?," they mean "Where you are from in Türkiye?" He came from Adana and just wanted to know whether I'm from Berlin. He laughed. "You don't look like someone from Gaziantep."

Arzu speaks of being self-conscious about her Turkishness, since there were not many Turkish families where she grew up. Coming to Berlin and experiencing Kreuzberg was a culture shock for her. She struggled with not being comfortable with either Turkishness or Germanness. A second experience, however, suggested a resolution to her struggle. As a graduate student, she encountered two doctoral students who lived in Türkiye. Through them, she realized that a person can be both German and Turkish and does not need to choose:

> There were two PhD students from Bilkent University. They were born and lived in Germany until they finished high school. Their Turkish was perfect. For the first time, I met people who could speak both Turkish and German, who know both Turkish and German cultures, who could move in both as if they had skates on their feet. I wanted to be like them. Meeting them totally changed my perspective. I started reading Turkish books. I became interested in Turkish. It was recuperative, as if I was sick and it cured me.

212 *Borderlands*

Arzu's third space also involves actual experiences she had in Türkiye, when she started going there as a journalist after the Izmit earthquake in 1999. She comments that after meeting colleagues in Türkiye, she realized that they had a life very similar to hers in Germany. The only real difference was location.

These accounts illustrate how Arzu's thoughts on Türkiye, Turks, and Turkishness have taken shape. She is now able to articulate what being, belonging, and difference mean for her. In the third places, she can gain distance from her lifelong search to understand her own differences.

Similarly, İrem encountered the question of being German or Turkish in a new way when she was in Canada. She talks about how she came to question the binary opposition of Turkishness and Germanness and how this boundary can be blurred:

> For the first time, I thought about this when I was in Canada ... I went there to represent Germany, to assist in a German language course. But ... Turkishness, Turkish values [became important], as if I was there to represent my Turkishness ... Everybody asked me where I come from. I had to decide whether to say where my *parents* are from, Türkiye, or where I am from, Germany and Berlin.

In looking at her experiences in Germany and in Türkiye from this third place, with the subjective distance that physical distance provides, İrem realized that the feeling of belonging changes from location to location:

> In Canada, I asked myself for the first time, What am I? I don't need to do that here in Kreuzberg. I don't feel assigned an identity in Kreuzberg ... But when I was in Canada for a workshop ... and I asked [my Italian friend], "What are you first?," she said, "First I'm Canadian, then I'm Italian." I asked, "How do you call yourself?" "Italian Canadian." I thought, "Unbelievable!" She asked me, "How do you call yourself?" I said, "I don't know" ... I realized that when a German asks, I say I am German to avoid giving them a chance to exclude me. But when a Turkish person asks, I feel embarrassed to say I'm German ... It is a bizarre feeling, maybe because being German is not accepted yet [among Turks].

This third-place encounter made İrem think about her affiliations – about other ways of being and belonging that are not acknowledged in the

Borderlands

simple Turkish/German binary. In the third place, when she searches for belonging, other identities are articulated as well, along with a new sort of Germanness. In the third place, she cannot take belonging to anywhere for granted.

Both Arzu and İrem realized that they experienced the same question differently in different contexts. In the perception of where they are from, locality makes a difference. In a third place, without the German ways of recognition or the participants' experiences as Ausländer, people ask questions differently. When Arzu and İrem are in a third place, they realize that they feel regret about being uncomfortable with their relationship to Germanness.

Homophobia: Fear of Going Home and Becoming Homeless

> Every bit ... [of self-confidence] I'd painstakingly gathered took a beating daily. Nothing in my culture approved of me.
>
> – Anzaldúa ([2007] 1987, 38)

The accounts of LGBTI+ Ausländer reveal that they are marginalized in multiple ways. They live in a borderland of another kind. Erkan, Ayşe, Barış, Müge, and Ayda all talk about how their gender identities are dually understood – as both a disease and a choice – and how they are hidden or silenced in both Türkiye and Berlin. They talk about how they are considered to be contaminated by a specifically "Western illness." They are seen as having chosen to infect themselves with this German disease, to betray their own culture by assimilating into a perverse Other. When he says: "This does not exist in Turkish culture; it never has existed in Islamic culture," Erkan means that Turkish culture and Islam do not recognize or approve of his experience.

Bali Saygılı was the federal appointee for Gays and Lesbians *aus der Türkei* (GLADT).[1] And he serves with the LSVD *(Lesben- und Schwulenverband in Deutschland)*, which is the federal organization for gays and lesbians in Germany.[2] His office handles the needs of gay migrant communities and their families. Whenever he travels to Berlin schools that have many Turkish students, the first reaction to any discussion of gender identities is, "We don't have gays in Türkiye, only in Germany." Erkan sees such denial as related to more than just Middle Eastern or Islamic traditionalism. He feels that oppression of LGBTI+ people in these cultures is "as in Europe, the key means of maintaining gender roles and reproduction."

214   *Borderlands*

In Türkiye, and in any patriarchal society, those who contest patriarchal gender roles are socially disgraced and excluded. *Ibne*, "effeminate men," are deemed sexually perverse because they do not fulfill patriarchal gender roles in public or in private life. Patriarchal Turkish society tolerates only occasional and discreet acts of gay sexuality. Very masculine men are permitted to engage in any sexual activity, because they sustain the stereotype of man as the active and dominant sexual being: "Nobody would consider himself as 'abnormal,' 'perverse,' 'sinful,' let alone 'homosexual,' for fucking an *ibne*" (Bochow 2004, 151). Erkan explains:

> In Türkiye, for military service, gay sexuality is accepted as an illness. If you are gay ... you can be excused from military service. To prove that you are gay, you need to present a document, either a picture or video. In that document, your face and position during the sexual activity should be shown clearly. To prove that this is an illness, you have to have these documents with more than one person. Even more interesting, only if you are passive in the relationship are you considered as homosexual. Then you receive a certificate. To show why you haven't had your military service, you have the document that says the reason is "Psychosexual disorder, homosexuality." And you have to carry this document with you, of course.

However, Erkan challenges the notion that Turkish culture is inherently homophobic. He explains how behaviours in the West that would be considered gay are embedded within Islamic cultures:

> For centuries, gender non-binary relations did exist in Islam and Arab culture. This is not taken into consideration, or it is not found strange. *Hamam* and harem are the places.[3] If it is hidden, it doesn't disturb anyone. Moreover ... [homoerotic relations can] strengthen your manhood. It is not what you did, but your position in the sex act that is about manhood. If you are active, no matter what you do and with whom you do it, you are a man. All the insulting names are for passive men.

In actuality, the Western homosexual-heterosexual binary does not exist in traditional Turkish society. Turkish men often engage in open displays of affection, like kissing and hugging with intimate male friends, which Western heteronormativity would consider gay.

Ayşe also argues that being lesbian and Turkish should not be seen as a paradox: "The first lesbian movie I saw was a Turkish movie. The first books

Borderlands 215

I read on gender non-binary sexuality were in Turkish. The first lesbians I met were Turkish lesbians. So it was not a paradox for me at all. What's more, it wasn't German at all: it was very Turkish." Yet Ayşe acknowledges that lesbians always question their experience in relation to culture. Which culture does it belong to? If sexual orientation does not have a culture, why then is it thought to be connected to a particular culture? As Ayşe explains it:

> The Turkish attitude is that if I don't like something, and it doesn't suit us, it belongs to Germans, *the Others,* who are bad ... If I accept that my child is gay, then I will have to deal with what does Türkiye mean to me ... It is better I don't question these aspects, and I will tell my child that you got this from Germans.

Similarly, DJ and queer activist İpek İpekçioğlu (2003, interview) frames the identity split between gay or lesbian and Turkish as an absurd paradox: "If [LGBTI+ Turks] are perceived to exist, then the heterosexual migrant community considers them as assimilated into the German dominant culture, or as 'fallen out' of the Turkish community and thus 'not a Turk anymore.' But LGBTI+ Germans use the same statement as a compliment – 'You're not Turkish at all!'"

The LGBTI+ participants' subjective negotiations involve their own sexuality and their own levels of acceptance by family and culture. They complain that their families sever financial ties, leaving them impoverished. As a prominent Turkish background LGBTI+ activist, Bali Saygılı, says: "Many times, those with the courage to come out to their parents are those with the luxury to be financially independent." But the fear of abandonment is more than financial for Ausländer gays and lesbians, as they negotiate from the borderlands of being, belonging, and difference. Writer Cem Rifat Sey (2004) would agree that being Turkish and gay or lesbian becomes a struggle that goes beyond just being excluded by family. Anzaldúa ([1987] 2007, 41–42) writes of a similar situation:

> Fear of going home. And not being taken in. We are afraid of being abandoned by the mother, the culture, *la Raza,* for being unacceptable, faulty, damaged. Most of us unconsciously believe that if we reveal this unacceptable aspect of the self, our mother/culture/race will totally reject us.

Many participants who are openly gay or lesbian express this fear of abandonment when they explain the difficulties that Turkish LGBTI+ people in

Germany have in coming out. For them, there is no moving away and finding a new home. Erkan explains how homelessness is different for Germans and Turks: "A queer German, born in a village, can move to a big city when their family doesn't accept them. In the city, they have a friendship circle to replace family ... and they continue their familiar life." Because LGBTI+ Germans by definition belong to the dominant German culture, they can easily find a substitute family within LGBTI+ communities, which reproduce the dominant culture and aesthetic. As İpek İpekçioğlu (2003) writes, even if they have to leave their biological family, Germans are not losing access to their culture and their positive self-image. For Turkish LGBTI+ people, however, family exclusion means losing access to the social connections to the family and to the migrant community that reproduces their culture of origin.

Due to a lack of alternative communities, Turkish LGBTI+ people commonly move further into self-isolation. Coming out transforms them into aliens – both in the mainstream German culture and in their migrant culture: "When you leave your parents, you cannot go to your relatives in Turkish culture. If I'm a problem for my parents, close relatives side with them. I also lose my religion, language, literature, and music" (Ayşe). As soon as they leave their family, they lose parents, siblings, and all their ties with Türkiye – with everything that is familiar to them. They are denied their roots and their identity. When they go to Türkiye without the approval of their families, whom will they visit? Where will they stay? They cannot do the things that German queers can easily do.

Saygılı observes that socialization leaves a unique imprint on gay Turks' views of their own sexuality, which many German counsellors have difficulty understanding: "Even today, many Turks who come out still think of their sexuality as somehow a disease." This shapes their self-confidence, lifestyle choices, and behaviour patterns. One study (Salman 1992) found that 64 percent of Turkish parents would rather their children were alcoholics (21 percent would prefer heroin addicts) than gay. According to another survey (Mercan 2004), when Turkish children come out as gay or lesbian, 38 percent of their parents ensure that the children get married, and 23 percent send them to a psychologist. As a result, as Barış, who is a social worker specializing in immigrant background LGBTI+ youth, observes: "Many attempt to mask the double lives they lead – as sexually active members of the gay community and as upstanding men of the Turkish community, sometimes as husbands and fathers."

Borderlands   217

Due to the profound personal and social toll of coming out, the vast majority of gay Turkish Ausländer in Germany maintain the taboo of silence and remain in the closet. Hakan Tandoğan, an organizer of the oldest and most successful gay Turkish dance event, *Gayhane* (gay house), looks back at his own coming out: "In the beginning, everybody led a double life." Many gay Turks remain in the closet to their families but come out in the gay community as they attempt to balance double lives as both gay men *and* good Turkish sons or brothers. Their sexuality is intensely restricted to private or anonymous gay spaces like underground bars, virtual chat-rooms, and private parties. The choice to be out in the gay community but not at home is sometimes painful and isolating, but they believe it is necessary.

Germans often find it difficult to accept the double lives of their Turkish partners, the paramount importance of their families, their taboos of silence, or their divergent expectations about coming out. In many cases, the German boyfriends of gay Turkish Ausländer do not understand why it is essential for their partners to keep the public and private sides separate. Instead of confronting these cultural misunderstandings, many gay Turks choose to pursue relationships exclusively with Turks: "A Turkish boyfriend understands all the little things that he had to explain to German partners all the time," Barış expresses.

When Saygılı came out, in Munich, in the 1980s, the gay mainstream society did not embrace gay Turks out of "fear and skepticism of foreign cultures." Saygılı regrets that Turks "still face racism in the [gay] scene" based on the criminal stereotypes of Turks as "pickpockets or callboys." A former board member of GLADT, Tarkan, believes that hidden racism or misperceptions of racism are a significant cause of breakups among inter-ethnic couples. Moreover, gay Turks point to openly racist policies at certain gay bars and clubs, which refuse to let Turks through the doors.

Gay Turks also experience exoticization, a form of "positive discrimination," according to Erkan. The German gay mainstream commonly ascribes certain attractive racial stereotypes to gay Turks. One needs look no further than the back-page personal ads of *box.de* magazine to see the fetishization of gay Turks in Germany – as dominant, bisexual, hairy, exotic lovers who act out the fantasies of ethnic Germans. Dating a Turk can be perceived as something special. Suat's German boyfriend introduced him to his German friends as "my cute little Turk." Erkan argues that such exoticization and objectification by the gay mainstream pigeonholes Turkish-background gays in the inferior role of exotic lovers or one-night-stands, and not as serious romantic partners. However, Bali Saygılı believes that the use of exoticized stereotypes, as well as racism against gay Turks, has diminished within the gay mainstream over the past twenty years.

Erkan explains that Turkish-background gays are a minority within a minority and, therefore, doubly homeless. Because of their sexual orientations, they are excluded from their mother culture. When they choose to live among German gay and lesbians, they are still subject to a different exclusion as an ethnic minority. When they claim, "My problems are different," they are held responsible for weakening the LGBTI+ cause, because "we LGBTI+ people have our common cause." Erkan continues: "Maybe you do not accept the common cause, such as the right to adopt a child, because your problems are totally different from theirs."

Barış feels that the problems of gay Turkish Germans exemplify the compounded forms of discrimination that cut across different minority and majority groups: racism and Islamophobia from the German heterosexual and gay community, and homophobia from the heterosexual German and Turkish migrant communities. It seems clear that Turkish LGBTI+ Ausländer belong to two societies, German and Turkish, and to certain gender minorities (LGBTI+), and that these various categories are deemed mutually exclusive. Such people seldom feel at home in any of these communities. To be accepted by one group, they are expected to reject the other(s), but they cannot.

Through negotiations of sexuality, ethnicity, and race, many participants make these parallel societies into borderland realities. Through their sexuality – which cannot be separated from ethnicity, race, or Ausländerness – they are forging a kind of belonging that recognizes openly gay Turkish men and women as full members of the societies they live in. While claiming their multiple, fluid sense of belonging and while facing double discrimination, they ask how they can open up this borderland, so that their multiple abandonments and compound discriminations can be frankly confronted.

Politicization of Subjective Struggle

When I was younger, not being regarded as a Turk did not bother me, but not being regarded as a [German] did. I wanted to belong, you know?

– Fatma

I believed that injustice and unfair treatment were all because I was Turkish.

– Arzu

Borderlands 219

At an early age, Ausländer children such as Fatma and Arzu, regardless of whether they were born in Germany, discover that Ausländer have few or even no legal rights. They realize that they may be characterized as less intelligent, as immoral, or even as subhuman. They have to work through the fact that they are the Other, that they do not belong, that they are different in fundamental ways. Teenagers are especially prone to reacting defiantly – often with provocative public behaviour. Selin explains: "They are saying, 'You don't like me anyway, so I don't care if you're offended.'" Nevertheless, they develop a strong sense of who they are. Fatma sees having all of these difficult experiences as a privilege: "If I hadn't, I wouldn't have questioned life, people, and being a woman as much."

For German-born Ausländer, this sort of struggle is internal, but it is played out in the external world. They know that awareness of their situation must come first from within; only then can there be changes in society. Anzaldúa ([1987] 2007, 109) says: "Nothing happens in the real world unless it first happens in the images in our heads." My analysis shows that diasporic people learn to situate themselves in history and in the contexts of their own experiences, so they can work through what is expected of them and determine what is just and fair. In this process, they come to know how to react. When asked for a definition of themselves, their responses recall Fanon's answer ([1952] 1967, 120): "I am one who waits; I investigate my surroundings, I interpret everything in terms of what I discover, I become sensitive." By working through their experiences, Ausländer gain a "stubborn will" (Anzaldúa [1987] 2007, 38).

The participants explain how they came to see that something was not right with how they were identified and expected to belong. They began to see that their responsibility was not to accept but to confront the situations they were placed in. Their confrontations began when they asked questions of themselves: "Is there such a thing as being like this, or is this something imposed on me?," as Ela states.

The participants argue they should determine their own issues, starting from themselves, not from what is expected of them. This struggle, they find, is political. Erkan explains:

> Individuals should solve things in their own minds so that a healthy solution for their identity can be possible. We have to transform this struggle into confidence. We have to determine our outlook, our world view, not starting from the majority but starting from ourselves ... We do this not because it is right, wrong, good, or bad, but because it is our own experi-

ence. This is not going to happen tomorrow. You have to make both the majority and the so-called minority accept this. First, you have to accept this yourself, and start from yourself to change the prejudices.

German-born Ausländer learn to distinguish their own understandings and experiences from the interpretations imposed on them by the groups and societies around them. The contradictions they see become resources for understanding how their struggles have affected them, how they can turn these struggles to their advantage, and how they can mobilize cultural capital to change their social and political surroundings.

Erkan's awareness has been influenced by his family's commitments to political consciousness and education: "I always have been political. It comes from my family. I always thought about the alternative ... It comes from my grandfather ... He used to provoke us to think." The acquisition of inner resources is a kind of cultural capital. As Bourdieu (1986) defines it, cultural capital represents the total of non-economic forces, such as family background, social class, education, and the various other resources that influence academic success. The diversity of diasporic lives can provide cultural capital.

The participants' narratives suggest how they can use their experiences of social inequality to their advantage. Reflecting on the inequalities they face is a matter of investing in self-understanding. Tunç explains his steps to becoming a political activist:

> I was going to become a soccer player, but I didn't have parental support. They were working, and they didn't have much to do with my life. They didn't know what I was doing outside ... Toward the end of 1980s ... I saw someone at school [doing graffiti]. I decided to try and I was hooked ... What we wanted was for people to see the graffiti at subway stations or on the walls in this space [Kreuzberg]. While I was doing graffiti, I met many artists, painters, directors. That led to my career in film.

Not always, but often, the sources of cultural capital include parental guidance and encouragement. Conflicts with family members and others can also generate capital. Many participants relate their initial involvement in personal activism to turning points in their family relations. Their families were often obstacles. In other cases, as in Erkan's, being critical was part of family life. Consciously or unconsciously, they grew up with cultural and social criticism, which turned into political criticism. Those experien-

Borderlands

ces became another kind of capital. Sociologist Nira Yuval-Davis (1997, 78; 2006) found that many feminists start out with an assumption that the public sphere is political, whereas the private sphere is a family domain, and women supposedly belong to the private sphere. Their transformation into feminists begins when the private sphere becomes political.

The struggle for critical awareness opens up the capacity to imagine alternatives. One might imagine a future in which German-born Turkish Ausländer form solidarities with people who are not like them, yet share their concerns. However, the struggles to realize their dreams in the real world often bring on *the worst* – strife, obstacles, fear, and hostility. In such struggle, dreamers seldom find ready support. But even if they cannot find anyone who supports them, the options of laziness, acceptance of inferior status, weakness, or surrender seem unacceptable. Most participants develop their skills as activists by proposing counter-arguments, going their own way, and questioning their own positions. Erkan describes some of his struggles:

> My German is perfect. My English is much better than my Turkish. I know some French, Spanish, and Italian. But speaking German much better than many Germans doesn't render me a German. In fact, I'm an exceptional Turk ... I cannot be ... an ordinary citizen. Indeed, doing ordinary things makes me extraordinary. This is first. The second thing is that as a person from Türkiye, when we criticize the Turkish state, government, culture, or Islam's patriarchal society, we are criticized by the Türkiyeli community. "How dare you criticize our country, homeland, state, traditions, and culture!" Because when we criticize these, it strengthens the prejudices against us. The Westerners see us as a big threat, and when you say LGBTI+ and women are oppressed, you strengthen their prejudices ... For example, you are forced to wear a headscarf, or you are told how bad the homosexuals are ... In my opinion, those oppressions must be revealed. Even though it strengthens the prejudices of the Westerners ... we have to tell the realities and be honest. To only protect Islam and to ignore the rights of the people in Muslim countries is a big injustice.

Erkan feels himself enmeshed in a complex, multi-sided struggle with a mix of demands and expectations coming from different sides. While being considered a representative of the Other culture, Erkan struggles to claim that "I belong here."

To a certain extent, the participants embrace Turkish, Anatolian culture. To have a healthy personality, they must say, "This is my culture." To deny it is to deny a real part of themselves. Even if they do not want it, they are considered representatives of that culture. However, their responses to cultural hegemonies take the form of a larger shift outward, to an articulation of a diasporic identity and the development of political subjectivity.

Many participants discuss how they have learned to negotiate among several layers of narratives. They tell their stories about discovering racist narratives. They articulate the marginalizations they have known. Their inner struggles change into a social struggle against being Othered. These people are thrown into situations where they must constantly think about their issues of identity. They become conscious that binary oppositions are artificial, and they realize that cultural identities are dynamic. Alp claims that because most Germans do not face these challenges, "German youth don't have such life experiences."

Most of the participants put a lot of energy into understanding the fluidity of identity. They play with identity as with playdough. Arzu, for example, has multiple identities: "When [Germans] denigrate Turks, I feel bad or try to defend them. When I'm in Türkiye, when people talk nonsense about Germans, I want to defend them. Both are important, and both flow into each other in me." Arzu and many other participants do not view cultures as separate entities, each in its own box with well-defined boundaries. Similarly, Milczarek-Desai (2002, 134) argues that people who are children of two cultures cannot think in such a polarized way. Turkish and German have been spilling into each other all their lives. The flexibility of identity is for them a source of hope that the future will be different.

I have discussed how participants negotiate Turkishness and Germanness. Being both Turkish and German, they attempt to find a third space, geographically, symbolically, or discursively. Understanding their negotiation with cultural identities is crucial to understanding their political claims.

When diasporic subjects struggle to reconcile competing discourses, it can result in what Bhabha (1994, 98, 131) refers to as a "splitting" of discourse, culture, and consciousness. This splitting is both problematic and productive. It can result in anxious subjects who struggle to achieve a strong sense of self but who must always rearticulate themselves in response to an Other. At the same time, such struggle for identity and selfhood is how "newness enters the world" (212).

If people are not constantly defined in relation to a dominant discourse, the struggle between and within different communities of discourse can become a productive hybrid cultural space. The third space is a bridge between all the places of belonging. It provides opportunities for hearing voices that

Borderlands 223

are typically marginalized. The third space supports diasporic subjects in exploring multiple sources of being and belonging. That space can be a site of cultural, social, and epistemological change, in which competing discourses are brought into conversation, and everyday relations can be challenged and reshaped. Encounters in the third space promote skills in critical awareness, as the German-born Turkish Ausländer move toward new identities. A third space that fosters these changes is one where everyday encounters are integrated with citizenship claims to construct new diasporic communities.

Conclusion: Ways of Belonging

> Every increment of consciousness, every step forward is a *travesía*, a crossing. I am again an alien in new territory. And again, and again. But if I escape conscious awareness, escape knowing, I won't be moving ... Knowing is painful because after it happens I can't stay in the same place and be comfortable. I am no longer the same person I was before.
>
> – Anzaldúa ([1987] 2007, 70), *emphasis in original*

In this chapter, I have analyzed how German-born Turkish Ausländer establish their unique belonging in borderlands as they work through their diasporic experiences. Their narratives of belonging in a borderland lead to self-discoveries and new social practices, which contribute to the political evolution of diasporic citizens. These narratives show how the discourses of displacement, in-betweenness, and belonging in a third space give rise to new, creative ways of belonging and relating.

The participants' criticisms regarding binary ways of understanding identity lead them beyond the comforts of traditional belonging. The lifestyles they choose are related to identities that tend to be subordinate to Germanness. These kinds of subordination arise from long histories of displacement and estrangement. Still, these Ausländer are marked by a profound sense of belonging to Germany and of having helped to build it. Although they may feel intimidated by Germany, at the same time they embrace it. They are altered by Germany, and they alter it. They have found ways to live with and accept their many identities. By challenging what is imposed on them, they have demonstrated that there is more than one way to create identity. Their ongoing struggle inspires a new kind of citizenship, which is the topic of the next chapter.

6 Forging Diasporic Citizenship

In the past, citizenship was largely a matter of civic responsibility within territorial administrative units. The boundaries of such units delimited the scope of civic identity and accountability. This kind of citizenship called for constricted loyalties and state-defined social identities. This chapter describes the emergence of a different kind of citizenship, which is based on the initiatives of people whose communities transcend political boundaries. In particular, this chapter examines the strategies that German-born Turkish Ausländer use to challenge traditional assumptions of identity, difference, and belonging. Through their everyday social acts, the participants are exploring the power of diasporicity, which nationality alone cannot grant. Just to reiterate, diasporicity is a quality of people who do not fit neatly into a nation-defined population. These people commonly show a kind of awareness that comes from a transnational, transborder perspective. I analyze how the participants redefine themselves in their social encounters through exerting their qualities of diasporicity. Investigating these encounters helps us to reveal the realities of diasporants' lives. Their experiences offer insights into how transnational people can, as Bakhtin (1993, 31) suggests, remake their world through promoting self-awareness. This kind of self-awareness is the catalyst and the muse for people to become diasporic citizens. Diasporicity is a fuel that incites the acts and practices of becoming political for a more inclusive community. Diasporic citizenship involves a

Forging Diasporic Citizenship 225

mode of being political by which Ausländer create moments of rupture in "the naturalness of the dominant virtues" (Isin 2002a, 275). By such ruptures in the prevailing context, they call the arbitrariness of ethnocentric standards into question.

Attributes of Diasporic Citizens

> I look at the ponytailed girl in a beige trench coat in the commercial posters and think to myself, I used to believe that when, one day, when I speak German really well, if I become very successful, I will become like this girl. When I was younger, I used to think I will become like them [Germans], one day. If you think about it, I do not have much in common with that girl. I don't dress like her, I don't look like her, but I still am waiting for that day that I will be like her ... When I look at myself from the outside as I'm thinking these thoughts, it is sad. But it is also kind of funny ... Maybe it is because one needs to live through the experience and think about it to really understand it. [When I was in my twenties,] I could comprehend [the social reasons behind] it, but it was only a heavy feeling, like envy or self-consciousness. But I am not sure if I was able to think about the social reasons behind it.
>
> – Arzu

Arzu is in her forties (in 2016) and is now better able to analyze her old feelings and doubts, as if from an outside viewpoint. Her lived experience provides a perspective that reveals how her feelings are more than personal emotions. They are also social, political, and perhaps universal aspects of experience that all of us need to deal with.

In this section, I analyze how the participants' everyday life experiences create a subjective understanding of what it means to be a political being. In other words, I look at how diasporicity transpires, turning what might look like a psychological state into a kind of political consciousness. Through experiencing estrangement and proximation (on the hostility-hospitality axis), these diasporants cultivate a capacity to recognize the everyday politics of the dominant discourses. They realize how these discourses have caused their own categorization, misrecognition, and marginalization. In response to that awareness, they renegotiate their displacement (on the homelessness–homesickness axis). Over time, they develop a mode of civic life that is suited to their own diasporic borderlands.

A diasporic citizen is *a practical reader* of the land (i.e., lands such as Berlin, Germany, Türkiye), of its associated features of identity (i.e., Germanness, Turkishness) and of belonging. These citizens express issues that are difficult to put into words (see Hall 2017). That kind of ability to read the land and its people is initially "nurtured as a tactic of survival" (Hall 2017, 203). Then, the awareness that diasporants cultivate becomes an intellectual/occupational motivation. Pursuing their concerns and insights puts them on a political trajectory. In finding their voices, they discover a sort of homecoming to what they are and can become. In this struggle, the German-born Turkish Ausländer are forging diasporic citizenship. Their stories or accounts will illustrate the awareness I call diasporicity and how it creates diasporic citizens.

Becoming Decisive and Assertive

When I left for England, I never wanted to come back [to Germany]. My being here was not my decision, but my mother's. I didn't like Germany ... And during a year-long au-pair program, I questioned my relationship with Germany ... But then, I realized that hearing German made me happy. I missed it. I appreciated, indeed, that German is a nice language ... Also, I realized that I could best advance my education in Germany. I asked, Do I feel close to Germany? Do I want to go back? My answer was yes, I do. So this is my re-migration here, as my own decision. My relation with Germany and the German language has changed after that. My anti-political attitude has disappeared. I came out as a lesbian. I felt comfortable to experience a lesbian lifestyle in a German community.

– Ayşe

Many of the participants describe how they came to change themselves and their relations to society. They have become practical readers and interpreters of their experiences. They describe how their initial reading of Germany and the German language has changed. Through learning from their encounters with the dominant stereotypes that previously defined who they were, they have cultivated a different awareness. For Ayşe, becoming decisive meant a practical re-reading and re-evaluating of her situation, which turned externally imposed choices into new choices of her own. Looking at her experience from the outside allowed Ayşe to decide again and *re-migrate* to Germany. At the same time, she emerged as a political agent for social change.

Forging Diasporic Citizenship 227

Sometimes, a particular event has a life-changing influence on a whole group or on public life in general. For example, the post-unification racist attacks spurred a new level of political activity and self-awareness for many Ausländer. Both İrem and Fatma explain that a particular murder – namely that of Mete Ekşi, who was beaten to death in 1992 by a neo-Nazi at *Adenauerplatz* in Ku'damm – spurred them to become social activists. İrem reports,

> I became political after the murder of a Turkish guy. It was 1992. I was eighteen ... We arranged a peace night for him. This was my first political activity. I never knew him. We learned later that he was coming from a conservative Turkish nationalist family ... We invited a Kurdish singer. But Mete's friends reacted to the Kurdish songs. Ironically, the night ended with a fight. Mete made me decide to be involved in the Turkish Parents' Association ... I'm also involved in the anti-racism caucus in the Alevi association.

In some cases, personal events have led the participants to political decisions that involve great personal risk. Barış had to decide whether to make his gay identity public, although he could lose his family and all relation to his homeland. Still, he knew that making LGBTI+ people visible in the diaspora was important for opening a space for acceptance in both the German and Turkish public spheres:

> In 1986, I was in Munich. We decided to attend CSD [Christopher Street Day]. I organized the "foreign background" part with Spanish and Italian groups, under the German LGBTI+ association. Journalists from the *Sueddeutsche Zeitung* and the *Frankfurter Allgemeine Zeitung* [internationally known papers from southern Germany] interviewed me and asked if they could use my real name. I said, "Yes, people should hear my name" without hesitating. But I never thought of the possible problems that would follow ... My older brothers, who didn't know I was gay, also read these papers. But I thought, "Let it be." I'm living by myself, and I'm responsible for my own acts ... Still, I didn't want to lose the love of my family, whose compassion I value the most.

As political subjects, İrem and Barış felt forced to make decisions in moments of crisis, when identities needed to be re-created. As Howarth and Stavrakakis (2000, 14; emphasis in original) explain: "It is in the process of this *identification* that political subjectivities are created and formed. Once formed and stabilized, they become those subject positions which 'produce' individuals with certain characteristics and attributes." Tunç describes his motives for taking on an assertive outlook. He now regards German-born Turkish Ausländer as members of a "club of challengers." They are different from one another in many ways, because of the choices they've made, but their lifestyles have become primary sites for contestation as they encounter others in society. This is how the personal becomes political. These people's confrontations and encounters in the course of everyday life evoke struggles that are both personal and social. They feel a need to deal with the complexity of their family histories and to claim their own hybrid worlds.

The participants' immigrant backgrounds – together with their personal accomplishments and their ethnic, class, racial, gender, and sexual identities – are interwoven into a tapestry of lived experience. For people of multiple identities, that sort of tapestry emanates diasporicity. The wisdom they gain from their experience becomes a form of social capital, which they can use to challenge the identities imposed on them. As they gain self-confidence, being political becomes more possible and, perhaps, even easy. Some of the participants become like Anzaldúa's ([1987] 2007, 86) mestizas and mestizos – "stubborn, persevering, impenetrable as stone, yet possessing a malleability that renders us unbreakable." Increasingly, diasporants become intolerant of ideologies that first create people as Othered minorities and then oppress them. In reacting against such ideologies of dominance, some of the participants go to war.

Of course, these people are aware that just being part of a minority does not necessarily make them right. Those they protest against also have shifting identities. In negotiating an unpredictable social landscape, these citizens find themselves "balancing on a thin string," as Barış puts it. In many cases, they find ways to weave the elements of their struggles into their work, reshaping their vocations and professions.

My analysis shows that the participants' understandings of social activism and political resistance differ from those of the more conventional activists. Rather than pursuing some definite end, these participants are evolving forms of resistance that can be incorporated into everyday life. They craft acts and practices to express who they are and how they belong in response to their constant, careful reading of the social landscape. They try to do this in a firm, honest way, standing up for themselves in the face of estrangement or confrontation. They deliberately and repeatedly practice

Forging Diasporic Citizenship

their acts of resistance and assertiveness, until these ways of responding become part of their personalities. For example, the Christian Democratic Union (CDU), which is the second-largest political party in Germany, has a very strict position on the citizenship law. It might be expected that no Turkish German could become a leader in this party. However, when Erkan calls for interrogating the boundaries of the CDU, he urges a kind of assertiveness that might change this party from within:

> Things can only change by immigrants being bolder and more demanding and saying, "I have rights for this." If I can't say that I want to do politics in the CDU, the CDU will never invite me to be with them. If I go there, force their boundaries, and expand their understanding, then they will start thinking. This is being activist ... We need more people doing this, so that German culture can change, grow flexible, and soften.

In this practical reading of a social issue, Erkan shows the vitality of redefining citizenship and of challenging what it means to be German. He dares to imagine the possibility of a flexible and even softened, compassionate German culture.

Ela defines integration differently from its usual interpretation. She aims to reclaim disadvantaged status as an advantage, thus turning a negative into a positive. She explains how she overcame her difficulty in claiming full membership in Berlin's Turkish community, due to her weak grasp of the Turkish language:

> I grew up in small places in Germany. We never had any Turkish family around us. After I came to Berlin, I entered into a Turkish community for the first time ... It was difficult, because their existence was different and I didn't know their rules. My Turkish was bad. I felt crushed, as I wasn't able to express myself. It meant being oppressed for me ... If you can't express yourself, other spokespersons emerge around you. I didn't want to give up my right to communicate.

After her experience of being unable to speak for herself, Ela decided to improve her Turkish. She wanted to show her strengths, not only to Germans but also to Turks. At university, she chose Turkish as her major: "I made being Turkish my job, working with Turkish people in any way, linguistically, sociologically." Ela sees her assertiveness as more than a matter of reclaiming her right to speak for herself. She also feels strongly about turning the Turkish language into a vocational asset that can give her a competitive edge within both German and Turkish circles: "We have to use this as a positive aspect of changing it from being a disadvantage ... When we get into a competition with Germans, if we are working with anything Turkish, economics, politics, or language, we will be stronger and better."

Active use of the Turkish language, which Turkish Ausländer have always nurtured as a survival tactic, became a motivating focus for Ela and eventually redirected her life's trajectory. For her, raising the profile of the Turkish language seemed more important than finding her own voice. In seeking to help other Ausländer find a greater voice, she found a new sense of being *at home* in Germany.

The perspective that comes with being a German-born Turkish Ausländer tends to enable or even force these people to reach creative decisions for enacting their diasporicity. As postcolonial theorist Chela Sandoval (2000, 15) argues, social assertiveness is driven by the ability to "read the current situation of power" and then "self-consciously ... [adopt] the ideological form best suited to push against its configurations." Behind this capacity lies what Sandoval calls "differential consciousness." On one hand, this involves an awareness of being discriminated against. On the other hand, it involves awareness that one's own life and way of being has a wider, even universal, significance.

Disrupting One's Own Politics

Maybe usual social movements like the May 1 protests are not meaningful any longer.[1] Because no society suits these movements any longer ... The content of being oppressed has changed, and these mass movements don't reflect our experiences any longer. There are many differences within and among women, workers, and LGBTI+ people. Once, one of the slogans on May 1 was "You don't need to bring workers from abroad; give work to Germans first." Why should I be in this protest?

– Erkan

Erkan explains that his strategies for change have less to do with being inclusive than with being reflexive and accountable. Diasporic activists call for reflexivity and accountability due to their struggles with their own prejudices. Those struggles stem from the awareness of having multiple experiences that do not peacefully coexist. For diasporic citizens, the struggle for self-awareness is an ongoing process. Leslie Sanders, African Americana and Black Canadian literature professor (2001, 176), argues that in this process of change, the sense of "responsibility is continual, it is expressed in what we buy, in where we shop, in what causes we choose to support, in what we say or do not say to friends and acquaintances." Responsibility (in terms of "responding well to others") requires reflexivity, which social worker and anti-racism activist Fairn Herising (2005, 136–37) describes as a resistance to generalizations and monolithic truth claims. Such a recognition – that all knowledge is tentative – is a necessary part of responsible political positioning. For filmmaker, literary theorist, and professor Trinh Minh-ha (1991, 12), reflexivity is a practice whereby we "interrogate the truthfulness of the tale, and provide multiple answers." Reflexivity subjects the politics of everyday life to serious examination.

In reflecting on his various struggles, Erkan argues that "being oppressed doesn't make you a good person. Someone might be both gay and racist, or sexist." In that case: "You have to struggle not only with your group ... but also with yourself to overcome that prejudice. You have to become conscious about it." For Erkan, a politics of accountability cannot proceed on the assumption that just because we practice some sort of activism or invest in a form of resistance, we are innocent of subordinating others. Accountability, as Sherene Razack (1998, 10; emphasis in original) defines it, requires "a recognition that we are implicated in systems of oppression that profoundly structure our understanding of one another." The ethics of accountability involve "exploring the histories, social relations, and conditions that structure groups unequally in relation to one another and *that shape what can be known, thought, and said.*"

Diasporic accountability reflects the apparent contradiction between seeing identity as socially constructed in multiple ways and maintaining that, nonetheless, there are identifiable oppressed groups. For example, as Fanon ([1952] 1967) noted, there is "a fact of Blackness." Therefore, while it is important to acknowledge that we are all simultaneously both dominant and subordinate, it is also important to realize the danger behind a postmodern understanding of difference, according to which all positions have equal validity, and there is no basis for judging that some people are being oppressed by others. As Razack argues, to declare that all people are simultaneously dominant and subordinate ignores the social hierarchies that exist in each social situation: "Such a response amounts to a statement that race

232   *Forging Diasporic Citizenship*

does not matter, an outright denial of the impact of white supremacy on the lives of people of colour" (Razack 1998, 161). Therefore, the self-questioning process must not lead to self-invalidation.

The politics of accountability involve "a recognition that we are each implicated in systems of oppression that profoundly structure our understanding of one another" (Razack 1998, 10). Razack (1998) adds that this kind of accountability involves tracing relations of privilege and penalty in a search for understanding on how we are complicit in the subordination of others. Such accountability requires asking questions about how we understand differences and what purposes those understandings serve (159, 170). Answering those questions requires "calculating not only who can speak and how they are likely to be heard but also how we know what we know and the interest we protect through our knowing" (10). Because systems of domination interlock and sustain one another, the political projects of diasporic citizenship can proceed only if diasporic citizens recognize their own habits of dominance and complicity. As Erkan says, we need to identify those moments when we are dominant and when we are subordinate.

In discussing the conflicting priorities seen in the May 1 demonstrations, Erkan notes that people can fight oppression while oppressing others at the same time. He urges people to examine the social hierarchies around them. That kind of accountability involves a process of self-analysis. Erkan asks himself, as an activist, to consider how he positions himself – to consider whether he is acting as a rescuer of those less fortunate. He therefore urges activists to reach beyond the contests for superiority that have commonly characterized the politics of inclusion.

During my fieldwork in 2003, the GLADT was invited to join other groups on an advisory commission to discuss a new anti-discrimination law. For the first time, the TBB (Turkish Organization of Berlin-Brandenburg, an umbrella organization for Turkish immigrants) invited GLADT's members to serve on such a panel of community leaders. This was a major step forward in acknowledging that discrimination is complex and multi-levelled. Previously, when planning how to draft the proposed law, the Berlin government had thought only in terms of ethnicity. It expected the advisory commission to include representatives from ethnic organizations and felt that this would deal with inclusivity. GLADT argued that the proposed law should not have a single focus, such as discrimination on the basis of ethnicity, age, sexual orientation, or race. Instead, the new law should recognize multiple discriminations. A GLADT representative explains:

Forging Diasporic Citizenship 233

> Even oppressed groups oppress those who are different among themselves. This is difficult to accept. If they oppress others among themselves, they do not deserve our solidarity even though they are oppressed. This situation makes thoughts, struggles, and being an activist difficult. We used to think if someone is oppressed, we have to be in solidarity.

Acknowledging this type of complexity challenges the logic of binary opposition and stereotyping. It changes the understanding of oppressed and oppressor, and it acknowledges the complexity of discrimination. The GLADT representative's position reminds me of Lowe's argument (2003, 132) that for patterns of hegemony to be transformed, alliances must be formed across lines of race, ethnicity, national origin, class, gender, and sexuality. Only such alliances – which require diasporic awareness – can expose the arbitrariness of all social barriers. Smith (1998, 124) argues: "Every individual is positioned vis-à-vis an irreducible plurality of communities and traditions, and ... every resistance is fashioned out of the traces of oppositional traditions."

My analysis supports the view that resistance, consciousness, and alternative discourses emerge from acknowledging and challenging multiple power relations. The multiplicity of differences and inequalities of and within classes, cultures, ethnicities, races, religions, and sexualities crosscuts the daily experiences of diasporic identity, structuring the ways that citizenship confers privileges.

A diasporic approach to accountability demands self-imposed responsibility, as those who can speak and be heard seek to identify with those who are absent or erased. In this kind of interchange, people can hold each other accountable for practices that benefit some but not others. Being accountable as a diasporic citizen means carrying the burden of challenging detrimental practices and recognizing the power that significations assign. So, for example, it is not the mere fact that someone is racialized as white that is relevant to identity and difference, but that their whiteness signifies privilege. This privileged signification benefits all those signified as white, regardless of whether this privilege is consciously exercised to impact people who are racialized or marginalized. Through exercising accountability in daily life and in public deliberation, it becomes possible to build alliances that are not dependent on presumably fixed identity markers but rather on shared commitments to finding mutual benefit.

Naturally, such accountability requires some level of action. For example, a movement for accountability can require the government to apologize

234

and provide restitution for those who have suffered from neo-Nazi attacks. Answerability requires transparency, with public acknowledgment of the injury done and of the ways that some have benefited from the injury of others.

At times, the acts and practices of accountability may be contentious. This, however, is part of the process of disrupting and challenging hegemonic systems for constructing identity and difference. Without contention, there is no discomfort, doubt, or anxiety, whereas uncomfortable, uncertain, and anxious encounters can disrupt prevailing assumptions about difference and identity. Nevertheless, the goal in causing discomfort is not to permanently silence people but to provoke critical self-reflection.

To practice this kind of accountability in the course of daily social life is an ambitious project. However, this kind of practice offers diasporic citizens a means of direct engagement, as opposed to appealing for institutionalized projects of inclusion such as government-backed integration or multiculturalism policies. Diasporic citizens want something more than official inclusion. The notion of inclusion begins with the premise that there is a core identity or a norm that others wish to belong to. Efforts for such inclusion tend to ignore the power dynamics behind the process of determining what is considered the norm. By contrast, the practice of direct accountability seeks to identify and disturb how meanings are structured in the first place. This approach involves finding the means of exposing, unsettling, and challenging the power of hegemonic meaning-making.

Critical self-analysis and self-awareness, along with decisiveness, assertiveness, reflexivity, and accountability, appear to be prerequisites for confronting and overcoming oppressions, prejudices, and their accompanying problems. Nothing is gained by flattening out ambivalent power relations or reducing them into a tidy binary of Ausländer versus Germans. Diasporic experiences are more complicated, fragmented, and blurred than that. Many patterns of subjugation persist in modern society, but at times, they are disrupted by German-born Turkish Ausländer who question these social and spatial boundaries. In these interactions, the dominant discourses are challenged, introducing a basis for renegotiating how people relate (Foucault 1978; McNay 2000; Stoler 1995; R. Young 1995).

Embracing Ambivalence and Resisting Labels

> We are so much in the life itself. Is it that easy to step outside of it even one foot and look at the past? Now [in 2016] I have two children, but is that the most important change that has happened in my life [since 2003]? We find

Forging Diasporic Citizenship

or pick something and make it stand for something but ... the details matter. I find it difficult to make things certain. Leaving room for uncertainty does not give you a clear course of action, so you have to choose some certainties to act on, but this is a significant difficulty, I think ... That's a fantasy.

– Arzu

Turkish Berliners have long resisted the labels placed on them. They have sought connection in a space between homesickness and homelessness. The participants insisted that I should capture their diversities at all levels. Many of them expressed a need for learning how to resist being labelled as one thing – as Turkish, as youths, or as immigrants. This kind of concern is what I refer to as claiming *ambivalence*. Ambivalence refers to the presence of conflicting ideas, attitudes, or emotions – a feeling of uncertainty. The sense of ambivalence indicates situations where steps can be taken toward forging alternatives. However, the sense of ambivalence also provides experience that is useful for mapping the complex structures of dominant discourses. A discordance of perspectives opens the situation to renegotiation. For Ausländer, ambivalence is especially strong when they seek to claim positions on the axis of homelessness–homesickness.

Ambivalence presents the participants with a double challenge. The first is to trespass into the centre of the dominant discourse. The second challenge is to bring their own backgrounds, languages, and idioms into this new sphere. With their sense of ambivalence, these diasporants claim the land and identity of the dominant community in Germany – by claiming that the dominant spaces and identities are just as ambivalent as their own. Haunted by their decentred selves, they seek to understand their condition and explain it to others. They face the ambivalence of their social encounters. In their confrontations with upholders of the dominant context, the participants tend to practice disruption and ambivalence as much as assertiveness and accountability.

The participants' ambivalence is informed by the multiplicity and fluidity of their identities, belongings, and differences, and by the hierarchies of ranking among them. Their accounts reveal how the conflicts among these identities entail what Derrida (1981, 41) calls a "violent hierarchy." Of course, we are all signified through systems of sexuality, gender, race, culture, and class. Many participants have come to realize, as Sherene Razack (1998, 14) explains, that one's own marginalization cannot be undone without dismantling all systems of oppression and privilege. Erkan, for example, recognizes his relationships to his multiple affinities but treats them as resources for his political engagement:

> The policies produced just because of being an immigrant, just because of being LGBTI+, just because of being Muslim, just because of being Jewish, or just because of being a woman are wrong. Because I'm not only one of these ... Maybe this is why these struggles are never easy, because you always have other thoughts.

Like Erkan, many of the participants find that their various struggles intersect, which changes the ways they view justice. They experience "the complex ways in which the multiple forms of exploitation and oppression intersect, overlap, combine, shape one another and contradict one another" (Smith 1998, 40). Diasporic politics is never easy. Diasporic citizens seek a balance, however precarious, between loyalties to their own cultures, races, ethnicities, classes, and sexual orientations and the broader norms of morality and human rights. Ali, a prominent name among Alevi's gay community, discusses what finding a balance means in terms of his own sexual orientation, class, ethnicity, and religion. In his task of producing policies on sexual orientation for the anti-discrimination law, his values come into conflict with another gay person's concerns:

> Maybe that person supports and follows a traditional family structure ... He can dream of a same-sex marriage, adopting a child, and sharing a house. As a gay person, I don't want that. Then my socialist side becomes more dominant. I say: "Okay, you are queer, and we are similar in that, but there is something else more important. When you live with someone, you pay less tax, and as I live alone, I pay more tax. This is unjust." This is not about being queer but about supporting individual freedom.

At the same time, Ali's issue produces conflicts with heteronormative leftists:

> When I talk to my leftist friends, they might be taking a heteronormative position, certain gender roles for women and men. This might bother me. And then, I can experience that my queerness becomes dominant. I might question them: "Where am I located as a gay person in this world view?" They might understand this in a certain way: "You sabotage the movement. First, we have to save the proletariat, and then we can deal with you."

Forging Diasporic Citizenship 237

Then, there are the conflicts of religious identity. Ali continues: "For example, if I'm an Alevi, I might hate to be defined as Muslim. Because [for most people] Muslim means Sunni. Maybe I can distance myself from Muslim groups."

However, it is also possible that all this ambivalence may enable Ali to negotiate a new set of shared community values. Several of the participants, including Ali, describe their own transformations from personal to political as a process of moving from an inner struggle to a kind of public mission, almost like going to war:

> These [issues] are indeed beyond one individual's capacity. Nobody can overcome a single one of these problems alone. And we have to struggle with all of these problems. Every day, we need to go to war over these issues. I mean war. Because the opposite side is much more effective, and in history, we are assumed not to exist. We weren't taken into consideration. And when we say "I'm this," we [gays] have been stoned or burned. All these remind me of a war.

This kind of public engagement requires an inner struggle. It takes struggle to recognize the power one holds as an individual in balance with the power of others. With this kind of awareness born of struggle, diasporic citizens can form groups that go to war for inclusion. Their challenge lies in maintaining the hybridity and flexibility required to articulate diasporic citizenship.

Emotional and Experiential Signs

> I was going to German language class with the book *German for Beginners* in my hand. Really basic ... And this guy was staring at me. I just found myself thinking about opening the newspaper and reading it so the guy would know that I speak German! ... Wouldn't think I am learning it, that I am new. Who cares, even if he does? But in the past, I would have felt the need to show proof of my fluency, and I would, let's say, take out my cell phone and make a phone call on the subway, so people would hear me speak German very well, so they would know. In the past, I would get that feeling and act to prove the watchers wrong. But now, I work through it in my head. I can, like, watch myself think.

> – Arzu

238   *Forging Diasporic Citizenship*

Mobilizing diasporicity is also about what diasporants *feel* and *experience* in their encounters. Arzu's feelings are reminders of how power impacts people's lives, and emotional responses can shape their awareness and their modes of action or resistance. Arzu's feelings are realities to deal with, not obstacles to be removed. The emotions that Arzu describes emerge as indications of society's emotional landscape, where she plays a role as a reader of the land. These feelings reveal conceptually and politically important aspects of the history of German-born Turkish Ausländer. Such emotions are political, for at least two reasons.

First, emotions and experiences of injury are indicators of real issues. In this sense, injured feelings express significations that emerge from actual experiences. Experiences and emotions involving injury, suffering, revenge, and frustration signify the *impact* of hostile agendas. These signifiers reveal the political effects of meanings that advance domineering, exclusionary, marginalizing, subordinating goals. Signs of injury emerge as emotional reactions, like the way Arzu reacts to a hostile gaze. These signs can thus be reflections of the violence inherent in the dominant systems. Emotional and experiential signs of injury are powerful tools for identifying and naming oppressive practices and their effects.

Second, although awareness regarding past injuries can produce a desire for revenge, it can also lead to constructive political action. Awareness of injury has the potential to go beyond powerlessness and the absence of agency, because such awareness is potentially motivating. As political scientist Susan Bickford (1997, 126–27) clarifies this experience: "Suffering and citizenship are not antithetical; they are only made so in a context in which others hear claims of oppression solely as assertions of powerlessness." Moreover, Bickford contends that identity is a source of productive power. Suffering is not the only thing that preoccupies or marks those signified as Others. It is often the *anger* over existing relations of power, the *desire* for change, and the *courage* to act that shape people's identities and social positions.

Suffering is real in the experiences of Othered people, and if suffering is exposed in sites of deliberation such as the media, it can evoke empathy. More importantly, the emotional response to suffering motivates opposition to injurious acts, practices, and institutions. Bickford (1997, 126) suggests that it is necessary to develop political practices of listening, so as to hear not only the pain but also the energy and initiative involved in demands for change. She states that "listening is best understood, not as an attempt to get at an 'authentic' meaning, but as participation in the construction of

Forging Diasporic Citizenship

meaning." Through listening, it becomes possible to understand not only the psychological pain but also the way in which emotions serve as powerful responses to subjugation. Emotions have the potential to incite action, resistance, and oppositional consciousness. Feminist and civil rights activist Audre Lorde ([1984] 2007, 41) sums this up by saying, "I am not only a casualty, I am also a warrior." So Ali's conception of going to war is not so exaggerated. For him, the historical experiences of Ausländer and their ongoing marginalization are sources of political, philosophical, and physical mobilization.

The acts and practices of diasporic citizenship require emotional engagement, assertiveness, and multiplicity. The participants are not simply "arriving at a scene, nor fleeing from it, but engaging in its creation" (Isin 2008, 27). These actors are creating themselves as agents who are responsible for the scenes they engage in. Cultivating such attributes and applying them in social acts and practices turns these agents into diasporic citizens.

Acts of Diasporic Citizenship

Acts, as I use the term, are deeds that challenge or rupture the normal context for social relations. Some acts are impulsive, emotional reactions to a situation; others are deliberate. The ruptures involve actors who play interactive roles in the scenes at hand. Such acts dramatize the agents' understandings of the complex ways in which racial, ethnic, linguistic, religious, class, and gender identities affect their lives. Acts reveal that identity is a work in progress, not an accomplished fact. As Stuart Hall (1990, 222) writes, such acts involve "a production, which is never complete, always in process and always constituted within, not outside representation."

Enactments generally begin with an encounter between dominant and alternative values. One party asserts prevailing assumptions, and the other calls them into question. The specific challenges that German-born Ausländer bring to these encounters give them political significance. Each encounter has a certain duration, position, and disposition. During the event, the participants demand to be redefined, not within some fixed category but with recognition of their hybridity. They assert a conception of identity that involves flexibility, multiplicity, and translocality. Such everyday encounters become sites for a "differential mode of resistance" (Sandoval 2000, 3). By means of these encounters, the participants produce themselves anew, reinventing the meanings of difference, identity, and belonging.

During an encounter, the participants recognize messages of estrangement and proximation. They renegotiate homelessness and homesickness on the fly, strategically affirming who they are. These encounters, whether hostile or hospitable, empower diasporic people to react and resist. The actors practice asserting their multiplicity more effectively, and these efforts become a significant part of their lives. Although they seek to manage their encounters in ways that express their own agendas, they are all challenging the notions of German citizenship, identity, difference, and belonging that are imposed on them. They use such encounters to make a scene, thereby transforming dominant messages into enactments of diasporicity.

The participants' acts range from forms of passive resistance to defiance. Some acts are responses to confrontations imposed by others, and some are self-initiated. Taking the initiative gives people the power to determine the agenda and often the outcome of the encounter. Some acts are short-lived, creating ephemeral ruptures in the dominant context but making no lasting difference and being quickly forgotten. Others are decisive acts that firmly articulate the perspectives of diasporicity. The more influential, context-altering encounters take place in public and tend to be performative events.

Passive Resistance

> Hearing ... [the comments on how we do not belong] became almost a habit. We got used to it. You are put in a position that you have to decide whether to say anything or not.
>
> – Güler

In analyzing social encounters and their hidden politics, we need to distinguish the different kinds of silences involved. Sometimes, the participants' voices are silenced by dominant discourses of racism and xenophobia. At other times, it is they themselves who highlight their different identities (of religion, ethnicity, gender, sexual orientation, or class) in ways that situationally silence others. These two forms of silencing – essentialist and situational – differ radically. They elicit different forms of acts and practices. There is also another, more violent way of silencing: internalized Ausländerness, through which the dominant discourses of marginalization and oppression are simply accepted.

Some participants, generally the younger ones, first internalize dominant stereotypes and later distance themselves from them. They may say, "There are ones who are like that, but I'm different from them." These young people establish an us-and-them distinction as a defence mechanism. For example, Arda does not want to be stereotyped, although her mother's story fits the stereotype:

Forging Diasporic Citizenship

> When my parents got divorced, we stayed in a women's shelter for about three years, at Schteglis ... It was about eleven years ago. Then, my mother and my stepfather had a Muslim marriage ceremony. They didn't officially get married, so that my mother continues to receive the social assistance as a single mother.

Arda believes she needs to keep her distance from Turks to be successful. She says it is difficult to find a job in Türkiye, and Türkiye is a dirty place. She has to posit such discrimination in order to feel a sense of connection with the dominant culture, or she may even adopt a superior position toward the Other, which is also herself. She does not want to live in Türkiye. Her life history reflects some stereotypes about Turks, and she assumes their truth. Many other participants do so as well, especially teenagers.

When Arda talks about the Berlin Wall and compares the eastern part of the city with Kreuzberg and Neukölln, the stereotypes are evident in her language. Clearly, Arda does not want to be associated with Turks who seem to fit German expectations. She first internalizes the stereotypes about Turks and then tries to distance herself from them. It is worth noting that Arda has a lighter skin colour. This helps her keep her distance. Internalizing the stereotypes and then distancing oneself from them is about accepting difference. It is a layered form of violence that becomes an integral part of everyday life – all in the name of belonging. Hegemonic discourses are voiced by these participants in a most violent way as they cope with internalized prejudice.

Most participants mention that they are never surprised or caught unprepared by the attitudes and comments they face about who they are and where they belong in German society. "You get used to it," as Ayla puts it. Yet, as Güler observes, people have to adapt their responses to the problems that arise in such encounters, and this requires careful choices. A succinct calculation informed by emotion is needed. Sometimes, the participants feel they have little choice but to keep quiet. At other times, they sense the power to intervene. Sometimes, they decide to remain passive; other times, they simply raise a question. Sometimes, they insist on correcting the misconception, which requires having a well-considered plan.

Selin describes the usual attitudes and comments she encounters as "negligible little problems" that she gets used to and just wants to forget: "Five days a week, I'm with Germans. During the weekends, when I'm with my friends, I want to forget the things that happened during the week." Damla, with a similar evocation, says, "I want to forget that my parents are from Türkiye" while she is at school. Passivity can be a coping strategy. Yet behind this mechanism lies a strong potential for dissent.

Remaining silent can also feel powerless. Funda says: "I get upset, but ... you can't make much difference as an individual." Seda refers to the negative comments about her headscarf: "They think of themselves as superior. If I'm alone, I feel powerless, but if I'm not, I sometimes react." Remaining passive might also mean making a deliberate choice – not to do something that others expect. Selin refers to being constantly watched and having to control her behaviour so as "not to give a chance to a German to treat me this way," adding that she would not be put in that position if she were not Turkish.

Silence can also mean choosing battles wisely. Ayla is aware of the types of injustice she witnesses at work, yet as a social worker she might strategically choose to remain passive, emotionally detached. To protect herself, Ayla says: "You have to divide work and private space. You let things happen in your work life that you would never tolerate in your private life." For her, this is the difference between "giving up" and "having to be cool-headed and objective." Tunç differentiates between his struggle as an artist and as a social worker. When I ask how he challenges social norms, he explains that he does it with his films: "I don't want to attract attention at my workplace by going beyond the norms. There are other issues that I have to focus on ... I leave my work, make my film, and I come back. Maybe someday I won't come back. My social network, film, and art are the places for change."

The silences described by Tunç and Ayla are well-thought-out acts and part of their choose-your-battles strategy. For Melissa, Yıldız, and Selin, decisions emerge from how they are positioned in relation to Germanness. Skin colour plays a significant role. Melissa's mother is Turkish; her father is German. Her first name is German; her last name, Turkish. Her light skin tone, her name, and her mixed heritage all enable her to manoeuvre between two affiliations. Her stories illustrate how she plays with "being able to be both." Yıldız, on the other hand, evaluates a situation before deciding how to act, using her perceptions to advantage:

> I think that among foreigners, Germans like Turkish people the least. If you are Spanish or Italian, they treat you with a little more respect. Once, I made somebody believe that I'm Spanish ... Unfortunately, I couldn't have made myself appealing to that person with my Turkish identity. I thought if he knew I was Turkish, he wouldn't have this type of conversation with me.

Forging Diasporic Citizenship

As she *decides* to pretend being Spanish, Yıldız turns the hierarchy to advantage by muting her Turkishness. That enables her to control the encounter, although the hierarchy and her position in it remain intact. Selin, however, is assumed to be German because of her complexion and hair colour. Selin says that when she hears someone making negative remarks about Turks in public: "Sometimes, I decide not to say anything, and sometimes I decide to confront them." Melissa, Yıldız, and Selin can become visible and claim ownership for a particular aspect of themselves – when and if they want. If they decide to, they can protect themselves. They can avoid suffering the consequences of their positions without challenging them.

Being passive involves significant mental calculations, which usually remain hidden. Passivity can be a coping mechanism to avoid marginalization. However, by their silence, the participants are, in fact, maintaining the status quo even if they don't accept it. What characterizes such encounters is that they are not chosen; they are imposed. The participants cannot avoid the assertion of rank and only choose whether to challenge it. On many occasions and in many ways, they do choose to challenge.

Ephemeral Ruptures

Many participants talk about the ways they have challenged stereotypes about Turks, either by persuasively disagreeing or logically arguing that individual cases should not be generalized into stereotypes. Sometimes, the participants have to explain how the stereotype is inaccurate in their experience. Other times, they make more direct, aggressive arguments to refute the stereotypes. Referring to her neighbour Therese, İrem complains, "No matter how close and friendly she is with us, she still has stereotypes." İrem explains how she argues against these perceptions, which leaves her neighbour amazed that İrem is "a graduate student and going to be a professor" although she is Turkish:

> I say: "Therese, I was born and raised here. How can I have an accent?" She says, "There are many with accents." She has a point. I say: "It is not these kids' fault. Have you ever gone to the schools? They put Turkish kids in the same classes. Do you know what they do in Canada? They have second-language projects. These kids attend regular classes, and there is extra money for them to take extra English classes for three to four hours a week so that they can catch up with their classmates ... Here, there are only Turkish and only German classes. The teacher who teaches Turkish does not even know any German."

İrem not only challenges her neighbour but also explains the situation that causes the preconception. In a similar way, Ayda talks about her sister's unusually unpleasant experience with a private school in Bremen, where she considered sending her daughter:

> At the open house, the principal proudly explained that the school has mostly European students, and they don't accept Turkish or Arab students ... My sister asked what he meant ... He said, "This shouldn't concern you." My sister said, "I asked you a question. I can decide whether it concerns me or not." He responded, "Turkish and Arab families are not attentive to their children's education." My sister said, "Why don't you then say the school accepts only the students whose families are attentive?" ... He still did not get why my sister kept arguing.

Another form of challenge is to show where the stereotypes come from. Ceyda refers to various incidents where people make clearly stereotypical statements about Turks:

> I responded once, "Why do you think that?" I didn't mean to defend being Turkish; I really wanted to understand why she thinks that. She thought I was angry. I said, "No, I'm not ... I don't take it personally" ... She said, "Many Turks are such and such." I asked: "How many Turkish people do you know? ... In every group, there are different kinds of people ... But you can't generalize and claim it is the truth." She said, "I generalize because I know a lot of cases." I said: "But if you give me a chance and get to know me, you will see I'm not like that." She said, "I know you; you are not like Turks."

Through this discussion, Ceyda wants to make her friend see that generalizations about the Turks do not reflect reality. She manages to get past the preconceived ideas that present obstacles for Turkish Ausländer in general, but her questioning still leads to estrangement. She compromises as she asks for a chance to explain herself, arguing that once this friend gets to know her, she will understand that Turks are not all the same.

Other times, the participants challenge ranking more directly, especially if they aim to present evidence against the dominant position. For example, the following exchange took place between politicians: "Herr Özdemir, you should tell your compatriots." To which Herr Özdemir replies, "Herr Lintner, you are my compatriot" (Mandel 2008, 11). In this exchange, a German

Forging Diasporic Citizenship 245

MP (Lintner) presumes to tell Özdemir (also a German MP, and the first German-born Turkish member of Parliament) about his relationship with Germans and Turks. Lintner puts Özdemir in the position of being obliged to represent *his compatriots* – Turks – and therefore not to represent Germans. He suggests that Özdemir can speak as a representative of Berlin's Turkish Ausländer, but this is the only voice available to him in German democracy. Behind Lintner's remark lies the assumption that Özdemir is not a *real* German; he does not have the same standing as a German MP. Özdemir effectively challenges Lintner's notions of Germanness and the category imposed on him. He is vocal, present, and visible. Özdemir claims that he is one of the people who Lintner considers his own. He confronts misrecognition and rejects it.

What is significant is not whether their truth claims are proved but what these participants do with their claims. Birgül claims a basic truth when she says: "They say we have to integrate; [but] there is not one person who is not integrated. Everybody is integrated in this society in their own way." She claims this even though she might not be able to prove it and knows that others might not agree with her. By asserting her own understanding of integration, Birgül asks that Turkish Ausländer's sixty years' lived experience in Germany be acknowledged. Similarly, İrem claims the value of her connections with Turkish culture and language in the following encounter with her neighbour and family friend:

> One day, I was watching a Turkish movie when Therese came. She asked, "Why do you watch Turkish TV? Watch German" ... I said, "Right now, I don't feel like watching German TV" ... She didn't understand. "Now, I feel like watching Turkish TV. And don't you forget that this belongs to me, like the tea you drink, the food you eat with us." "I love it," she said. I said, "I do too! But I love this too. You can like this too!" She said, "But I don't understand Turkish." "If you want to watch with me, I can help you understand. But you have to understand that this belongs to us. However much we seem like a new German generation to you, we are still different, maybe, compared to you. I might want to talk to my mom in Turkish. I wouldn't call her 'Mutti' [mom in German]. I call her 'anne' [mom in Turkish]."

İrem challenges her neighbour when she demands that İrem watch German TV, which might imply a demand for İrem to improve her German or to integrate more fully. Perhaps the neighbour sees Turkish TV as an obstacle. İrem presents herself as a well-integrated young Turkish person. Nevertheless, she still claims that what others might see as an obstacle, she sees as a possession, and a positive one at that. İrem puts German and Turkish TV on the same level. She also connects Turkish TV with the Turkish cuisine that her neighbour likes.

Many participants refer to comments such as "How did you learn German?"; "Do you know Turkish as well?"; and "Your German is really good!" Germans express surprise that the Other can speak the authoritative language so fluently and even without an accent. This is assumed to be unusual. Being utterly surprised by a German-born Ausländer's language skills overlooks the fact that Turks have lived in Germany since the 1960s, and someone who is sixty could well be born and raised in Germany. Just by being who they are, German-born Ausländer disrupt what being German and Ausländer represent. Melda says: "Once a German woman said, 'Your German is very good!' She was surprised and complimented me. She must have thought I would be grateful for the compliment. I responded, 'So is yours.' She looked puzzled. Then I said, 'Of course, this is my language.'"

While being pleasantly surprised that a Turkish girl speaks German well, with no accent, the woman never expected that Melda would claim possession of the language. By responding, "So is yours," Melda made speaking German well an equal achievement for both of them and claimed ownership of the language for herself. She turned the binary opposition against the German woman, opened a space of resistance, and reversed the enactment of Germanness. Melda's claiming the German language produced ambivalence in the woman and altered the hierarchy of power.

#MeTwo: Stories of Everyday Racism

As far-right protests continued in Germany in July 2018, Mesut Özil, a prominent football player, resigned from the German national team, claiming that he had been subjected to racial discrimination from football authorities after posing in a picture with President of Türkiye Recep Tayyip Erdoğan. His resignation led to a social media campaign called "#MeTwo" – a play on #MeToo, used by survivors of sexual assault. The phrase *#MeTwo* was coined as a diasporic claim to having two nationalities, one of which is Germanness. It was meant to challenge the old assumption that one "must leave behind the traditions of their forebearers to be fully German" (Noack and Beck 2018, para. 5). In this campaign, thousands of people of colour tweeted their stories of everyday racism, drawing attention to the extent of racist harassment and violence in Germany.

Forging Diasporic Citizenship

The everyday expressions of racism described in these tweets were meant to remind multinational people that they did not belong in German society. Many participants reported that when they voiced their experiences with racism, they were told if they didn't like it in Germany they should leave. Many of them shared stories of the racist slurs that they bore on a daily basis, such as being singled out by police to show identification documents on a train full of white people, or being asked by teachers about when their parents would be forcing them to marry. Others told how they replaced their ethnic names with German names, to avoid the constant questions regarding their origin in everyday life. One participant explained that constant questions about her non-German name give her feelings of "'This is not where I should be and this is not where I deserve to live' ... And these questions don't come from authorities, they come up in everyday life" (Starkarat, in Sharma 2018, para. 11). The #MeTwo stories told how people feel when "their personal boundaries are regularly crossed, with comments about their skin tone, knowledge of the German language, and questions about where they are 'really from' in social settings, workplaces or as they go about their day" (Sharma 2018, para. 6).

Over 200,000 tweets containing anecdotes of everyday racism were shared on social media by the end of July 2018 (Noack and Beck 2018). These stories mirrored the experiences reported in my earlier research dating back to 2003, and the #MeTwo campaign showed that this problem is not restricted to children of Turkish immigrants. An ethnic Russian woman reported: "My German teacher was guessing the future professions of pupils in the class (10th grade): 'Well ... Veronika, you are going to be a Russian porn actress ... ' No one was laughing. 'Joke' #MeTwo" (Veronika 2018).

Other media reports have shown that Black people commonly avoid travelling to certain areas, as they fear being attacked. Concerned citizens have sent a clear call for the school system, the police force, and the state and federal authorities to accept and deal with the fact that institutionalized, commonplace racism is pervasive in Germany. The hope is that since July 2018, the stories shared and the voices raised will contribute to an understanding among white Germans that non-white citizens experience daily, often institutionalized encounters with racism (Sharma 2018; Noack and Beck 2018).

These stories help to demonstrate that very many Germans still understand their national identity in racial terms. To address racism and structural discrimination, society needs to explore the roots of these sentiments. People need to examine the role that racism has played in German society, in the collective memory of the Nazi regime, and in the history of anti-Semitism.

Emine Aslan, an anti-racist activist from Frankfurt, argues: "People think that we have dealt with that, so racism no longer exists ... [The Nazi history] is just a feeling of guilt, and [people have] a very narrow understanding of how it came to the Holocaust ... " (Sharma 2018, para. 34–35). #MeTwo is a disruption of German assumptions about whiteness. It is a rupture in the perception that raising the issue of racism is an accusation. Actually, it is an act of uncovering societal complicity in racism.

Such creative acts articulate inclusive being and belonging, and they do so in dynamic, concrete, critical ways. Ephemeral events do not, of course, cause immediate structural change: they are small, everyday acts without long-term political effects. Nevertheless, these acts open momentary ruptures in the socio-historical patterns of citizenship and identity. They interrupt established routines, creating disorder and deviance from the dominant discourse. Although their significance is limited, even short-lived acts require courage, creativity, and a sense of justice. Such acts suggest the possibility of social transformation, and many German-born Ausländer have faith that the accumulation of such ruptures in everyday life can lead to more enduring breaks in patterns of recognition. When Ausländer become claimants in the routines of everydayness, they provide memorable demonstrations of diasporic citizenship.

Practices of Diasporic Citizenship

Unlike momentary *acts*, the *practices* of diasporic citizenship are long-term lifestyle or vocational choices that emerge from the participants' agency and their lived experiences in being practical readers of the land who aim to advance longer-term social change. Such practices can become priorities in the participants' lives and may even shape their professional careers. Some participants engage in practices that involve creative media, the visual arts, music, literature, or film. Others have become effective agents of diasporic citizenship as writers and intellectuals. These people creatively employ artistic, literary, and intellectual practices to defend existing rights or to claim new ones.

Unlike acts, practices involve being *out there* as a lifestyle choice. I will examine examples of this from the fields of journalism, literature (Dilek Güngör); film, media (Neco Çelik); and music (Aziza A). I will also examine the formation and practices of a group that represents LGBTI+ Turkish Ausländer (and more recently POC LGBTI+ Ausländer). Such groups exemplify how advocacy organizations can shape and express diasporic citizenship.

My Father and I

When I first met Dilek Güngör, she was a journalist for a major Berlin newspaper, writing a weekly column that criticized how mainstream Berlin society sees its Ausländer. Once a week, she told witty, partly fictional stories in her column, *Unter Uns* (Among Us), which was inspired by her father. In 2013, she wrote:

> My father likes to listen to Turkish radio while he cooks. But the radio is not strong enough to get the stations from Türkiye. All we hear are a few Turkish words now and then, and then Arabic music, and buzzing sounds, and then someone says something that we don't understand, but somehow this is enough for my father. Maybe he is getting the real news from those buzzing sounds! Why can't I understand? ... He is the only one who has that skill in the family.

In such articles, Güngör made her father look inadequate at the beginning, such as when describing how he could not fill out German forms without Güngör's help. But he always turned out to be smarter, better – the one who got it right in the end. His insufficient language skills did not matter. Güngör reclaimed the guest-worker identity in a way that was political. She took the readers in a predictable direction at first, giving the impression that her father was ignorant and did everything wrong, but then events unexpectedly proved him right. The reader was left feeling "This is also right; this is another way of doing it." Güngör (2003) showed great candour describing her father's ordinary limitations:

> Once, I wrote about how I cannot talk to him on the phone. If he answers, he says, "Wait, I am giving it to your mother." I love my father, but our relationship is through my mother. I tell my mother, then she tells my father; my father tells her, then she tells me. Some [German] friends reacted, "My father does the same thing! ... We can never talk!" Then maybe, all fathers and daughters experience similar issues ... It has nothing to do with being Turkish, or being a Turk in Germany.

Through these stories, Güngör's father was transformed from a guest worker into a human character that many could relate to. She received letters saying how much readers liked her father and wished to meet him. A colleague said she would have married Güngör's father if she had met him. People looked forward to her next story. The impact of her column exceeded Güngör's own expectations. She got letters from a great diversity of readers – from outside of Berlin, rural Germany, people from the east, and from older people. Güngör confessed that she had assumed "a Turkish girl's relation with her father might be interesting for people in Kreuzberg, or leftists, who are interested in cultures." In 2003, Güngör said she planned to expand on this theme as soon as she got a bigger column: "Maybe I will think of a grandmother who comes to Germany for the first time, and I show her Germany. Maybe I will approach her as if she came from the village and she does not know anything, but she is much smarter than I am."

In 2003, Güngör also spoke about how she strategically used her Turkish-German perspective in shaping news stories about the Turks of Berlin. She explained how news writing has often perpetuated stereotypes:

> The paper receives daily fax messages from the police department about what is going on in the city. If the identity [of a suspect] or where they came from is not relevant, I always delete this information. For example, a sixteen-year-old man stole a woman's purse on the street. Here, that guy's citizenship is irrelevant ... The other day, during a wedding, while having a barbeque, three big families got into a fight, and someone was injured. Here, whether you say they are Turkish or not, people will assume so, as big families and barbeques fit the image of Turkish people. As you already gave that information, there is no need to mention that they were Turkish.

Also, when she needed to describe some person or group in relation to their Turkishness, she never wrote "Turks," but "Berliners from Türkiye," or "Berliners whose parents came from Türkiye." Similar strategies were also reflected in the topics she chose to write on. In 2003, she shared:

> While assigning the topic of Türkiye's getting first place at the Eurovision Song Contest, they asked me to talk to the people in Kreuzberg, as if I'm the expert ... But I didn't want them to send me to Kreuzberg and have me ask people on the street how they feel. The people would say, "I feel good. We are one step closer to Europe, we did something good!" while driving through downtown with flags. This implies that the Turks here have a complex ... But sometimes, I think I'm exaggerating. If people are thinking like this, I have to write it.

Forging Diasporic Citizenship 251

According to Güngör in 2003, being a Turkish journalist has also opened a space for Güngör to act as a bridge between Turks and Germans:

> I knew I was hired because of my fluency in Turkish. I was afraid they would ask me to write only about the news in Kreuzberg or the neighbourhoods in which Turks live. But they did not ... Sometimes, when the soccer teams came here, they asked me to go to the coffee houses and talk to the people there. I tried to avoid that. Yet when Germans did it, I realized they did not do a good job. Because they don't know Turkish, or they approach it as if they understood the situation of Turkish people when they don't ... Of course, when I go for interviews, when they find out I know Turkish and come from a Turkish family, Turks feel closer, and they see me as one of themselves ... They think they do not need to explain themselves ... I do not ask unnecessary questions. Or they feel I am less likely to see something and misunderstand ... This also made my job easier.

Güngör argued for the need to go beyond being reactive and defensive about the experiences of Turkish Berliners. She encouraged people to look at themselves in a humorous way, to make fun of themselves, and to avoid being defensive or assuming that they are always looked down on. She said: "This much-needed approach is missing. We have that self-pity. We cannot look at ourselves in a self-deprecating way. We should be able to see our own mistakes and make fun of ourselves while being at peace with ourselves."

Güngör went to England in 2003 for a year of master's studies, and she continued to write her column that year. Her first book, *Ganz Schön Deutsch* (Very Nice German), was inspired by her column. The response she received encouraged her to write her first novel, *Das Geheimnis Meiner Türkischen Großmutter* (The Secret of My Turkish Grandmother), which came out in 2007 and has since gone through at least eight editions. She attempted to rewrite this story as the script for a film but encountered many setbacks. Then, she decided to continue writing fiction and started a second novel. But after her daughter was born in 2007, she could not find a publisher for it and after many failures started a third novel. She is still trying to get this book and her screenplay published in 2016, I asked her why she hasn't given up, and she explained:

> This stuff kind of becomes myself. I own these things in my thoughts. Everything I engage in, the stuff I listen to, hear, all about the same issues.

Always identity, belonging, language, always these topics. Before I used to think that this was special, but then I have realized it is not that special after all. It wasn't that unique. These small vignettes are not only about my experiences – there is also a universality to them. It is not only about immigrants of Turkish background but also about any diasporic person who goes from one place to another, living and speaking the language. This feeling of foreignness. You can feel like a foreigner in your own culture and in your own language. I want to capture that.

Alltag (Everyday)

Neco Çelik is a former graffiti artist and youth gang member (in a gang called the "36 Boys" – named after a Berlin postal address number). He is now a film and drama producer who also works as a media educator at the Naunyn Ritze Youth and Cultural Centre (Şeker 2008). One reviewer says that Çelik is "from Little İstanbul, [and] has gained a reputation as the Spike Lee of his time and place, with his debut film [*Alltag*]" (Schlagenwerth 2006). When asked if he feels integrated as a Turk, Çelik objects:

No one can tell me how I should live and behave. That is for me to determine. Period ... No one has said exactly where integration ends or at what point someone has finally made it ... To me, the word is like a bar of soap – it always slips away ... Of course, it is important that if you can't speak German, then your radius is limited in Germany – that's clear. (Şeker 2008)

Çelik is not interested in a storybook that is focused on ethnic conflict. If ethnic identity is part of the theme, if it has a political background, he uses it but does not put it at the centre. The main thing is people going beyond the social norms:

My stories are about people living through some particular experience, or who have a certain problem that has to be resolved in Germany. This problem has nothing to do with integration, immigration, or any other culture. I would never tell an immigrant story. But this is where it gets difficult. The public sees a character with dark hair and assumes they're an immigrant. Therefore, I must be telling only immigrant stories. (Şeker 2008)

In our interviews in 2003, Çelik told me about how he challenges various stereotypes:

Forging Diasporic Citizenship

In films, Turkish youth are portrayed as depressed, melancholic. But I don't want to do that. I want to show them in a way that everyone wants to be like them. In *Alltag*, I used classical music instead of pop music. They were puzzled to see classical music in the movie. They said they didn't understand. Because the German and the Turk were at the same level. A little nuance between bad and good is a thin line. Even if they are bad, at the end they are the ones who are right. The Turkish character dies as a hero in the movie.

Alltag is set in Kreuzberg, in a rough neighbourhood. It centres on a deadly competition between two men, one a German and one a Turk, for the love of a beautiful Turkish woman: "The space is important. The first space was graffiti. There is always humour. The last scene was at this intersection here. A girl has to decide between two guys. She can't. And the guys have a duel. They solve their problems with the laws of the streets. This is the most dramatic part in the film."

Çelik's work reflects the gap between mainstream German culture and the culture of Kreuzberg. As Bernstein (2003) explains: "In Alltag, there is only one culture, the desperation-tinged youth culture of Kreuzberg itself, and while that may not exactly correspond to real life, it is Kreuzberg's separateness from the rest of Germany, and not the separateness of those who live within the district, that Mr. Çelik wanted to depict."

Çelik complains that everything a German-born Ausländer does becomes a phenomenon, and he argues that challenging this mindset is their main task. He directed a theatre play, a German version of *Romeo and Juliet*, written by Feridun Zaimoğlu and Günter Senkel:

Feridun only made the Capulets into Christians and the Montagues into Muslims. In the original, there is no religious conflict – the families simply hate each other. Here, the hate is based upon religion. They hate each other because they adhere to different faiths, and is each convinced that their own culture is superior to the other. And in the middle of all of this, their children fall in love. Something has to burn. It is very provocative and it should be. (Şeker 2008)

Through his work, Çelik challenges what is considered normal and shows that Kreuzberg's existence is already normal. He wants to make Germans realize that these people are normal without Ausländer having to insist on it. In 2003, Çelik told me that for him the important task is not staking a

254 Forging Diasporic Citizenship

claim to being considered as normal but rather to challenge what is imposed as normal:

> If I make a movie and appear on TV, I become a phenomenon. We shouldn't constantly say "We are not a phenomenon, we are normal." They have to see us as normal, without us claiming it. Recently, newspapers are writing these ideas. They even say, going too far, "These people will save us" ... but the most important thing is doing it with a future perspective in mind ... Then, you are in the "challenging club" in every aspect, including film, politics.

Çelik's work in general, and *Alltag* in particular, shows that subcultures such as those of Turkish-background Germans are creating new identities that mix Turkish, German, and African-American cultures. This creativity sets an environment for the growth of hip-hop in Germany (Pennay 2001). Turkish-German Kreuzberg is enthralled with the sounds and styles of the US ghetto. Rap music, graffiti, breakdancing, and gangs are all present in Kreuzberg and are depicted in Çelik's film (Brown 2006).

In 2006, Çelik staged Feridun Zaimoğlu's *Black Virgins* (Schwarze Jung-frauen), which tells the story of five Muslim women caught in a conflict between religion and sexuality (Schlagenwerth 2006):

> It went off like a bomb. I think it was just too demanding for the public. They probably never heard anything like it ... The shock wasn't portrayed in a single situation, but was let loose by the avowals to individuality on the stage ... There were very fierce reactions in discussions with the public. I had never before heard or seen anything so xenophobic. First came questions like: "Why did you perform something like this in our theatres?" Where did they get the idea that these were "their" theatres? Theatres are subsidized with our money, from your taxes and mine. And then came the idea that the actors playing the characters in the piece weren't really actors, but were actually the women portrayed. Others were even oblivious to the fact that it was a work of theatre. (Şeker 2008)

In 2007, Çelik made *Ganz oben. Türkisch – Deutsch – Erfolgreich*, a documentary for the TV network 3Sat, about the success stories of five Turks in Germany (Öztürk and Bengi 2009). In June 2009, at the *Almancı Festivali* in İstanbul, he staged a Brechtian musical that Gazino Arabesk set in Kreuzberg, with a hip-hop twist featuring Turkish Arabesk songs performed with German lyrics (Öztürk and Bengi 2009).

Aziza A's Oriental Hip-Hop

Es ist Zeit ["It Is Now Time"] [2]

I have brown eyes, have black hair.
And come from a country where the man stands over the woman and
*   there does not blow a completely different wind like here!*
In the two cultures I grew up in, my dear sisters tend to lose out, because
*   not only the two cultures crash, because even fathers watch over their*
*   daughters: "You are the honor of the family, clear, obedient, silent as*
*   your mother used to be. "*
Such a crap, you're scared, no branch you can hold on to is in sight ...
You think: is it my duty to live the life of my parents as they strive?
*   With authority to glue my mouth to me!*
Yes, yes, now I take my liberty!
AZIZA-A. does what she thinks right, even if she falls out of sight of the
*   whole clan and nobody counts her among the obedient women!*
I do not care, I have to say what I think, and indeed ...
Wife, mother, and girl or child, no matter what country they came
*   from: everyone a man who can think independently, you understand*
*   man!*
Look and see what happens: nothing, no difference!
It's time, get up! Face to face, recognize: we have the weight!
Mixed with hip-hop, my voice also echoes the ears of those who drill their
*   fat fingers into their ears. Seeing nothing, not wanting to hear, like the*
*   three monkeys, with one difference: they talk without knowing what is*
*   happening in us!!!*

– Aziza A (Bradham, 2018)

Aziza A is the first German female rapper and hip-hop artist with a Turkish background. Aziza A has developed the "Oriental hip-hop" genre by blending in traditional Turkish features. By identifying her music as *Oriental*, Aziza A turns the term on its head. She reminds us that even though the everyday use of the word *Oriental* may seem to be in decline, a deep distaste toward certain Ausländer is very much well and alive. At the same time, she put Oriental hip-hop in the German language, blending Turkish in the refrain. Her Oriental hip-hop ruptures Germanness and alters what it means to be German. In her music, she talks about the problems with migration and the lives of modern, second-generation Turkish people in Germany. Her song "Es ist Zeit" (It Is Time) came out in 1997.

In Arabic, *Aziza* can mean "beloved," "precious," or "mighty." The "A" re-fers to the Turkish word *abla* (big sister). In her songs, Precious Big Sister raps out against clichés. Although she is not a strident feminist, she raps in Turkish and German about migration and the desires of Turkish women born in Germany: "To be able to say, 'I am not this system's woman' is difficult for many, because it might mean not being taken seriously. A woman has to be with a man to be taken seriously. Everything becomes a struggle when you question: 'Then why?'" (Aziza A, interview in 2003). In daily life, on television, and on stage, Aziza A urges women to have more self-confidence (culturebase.net 2010).

Aziza A started doing hip-hop in Kreuzberg in the 1980s and developed her own style. She says: "There is no boundary and limit in music ... The social critique is in the words." She uses this medium to speak out about life between two worlds, questioning the unidimensional German image of Turkish women. Her lyrics, like those in the song titled "Es ist Zeit" ("It Is Time"), often concern the situation of Turkish women living in Germany, but she does not take a feminist stance so much as her own stance, as in "Kendi Yolum" ("My Own Way"). In a newspaper interview, she says:

> I have a lot of experience to pass on, a lot to speak about ... But I'll never yell from the stage to a woman: "Stick up for your rights!" Rather I'll say: "Look how you are living. If you like it, fine. But don't think it's everything, you could do a lot more." I don't go onstage to tell women to do things, but I show them what I am doing, and I speak directly: "You could, if you wished to, do the same in your own way." (culturebase.net 2010)

Her central message is the need to see human beings as special, unique individuals, not as stereotypes or members of groups, as she told me in 2003:

> The list is created by the society. The system locates individuals higher, lower, right, or left. Not everybody can fit in the categories listed. The people who cannot fit into these lists are the ones who are oppressed and constantly struggling. Society and the system think for the people; people do not think for themselves but follow what is expected of them.

Music is Aziza A's tool to critique how the lists of rank are created by society. She reflects the struggles of people who cannot and do not want to fit into lists. As well as being a means of resistance, her music creates space for it.

Forging Diasporic Citizenship

When I reminded Aziza A that we met in 2003, and suggested that we start from there, she paused: "Oh, my, that long ago, eh?" In 2006, she went to İstanbul to continue working on her second album. For several years, she moved back and forth between Germany and Türkiye. After her son was born, she focused on raising him. She did not write or make music for a while, but now she is continuing her career. In 2016, she told me:

> If I think about these issues in relation to music, I can see there are changes. There are more young girls who are into rap. It was only me when I started doing it. They are doing this with more engagement, pride, and they love what they do. They don't feel the need to be masculine while doing rap. This doesn't mean it has become easier, but it is more accepted. It is not mainstream per se, but hip-hop has become more visible. There is a market for hip-hop. It is not as big as pop music; it is still underground. However, I don't see anyone [else] in Berlin doing rap in Turkish. Now, everyone is doing rap in German. Turkish is not a sexy language. You never see any song in Turkish on the charts, whereas you can come across Spanish or Italian songs on the charts.

Today, communications technology, computers, the Internet, and the media have a significant role in distributing political ideas or claims, which makes individual acts more effective. The three examples of practices of Dilek Güngör, Neco Çelik, and Aziza A illustrate that one significant way of being out there as diasporic citizens is through the media, including art, music, literature, film, and other formats.

These various long-term practices are not necessarily built on pre-existing public platforms. The practices themselves can become platforms, even if they are conveyed through specific media. Diasporic citizens do not depend on institutional approval or the support of political parties and other organized groups. Through the Internet, individuals can reach unlimited audiences by putting their personal views into blogs. They can have an impact just by speaking for themselves, without having to claim that they speak for all members of a community.

In the preceding pages, I have focused on individual acts and practices. However, practices at the group level are also significant. Therefore, let's consider a significant example: organizations representing Turkish-background gays and lesbians in Berlin. These are not, of course, the only groups that articulate diasporic citizenship. However, gays and lesbians

258   *Forging Diasporic Citizenship*

have contributed significantly to my understanding. They challenge all our categories of identity. They are a unique group that truly confronts the whole range of prevailing conceptions of race, ethnicity, religion, class, gender, and sexual orientation.

Breaking Out Queer

Ayşe is a social worker, academic, and DJ. She plays "Oriental" music at Gayhane (gay house), a nightclub in Kreuzberg:

> We live in Germany, but we exist as Türkiyeli Orientals. Wherever we go, it's always Western music. The music I relate to is not played ... When I want to experience my Turkishness, I have to be with Turks. But with other German lesbians and other Oriental gays and lesbians as a subculture, I want to experience my Turkishness as well. It was around the end of 1980s. They were organizing a dance party with the Oriental music theme, and they needed a DJ. The organizers asked me. As I can relate myself to both gay-lesbian culture and Türkiyeli culture, I thought this might be a chance to combine both with music.

In recent decades, gay Turkish dance parties have become popular sites of integration between communities. These events have greater appeal than discussion groups, cultural organizations, or counselling services. Since 1996, the popular club SO-36, located at the nexus of the LGBTI+ and Turkish communities on Oranienstrasse in Kreuzberg, has hosted the Gayhane, an Oriental gay party, on the last Saturday of every month. Hakan Tandoğan, an organizer and renowned cross-dressing belly dancer of Gayhane parties, points to the dance floor as a symbol of the possibilities of integration for many people: "Gayhane, which started for Turks, has ended up drawing everybody you can think of: Arabs, immigrants, Germans, anyone who feels like partying with us" (Tandoğan). This is an example of how the GLADT organization, through its member initiations, can make rights claims through something as simple as a dance party. The event puts the personal struggle of being gay or lesbian at the centre. Gayhane at the SO-36 is forming a third space for claiming how the personal is political: "If my private life is a reason for the dominant culture to be offended, then it is political" (Ayşe).

If it is kept private and hidden, what is personal does not disturb social norms. The personal only becomes political by pushing the margin to the

Forging Diasporic Citizenship 259

centre and making the hidden seen. The GLADT movement and its related organizations challenge heterosexist discourses in both German and Turkish contexts. They also challenge the marginalization of Turkish immigrants among ethnic German gay and lesbian groups, along with prejudice in German society at large.

GLADT was initially founded in 1997 as part of the formation of LSVD (*Lesben- und Schwulenverband*), which is an umbrella organization for gays and lesbians. Later, GLADT broke away and become independent. LSVD still retains MILES, *Zentrum für Migranten, Lesben und Schwule* (Centre for Immigrants, Lesbians and Gays), which is an office dedicated to the needs of LGBTI+ people from migrant backgrounds.

The stance on homophobia among Turks has become a dividing line between MILES and GLADT. MILES identifies the problem of homophobia in the Turkish community as a cultural issue and insists on discussing this openly. In contrast, GLADT's leaders consider that there is nothing ethno-specific in homophobic acts by people of Turkish descent. In their view, ascribing special homophobic tendencies to Turkish culture is discriminatory, if not outright racist. GLADT's leaders hint that MILES, as a subsection of LSVD, has been unable to resist or oppose the prejudices of German mainstream gays. This disagreement came to a boiling point when, after a MILES publication discussed Turkish homophobia, GLADT refused all contact with LSVD and distanced itself from MILES (Saygılı and Erkan, in 2003).

Despite having different positions on certain issues, both GLADT and MILES work by making individual struggles into public causes. As Erkan explains: "We aim to take our issues from the individual level to the societal level. They can become social issues, not just individual problems, only when we start discussing them on a public platform ... If it is hidden, you bring it to the centre. Sometimes, we have a little success."

Specialized organizations such as GLADT and MILES also attempt to remedy what İpekçioğlu (2003) calls the lack of substitute communities within the gay community. MILES stages social activities, such as parties, Eid (a Muslim festival) celebrations, hamam nights, and movie nights. At the Christopher Street Day (CSD) and LGBTI+ honour day parades, MILES has its own float. During the big street festival at the end of June (one week before CSD), they have their own stands.

In November 2003, MILES organized the first conference of Turkish LGBTI+ people, with more than three hundred attendees from throughout Europe. This event culminated in the publication of a series of essays called *Muslims under the Rainbow*. In 2004, MILES took its first step in cooperating with the Turkish Union of Berlin-Brandenburg (TBB), an umbrella organization for associations respresenting the interests of Berlin and Brandenburg citizens of Turkish origin, through an awareness campaign aimed at breaking the silence among gay migrants and their home communities. MILES displayed posters and billboards all over Berlin showing a group of gay youths with the motto *"Kai ist Schwul und Murat auch. Sie gehören zu uns, jeder Zeit"* (Kai is gay, so is Murat. They are a part of us, always). In 2005, another version of these posters featured young women. This campaign produced a mixed response. Volunteers hanging posters in Kreuzberg and Neukölln encountered verbal and physical aggression (Hairsine 2004). The campaign received many positive phone calls from Turkish gays, lesbians, and their families, asking for information and counselling: "We had parents calling, 'My son just told me he is gay; how do I react?' or 'How can we reconnect with our child?'" (Barış).

MILES also cooperates with other LGBTI+ organizations. The media is showing interest in their activities. Associations such as the TBB invite MILES members to participate in various events. Erkan says, "This was impossible in the 1990s. There is some change." The activities of GLADT and MILES reveal how the local micro-politics of the diasporic public sphere have intertwined with transnational diasporic political activism. Transcending any construction of their identity as "victims," or as a doubly oppressed racialized minority group, the LGBTI+ Turkish Ausländer activists I met were redefining their social position in Germany and elsewhere. As they rightfully claim a place in the public sphere, these activists have rewritten the moral terms of their citizenship, moving from passive to active membership. To achieve all this, groups affiliated with LGBTI+ from Türkiye have organized to work for diasporic causes beyond their personal issues of sexual orientation. As they encounter mainstream resistance to their work, their efforts include holding public marches against discriminatory events that happen in Türkiye.

LGBTI+ People of Colour
Many LGBTI+ people with immigrant backgrounds maintain a political stance of refusing to embrace racism in the name of challenging homophobia. Therefore, many LGBTI+ participants are increasingly engaged in anti-racist activism – a noticeable change since 2003. Following the various debates around integration of LGBTI+ people, the participants in my

Forging Diasporic Citizenship

research grew discouraged with the LGBTI+ movement, and for many, the anti-racist movement is now their home.

For example, Koray Yılmaz-Günay has sought to address two central issues regarding the tremendous rise of Islamoracism since 9/11: first, the perception that Muslims are homophobic; and second, that they are anti-Semitic. These concerns have driven Yılmaz-Günay's efforts to document various forms of anti-racist activity in literature and art:

> Regardless of their level of religiosity or, in fact, whether they are Muslims or not, immigrants with Turkish, Arab, Bosnian, Albanian, or Iranian backgrounds have been presented as particularly homophobic. This argument seems to be here to stay. Islamoracism among the LGBTI+ movement has become mainstream. In the past, while challenging homophobia, the LGBTI+ movement stood with anti-racist activism. Now, they ask how homophobia can be included in anti-racist studies. But the movement is dominated by white Christian men. Even white lesbians don't feel at home there. Neither do trans people, nor immigrants.

Yılmaz-Günay also responds to the popular concern over "anti-Semitism in Islam," which has grown exponentially since 9/11:

> It is like: "We learned from our history and we overcame anti-Semitism, but these dark-heads are bringing this issue back into our country." This is really current right now. Especially since the attacks in Brussels and Paris. It is always current, and it is an increasingly talked-about argument ... Islamoracism has greatly increased. Even though in German history the Jews were the most hated and abused people, today they are accepted as "one of us" by the white society. The Muslims are the Other now.

Now that traditional anti-Semitism among Christian Germans has been largely renounced, Muslims are labelled as the Jews' greatest enemies. With that, traditional prejudice against Muslims has gained a new justification – as protest against the racist anti-Semitism attributed to Islam. Islamoracism has been rebranded as a movement to oppose the racism of non-Westerners.

By 2018, LGBTI+ groups representing racialized minorities had multiplied, all of them critical of structural and governmental violence against racialized minorities. GLADT still works very successfully to deal with the issues of multiple discrimination, homophobia, transphobia, sexism, and racism.

Other groups exist as well. *LesMigraS* (lesbian/bisexual migrants, Black lesbians, and trans people) is an anti-violence, anti-discrimination division of *Lesbenberatung Berlin* (Berlin Lesbian Counselling Center, a diverse team with different qualifications in social education, psychology, and therapeutic training). For more than ten years, LesMigraS has worked to oppose multiple discrimination, promote self-empowerment, and support anti-racist labour policy. SUSPECT is a new group of queer and trans migrants, Black people, people of colour, and their allies, whose leaders maintain that the fight against homophobia requires fighting racism as well. This group's aim is to monitor the effects of hate crimes, conduct debates, and build communities that are free from violence in all its interpersonal and institutional forms. ReachOut is a counselling centre for victims of right-wing extremist, racist, anti-Semitic, homophobic, and transphobic violence in Berlin (Vail 2010).

The diasporic citizens who support such groups emerge from multiple backgrounds. They are preoccupied with making sense of the multiple worlds they experience in the cultural borderlands. Like Agathangelou and Ling (2009), I found that people subject to hegemony can be resilient and creative. Diasporic citizens are among those who "bear the biggest burden of negotiating the multiple worlds of language, culture, class, and gender ... despite the systemic discrimination and obstacles ... Still, they are able to exercise internal reserves of freedom, thought and action" (Agathangelou and Ling 2009, 89).

Diasporic Citizenship Politics

> You know what, I don't want to look back to the old days and be stuck there or compare necessarily ... I am improving myself; I want to share what I improved ... I want to make my contributions with the youth in my work. I don't want to start from "You have treated me as a second-class citizen" or "You have discriminated against me." This is very tiring and takes a lot of energy; it brings one's very personality down. So even when I face these stereotypes and perceptions, I challenge them by claiming that "I am German." Or I ask them back, "Where are *you* from?" I also like to say, "I am a Berliner" to throw them off a little. It is like a game, you know.
>
> – Leyla

Forging Diasporic Citizenship 263

The politics of diasporic citizenship that I analyze here aim to create a platform for changing norms and building solidarity with others. These diasporic citizens seek to connect with other people who feel alone in their struggles, to take their issues from the personal to the public level, and to challenge the attitudes of both Germans and German Turks. The everyday acts of diasporic citizenship serve these aims by causing ephemeral ruptures in the established context. Organized practices such as those of MILES, GLADT, Dilek Güngör's *Unter Uns,* Aziza A's music, and Neco Çelik's films provide platforms for this movement. The particular platforms may disappear as a particular act or a practice concludes, or they may open up new encounters – with the families of gay and lesbian teens, with Germans in rural parts of eastern Germany, with young Turkish women, or with mainstream society. Platforms for diasporic awareness encourage people to become more visible, resistant, transgressive, and disruptive. They invite people to risk evoking reactions.

I understand the various enactments of diasporic citizenship – actions, silences, thoughts, perceptions, or words – not in terms of right or wrong ideas, but as experiments in political self-expression. Acts and practices can involve combinations of the visible and invisible or of speech and noise, which can determine the sites and the stakes of political life. In *The Politics of Aesthetics,* Rancière (2004, 13) writes that "politics revolves around what is seen and what can be said about it, around who has the ability to see and the talent to speak, around the properties of spaces and the possibilities of time." The politics of diasporic citizenship is finally just a matter of being out there and interacting with the world.

Being out There on the Streets
The politics of diasporic citizenship articulates itself mainly in cities. Given its complex history, Berlin is a special site for encounters that transgress spatial, temporal, geographic, and national boundaries. It is a meeting place where the politics of proximation and estrangement affect a vast diversity of people, with implications for their social and political narratives of ethnicity, identity, community, class, and religion. Within this city, the diasporic public space is articulated as an arena where private individuals meet to deliberate on matters of public significance. The city is the major site for negotiating and renegotiating citizenship. Groups and individuals make claims to the city – to establish or unsettle patterns of difference and belonging. They appropriate spaces that they claim as their own, occupy spaces that

others claim, and form solidarities in public places. In the everydayness of their encounters, they challenge the identities, differences, and belongings that have emerged on the level of the nation-state.

In the city, Isin finds an emerging "difference machine" (2002a, 1–51), in which groups and individuals generate encounters as they take up positions, orient themselves for and against one another, invent and assemble strategies, and mobilize various forms of capital. The city is neither a background *against which* they wage their struggles nor a foreground *for which* they struggle. It is the battleground *through which* groups and individuals define their identities, stake their claims, and articulate citizenship rights and obligations. Therefore, Berlin is Germany's primary site for the formation and re-formation of German-born Turkish Ausländer as diasporic citizens. Its streets are special zones of resistance, disruption, and conflict. In Kreuzberg, Turkish Ausländer turn their displacement into a process of engagement and negotiation with urban spaces. Their presence and involvement disrupts the social and cultural structures of the city. All of this sends a message to the whole nation.

Many have argued that discussing individual matters on public platforms is more important than achieving a specific result. Therefore, using the streets for political purposes means taking personal issues and making them into public concerns for both Germany and for a diasporic homeland. To be out there on the streets is important: what matters is not whether *it is nice* but what difference it makes. In raising their issues, diasporic subjects tend to drive a wedge between the spaces of the nation and those of the city. Urban groups have a different relationship to global concerns than nation-states. The city streets conflate their identities of territory with those of race, religion, class, culture, and gender to produce the ingredients of both progressive and reactionary movements. The city represents the localization of claims for belongings and rights. It is a condensed articulation of the nation's priorities, resources, and changing population. It is everyday life in the globalized world.

The public space of diaspora, in its multiplicity and fluidity, is partly constituted by political meetings and commemorative events, but mainly it appears in everyday encounters. Seyla Benhabib (1992, 94) argues that we need to recognize the public sphere's increasing porosity and complexity, which arises because "neither access to it nor its agendas for debate can be predefined by criteria of moral or political homogeneity." Concerning this public sphere, I agree with Werbner (1998) that it mainly involves private

Forging Diasporic Citizenship   265

citizens who gather to contest or deliberate issues of general public concern, whether these are issues of citizenship and political democracy in Türkiye, of the economic opportunities and problems facing the Turkish business community in Germany, or the rights of gays and lesbians. But this public arena is also a sphere in which private issues become both public and political. There are no substantive limitations on the topics openly debated. They can include arranged marriages, violence against women, or breaking the silence about non-heteronormative sexualities.

Being Dialogical, Vocal, and Media Savvy

Acts and practices are expressions of the need to be heard (Reinach 1983, 19–20), and therefore they are inescapably dialogical. These politics emerge from the various situations that the participants are thrown into or from conditions that emerge over time and need to be discussed. The participants' claims regarding truths, values, and rights may be expressed discursively, but they also use the language of bodies, signs, and spaces.

Naming means disclosure, as in *coming out*. For example, being openly gay is an important step in being recognized and becoming active. Naming also puts things that were marginal and unmentioned at the centre of attention. Therefore, Bali Saygılı wants his actual name to be openly used in this research. Using his name openly means being heard and acknowledged within the gay-lesbian movement. It also means becoming a role model. For Saygılı, it means proving to the German LGBTI+ community that he is not stepping back from honesty and is willing to take its consequences. Naming is a significant act of transgression in becoming a diasporic citizen. The act of naming in this context presents an interesting contrast to the ways that many diasporic parents name their children. Erkan explains the importance of naming in the context of queer identity and cultural relations:

> If you don't say, "I am gay," you are heterosexual in the eyes of people. It is known but unspoken. Being out there, on the street, is significant. On the street means openly, in public, taking risk ... Heterosexuals have the power, and non-heterosexuals do not share it, or they are not involved in it. The people on the street don't see that. Saying that you are gay every chance you get is important. Not because it is nice or not but to remember that you are different. If you are seen as different, you are seen as a minority. Being seen as a minority is always a disadvantage ... Heterosexuals do this every day

but not consciously. "I'm like this, my life is wonderful, and everybody should have the life that I have." It is like whiteness. Going to the streets and marching to protest against this privilege is significant.

Many of the people who participated in this research argued that they needed to become more prominent in the media, which has the power to make their issues into matters of public discussion. Many participants explained that they look for ways of accessing the media or of planning unexpected acts that convey diasporic messages. They want to make themselves understood and make their causes visible through significant public acts. They have different ways to use various media as their platforms for diasporic politics, such as holding press conferences or street festivals. Sometimes, they seek to attract media attention by involving political figures, hoping to convey their claims to society through encounters with such leaders.

Tunç believes that journalists are aware that a different kind of human being is emerging among these German-born activists of Turkish background: "[Germans] are not [global thinkers] like [our diasporic children]. And some journalists are well aware of that ... Being connected with these journalists is important so that you can make sure that they understand you." Tunç describes how he negotiates with journalists. He does not try to get a journalist on his side. Rather, he wants the journalist to encounter his ideology and then spread word of that encounter. "I know they want to use me. I'm using them in the same way ... But you shouldn't see this as simple or negative. It is a strategy." Erkan also argues that since the majority population uses the media to spread its ideology, he should do it too. People should get their messages across and use many different means of communication to do it.

To demonstrate the importance of mass media, Bali Saygılı describes a transgressive act carried out during the international CSD parade:

During the gay parade, we wore blue veils, and it got enormous media attention ... Does that mean we are Orientalist? No. But if they look at you [with an Orientalist gaze] you can use that. We gave a political message below the car we were in. Our banner read: "asylum rights for transvestites in Türkiye." In Türkiye, homosexuality is not forbidden. So it is not a reason to seek for asylum. [Even] if you say, "My family wants to kill me," they look it up in the law, they see it is not forbidden, and they deny your application.

Forging Diasporic Citizenship

> When we had these garments covering us from head to toe, everyone, including the media, came and took our pictures. But at first, it seemed ridiculous. People didn't understand why we did it. But when you wore these garments in that car, it wasn't only the veils that were seen but also the political message we wanted to give. Many people criticized this. They said, "You are making fun of people's religious beliefs or of women," but at the end, everybody looked at us; everybody saw us. It is what matters: to be seen and to exist.

Here, Saygili expresses an awareness of how the media makes news. Behind this transgression is the conviction that media should be considered a tool for interacting and creating a platform, and it should be used as such. By wearing blue veils, the Türkiyeli gays of Berlin can also exploit the media to create a platform, get media attention, and use this attention to send a political message, as their banner read "asylum rights for transvestites in Türkiye." In these new forms of being political, as the struggle becomes more media savvy, the street becomes a diasporic platform for claiming rights by turning Orientalism and media bias into a publicity tool.

Being Resistant and Transgressive

Many of the practices and acts analyzed here demonstrate that challenging the dominant processes involves an intention to change some particular obstacle or to advance some particular claim. Whether that potential is realized depends on the effect it has on the surrounding power relations. An act or practice is effective if it alters established social structures or lessens their dominating effects. James Scott (1986) contends that any definition of everyday resistance requires some reference to the intentions of the social actors.

Human geographer Tim Cresswell's (1996) concept of transgression is useful in thinking about how to identify the potential for resistance and how to describe moments of social destabilization in everyday acts and practices. Cresswell (1996, 9) defines social transgression as a "form of politics that questions the normative world by underlining what values and norms are considered correct and appropriate." This activity involves an opposition that contests the hegemonies of everyday life, crosses conventional social or spatial boundaries, and confounds the "common-sense" understandings of our world. For Foucault (1977), transgression is a kind of boundary crossing that serves to clarify discursive limits and expose what is excluded by discourse. Such transgression highlights how identities, difference, and belonging are reconfigured through boundary negotiations. This kind of activity destabilizes the assumed meanings, the boundaries around those meanings, and the social relations formed through those contexts. Such boundary crossings may involve responding to the comment "Your German is very good!" with "So is yours." It may mean wearing blue veils to send a political message during a parade or claiming a Kreuzberg culture beyond ethnicity in a film like *Alltag*. Foucault and Cresswell envision transgression not as a rebellion that seeks to destroy boundaries, but as an act that reveals the limits placed by social parameters and prohibitions. Boundaries have the ability to exclude, but they are also vulnerable to exposure as limited perspectives. Thus, boundaries can be enabling as well as constraining.

These disruptive acts and practices are political in that they expose the arbitrary foundations of the boundaries that define categories. However, these acts are not political in the sense usually envisaged by the dominant culture. They are not about establishing control or rank. Instead, diasporic citizens aim to change the quality of human relations. Disagreeing with a friend can be a political act. Güngör's *Unter Uns*, Çelik's *Alltag*, Aziza A's songs, Gayhane parties at the SO-36, and #MeTwo stories are all platforms for disruptive acts, in which diasporic activists put the focus on things that are generally ignored or disparaged. In Cresswell's (1996, 26) words: "Derivations from the dominant ideological norms confuse and disorient, and therefore reveal the historical and mutable nature of what is considered 'the way things are.'"

The transgressors' responses to their own acts are also important. Social actors may or may not seize the opportunities presented for questioning judgments or exploring new relations. The political significance of their transgressions depends on what awareness emerges in the midst of the disruption. During their transgressive acts, the participants engage in boundary-challenging behaviours in ways that may be neither intentional nor antagonistic. Hence, as Cresswell (1996, 23) argues, their disruptive effects often depend on the responses made to those particular behaviours or on what the actors and other witnesses do after the boundary challenge happens.

In reacting to some expression of power, the research participants intentionally or unintentionally cross lines that should not be crossed, and

Forging Diasporic Citizenship 269

such crossings do not always offer alternative proposals. Instead, the line crossings are arbitrated by everyone involved. The effectiveness of a transgression lies in its ability to explore alternative topographies of power or to challenge common-sense assumptions about the way things are, but these effects depend largely on people's spontaneous reactions.

The effort to destabilize socio-spatial boundaries may not lead to social transformations, especially when boundary-defenders quickly explain the transgressions away. In most cases, transgression involves a temporary, ephemeral disruption rather than a radical rupture of world views. To effect lasting social changes, transgressive boundary challenges need to become more regularized or institutionalized. German-born Turkish Ausländer need to build on their incidental disruptions, seek to alter structural constraints, and achieve a greater agency.

Transgressive politics allows for a range of possibilities, depending on what it is that people are seeking to disrupt. In some cases, diasporic citizens may need to unburden themselves from an excessively ascribed or constructed identity. In other cases, they may want their hitherto underacknowledged distinctiveness taken into account. In still other cases, they may need to shift the focus to critically examine the dominant or advantaged groups and *out* these groups' distinctiveness as another ethnocentric standard, rather than a universal standard. The diasporants may need to deconstruct the terms in which attributed differences are presently elaborated.

Boundary challenges do not necessarily produce new modes of living and knowing. They can, however, foster new ways of relating if the questions they raise are considered, rather than simply invalidated. Such challenges are sometimes *corrected* in reactionary ways by simply reasserting the established systems of meanings. At other times, however, boundary challenges provoke a greater awareness, and the boundaries shift.

In seeking to challenge the social context, diasporic people find it necessary to shift from a binary conception of difference to a more complex understanding, which recognizes that variable contexts determine the degrees and forms of social difference. The politics of diasporic citizenship reveals how and why one form of difference is implicated in the meanings of other forms of difference. Representations of subjectivity and subjection are situated in many differentiating schemes that variously privilege and penalize people, where the privileges assigned to some are fundamentally tied to the disadvantages assigned to others. People are therefore not simply either dominant or subordinate: they embody *relative* representations of dominance and subordination (Dhamoon 2009, 65–66). In considering this relativity, Sherene Razack (1998, 10) calls for an account concerning which voices are given legitimacy, how they are heard and reinterpreted (or misinterpreted) by others, and how the images we hold of Others protect certain interests. As Razack (1998, 10) argues, protesters need to communicate across social hierarchies, to disturb relations of domination, and to challenge "hegemonic ways of seeing through which subjects make themselves dominant." The aim, according to Razack (1998), is to recognize how we are *implicated* in the subordination of other[s]. Acts and practices can clarify how we are implicated in structures of difference and help to establish relations of accountability.

Being Aware of Vehicles of Power

The acts and practices of diasporic citizenship are all power driven, but they are driven in diverse ways. The narratives analyzed here present accounts of how the vehicles of power produce varied social relations, with their criteria of ranking by sexual orientation, gender, class, culture, and race. For example, the category of "Ausländer" (as a particular variation of immigrant) is clearly established as an important marker of recognition in Germany, which shapes social, economic, and political life. Yet, as the acts and practices analyzed here demonstrate, it is necessary to rethink how German-born Ausländer are considered and to do so beyond the scope of narrow binary oppositions of identity and citizenship based on culture. To conceptualize the experiences of diasporic subjects primarily through the lens of culture, or through any other singular mode of difference, is to interpret social representation too narrowly. An overly narrow view obscures how othering occurs. The representations of German-born, Turkish-background subjects vary according to how their diasporicity operates within specific contexts and in relation to various norms related to culture, language, accent, skin colour, gendering, whiteness, class, and religion. Attention to these variations, as Dhamoon reminds us (2009, 91), simultaneously challenges the singular preoccupation with culture and enables a better understanding of how the representations of Otherness and the representations of national norms are "mutually constituted." When dominant discourses indicate that "one mode of identity is politically more important than another, it is crucial to examine what specific agenda is being advanced, which norms are being protected or privileged, and what is at stake for the state in regulating that particular form of difference."

Being Critical and Deliberative about Shared Citizenship

> But when journalists want to reduce me to my Turkish descent, then I ignore it. You have to show people that it doesn't matter where your parents come from, but rather what you as an individual can do.
>
> – Neco Çelik, in Şeker 2008

Conceptualizing identities as active, contestable, dialogical sites of politics suggests a particular political view of citizenship. Diasporic citizenship requires some flexibility, contingency, and accommodation for plural significations. It does not eliminate the moral or political reasons for alliances, or for sharing, bonding, and belonging. However, it does alter the space in which the meanings of citizenship are negotiated. To fully understand the multiplicity and contingency of the meanings given to shared citizenship, it is critical to disrupt the relations of dominance from which the current practices of citizenship, immigration, and multiculturalism are derived. The processes and sites of critical reflection are crucial for facilitating such discussions about the meanings related to shared citizenship, both among and between groups.

The production or reproduction of social meaning is part of everyday life. It takes place through subtle forms of engagement in educational spaces, social settings, and everyday encounters. The acts and practices involved do not necessarily require formal, institutional democratic deliberation. Even everyday casual acts and practices can be influential, because the quality of human relations sets the tone for society from the ground up. Also, especially for people whom conventional society denigrates, it is often safer, physically, emotionally, and materially, to work through private channels and avoid encounters in public spaces, however unthreateningly deliberative they might appear to be.

It seems reasonable to expect that democratic institutions offer public acknowledgment and disclosure regarding the issues at stake, a willingness to listen to others, a desire to resolve collective problems, and openness of mind. But this is not the starting point for the many people who face marginalization, discrimination, and oppression. As the terms of reasonable deliberation or disagreement are shaped by power, these people have grounds for mistrust and uncertainty. Whether or not there is reasonable disagreement and dialogue, meanings continue to be produced, both formally, through deliberation, and through other modes of interaction such as private conversations, socializing, and travelling (Young 2000, 57–77).

Even when recognition and agreement are not achieved, reciprocal disclosure and acknowledgment is "an important achievement in its own right for all the actors involved" (Tully 2001, 22). Disclosure of concerns and objections "forces minorities to convert their alienation into public argumentation rather than into private frustration" (Maclure 2003, 7). Diasporic citizens, as both individuals and groups, need to articulate and publicly justify their meanings, both to other members of their groups and to those outside their groups, including the dominant meaning-makers. Mutual disclosure and acknowledgment can "generate levels of self-empowerment, self-worth, and pride that can overcome the debilitating and psychological effects of misrecognition" (Tully 2000, 479). For Benhabib (1996, 71), the "procedure of articulating a view in public imposes a certain reflexivity on individual preferences and opinions." Listening to alternative perspectives can lead one to alter one's position, as the intersubjective aspects of deliberation provide opportunities to re-evaluate or refine an argument.

Disruptive Acts and Practices
Diasporic citizenship, as expressed through the politics of meaning-making around identity and difference (cf. Dhamoon 2009), embodies ongoing deliberation as individuals engage in the activities and practices of signification in their everyday lives. This kind of politics – which entails focused, conscious, premeditated disruptions – is not necessarily limited to the public realm. Nor are the more personal and spontaneous politics of subtle, indirect, subconscious, or unintended claim-making necessarily limited to the private realm.

In democratic political systems, the category of "the people" is not a predefined, permanent reality. It is a changing concept that is given meaning through historically rooted discourses concerning law, politics, citizenship, nation, gender, racialization, and economics (Canovan 2005, 60). Dhamoon (2009, 144) argues that "due to this contingency, particular groups in society claim the authority to determine who the people are ... and to do so by constituting differences between subjects." In this sense, claims about the people are changeable myths with real political implications. Diasporic citizenship constantly reveals the contingency and fluidity of such myths.

When questions of political identity, difference, and belonging arise, the issue at stake is not simply the relations between majority and minority groups, the state and the people, or *our* culture versus *yours*. The bigger questions are how practices of signification constitute "the people" and the

Forging Diasporic Citizenship

citizen, how these practices affect different people, and how a better basis for social relations can be found. This is the political potential explored through diasporic acts and practices. When citizenship is defined as an entity or ideal, rather than an activity, the practices of signification involved in that delimited definition seem to be placed beyond questioning. The choices of inclusion or invalidation, together with the whole process of negotiating hostility–hospitality, or homelessness–homesickness, remain concealed and unacknowledged.

The enactments of diasporic citizenship are disruptive forms of critique that contest dominant significations. They question the authority, stability, and character of any particular representation. Their disruptive quality invites individuals, as participants and agents of everyday enactments, to critically examine their own positions as dominant or dominated. These encounters expose the discourses of hostility–hospitality and homelessness–homesickness, showing how these axes are constituted through meanings attached to various human beings. Acts of diasporic awareness disrupt the conditions that structure these axes, rather than merely challenging one dimension or polarity of difference.

Diasporic acts and practices do not produce something new that did not already exist; nor do they provide ideal alternative options for the future. They just open doors for new ways of relating by denaturalizing and disrupting the conditions that produce privileging or penalizing characterizations. The disruptions they create do not necessarily lead to the rejection of any particular identity, difference, or sense of belonging. Disruption is not always explicitly confrontational. Questioning bias can be conversational, entertaining, or quite hostile. Such challenges are varied in character and form precisely because meanings are contextually and relationally produced, contingent in nature, and shaped by the specific forces of power at play.

Since diasporic acts and practices happen within particular social contexts, but all social contexts are related, the disruption of a participant's own position necessarily disrupts the whole social process of signification. As people examine their own contexts and roles, they demystify and disrupt the broader social circumstances that create their representations of identity, difference, and belonging – not just their private sense of self. Thus, accounts of meaning-making are less person-centred than power-centred. Person-centred inquiries concern individual blame or responsibility. They serve to idealize persons, generate essentialist conceptions of identity, and obscure understandings of how and why personal differences become relevant in social hierarchies.

Inquiries regarding diasporic citizenship centre on issues of social power rather than individual worthiness. Diasporic citizenship suggests that no one can avoid being caught up in creating and perpetuating the relations of penalty and privilege, because any positioning for advantage obviously involves everyone in the picture, and everyone has to occupy some position. Being implicated in this struggle means that all subjects have differing types and degrees of privilege, that difference has many manifestations, and that it is relationally varied (Dhamoon 2009, 148).

Having been defined by negative stereotypes themselves, diasporic citizens are commonly unwilling to project similar essentializing notions onto others. They are typically reluctant to define individuals who occupy dominant positions as inherently evil or even intentionally oppressive. Just as dominated people are caught in a role, so dominators are caught up in the process that produces domination. Rather than demonizing individuals, diasporants tend to look for the social conditions that structure the relations of penalty and privilege. Thus, regardless of whether individuals and groups deliberately enact forms of domination, the process of subject formation is always conditioned by power. No subject in this process is ever completely powerless.

As Fellows and Razack (1998, 340) argue, it *is* a risk for marginalized people to examine their own responsibility in the oppression of others. Their own claims for justice are likely to be undermined if they acknowledge the competing claims of others who wish to position themselves as dominant. Given this reality, it is normally difficult to evaluate how people become caught up in social relations of domination. This kind of interaction, as Dhamoon (2009, 149) argues, requires "an ethical commitment to accountability, and to responsibility" for disrupting the conditions that make people participants in normalizing their own subjection.

Demanding Dialogical Alliances

I don't provoke things to get attention, but I do provoke things so that social problems and concerns can be talked about socially. Nobody says we have to get together and make the society a better place, and we can solve these problems. But this is logical. You don't have to be oppressed to rebel ... As a society, it is necessary to reach a better and more just level. And it isn't only about Germany or Türkiye ... This has to be done globally.

Forging Diasporic Citizenship

Although politics functions mainly through groups, my analysis shows that individual activism and personal viewpoints are also very important. The most commonly seen expression of diasporic citizenship involves individual initiative, as people confront the social contexts around them during the course of their everyday activities. Whenever individuals take critical positions toward the prevailing context, they inject the politics of diasporic citizenship into their groups. Ali continues:

> If I had worked at TBB and said that I'm a gay, this would have been a great shock for them, maybe. My German friends always say: "You are one of us, you speak German better than we do, you dress the same, and you eat the same food." And I resist that. Maybe a lot of my personality is much closer to Germans than Turkish people; but if I say I'm not one of you, at that moment I'm transferred to a specific position. Or I transfer myself.

In the context of multiple discriminations, creating shared agendas with immigrant associations involves demanding to have and share power. A good example is the interaction regarding the anti-discrimination law. German LGBTI+ organizations have claimed that "adaptation and immigration are not our issues." LGBTI+ Ausländer have answered: "We are members of this society; adaptation and immigration are our business, and they concern us." In the dominant discourse, adaptation means assimilation. It means making people look like Germans and only then seeing them as equal. But building alliances involves working through such differences by giving all parties a voice.

Diasporic solidarity is the unity and agreement that these individuals find with each other in supporting actions and struggles for recognition. Such solidarity can be formed implicitly during individual encounters or explicitly as groups are formed to make claims in public. The resistance and pressure generated in either of these ways helps to create the willingness in society to shift toward an understanding of ambivalence, fluidity, and the intersectionality of being and belonging together. Therefore, a critical understanding of solidarity leads to forming dialogical alliances.

The solidarity that the participants envision involves two sensibilities: The first is an awareness of how the current structures favour citizens of the dominant group, who have positions of power over people who are deemed as "the Others." The second kind of sensibility comes from presenting people with a mirror so they can see how this *Othering* looks to those who are Othered.

That perspective allows people to build alliances that challenge the existing dominant ideologies and oppressive restrictions within their societies. This type of alliance building calls for utilizing an intersectional approach in shaping the acts and practices of diasporic citizenship. This building of intersectional partnerships enables diasporic individuals to form communities of resistance that include others who were once alienated within competing movements for social change. The acts and practices of diasporic resistance to state oppression reveal how marginalization has been structurally embedded within society. Some activists and institutions that claim to be intersectional actually participate in discrimination against minority people.

Diasporicity reminds us of the value of co-resistance, and it suggests how we can become partners rather than competitors. Diasporic acts and practices demand that people in privileged positions improve themselves by considering issues that may not directly affect them. Such acts and practices suggest two principles for inclusiveness: coming together under a common idea or core value (Edgell and Tranby 2010), and then acknowledging and fighting to change structures that privilege some over others (Snelgrove, Dhamoon, and Corntassel 2014). Even among people who engage in such action, some groups and individuals may be marginalized. The priorities of some may dominate, and others can feel forgotten and cast aside. Therefore, diasporicity demands a kind of solidarity that includes and honours those who are marginalized within activist work (Malseed 2008).

Conclusions: What Makes Diasporic Citizens

Stuart Hall (2017) explains that identities of displacement are formed as much by the subjective self-judgments of diasporic subjects as they are by struggles against conditions of subordination. It is the paradox of being a permanent familiar stranger that makes diasporic citizens. Through their everyday acts and practices, the German-born Turkish Ausländer who participated in this research have actively positioned themselves as agents who are able to judge what is fair. They are engaged in examining the patterns of marginalization and misrecognition that are imposed on them. They evaluate and react to these patterns, finding ways to open ephemeral ruptures in the prevailing contexts. This ability to open a rupture in the context is the essence of a diasporic act. Most of the time, such acts are spontaneous. At other times, these acts are more like practices, which are planned, through and through, and intended for making a more permanent disruption of social patterns.

Of course, these various acts and practices are not the sole cure for categorizing, misrecognition, or marginalization. Still, these activities reveal an integral relation between the knowledge gained from historical experience and the knowledge generated from everyday living. Designating the Ausländer as a separate form of humanity and subjecting them to the politics of accommodation have been everyday practices in Germany, and these practices have affected every sphere of the Ausländer's lives. Diasporic acts and practices promote extending citizenship not just to include a wider range of subjects, but also to radically reassess the historically specific regimes through which social categories are constructed.

The diasporants' acts and practices do not resolve all conflicts between self-directed and externally imposed dichotomies, such as Ausländer versus German, queer versus heteronormative, or citizen versus non-citizen. Indeed, their practices are not intended to resolve conflicting meanings. They do not necessarily lead to conclusions that reorder or reverse the existing representations of difference. Most of the German-born Ausländer participants feel that it is simplistic to suggest that Ausländer-centred modes of intentionality should be privileged over German-centred modes – or that conventional meanings (such as those attached to male and female or to cisgender and gender nonconforming) should be switched. These people tend to avoid obscuring how marginalized subjects enact their own agency, and they reject the logic that some modes of representation are *intrinsically* better than others. They do not wish to simply exchange existing formations of dominance for new ones, as this would leave the basic structure of dominance in place. The acts and practices of diasporic citizens have a greater potential – to reassess the entire pattern that gives rise to such structures. Acts and practices can challenge the specific practices, institutions, or agents that set up relations of penalty and privilege. These interventions can potentially open up other ways of being and belonging, while destabilizing contexts that limit our understandings of difference to conventional binaries such as male versus female and citizen versus non-citizen.

Underlying the unidimensional, additive, or hierarchical approaches to citizenship is an assumption that the various aspects of being and belonging can be quantified, categorized, and ranked in bounded ways (Collins [1990] 2015, 225). By contrast, the intersectional approach that many diasporic citizens embrace starts from a different understanding: representations of being and belonging are performed through systems of identification and power that cannot be owned and ranked. As the process of ranking is biased,

278   *Forging Diasporic Citizenship*

the rankings that result are clearly choices that can be changed. This is not to say that identity and power are indistinguishable; it is to recognize that competing systems of oppression and privilege function interactively to position each other (Fellows and Razack 1998, 340; Brah and Phoenix 2004).

Through their acts and practices, the diasporic people who participated in this research imply that their politics cannot be driven simply by desire for inclusion or a simple opposition to the practices of exclusion. Instead, they acknowledge that these practices are central to all political relations, and their response is to raise consciousness regarding the contexts of power. For them, rights can be reconceived, not as final goals but as instruments that provide opportunities to create, organize, and articulate the significations they find desirable. As expressions of citizenship, these people's everyday interactions can be contingent, flexible, and transgressive. They can be tied to democratic practices that facilitate contestation. Acts and practices have the potential to both acknowledge and disclose the processes that shape the context of power, to expose the agendas of meaning-makers, and to uncover the stakes involved in political struggle. In their sites of deliberation, these boundary-crossing people stand for accountability in the decisions that affect privilege and oppression. Finally, their own experiences and emotions are central to their deliberative acts and practices because personal experience is what reveals the effects of diasporic displacement, and emotion can be a source of political action toward a more inclusive, diasporic kind of citizenship.

Conclusion
Becoming a Chameleon

I belong to this neighbourhood ... I'm about all these traditions and folklores ... Whoever sits with me, they are comfortable. I don't try to change them. I can talk and discuss anything ... I can communicate with and adapt in every culture, like a chameleon ... I know every language ... I am dynamic ... I am like a shark, smarter, more aware, and faster ... I am the pioneer of Europe.

– Tunç

Like the German-born Turkish Ausländer, the children of immigrants who were born in their countries of destination are emerging diasporic citizens. These native-but–non-native people profoundly affect global politics, because they enable the deconstruction of our traditional binary, oppositional ways of understanding identity, belonging, and citizenship. They increasingly recognize how the traditional operations of citizenship involve a social construction of sameness as opposed to Otherness, and this is the human division they struggle to transcend. In Germany, these people are principal actors in transforming the identities of both Germans and Turks into something broader and more flexible. They hold citizenship close to themselves, even as they insist on a critical distance. The struggles of these diasporic citizens are constant reminders of how difficult it is to address the contemporary dilemmas of identity and belonging in a nation-state. They exemplify the challenges that nations face in their choices of whether to restrict or expand their relations with a transnational people.

Perhaps the most important social development of the current century is the creative response of diasporic people to traditional forms of political, social, and cultural domination. At this point in history, the rise of diasporic

280   *Conclusion*

awareness shows that it is still possible to prioritize partnership values, rather than struggle over which groups should be dominant. Despite our violent heritage of conflict for advantage over others, it is still possible to make the quality of our mutual relations our central concern. New partnerships and collaborations appear whenever communities of struggle call the narratives of domination and hostility into question. Therefore, diasporic citizenship is both an epistemological and a political project. It is a matter of thinking (critical awareness) and doing (co-resistance and collaboration). The rising new forms of racism underscore the urgent need for cultivating these new ways of understanding, relating, and resisting. As Tunç's words (quoted above) illustrate, the German-born Turkish-background Ausländer have developed the attributes of diasporic citizenship.

In this conclusion, I have three interrelated aims. First, I want to review the various ways this book contributes to studies on citizenship and diaspora. Second, I want to reassess the ways that communities of struggle can learn from diasporic citizens as they seek to form collaborations for social justice. Third, I want to summarize the reasons why Germany needs to redefine citizenship beyond the realm of the nation-state.

Citizenship Politics through Everyday Acts and Practices

I have examined how the subjectivity of German-born Ausländer is discursively informed, practically performed, and historically situated in contemporary Berlin, Germany, Türkiye, and elsewhere. I have described these processes as an emergence of diasporicity – a critical awareness. This kind of awareness among German-born Turkish Ausländer reminds us that any dichotomy of inclusion/exclusion oversimplifies the processes by which people interact and belong together. Diasporicity appears as "a perpetual reminder of the losses which enable citizenship to flourish" (Cho 2007a, 105).

The evolution of human society depends on being open to learn from other people's experiences, especially from those we have tried to exclude and who occupy ambivalent spaces in our society, as we encounter their everyday acts and practices. These people's expressions of belonging reveal the challenges that German society faces in defining national identity and citizenship through culture. Exploring the participants' everyday encounters and examining the discursive repertoires that have categorized, defined, and (mis)recognized them has helped me to understand their emerging awareness. My analysis of their expressions, as mapped on the

Becoming a Chameleon

axes of hostility–hospitality and homelessness–homesickness, has helped to expand the discussion of how diasporic subjects are positioned within transcultural fields of power in contemporary Western cities. Their narratives question the dominant discourses that represent Ausländer as the Other in terms of race, ethnicity, religion, gender, sexual orientation, and class. I have shown how the participants' acts and practices are implicated in various operations of power, which appear in the context of everyday encounters. Through reporting these encounters and responses, I have illustrated how diasporic citizenship is already shaping a broader context for belonging and relating in society.

Examining everyday encounters as expressions of diasporic citizenship advances the study of citizenship politics in significant theoretical and practical ways. This analysis provides ways of rethinking key social categories of difference as they relate to aspects of citizenship, and it does so through examining how these categories are constituted beyond the scope of culture. This approach challenges the logic of exclusion that treats identities as fixed categories, with either dominant or subordinate rankings. The investigation shows how encounters with diasporic awareness reveal a process by which structures of difference, identity, and belonging are produced, de-formed, and re-formed as society changes. These encounters expose options beyond fixed, totalizing views of identity. They allow variable choices concerning Otherness and normality.

The acts and practices of diasporic people are not merely cultural or social expressions, but also political statements. In these expressions, people are claiming rights that they do not have. They are resisting attempts to assimilate their human differences into sameness, and their resistance is commonly seen as divisive rather than affirmative. Their expressions emerge almost randomly, as various individuals or groups feel moved to speak or act out their transgressive, resistant, deliberative ways of relating. In many cases, their responses are complicated, fragmented, or misunderstood. Driven by paradoxes, these people demonstrate how citizenship involves choices among complicated sets of options and not just simple choices between opposition or loyalty.

Diasporic acts and practices reveal how power, subjection, and justice work. The actors push back against the boundaries of traditional liberal-democratic ideas regarding the nation-state and liberal citizenship, including the idea of multiculturalism (cf. Dhamoon's conception of identity/difference politics in 2009). These protests raise deeper questions of what identity, difference, and belonging mean, and this kind of active questioning introduces a significant shift of focus – from the problem of accommodation to a dominant culture, to the problem of renegotiating power relations. This kind of questioning exposes and identifies the political choices and discourses that underlie assumptions about inclusion, exclusion, and accommodation. That exposure of unstated presumptions makes it possible to diagnose existing relations of power and to open up new possibilities for responding to such issues of power. Therefore, analyzing the experiences, acts, and practices of diasporic citizenship provides a critical framework for naming, criticizing, challenging, and dismantling the expressions of power that privilege some and subjugate others.

Diasporic citizenship is not a new ideology or doctrine. Neither is it a model or an ambitious policy for mandating an improved form of cosmopolitan citizenship. It does not replace the quest for minority rights, or revive the notion of multiculturalism, or promote a new group-differentiated citizenship. Instead, diasporic citizenship aims to disrupt narrowly defined forms of citizenship and to explore a more practical, experiential understanding of citizenship through trial and error from the ground up. In reflecting on the understanding of worldism as expressed by Agathangelou and Ling (2009, 136–37), I propose that diasporic citizenship is a process of social dialogue that contests the boundaries and identities that have defined individuals.

Of course, diasporic citizenship cannot serve as the remedy for the nation-state's failures to protect human rights. It is not a universal solution for the contradictions inherent in the concept of modern citizenship. The aims of diasporic citizenship are much more modest. Rather than proposing a formal ideology or organizing a political movement, diasporic citizens simply engage in creative encounters, expressing an awareness based on standing in the borderlands between national and other identities.

Diasporic citizenship involves awareness of contradictions and possibilities. That awareness comes from perceiving the profound problems with traditional citizenship and experiencing the difficulties that result from the conventional project of citizen-making. This new kind of citizenship reminds us that *nations are made, not born.* It takes account of what people lose in efforts to conform with others. In addition, besides challenging nation-state and disrupting traditional citizenship, diasporic citizenship is also a model for communities of struggle in ways of forming collaborations for social justice.

Forming Partnerships and Communities of Resistance

My analysis explores how we can take part in a self-reflexive mode of questioning on the individual and group level. Such self-reflexivity disrupts how subjects understand their own social positions. It helps us to clarify why a particular meaning of identity, difference, or belonging is of value to an individual or social group. This praxis of taking signification into account fosters active engagement in politics. It does this by exposing and disrupting the ways that power produces differences and does so in repressive, agency-reducing ways. The activity of disruption is a response to the dominant context of hostility–hospitality toward Others. It is a form of resistance and a means of liberation (Dhamoon 2009, 150–51).

As a self-reflexive and politically engaged praxis, the action-oriented practice of diasporic citizenship can involve even those who feel insecure about expressing themselves. Many marginalized people know they are vulnerable and that challenging power may bring material losses or severed relations. Even so, these people realize that they have a choice. Those who are most at risk are often the most willing to take risks. As Allen (1999, 33; emphasis in original) refers to Foucault's insights: "Individuals are both *subject* to the constraints of social relations of power and simultaneously enabled to take up the position of *a subject* in and through those constraints."

Diasporic citizenship, however, is not a project to rescue diasporic subjects from contestation or from difference itself. The disruption it causes is not directed toward erasing or reducing power. Instead, diasporic citizenship confronts the ways and systems that create and maintain relations of domination, thereby allowing the Ausländer to experience new, alternative ways of creating themselves. Domination needs to be resisted, as it constrains the range of possibilities for interpreting identity, difference, and belonging. New ways of constituting the self are opened up by critiquing patterns of dominance and then subjecting new patterns to criticism as well (cf. Dhamoon 2009, 151).

Diasporic acts and practices provide understanding of how our modes of difference function through one another, of how differences can vary in content and form, and why one interpretation of difference is not reducible to another. Cultural differences, for example, are not reducible to differences of gender, class, or religion (Yuval-Davis 2006, 195, 200).

The self-understandings that diasporic citizens articulate are themselves subject to critique because they, too, overlap with relations of power. As

Dhamoon argues (2009, 152): "If representations and structures of difference can be imagined beyond the scope of what seems entrenched and natural, it is possible for new forms of subjectivity (including new ways of imagining 'the people') to emerge." The forms of politics that diasporic citizenship enhances disrupt the relations of power in the context of everyday life. These practices do not eradicate power in human relations; they just allow it to be contested. As Foucault (1978, 95) asserts, power makes resistance possible, because resistance, critique, and deconstruction involve using power mechanisms that produce relations of domination or partnership.

Finally, diasporic citizenship is responsive to disruption and contesting. Openness to disruption leaves space for contestation and for plurality among sometimes conflicting interpretations of difference. A subject may commit to one interpretation in one context and adopt another interpretation in another context. Such acts and practices expose the identity politics of meaning-making as disruptable rather than fixed or final. By taking account of lived experience, the acts and practices of diasporic citizens point to plural, open-ended, contingent meanings. The disruption of dominant processes opens rather than forecloses. It is a way of being *responsive* to critique by re-examining how, when, and why interpretations of differences are foreclosed or opened up. As Selim puts it: "You need to talk to different people from different backgrounds. Avoid generalizations and being one-sided. We still have a common ground connecting us."

In my recent visits, the participants spoke about the racism that has increasingly flowed between the lines of public discourse. They discussed the obvious fear-mongering in the media, with alarmist politicians deliberately arousing public fears about Muslims, refugees, and immigrants. At the same time, the participants expressed their hope for a positive outcome. Although certain issues are becoming more difficult to deal with in Germany, resistance against racism and discrimination is also growing. People are articulating new forms of resistance and empowerment through creative acts and ways of working together. As Alp explained: "We, the people who are discriminated against, did not witness all these changes helplessly. We started forming reactions and resistance against racism and discrimination. We react both at individual levels and at group levels, as civil organizations, as well."

Although people's attitudes are changing, their ways of organizing are often mired in the past. New structures of activism have generally failed to emerge. People who become politically active are still organizing mainly around political parties, associations, and civil societies. In Berlin, for instance, political parties target the immigrant youth and population. In the past, immigrant communities tended to organize along ethnic lines. Now, the different ethnic groups are starting to form alliances. When I started my research in 2003, there was no real intercommunity work. Now, it is widespread. For example, Latin Americans and Türkiyeliler are working together; Arab and Russian immigrants are also working together and so on. As Erkan explains: "Everyone is experiencing a different kind of racism, and there is an understanding that we cannot overcome one kind without overcoming all of the racisms. This is beautiful."

These collaborative responses remind us of Said's (1998, 9) call for maximizing a spirit of cooperation and moving toward "a profound existential commitment and labour on behalf of the other." Today, we live in a world of mixtures, of migrations and crossings-over, of boundaries traversed. The emerging collaborative responses to the threats of contemporary racism are building on local acts and practices of diasporicity. It is not surprising that the practices of overcoming divisiveness can best be found in communities of struggle among the very people who are the targets of hostility.

In responding to the revival of ethnocentric hate, there is an urgent need for understanding the tension between European society and the politics of resistance, and nowhere is that need more pressing than in Germany. Accordingly, greater attention from scholars and the media must be directed toward the collective resistance practices of activists in German cities as they struggle to deal with marginalization, discrimination, and racism.

There is an urgent need for more research concerning activists who are engaged in an emerging network of political struggle on behalf of migrants and minorities of every kind. During my update research in 2016, I discerned a shift from a discourse on identity, belonging, and citizenship to a new politics of partnership among different groups of migrants. The tropes of fearful hate and the practices of collective resistance had both grown more pronounced. Where the context of social inequality had once been broadly accepted, now the tensions between ethnocentric fear and diasporicity have grown more pervasive (Halm 2013; Mühe 2016; Adam 2015; Jackson 2012; Meng 2015).

This book has explored an alternative theoretical avenue for investigating what types of collaborations diasporic citizenship requires. This new avenue is important because the partnerships among anti-racist, feminist, queer, and other movements have the potential to disrupt the dominant conditions, but they can do so only if their collaborations remain fluid and if the participants feel free to retain their autonomy. The strengths and weaknesses of partnerships between various defenders of difference need to be further examined and theorized.

Through this kind of study, we can also see how group identities tend to grow and mutate into new constellations of subtle, often permeable, intersecting collaborations. Such developments encourage us to share in a self-reflective mode of questioning. An awareness of boundedness helps people to realize themselves as a group, and it bestows a sense of diasporic *we-ness*. However, when we consider the characteristics of German-born Turkish Ausländer as diasporic citizens, it is clear that the boundaries of groups are always permeable and intersecting. Analysis of such groups reveals that communities are both the products and sites of intentionality. By recognizing the temporary and limited nature of their partnerships, diasporic activists open up ways to question their own group identities. They avoid habits of oppositional consciousness that designate particular individuals or groups as members of a particular community. They become free to examine how politically shared histories of displacement and exclusion give rise to new representations regarding the community of Turkish Ausländer in Berlin, even as they deconstruct the idea that this community is homogeneous.

In addition to being sites of displacement, exclusion, and struggle, diasporic communities commonly help to insulate individuals and groups from hostility. These communities can provide a sense of home and belonging, help members interpret their lives, and serve as a base for political mobilization. As Phelan (1994, 95) says, being a member of a community provides a sense of belonging, even for individuals who are not fully accepted by all members or who are members of more than one community. Thus, like any communities, diasporic communities are marked by both internally and externally generated meanings. They negotiate what they share and how they share it, rather than relying on fixed notions of what they have in common.

The politics of diasporic citizenship are useful not only for minority communities but also for analyzing the significance of any set of social conventions. As Dhamoon's (2009, 56–57) analysis suggests, such politics are useful for challenging power, regardless of whether one's community is fragmented, tightly knit, or seems to be some amorphous hybrid in the making.

Reimagining Germany, If German Is Just an "Other"

> What is at stake is not only the hegemony of Western cultures, but also their identities as unified cultures; in other words, the realization that there is a Third World in every First World, and vice-versa. The master is made to recognize that His Culture is not as homogeneous, not as monolithic as He once believed it to be; He discovers, often with much reluctance, that He is just an other.
>
> – Trinh T. Minh-ha (1986, 3)

Around the time that Trinh T. Minh-ha wrote the powerful lines above, most of the participants were attending primary school classes designed for "Ausländer" children, who would presumably go back to Türkiye one day with their guest-worker parents. More than thirty years later, Minh-ha's diagnosis is still applicable – and not just to Germany but to all of Europe. It might seem that since Minh-ha wrote those lines, or since 2002 when I first started collecting the narratives of German-born Ausländer, not much has changed in Germany. Or maybe things have changed mainly for the worse. The politics of domination have a way of covering over all the dialogical work of social change and reclosing the openings in local people's lives.

Still, some significant changes have appeared in people's understanding of Germanness and the various types of Otherness (Meng 2015). The identities of *the Others* have been increasingly policed and also more strongly asserted (Shoshan 2014). The social experience and political conscious-ness of Germans with immigrant backgrounds have grown more complex and mature (Çalışkan 2014). Clearly, people born and raised in Germany have diverse histories of migration, but they also share a common concern for social justice in their everyday lives.

The truth is that global movements of people in the postcolonial era have already shown that citizenship is no longer a matter of ethnic homogeneity or accommodation, if it ever was. This book has illustrated how German-born Turkish Ausländer represent a growing population of uprooted, trans-local people who are accentuating this broader awareness by expressing a kind of belonging that transcends nationality. Even though the narratives analyzed here are drawn from a particular group, time, and space, they speak to an omnipresent reality, namely that the whole nature and iden-tity of the ethnic nation-state is coming under question. This is because such an imagined monolithic culture does not fit the wider realities of human relations.

As a part of Europe, Germany has long been "a postcolonial locus of multiple diasporas" (Werbner 1997, 263). German culture has never been a unified, consensed social reality. The country remains torn between aspiring to overcome the fundamental incompleteness of German identity and denying the existence of any such incompleteness altogether. In the meantime, the renegotiation of internal differences has become an integral feature of Germanness. In the past, Germany's main strategy was to push non-conformant lives outside the imagined boundaries of German culture, even though everyday life in Germany has made these lives ever more integral to German society.

Germany as a nation-state has monologically understood itself as "corresponding to a single and unified authorial consciousness" (Bakhtin 1984, 9). The narratives from German-born Turkish Ausländer interrogate the monologism of this dominant discourse. They expose "the sheer heterogeneity of the diverse social forces" (Mercer 2018, 207) in Germany. From inside out, and from margin to centre, these voices challenge Germans to come to terms with the fact that there is a world of Ausländer on every corner, and Germany is an integral part of this foreign world. These worlds where German and Ausländer flow into each other challenge the make-believe notion of a monolithic culture where the ethnic German participants can presume to be masters of the house. Despite any measured reluctance to admit it, the German has long been just *another Other* in the land. The narratives of Germany's *other Others* have shown us how understanding citizenship as something flexible, fluid, and multiple is not only possible, but also crucial if Germany hopes to comprehend, reinvent, and revitalize itself.

Diasporicity reminds Germany that it can never be complete in isolation. Only when it overcomes its monologism and understands the fundamental incompleteness of Germanness will the country accept a greater wholeness of diasporic awareness. Then, perhaps the country can stop trying to constantly cover up the fact that it has long been a home for multiple diasporas, as has the rest of Europe.

The contemporary rise of right-wing extremism – with its language of fear and acts of violence against marginalized, vulnerable groups – is intimately connected to the crisis of the West. Right-wing extremism is a broad term that describes the many movements, groups, and parties devoted to the notion that an ethnic, racial, or a national identity determines one's

Becoming a Chameleon 289

value as a human being. This resurgence of ethnocentric values is witnessed most dramatically in the contemporary rhetoric of fear toward Muslims. The increasing prominence of the PEGIDA movement (Patriotic Europeans Against the Islamization of the West), the recent political gains of the AfD (Alternative für Deutschland), and the growing number of violent attacks on minorities all indicate that right-wing extremism is on the rise in Germany.

Regardless of how politicians or opinion-makers try to brand the reality, most of them realize they cannot simply expel migrant populations from their countries. Therefore, all efforts to generate greater hostility for non-German residents can only deepen social divisions. Accusing immigrants (especially Muslims) of making Germany stupid, or calling for a führer with a strong hand to control minorities, will only repeat the past's costly mistakes.

These contemporary arguments of fear and hatred in Germany exemplify the broader problem that Europe and the West face. There is no way of achieving a unified, homogenous community by claiming and enforcing the hegemony of one group over others. In Germany's past, treating other people as *social pollution* has been the problem, not the solution. Reinventing Germany requires a fundamental mindset shift. Instead of assuming that the problem is with people who fail to fit in with a single definition of Germanness, the challenge of the future is in learning how to develop more mutually beneficial relations among all its different peoples.

The emergence of diasporic citizenship challenges German politicians to rethink old definitions of German identity and old policies of accommodating Ausländer. Diasporic citizenship is a broader network of relations, and German-born Turkish Ausländer are very forcefully challenging politicians and opinion-makers to open themselves up to a different kind of citizenship. People across the world are exploring forms of citizenship that are fluid and by nature always under construction.

Germans have a lot to learn from diasporicity as a particular type of awareness that provides an alternative to nationality. Nationality has involved a monologist awareness of belonging based on the imagined dominion of one cultural group. In contrast, diasporicity involves an awareness regarding the worldwide struggle of migrants and their descendants who occupy ambivalent spaces – sometimes being included and other times excluded – yet are able to transcend the limits of any particular culture (Dhamoon 2009). Diasporic citizenship emerges from these people's awareness that national collectivities have to be questioned and new alliances have to be formed. Different ways of reading the same land need to be incorporated into the dialogue among citizens. Otherwise, we will continue the ancient battle over which people will be silenced or excluded in our communities.

Although I am sympathetic to the principles of diversity and pluralism that underpin multiculturalism, I assert that multiculturalism cannot go far enough in addressing the key issues of power. At best, multiculturalism only partially captures the complexity of culture-based differences. At worst, it so narrowly defines the territories of identity, difference, and belonging that it becomes a means for accommodating the desire for social segregation. The politics of multiculturalism needs to go beyond simply affirming, accommodating, managing, and softening culture-based differences. To relate as equals, people who are different need to fundamentally question and reconstitute their relations of power.

The contemporary practices of multiculturalism around the world have shown that this political strategy is fundamentally limited in its potential for offering answers to the challenges Europe faces. Diasporic citizenship serves to disrupt any singular narratives of nations or cultures. Multicultural citizenship simply treats different cultures as collective entities to be accommodated. Perhaps it is not that multiculturalism has failed but that the Ausländer are creating something better, which Germany can no longer ignore. Like the Ausländer, as Minh-ha (1986) would say, the German *is just an other.*

Notes

INTRODUCTION

Note: The participants were assigned pseudonyms. First names are used so that readers may track the comments of participants across quotes. If the participants are publicly known figures or stated that they want to be referred to by their real names in the text, then I use their real names.

1. During my follow-up research, I applied my extensive experience with narrative interviewing (Çalışkan 2015, 2018) and relied on my previously built rapport with the participants. I also approached some of the public figures who had participated in my original research. In general, I followed the same methodology that I had applied in the initial study. The respondents talked about their experiences relevant to the research topic. Then I encouraged them to reflect on their experiences, which led to discussions of their political activities. Although I avoided imposing a rigid structure, I had a list of themes prepared. When necessary, I broached these themes by asking open-ended questions (Çalışkan 2018).

   Using Skype made the interviewing process more accessible, more flexible, and less expensive. With Skype, the researcher gets to have face-to-face contact, as in a one-on-one interview, and the participants can participate in a setting where they feel comfortable. One concern about Skype is the perceived reliability and quality of the program itself (Weller 2015). Internet access can be lost midway through an interview, and sometimes the program freezes temporarily. Another concern with Skype interviews is the involvement of the participant (Weller 2015). As the researcher and participants are not actually face-to-face, the researcher cannot guarantee that the participants will give undivided attention to the interview.

292   Notes to pages 9–214

2 *LGBTI+* is an inclusive term representing Lesbian, Gay, Bisexual, Trans (gender), and Intersex. It also includes other groups relating to sexual orientation and gender identity including, but not limited to, Asexual, Non-Binary, Queer, and Two-Spirit.
3 Parts of this section have been previously published (Çalışkan, 2015).

CHAPTER 2: CONSTITUTING GERMANS AND OUTSIDERS
1 In these statistics, it is not clear if Turks are considered as coming from Europe or Asia.

CHAPTER 3: HOSTILITY–HOSPITALITY
Acknowledgment: An earlier version of this chapter was published in *International Review of Sociology: Revue Internationale de Sociologie*, titled "Accommodating 'Foreigners': Narrative Accounts of Berlin's German-born Turkish Ausländer" (2014). This chapter has had substantial updates since then.
1 This category is largely symbolic, as the number of German Jews is quite small, and they require a different analysis, which is beyond the scope of this project. Still, I want to highlight that the historic treatment of Jews (from medieval times forward) is directly relevant to the treatment of new minorities.
2 See Judith Goode (2018) for an ethnographic critique of Lewis's theory.
3 See, for example, Citlak, Leyendecker, Schölmerich, Driessen, and Harwood (2008); and Mueller (2006).
4 Kurdish identity and its place in political, cultural, and social landscapes of Türkiye is a complex issue beyond the scope of this study. There is a separatist Kurdish movement in Türkiye.
5 Antalya, a Mediterranean city, is a main holiday destination for both Germans and Turks living in Germany.

CHAPTER 4: HOMESICKNESS–HOMELESSNESS
1 *Ladino* is a Romance language with a vocabulary derived mainly from Old Castilian, Hebrew, Turkish, and some French and Greek. Speakers are currently almost exclusively Sephardi Jews, for example, in or from Thessaloniki, İstanbul, and İzmir. http://en.wikipedia.org/wiki/Ladino_language.
2 A *Cemevi* (pronounced Djemevi) is a house of gathering in Turkish, which is a place of fundamental importance for Türkiye's Alevi and Bektaşi populations. Strictly speaking, it is not a place of worship but rather a place of assemblage (http://en.wikipedia.org/wiki/Cemevi).
3 In April 2010, Lower Saxony's CDU government appointed Germany's first cabinet minister with a Turkish heritage. Born in the northern German city of Hamburg to Turkish immigrant parents, Aygül Özkan, a lawyer and a practising Alevi Muslim, said she chose the CDU because she shares the party's values about family and compassion for neighbours (Dernbach and Wallbaum 2010).

CHAPTER 5: BORDERLANDS
1 GLADT is a non-profit organization based in Berlin, which is run by and for Black and of colour lesbians, gays, bisexuals, trans people, and queers. This organization

Notes to pages 214–57 293

started as an independent, self-organized group of gay men, lesbians, bisexuals, and trans people (LGBT) with family links to Türkiye. GLADT began meeting in 1997 and has been a registered nonprofit organization since 2003. It engages on various levels in the fight against racism, sexism, trans- and homophobia, ableism, and other forms of discrimination. http://www.gladt.de/index.php?option=com_content&view =article&id=43&Itemid=38, https://www.facebook.com/pg/gladt.de/about/?ref=page _internal.

2 LSVD is the largest civil rights organization of LGBTI+ in Germany. It was founded in 1990 as a gay association in the GDR, by former opposition activists against the communist government. The organization became known throughout Germany for its campaign to legalize gay marriage in 1992. http://en.wikipedia.org/wiki/LSVD.

3 Hamam, also known as Turkish bath, is "a bath in which the bather passes through a series of steam rooms of increasing temperature and then receives a rubdown, massage, and cold shower." https://www.merriam-webster.com/dictionary/Turkish%20 bath. *Harem* here refers to "a usually secluded house or part of a house allotted to women in some Muslim households." https://www.merriam-webster.com/dictionary/ harem.

CHAPTER 6: FORGING DIASPORIC CITIZENSHIP

1 May 1 is the European and International Labour Day. This commemoration has strongly Marxist connotations of class struggle and labour solidarity.

2 Translated from the German.

References

Abadan-Unat, Neriman. 1976. *Turkish Workers in Europe (1960–1975)*. Leiden: E.J. Brill.

—. 2002. *Bitmeyen göç: Konuk işçilikten ulus-ötesi yurttaşlığa* [Endless migration: From guest-worker to transnational citizenship]. İstanbul: İstanbul Bilgi University Press.

Adam, Heribert. 2015. "Xenophobia, Asylum Seekers, and Immigration Policies in Germany." *Nationalism and Ethnic Politics* 21, 4: 446–64.

AFP/The Local. 2016. "One in 10 Germans Wants Country to be Ruled by 'Führer.'" The Local Germany, June 15, 2016. https://www.thelocal.de/20160615/one-in-every-ten-germans-wants-to-be-led-by-fuhrer.

Agathangelou, Anna M., and L.H.M. Ling. 2009. *Transforming World Politics: From Empire to Multiple Worlds*. New York: Routledge.

Ahmed, Sara. 2000. *Strange Encounters: Embodied Others in Post-coloniality*. London: Routledge.

—. 2004. *The Cultural Politics of Emotion*. Edinburgh: Edinburgh University Press.

—. 2007. "The Language of Diversity." *Ethnic and Racial Studies* 30, 2: 235–56.

Aisch, Gregor, Adam Pearce, and Bryant Rousseau. 2016. "How Far Is Europe Swinging to the Right?" *New York Times*, updated October 23, 2017. http://www.nytimes.com/interactive/2016/05/22/world/europe/europe-right-wing-austria-hungary.html?_r=0.

Albrecht, Richard. 1982. "Was ist der Unterschied zwischen Türken und Juden? (Anti-) Türken- witze in der Bundesrepublik Deutschland" [What is the difference between Turks and Jews? (Anti-) Turkish jokes in the Federal Republic of Germany]. *Zeitschrift für Volkskunde* 78: 220–29.

References

Allain, Kristi A., Rory Crath, and Gül Çalışkan. 2020. "Speaking Welcome: A Discursive Analysis of an Immigrant Mentorship Event in Atlantic Canada." *Ethnicities* 20, 6: 1197–217. https://doi.org/10.1177/1468796819833398.

Allen, Amy. 1999. *The Power of Feminist Theory: Domination, Resistance, Solidarity.* Boulder, CO: Westview Press.

Alsultany, Evelyn. 2002. "Los Intersticios: Recasting Moving Selves." In *This Bridge We Call Home: Radical Visions for Transformation,* edited by Gloria Anzaldúa and AnaLouise Keating, 106–10. New York: Routledge.

Amt für Statistik Berlin-Brandenburg. 2020. Accessed January 4, 2021. https://www.statistik-berlin-brandenburg.de/a-i-9-j.

Anderson, Benedict. 1983. *Imagined Communities: Reflections on the Origins and Spread of Nationalism.* London: Verso.

Anthias, Floya. 1998. "Evaluating 'Diaspora': Beyond Ethnicity?" *Sociology* 32, 3: 557–80.

—. 2018. "Evaluating 'Diaspora': Beyond Ethnicity?" In *The Routledge Diaspora Studies Reader,* edited by Klaus Stierstorfer and Janet Wilson, 157–62. Abingdon, Oxon: Routledge.

Anzaldúa, Gloria. (1987) 2007. *Borderlands/La Frontera: The New Mestiza,* 3rd ed. San Francisco: Aunt Lute.

Appadurai, Arjun. 1996. *Modernity at Large: Cultural Dimensions of Globalization.* Minneapolis: University of Minnesota Press.

Arneil, Barbara. 2007. "Cultural Protections vs. Cultural Justice: Post-colonialism, Agonistic Justice and the Limitations of Liberal Theory." In *Sexual Justice/ Cultural Justice: Critical Perspectives in Theory and Practice,* edited by Barbara Arneil, Monique Deveaux, Rita Dhamoon, and Avigail Eisenberg, 50–66. London: Routledge.

Asgharzadeh, Alireza. 2004. "Islamic Fundamentalism, Globalization, and Migration: New Challenges for Canada." In *Calculated Kindness: Global Restructuring, Immigration and Settlement in Canada,* edited by Rose B. Folson, 130–50. Halifax, NS: Fernwood.

Ashkenazi, Abraham. 1990. "The Turkish Minority in Germany and West Berlin." *Immigrants and Minorities* 9, 3: 303–16.

Bakare-Yusuf, Bibi. 2008. "Rethinking Diasporicity: Embodiment, Emotion, and the Displaced Origin." *African and Black Diaspora: An International Journal* 1, 2: 147–58.

Bakhtin, Mikhail M. 1981. "Discourse in the Novel." In *The Dialogic Imagination: Four Essays,* edited by Michael Holquist, translated by Caryl Emerson and Michael Holquist, 259–422. Austin: University of Texas Press.

—. 1984. *Problems of Dostoevsky's Poetics,* edited by Caryl Emerson. Minneapolis: University of Minnesota Press. https://doi.org/10.5749/j.ctt22727z1.

—. 1993. "Toward a Philosophy of the Act." In *Toward a Philosophy of the Act,* edited by Vadim Liapunov and Michael Holquist, translated by Vadim Liapunov, 1–76. Austin: University of Texas Press.

296 References

Ballard, Roger. 1996. "Islam and the Construction of Europe." In *Muslims in the Margin: Political Responses to the Presence of Islam in Western Europe*, edited by Wasif Abdelrahman R. Shadid and P.S. van Koningsveld, 15–51. Kampen, Netherlands: Kok Pharos.

Baumgartl, Bernd, and Adrian Favell. 1996. "Europe: National Visions, International Perspectives and Comparative Analysis." In *New Xenophobia in Europe*, edited by Bernd Baumgartl and Adrian Favell, 378–99. London: Kluwer Law.

Bax, Daniel. 2008. "Pietät und Populismus: Wegen des Brands in Ludwigshafen wird eine 'Tatort'-Folge verschoben. Das ist nicht so absurd, wie es demnächst scheint" [Piety and populism: Because of the fire in Ludwigshafen, a "Tatort" episode is postponed. This is not as absurd as it will soon seem]. *Die Tageszeitung*, July 2, 2008. https://taz.de/!5187022/.

BBC. 2011. "Thilo Sarrazin Live from Berlin" (broadcast episode). World Have Your Say. January 18, 2011. http://www.bbc.co.uk/programmes/p00d0fbj.

Becker, Birgit. 2009. "Immigrants' Emotional Identification with the Host Society." *Ethnicities* 9, 2: 200–25.

Benhabib, Seyla. 1992. "Models of Public Space: Hannah Arendt, the Liberal Tradition and Jurgen Habermas." In *Habermas and the Public Sphere*, edited by Craig Calhoun, 73–98. Cambridge, MA: MIT Press.

–. 1996. "Towards a Deliberative Model of Democratic Legitimacy." In *Democracy and Difference: Contesting the Boundaries of the Political*, edited by Seyla Benhabib, 67–94. Princeton, NJ: Princeton University Press.

–. 2002. *The Claims of Culture: Equality and Diversity in the Global Era*. Princeton, NJ: Princeton University Press.

Berger, John, and Jean Mohr. 1975. *A Seventh Man: A Book of Images and Words about the Experience of Migrant Workers in Europe*. London: Penguin.

Berlin.de. n.d. "Berlin after 1945." Berlin in Brief. Accessed February 2, 2010. http://www.berlin.de/berlin-im-ueberblick/geschichte/1945.en.html.

Bernstein, Richard. 2003. "The Saturday Profile; A New Bold View of German-Turkish Youth." *New York Times*, April 12, 2003. https://www.nytimes.com/2003/04/12/world/the-saturday-profile-a-bold-new-view-of-turkish-german-youth.html.

Bhabha, Homi K. 1990. *Nation and Narration*. London: Routledge.

–. 1994. *The Location of Culture*. New York: Routledge.

Bickford, Susan. 1997. "Anti-anti-identity Politics: Feminism, Democracy, and the Complexities of Citizenship." *Hypatia* 12, 4: 112–31.

Board on Children and Families. Commission on Behavioural and Social Sciences and Education. National Research Council. Institute of Medicine. 1995. "Immigrant Children and Their Families: Issues for Research and Policy." *Future of Children* 5, 2: 72–89.

Bochow, Michael. 2004. "Junge schwule Turken in Deutschland: Biographische Bruche und Bewaltigungsstrategien" [Young gay Turks in Germany: Biographical breaks and coping strategies]. In *Muslime unter dem Regenbogen: Homosexualitat, migration und Islam* [Muslims under the rainbow: Homosexuality, migration and Islam], edited by LSVD Berlin-Brandenburg e.V, 168–88. Berlin: Querverlag.

References 297

Boston, William. 2010. "Top German Banker's Attack on Immigrants Causes a Stir." *Time,* September 3, 2010. http://content.time.com/time/world/article/0,8599, 2015866,00.html#ixzz1YYZvG5P6.

Bourdieu, Pierre. 1973. "Cultural Reproduction and Social Reproduction." In *Knowledge, Education, and Cultural Change: Papers in the Sociology of Education,* edited by Richard Brown, 71–112. London: Tavistock.

–. 1986. "The Forms of Capital." In *Handbook of Theory and Research for the Sociology of Education,* edited by John G. Richardson, 245–58. New York: Greenwood Press.

Boyarin, Jonathan, and Daniel Boyarin. 2002. *Powers of Diaspora: Two Essays on the Relevance of Jewish Culture.* Minneapolis: University of Minnesota Press.

Boyle, Darren. 2016. "'Go Naked in Saudi Arabia and See What Will Happen to You': French Mayor Vows to Ignore Burkini Ban Court Ruling." *Daily Mail,* August 31, 2016. http://www.dailymail.co.uk/news/article-3766672/Go-naked -Saudi-Arabia-happen-French-mayor-vows-ignore-burkini-ban-court-ruling. html.

Bradham, Journey. 2018. "Aziza A, Women's Woes- Feminism in the Pre-modern and Modern Middle East: Es Ist Zeit." *Journey Bradham: Agnes Scott College* (blog), December 6, 2018. https://journeyb.agnesscott.org/his-207/ es-ist-zeit/.

Brady, Kate. 2016. "Almost Two Thirds of Germans Believe Islam 'Does Not Belong in Germany', Poll Finds." *DW,* May 12, 2016. http://www.dw.com/en/almost-two -thirds-of-germans-believe-islam-does-not-belong-in-germany-poll-finds/a -19251169.

Brah, Avtar. 1996. *Cartographies of Diaspora: Contesting Identities.* London: Routledge.

–. 2018. "Cartographies of Diaspora." In *The Routledge Diaspora Studies Reader,* edited by Klaus Stierstorfer and Janet Wilson, 235–38. Abingdon, Oxon: Routledge.

Brah, Avtar, and Ann Phoenix. 2004. "Ain't I a Woman? Revisiting Intersectionality." *Journal of International Women's Studies* 5, 3: 75–86.

Braziel, Jana E., and Anita Mannur. 2003. "Nation, Migration, Globalization: Points of Contention in Diaspora Studies." In *Theorizing Diaspora: A Reader,* edited by Jana E. Braziel and Anita Mannur, 1–22. Malden, MA: Blackwell.

Brown, Timothy S. 2006. "'Keeping It Real' in a Different 'Hood: (African-) Americanization and Hip Hop in Germany." In *The Vinyl Ain't Final: Hip Hop and the Globalization of Black Popular Culture,* edited by Dipannita Basu and Sidney J. Lemelle, 137–50. London: Pluto Press.

Brubaker, Rogers. 2017. "Between Nationalism and Civilizationism: The European Populist Moment in Comparative Perspective." *Ethnic and Racial Studies* 40, 8: 1191–226. doi:10.1080/01419870.2017.1294700.

Bulletin. 1976, June 29. Federal Republic of Germany, Press and Information Office, 179.

Bundeszentrale für politische Bildung. 2016. "Dossier, Rechtsextremismus: Mehr als 50 Jahre rechtsextrem" [Dossier, Right-wing extremism: More than 50 years

of right-wing extremism]. https://www.bpb.de/politik/extremismus/rechtsex
tremismus/222499/mehr-als-50-jahre-rechtsextrem.

–. 2018. "25 Jahre Brandanschlag in Solingen" [25 years after arson attack in Sol-
ingen]. https://www.bpb.de/politik/hintergrund-aktuell/161980/brandanschlag
-in-solingen.

–. 2021. "Bevölkerung mit Migrationshintergrund: In absoluten Zahlen, Anteile
an der Gesamtbevölkerung in Prozent, 2020" [Population with migration background: Absolute figures in percentages of the total population, 2020]. https://
www.bpb.de/nachschlagen/zahlen-und-fakten/soziale-situation-in-deutsch
land/61646/migrationshintergrund.

Butler, Judith. 1993. *Bodies That Matter: On the Discursive Limits of "Sex."* New York:
Routledge.

Çağlar, Ayşe. 1995. "German Turks in Berlin: Social Exclusion and Strategies for
Social Mobility." *New Community* 21, 3: 309–24.

Çağlar, Ayşe, and Levent Soysal, eds. 2003. Turkish Migration to Germany: Issues,
Reflections, and Futures [Special Issue], in *New Perspectives on Turkey* 29,
Spring–Fall.

Çalışkan, Gül. 2014. "Accommodating 'Foreigners': Narrative Accounts of Berlin's
German-born Turkish Ausländer." *International Review of Sociology: Revue
Internationale de Sociologie* 24, 3: 450–70. doi:10.1080/03906701.2014.954329.

–. 2015. "Politics of Narrating Everyday Encounters: Negotiating Identity and
Belonging among Berlin's German-born Turkish Ausländer." *Narrative Works:
Investigations and Interventions* 5, 2: 25–49.

–. 2018. "Conducting Narrative Inquiry in Sociological Research: Reflections from
Research on Narratives of Everyday Encounters." In *SAGE Research Methods
Cases.* http://dx.doi.org/10.4135/9781526445513.

Çalışkan, Gül, and Kayla Preston. 2017. "Tropes of Fear and the Crisis of the West:
Trumpism as a Discourse of Post-territorial Coloniality." *Postcolonial Studies*
20, 2: 199–216.

Canovan, Margaret. 2005. *The People.* Cambridge, UK: Polity Press.

Çelik, Neco. dir. 2003 *Alltag* [Everyday]. Film. Berlin: Bayerischer Rundfunk (BR).

Charles, Hawley. 2006. "Muslim Profiling a German State Quizes Muslim Immigrants on Jews, Gays and Swim Lessons." *Spiegel International,* January 31, 2006.
http://www.spiegel.de/international/muslim-profiling-a-german-state-quizes
-muslim-immigrants-on-jews-gays-and-swim-lessons-a-397482.html.

Cho, Lily. 2007a. "Diasporic Citizenship: Contradictions and Possibilities for Canadian Literature." In *Trans.Can.Lit: Resituating the Study of Canadian Literature,* edited by Smaro Kamboureli and Roy Miki, 93–109. Waterloo, ON: Wilfrid
Laurier University Press.

–. 2007b. "Diasporic Citizenship: Inhabiting Contradictions and Challenging Exclusions." *American Quarterly* 59, 2: 467–78.

Chrisafis, Angelique. 2016. "France's Burkini Ban Row Divides Government as
Court Mulls Legality." *Guardian,* August 25, 2016. https://www.theguardian.
com/world/2016/aug/25/frances-burkini-ban-row-divides-government-court
-mulls-legality.

References

Citlak, Banu, Birgit Leyendecker, Axel Schölmerich, Ricarda Driessen, and Robin L. Harwood. 2008. "Socialization Goals among First- and Second-Generation Migrant Turkish and German Mothers." *International Journal of Behavioural Development* 32, 1: 56–65.

Clifford, James. 1994. "Diasporas." *Cultural Anthropology* 9, 3: 302–38.

Coburn-Staege, Ursula. 1979. "Ausländerkinder als Aussenseiter in der Schule und Moglichkeiten ihrer Integration." *Pädagogische Welt* 33, 12: 756.

Cohen, Rina, and Gerald Gold. 1997. "Constructing Ethnicity: Myth of Return and Modes of Exclusion among Israelis in Toronto." *International Migration/ Migrations Internationales/Migraciones Internationales* 35, 3: 373–94.

Cohen, Robin. 2018. "Solid, Ductile and Liquid: Changing Notions of Homeland and Home in Diaspora Studies." In *The Routledge Diaspora Studies Reader,* edited by Klaus Stierstorfer and Janet Wilson, 239–43. Abingdon, Oxon: Routledge.

Cohen, Robin, and Paul Kennedy. (2000) 2013. *Global Sociology.* New York: New York University Press.

Collins, Patricia Hill. (1990) 2015. *Black Feminist Thought: Knowledge, Consciousness, and the Politics of Empowerment.* London: Routledge.

Connolly, Kate. 2015. "Pegida: What Does the German Far-right Movement Actually Stand For?" *Guardian,* January 6, 2015. https://www.theguardian.com/world/shortcuts/2015/jan/06/pegida-what-does-german-far-right-movement-actually-stand-for.

Council of Europe. 1980. *The Federal Republic of Germany: Education for Migrant Workers' Children.* Newsletter. Strasbourg: Documentation Centre for Education in Europe, February.

Coy, Jason P. 2011. *A Brief History of Germany.* New York: Facts on File.

Crenshaw, Kimberlé. 1991. "Mapping the Margins: Intersectionality, Identity Politics, and Violence against Women of Color." *Stanford Law Review* 43, 6: 1241–99.

Cresswell, Tim. 1996. *In Place/Out of Place: Geography, Ideology and Transgression.* Minneapolis: University of Minnesota Press.

culturebase.net: The International Artist Database. 2001. "Emine Sevgi Özdamar: Artist Portrait." Accessed September 2010. http://www.culturebase.net/artist.php?629.

–. 2010. "Aziza A Artist Portrait." Accessed September 2010. http://www.culturebase.net/artist.php?347#article.

Dağtaş, Mahiye Seçil. 2007. "Married to the Military: Family, Nationalism and Women's Political Agency in Turkey." Master's thesis, York University.

Dale, Gareth. 1999. "Germany: Nation and Immigration." In *The European Union and Migrant Labour,* edited by Gareth Dale and Mike Cole, 113–46. Oxford: Berg.

Day, Richard. 2000. *Multiculturalism and the History of Canadian Diversity.* Toronto: University of Toronto Press.

de Hart, Betty. 2007. "The End of Multiculturalism: The End of Dual Citizenship? Political and Public Debates on Dual Citizenship in the Netherlands (1980–2004)." In *Dual Citizenship in Europe: From Nationhood to Societal Integration,* edited by Thomas Faist, 77–102. Hampshire, UK: Ashgate.

300 References

Der Spiegel. 2008, February 7. "An Opportunity in Tragedy." http://www.spiegel.de/international/germany/german-press-reactions-an-opportunity-in-tragedy-a-533748.html.

Dernbach, Andrea, and Klaus Wallbaum. 2010. "Ministerin für Integration: Wer ist Aygül Özkan?" *Der Tagesspiegel,* April 25, 2010. https://www.tagesspiegel.de/politik/ministerin-fuer-integration-wer-ist-ayguel-oezkan/1808134.html.

Derrida, Jacques. 1981. *Positions,* translated by Alan Bass. London: Athlone Press.

Derrida, Jacques, and Anne Dufourmantelle. 2000. *Of Hospitality: Anne Dufourmantelle Invites Jacques Derrida to Respond.* Stanford, CA: Stanford University Press.

Deutsche Welle. 2016. "Hundreds of Right-wing Asylum-related Attacks in 2016." November 13. http://www.dw.com/en/hundreds-of-right-wing-asylum-related-attacks-in-2016/a-36377046.

–. 2017. "AfD, PEGIDA Hold Side-by-side Events in Dresden." May 9. http://www.dw.com/en/afd-pegida-hold-side-by-side-events-in-dresden/a-38761338.

Dhamoon, Rita. 2009. *Identity/Difference Politics: How Difference Is Produced and Why It Matters.* Vancouver: UBC Press.

Die Bundesausländerbeauftragte. 2022. "Integration in Deutschland" [Integration in Germany]. http://www.bundesauslaenderbeauftragte.de/integration.html.

Diener, Alexander C., and Joshua Hagen. 2009. "Theorizing Borders in a 'Borderless World': Globalization, Territory and Identity." *Geography Compass* 3, 3: 1196–216.

Dion, Karen K., and Kenneth L. Dion. 2004. "Gender, Immigrant Generation, and Ethnocultural Identity." *Sex Roles* 50, 5/6: 347–55.

DOMiD. n.d. "Migration History in Germany." Documentation Centre and Museum of Immigration in Germany. https://www.domid.org/en/migration-history-germany.

DuBois, W.E.B. (1903) 2017. *The Souls of Black Folk.* Brooklyn, NY: Restless Classics.

Dundes, Alan, and Thomas Hauschild. 1983. "Auschwitz Jokes." *Western Folklore* 42, 4: 249–60.

Dziadek, Francesca. 2012. "Germany Grapples with Diversity." Inter Press Service: News Agency, December 7, 2012. http://www.ipsnews.net/2012/12/germany-grapples-with-diversity/.

Edgell, Penny, and Eric Tranby. 2010. "Shared Visions? Diversity and Cultural Membership in American Life." *Social Problems* 57, 2: 175–204.

Egorova, Yulia, and Fiaz Ahmed. 2017. "The Impact of Antisemitism and Islamophobia on Jewish-Muslim Relations in the UK: Memory, Experience, Context." In *Antisemitism and Islamophobia in Europe: A Shared Story?,* edited by James Renton and Ben Gidley, 283–301. London: Macmillan.

Fabb, Richard. 2013. "How New UK Spouse Visa Rules Turned Me into an Englishman in Exile." *Guardian,* July 8, 2013. https://www.theguardian.com/commentisfree/2013/jul/09/uk-australia-spouse-visa.

Faist, Thomas. 2007. *Dual Citizenship in Europe: From Nationhood to Societal Integration.* Hampshire, UK: Ashgate.

References 301

Fanon, Frantz. (1952) 1967. *Black Skin: White Masks*. New York: Grove Press.

Farahat, Anuscheh, and Kay Hailbronner. 2020. Report on Citizenship Law: Germany [Global Governance Programme], Globalcit, Country Reports, 2020/05 [Global Citizenship]. Retrieved from Cadmus, European University Institute Research Repository, at: http://hdl.handle.net/1814/66430.

Federal Anti-Discrimination Agency. 2006. "The General Act on Equal Treatment." Accessed June 2, 2018. http://www.antidiskriminierungsstelle.de/EN/AboutUs/TheAct/theAct.html.

–. 2009. *Act Implementing European Directives Putting into Effect the Principle of Equal Treatment*. August, 2009. http://www.antidiskriminierungsstelle.de/SharedDocs/Downloads/EN/publikationen/agg_in_englischer_Sprache.pdf?__blob=publicationFile&v=1.

Fekete, Liz. 2004. "Anti-Muslim Racism and the European Security State." *Race and Class* 46, 1: 3–29.

Fellows, Mary Louise, and Sherene Razack. 1994. "Seeking Relations: Law and Feminism Roundtables." *Signs: A Journal for Women in Culture and Society* 19, 4: 1048–83.

–. 1998. "The Race to Innocence: Confronting Hierarchical Relations among Women." *Journal of Gender, Race and Justice* 1, 2: 335–52.

First Post. 2012, March 12. "Sarkozy Threatens French Pullout of Visa-free Zone." http://www.firstpost.com/politics/sarkozy-threatens-french-pullout-of-visa-free-zone-240544.html.

Foucault, Michel. 1977. "A Preface to Transgression." In *Language, Counter-Memory, Practice*, edited by Donald Bouchard, 29–52. Ithaca, NY: Cornell University Press.

–. (1977) 1995. *Discipline and Punish: The Birth of the Prison*, translated by A. Sheridan. New York: Vintage Books.

–. 1978. *The History of Sexuality: An Introduction*. Vol. 1. Translated by R. Hurley. New York: Vintage Books.

–. 1980. *Power/Knowledge: Selected Interviews and Other Writings, 1972–1977*, edited by Gordon Colin. New York: Pantheon.

Furlong, Ray. 2006. "German 'Muslim Test' Stirs Anger." BBC News, February 10, 2006. http://news.bbc.co.uk/2/hi/europe/4655240.stm.

Gebauer, Matthias. 2001. "Klage gegen Abschiebung: `Mehmet' will bis zum Ende kampfen" [Lawsuit against deportation: "Mehmet" wants to fight to the end]. *Der Spiegel*, April 24, 2001. https://www.spiegel.de/panorama/klage-gegen-abschiebung-mehmet-will-bis-zum-ende-kaempfen-a-130183.html.

Gerdes, Jürgen, Thomas Faist, and Beate Rieple. 2007. "We Are All 'Republican' Now: The Politics of Dual Citizenship in Germany." In *Dual Citizenship in Europe: From Nationhood to Societal Integration*, edited by Thomas Faist, 45–76. Hampshire, UK: Ashgate.

Gerhards, Jürgen, and Silke Hans. 2009. "From Hasan to Herbert: Name-giving Patterns of Immigrant Parents between Acculturation and Ethnic Maintenance." *American Journal of Sociology* 114, 4: 1102–28.

Germany Visa: Information, Requirements, Application Form. n.d. https://www.germany-visa.org/.

302 References

GHDI. 1982, March 4. "The Heidelberg Manifesto of Xenophobic Professors." http://ghdi.ghi-dc.org/sub_document.cfm?document_id=857.

Giddens, Anthony. 1997. *Sociology*. London: Polity Press.

Gilroy, Paul. 1993. *The Black Atlantic: Modernity and Double Consciousness*. London: Verso.

Gitmez, Ali S. 1979. *Dişgöç Öyküsü*. Ankara, Turkey: Maya Matbaacilik Yayıncılık.

–. 1983. *Yurtdişina Işçi Göçü ve Geri Dönüşler: Beklentileri Gerçekleşenler*. İstanbul: Alan Yayıncılık.

Goode, Judith. 2018. "How Urban Ethnography Counters Myths about the Poor." In *Urban Life: Readings in the Anthropology of the City*, edited by George Gmelch and Petra Kuppinger, 195–211. Prospect Heights, IL: Waveland Press.

Gordon, Milton. 1964. *Assimilation in American Life: The Role of Race, Religion and National Origins*. Oxford: Oxford University Press.

Goulard, Hortense. 2016. "Manuel Valls Scolds Minister for Criticizing Burkini Ban: French PM Repeated That All-body Swimwear Is 'Enslavement of Women.'" *Politico*, August 25, 2016. http://www.politico.eu/article/manuel-valls-slams -minister-criticizing-burkini-ban-najat-vallaud-belkacem-national-cohesion-islam/.

Green, Simon. 2003. "The Legal Status of Turks in Germany." *Immigrants and Minorities* 2–3 (July): 28–46.

Groenendijk, Kees. 1997. "Regulating Ethnic Immigration: The Case of the Aüssiedler." *Journal of Ethnic and Migration Studies* 23, 4: 461–82. doi:10.1080/ 1369183X.1997.9976606.

Gunkel, Henriette, and Ben Pitcher. 2008. "Editorial: Racism in the Closet – Interrogating Postcolonial Sexuality." *Darkmatter: In the Ruins of Imperial Culture*, May 2, 2008. http://www.darkmatter101.org/site/2008/05/02/racism -in-the-closet-interrogating-postcolonial-sexuality/.

Güvenç, Bozkurt. 1993. *Türk Kimligi: Kültür Tarihinin Kaynaklari* [Turkish identity: Sources of cultural history]. Ankara, Turkey: Kultur Bakanligi Yayinlari.

Habbe, Christian. 1983. *Ausländer: Die verfemten Gäste, Spiegel-Buch* [Foreigners: The ostracized guests, Spiegel book]. Reinbek, Germany: Rowohlt.

Hairsine, Kate. 2004. "Being Turkish and Gay in Germany." Deutsche Welle, September 9, 2004. https://www.dw.com/en/being-turkish-and-gay-in-germany/a -1336100.

Hall, Alan. 2010. "Multiculturalism in Germany Has 'Utterly Failed,' Claims Chancellor Angela Merkel." *Daily Mail*, October 18, 2010. http://www.dailymail.co. uk/news/article-1321277/Angela-Merkel-Multiculturalism-Germany-utterly -failed.html#ixzz1DrUfXCUi.

Hall, Stuart. 1990. "Cultural Identity and Diaspora." In *Identity: Community, Culture Difference*, edited by Jonathan Rutherford, 222–37. London: Lawrence and Wishart.

–. 1995. "Negotiating Caribbean Identities." *New Left Review* 209 (January– February): 3–14.

–. 1997. "Old and New Identities, Old and New Ethnicities." In *Culture, Globalization and the World System: Contemporary Conditions for the Representa-*

References 303

tion of Identity, edited by Anthony King, 31–68. Minneapolis: University of Minnesota.

Hall, Stuart, with Bill Schwarz. 2017. *Familiar Stranger: A Life between Two Islands.* Durham, NC: Duke University Press.

Halm, Dirk. 2013. "The Current Discourse on Islam in Germany." *Journal of International Migration and Integration* 14, 3: 457–74.

Hancock, Ange-Marie. 2007. "When Multiplication Doesn't Equal Quick Addition: Examining Intersectionality as a Research Paradigm." *Perspectives on Politics* 5, 1: 63–69.

Hanru, Hou. 2006. "Wherever They Go, They Create a New World – Fragmental Notes on Migration, Cultural Hybridity and Contemporary Art." Accessed December 30, 2006. http://www.sfaiart.com/News/NewsDetail.aspx?newsID=1178&navID=&sectionID=8.

Harding, Sandra. 2004. "Introduction: Standpoint Theory as a Site of Political, Philosophic, and Scientific Debate." In *The Feminist Standpoint Theory Reader: Intellectual and Political Controversies,* edited by Sandra Harding, 1–15. New York: Routledge.

Haritaworn, Jin. 2010. "Queer Injuries: The Racial Politics of 'Homophobic Hate Crime' in Germany." *Social Justice* 37, 1: 69–89.

Haritaworn, Jin, and Jen Petzen. 2011. "Invented Traditions, New Intimate Publics: Tracing the German 'Muslim Homophobia' Discourse." In *Islam in Its International Context: Comparative Perspectives,* edited by Stephen Hutchings, Chris Flood, Galina Miazhevich, and Henri Nickels, 48–64. Cambridge, UK: Cambridge Scholars.

Haritaworn, Jin, Tamsila Tauqir, and Esra Erdem. 2008. *Gay Imperialism: Gender and Sexuality Discourse in the 'War on Terror.'* York, UK: Raw Nerve Books.

Herising, Fairn. 2005. "Interrupting Positions: Critical Thresholds and Queer Pro/positions." In *Research as Resistance: Critical, Indigenous, and Anti-oppressive Approaches,* edited by Leslie Brown and Susan Strega, 127–51. Toronto: Canadian Scholars' Press.

Hignett, Kelly. 2011. "50 Years On – Commemorating the Construction of the Berlin Wall." *The View East* (blog), August 11, 2011. http://thevieweast.wordpress.com/tag/mauer-im-kopf/.

Holstein, James A., and Jaber F. Gubrium. (1995) 1997. *The Active Interview.* Thousand Oaks, CA: Sage.

–. 2012. *Varieties of Narrative Analysis.* Los Angeles: Sage.

Holton, Robert J. 2013. "Multicultural Citizenship: The Politics and Poetics of Public Space." In *Democracy, Citizenship and the Global City,* edited by Engin F. Isin, 189–202. New York: Routledge.

House, Jim. 1997. "Muslim Communities in France." In *Muslim Communities in the New Europe,* edited by Gerd Nonneman, Tim Niblock, and Bogdan Szajkowski, 219–39. Reading, UK: Ithaca Press, an imprint of Garnet.

Howarth, David, and Yannis Stavrakakis. 2000. "Introducing Discourse Theory and Political Analysis." In *Discourse Theory and Political Analysis: Identities,*

Hegemonies and Social Change, edited by David Howarth, Aletta J. Noval, and Yannis Stavrakakis, 1–23. Manchester, UK: Manchester University Press.

Hunter, Margaret L. (2005) 2013. *Race, Gender, and the Politics of Skin Tone.* New York: Routledge.

Huntington, Samuel P. 1993. "The Clash of Civilizations?" *Foreign Affairs* 72, 3: 22–49.

Independent Commission on Migration to Germany. 2001, July 4. *Structuring Immigration, Fostering Integration.* Berlin: Druckerei Conrad.

İpekçioğlu, İpek. 2003. "Türkeistämmige Lesben und Schwule in Bundesrepublik." *Dokumentation des 1. Bundeskongresses türkeistämmiger Lesben, Schwuler, Bisexueller, Transsexueller und Transgender.* Berlin: LSVD & MILES.

Isin, Engin F. 2000. "Introduction." In *Democracy, Citizenship and the Global City,* edited by Engin F. Isin, 1–21. London: Routledge.

–. 2002a. *Being Political: Genealogies of Citizenship.* Minneapolis: University of Minnesota Press.

–. 2002b. "Ways of Being Political." *Distinktion* 4: 7–28.

–. 2008. "Theorizing Acts of Citizenship." In *Acts of Citizenship,* edited by Engin Isin and Greg M. Nielsen, 15–43. London: Zed Books.

Isin, Engin F., and Brian Turner, eds. 2002. *Handbook of Citizenship Studies.* London: Sage.

Jackson, Jennifer K. 2012. "Introduction: Creating the 'Other' in Germany and Britain – A Comparison of Discourses from the Interwar and Contemporary Periods." *Studies in Ethnicity and Nationalism* 12, 2: 363–65.

Jacobs, Jane M., and Ruth Fincher. 1998. "Introduction." In *Cities of Difference,* edited by Ruth Fincher and J.M. Jacobs, 1–25. New York: The Guilford Press.

James, Carl E. (2003) 2010. *Seeing Ourselves: Exploring Race, Ethnicity and Culture.* Toronto: Thompson Educational.

JAN Trust. 2016, September 1. "Burkini Ban Busted!" https://jantrust.wordpress. Com/2016/09/01/burkini-ban-busted/.

Jones, Timothy. 2018. "Germany Sees Almost 1,000 Anti-muslim Crimes in 2017." Deutsche Welle. March 3, 2018. http://www.dw.com/en/germany-sees-almost -1000-anti-muslim-crimes-in-2017/a-42810445.

Joppke, Christian. 2002. "Multicultural Citizenship." In *Handbook of Citizenship Studies,* edited by Engin F. Isin and Brian Turner, 245–58. London: Sage.

Kaya, Ayhan. 2007. "German-Turkish Transnational Space: A Separate Space of Their Own." *German Studies Review* 30, 3: 483–502.

–. 2011. "Euro-Turks as a Force in EU–Turkey Relations." *South European Society and Politics* 16, 3: 499–512.

–. 2012. "Transnational Citizenship: German-Turks and Liberalizing Citizenship Regimes," *Citizenship Studies* 16, 2: 153–72.

–. 2018. "Right-wing Populism and Islamophobism in Europe and Their Impact on Turkey–EU Relations." *Turkish Studies* 21, 1: 1–28. doi:10.1080/14683849.2018. 1499431.

Kaya, Ayhan, and Ayşe Tecmen. 2019. "Europe versus Islam?: Right-wing Populist Discourse and the Construction of a Civilizational Identity." *Review of Faith*

References   305

and International Affairs 17, 1: 49–64. https://doi.org/10.1080/15570274.2019. 1570759.

Keyes, E. Rodriguez. 2006. "A Qualitative Study on How Second-Generation Puerto Rican Women Negotiate Living between Two Cultures." Master's thesis, Smith College School for Social Work.

Klimt, Andrea C. 1989. "Returning 'Home': Portuguese Migrant Notions of Temporariness, Permanence, and Commitment." Special issue, *New German Critique* 46 (Winter): 47–70.

Kramer, Heinz. 1997. "The Institutional Framework of German-Turkish Relations." In *The Institutional Framework of German-Turkish Relations, the Parameters of Partnership: Germany, the U.S. and Turkey: Challenges for German and American Foreign Policy,* 11–31. Conference paper. Washington, DC/Baltimore, MD: American Institute for Contemporary German Studies, Johns Hopkins University.

Kurt, Kemal. 1998. "Not an Oriental (Fairy) Tale." In *Fringe Voices: An Anthology of Minority Writing in the Federal Republic of Germany,* edited by Antje Harnisch, Anne Marie Stokes, and Friedemann Weidauer, 264–71. Oxford: Berg.

Kymlicka, Will. 1989. *Liberalism, Community and Culture.* Oxford: Oxford University Press.

–. 1995. *Multicultural Citizenship.* Oxford: Oxford University Press.

–. 2007. *Multicultural Odysseys: Navigating the New International Politics of Diversity.* New York: Oxford University Press.

Laguerre, Michel S. 2016. *Diasporic Citizenship: Haitian Americans in Transnational America.* New York: St. Martin's Press.

Le News. 2016, August 25. "Wearing Burkinis Is against Social Cohesion and Integration, Says Geneva Councillor." *Tribune de Genève,* August 25, 2016. https:// lenews.ch/2016/08/25/wearing-burkinis-is-against-social-cohesion-and -integration-says-geneva-councilor/.

Lewis, Bernard. 1990. "The Roots of Muslim Rage." *Atlantic,* September 1990, 47–60.

Lewis, Oscar. 1966. *La Vida: A Puerto Rican Family in the Culture of Poverty, San Juan and New York.* New York: Random House.

–. (1963) 1998. "The Culture of Poverty." *Society* 35, 2: 7–9.

Linde, Charlotte. 1993. *Life Stories: The Creation of Coherence.* New York: Oxford University Press.

Linke, Uli. 1999. *German Bodies: Race and Representation after Hitler.* New York: Routledge.

–. 2011. "Technologies of Othering: Black Masculinities in the Carceral Zones of European Whiteness." In *Europe in Black and White,* edited by Manuela Ribeiro Sanches, Fernando Clara, João Ferreira Duarte, and Leonor Pires Martins, 123–42. Bristol, UK: Intellect.

Local Germany. 2015, 16 March. "Number of Foreigners in Germany Hits Record High." https://www.thelocal.de/20150316/number-of-foreigners-in-germany-hits -record-high.

Longman, Jere. 2006. "Surge in Racist Mood Raises Concerns on Eve of World Cup." *New York Times,* June 4, 2006. https://www.nytimes.com/2006/06/04/sports/soccer/04racism.html.

Lorde, Audre Geraldine. (1984) 2007. *Sister Outsider: Essays and Speeches.* Berkeley, CA: The Crossing Press.

Lowe, Lisa. 2003. "Heterogeneity, Hybridity, Multiplicity: Marking Asian-American Differences." In *Theorizing Diaspora: A Reader,* edited by Jana E. Braziel and Anita Mannur, 132–55. Malden, MA: Blackwell.

Lynch, Sandra. 2002. "Aristotle and Derrida on Friendship." *Contretemps* 3 (July): 98–108.

Maclure, J. 2003. "The Politics of Recognition at an Impasse? Identity Politics and Democratic Citizenship." *Canadian Journal of Political Science* 36, 1: 3–21.

Malseed, Kevin. 2008. "Where There Is No Movement: Local Resistance and the Potential for Solidarity." *Journal of Agrarian Change* 8, 2–3: 489–514.

Mandel, Ruth. 1989. "Ethnicity and Identity among Migrant Guestworkers in West Berlin." In *Conflict, Migration and the Expression of Ethnicity,* edited by Nancie L. Gonzales and Carolyn S. McCommon, 60–74. Boulder, CO: Westview Press.

–. 2000. "Turkish Headscarves and the 'Foreigner Problem': Constructing Difference through Emblems of Identity." *New German Critique* 46: 27–46.

–. 2008. *Cosmopolitan Anxieties: Turkish Challenges to Citizenship and Belonging in Germany.* Durham, NC: Duke University Press.

Markell, Patchen. 2003. *Bound by Recognition.* Princeton, NJ: Princeton University Press.

Martin, Philip. 2006. "Managing Labour Migration: Temporary Worker Programmes for the 21st Century." Paper presented at the International Symposium on International Migration and Development, Population Division, Department of Economic and Social Affairs, United Nations Secretariat, Turin, Italy, June 28–30, 2006. http://www.un.org/esa/population/migration/turin/Symposium_Turin_files/P07_Martin.pdf.

Mayer, Frederick W. 2014. *Narrative Politics: Stories and Collective Action.* New York: Oxford University Press.

McKenzie, Sheena. 2016. "Germany Could Impose Partial Ban on Face Veils, Officials Say." CNN, August 19, 2016. https://www.cnn.com/2016/08/19/europe/germany-veil-ban/index.html.

McNay, L. 2000. *Gender and Agency: Reconfiguring the Subject in Feminist and Social Theory.* Cambridge, UK: Polity Press.

McQueen, Fraser. 2016. "France's Burkini Ban Could Not Come at a Worse Time." *The Conversation,* August 24, 2016. https://theconversation.com/frances-burkini-ban-could-not-come-at-a-worse-time-64249.

Meng, Michael. 2015. "Silences about Sarrazin's Racism in Contemporary Germany." *Journal of Modern History* 87, 1: 102–35.

Mercan, Abdurrahman. 2004. "Identitat und Emanzipation bei turkischen Homosexuellen am Beispiel von TurkGay & Lesbian LSVD" [Identity and emancipation among Turkish homosexuals using the example of TurkGay & Lesbian LSVD]. In *Muslime unter dem Regenbogen: Homosexualitat, Migration und*

Islam [Muslims under the rainbow: Homosexuality, migration and Islam], edited by LSVD Berlin-Brandenburg e.V, 152–67. Berlin: Querverlag.

Mercer, Kobena. 2018. "Diaspora Culture and the Dialogic Imagination: The Aesthetics of Black Independent Film in Britain." In *The Routledge Diaspora Studies Reader,* edited by Klaus Stierstorfer and Janet Wilson, 204–8. Abingdon, Oxon: Routledge.

Michaels, Walter Benn. 2006. *The Trouble with Diversity: How We Learned to Love Identity and Ignore Inequality.* New York: Metropolitan/Holt.

Milczarek-Desai, Shefali. 2002. "Living Fearlessly with and within Difference: My Search for Identity beyond Categories and Contradictions." In *This Bridge We Call Home: Radical Visions for Transformation,* edited by Gloria Anzaldúa and AnaLouise Keating, 126–35. New York: Routledge.

Miller, Toby. 2002. "Cultural Citizenship." In *Handbook of Citizenship Studies,* edited by Engin F. Isin and Brian Turner, 231–43. London: Sage.

Minh-ha, Trinh T. 1986. "Introduction." *Discourse* 8: 3–10. http://www.jstor.org/stable/44000268.

–. 1991. *When the Moon Waxes Red: Representation, Gender and Cultural Politics.* New York: Routledge.

Mishra, Vijay. 1996. "The Diasporic Imaginary: Theorizing the Indian Diaspora." *Textual Practice* 10, 3: 421–47.

Mocan, Naci, and Christian Raschke. 2016. "Economic Well-being and Anti-Semitic, Xenophobic, and Racist Attitudes in Germany." *European Journal of Law and Economics* 41, 1: 1–63. https://doi.org/10.1007/s10657–015–9521–0.

Moghissi, Haideh. 1999. *Feminism and Islamic Fundamentalism: The Limits of Postmodern Analysis.* London: Zed Books.

Mohanty, Chandra Talpade. 2003. *Feminism without Borders: Decolonizing Theory, Practicing Solidarity.* Durham, NC: Duke University Press.

Mueller, Claus. 2006. "Integrating Turkish Communities: A German Dilemma." *Population Research and Policy Review* 25, 5–6: 419–41.

Mühe, Nina. 2016. "Managing the Stigma: Islamophobia in German Schools." *Insight Turkey* 18, 1: 77–95.

Mummery, Jane. 2018. "Being Not-at-home: A Conceptual Discussion." In *The Routledge Diaspora Studies Reader,* edited by Klaus Stierstorfer and Janet Wilson, 230–34. Abingdon, Oxon: Routledge.

Noack, Rick, and Luisa Beck. 2018. "Germany's #MeTwo Hashtag Has the Country Asking: How Racist Are We?" *Washington Post,* August 1, 2018. https://www.washingtonpost.com/news/worldviews/wp/2018/07/31/germanys-metwo-hashtag-has-the-country-asking-how-racist-are-we/?noredirect=on&utm_term=.c0dca28a501e.

Nonneman, Gerd. 1997. "Muslim Communities in the New Europe: Themes and Puzzles." In *Muslim Communities in the New Europe,* edited by Gerd Nonneman, Tim Niblock, and Bogdan Szajkowski, 3–23. Reading, UK: Ithaca Press, an imprint of Garnet.

Oliver, Kelly. 2000. "Beyond Recognition: Witnessing Ethics." *Philosophy Today* 44, 1: 31–43.

Open Society Institute. 2010. *Muslims in Europe: A Report on 11 EU Cities.* At Home in Europe Project. New York/London/Budapest: Open Society Institute.

Özcan, Veysel. 2004. "Germany: Immigration in Transition." *Migration Information Source,* July 1, 2004. https://www.migrationpolicy.org/article/germany-immigration-transition/.

Özdemir, Cem. 2003. "Mehmet and Edeltraud Too: Prospects for a Multicultural Germany." https://www.opendemocracy.net/en/article_1255jsp/.

Öztürk, Çiğdem, and Derya Bengi. 2009. "Germany Psyched Us Out [Bizi Almanya manyak etti]." *Roll* 13, 142: 45–49.

Parekh, Bhikhu. 2000. *Rethinking Multiculturalism: Cultural Diversity and Political Theory.* Basingstoke, Hants: Macmillan.

–. 2005. "Dialogue between Cultures." In *Democracy, Nationalism and Multiculturalism,* edited by Ramón Máiz Suárez and Ferrán Requejo Coll, 13–24. London: Frank Cass.

Park, Robert Ezra, and Herbert Miller. 1921. *Old World Traits Transplanted.* New York: Harper.

Patel, Romil. 2016. "Top Catholic Bishop Blasts France's 'War on Symbols' Following Controversial Burkini Ban: Bishop Nunzio Galantino Criticised the 'Vulgar Ridiculing of the Religious Sensitivity of Others.'" *International Business Times,* August 19, 2016. http://www.ibtimes.co.uk/top-catholic-bishop-blasts-frances-war-symbols-following-controversial-burkini-ban-1576888.

Peck, Jeffrey M. 1992. "Rac(e)ing the Nation: Is There a German Home?" *New Formations: A Journal of Culture/Theory/Politics* 17 (Summer): 75–84.

Peck, Jeffrey, Mitchell Ash, and Christiane Lemke. 1997. "Natives, Strangers, and Foreigners: Constituting Germans by Constructing Others." In *After Unity: Reconfiguring German Identities,* edited by Konrad H. Jarausch, 61–102. Providence, RI: Berghahn.

Pécoud, Antoine. 2002. "'Weltoffenheit schafft Jobs': Turkish Entrepreneurship and Multiculturalism in Berlin." *International Journal of Urban and Regional Research* 26, 3: 494–507.

Pennay, Mark. 2001. "Rap in Germany." In *Global Noise: Rap and Hip Hop Outside the USA,* edited by Tony Mitchell, 111–13. Middletown, CT: Wesleyan University Press.

Perry, Barbara P. 2014. "Gendered Islamophobia: Hate Crime against Muslim Women." *Social Identities* 20, 1: 74–89.

Persky, Stan. 1999. "Mehmet Is Gone." *Vancouver Sun,* May 10, 1999. http://www.stanpersky.de/Europa/19990510.E001TURK.html.

Peter, Frank. 2012. "Nation, Narration and Islam: Memory and Governmentality in Germany." *Current Sociology* 60, 3: 338–52.

Petzen, Jennifer Lee. 2009. "Gender Politics in the New Europe: 'Civilizing' Muslim Sexualities." PhD diss., University of Washington. Proquest (UMI Microform 3328436).

Pfaff, Carol W. 1984. "On Input and Residual L1 Transfer Effects in Turkish and Greek Children's German." In *Second Languages: A Cross-linguistic Perspective,* edited by Roger W. Anderson, 271–98. Rowley, MA: Newbury House.

References

Phelan, Shane. 1994. *Getting Specific: Postmodern Lesbian Politics*. Minneapolis: University of Minnesota Press.

Phillips, Anne. 2007. *Multiculturalism without Culture*. Princeton, NJ: Princeton University Press.

Pile, Steve, and Michael Keith. 1993. *Place and Politics of Identity*. London: Routledge.

Platen, H., and J. Gottschlich. 2008. "Türkischer premier in ludwigshafen: Nach brand droht diplomatische krise." *Die Tageszeitung*, February 7, 2008. http://www.taz.de/!5187035/.

Polletta, Francesca. 2006. *It Was Like a Fever: Storytelling in Protest and Politics*. Chicago: University of Chicago Press.

Porter, John. 1965. *The Vertical Mosaic: An Analysis of Social Class and Power in Canada*. Toronto: University of Toronto Press.

Puar, Jasbir. 2007. *Terrorist Assemblages: Homonationalism in Queer Times*. Durham, NC: Duke University Press.

Purdie-Vaughns, Valerie, and Richard Paul Eibach. 2008. "Intersectional Invisibility: The Distinctive Advantages and Disadvantages of Multiple Subordinate-group Identities." *Sex Roles* 59: 377–91.

Radhakrishnan, R. 2003. "Ethnicity in an Age of Diaspora." In *Theorizing Diaspora: A Reader*, edited by Jana E. Braziel and Anita Mannur, 119–31. Malden, MA: Blackwell.

Rancière, Jacques. 2004. *The Politics of Aesthetics*, translated by Gabriel Rockhill. London: Continuum.

Razack, Sherene. 1998. *Looking White People in the Eye: Gender, Race, and Culture in Courtrooms and Classrooms*. Toronto: University of Toronto Press.

–. 2005. "Geopolitics, Culture Clash, and Gender after September 11." *Social Justice* 32, 4: 11–31.

–. 2007. *Casting Out: The Eviction of Muslims from Western Law and Politics*. Toronto: University of Toronto Press.

Reinach, Adolf. 1983. "The Apriori Foundations of Civil Law." *Aletheia* 3: 1–142.

RFI. 2016. "Poll Shows Mistrust of Islam in France, Germany." Radio France Internationale, April 30, 2016. http://en.rfi.fr/france/20160430-poll-shows-mistrust-islam-france-germany-1.

Rist, Ray C. 1978. "On the Education of Guestworker Children in Germany: A Comparative Study of Policies and Programs in Bavaria and Berlin." Paper presented at the Annual Meeting of the American Educational Research Association, Toronto, Ontario, March 27–31, 1978.

Rothwell, James. 2016. "German Far-Right Extremists Teaming Up with Gangs in America and Europe to Plan Attacks, Intelligence Chief Warns." *Telegraph*, November 16, 2016. https://www.telegraph.co.uk/news/2016/11/16/german-far-right-extremists-teaming-up-with-gangs-in-america-and/.

Rushdie, Salman. 2018. "Imaginary Homeland." In *The Routledge Diaspora Studies Reader*, edited by Klaus Stierstorfer and Janet Wilson, 227–29. Abingdon, Oxon: Routledge.

Rygiel, Kim. 2003. "Globalizing Inequality: Citizenship Politics of Diasporic Women in Globalized Cities: The Case of Homeworkers in Toronto's Garment Industry."

Paper presented at the Citizenship Studies Symposium, Citizenship Studies Media Lab, York University, Toronto, Canada, January 15, 2003. https://yfile. news.yorku.ca/2003/01/13/citizenship-studies-symposium-inaugurates-new -media-lab-at-york/.

Safran, William. 1991. "Diasporas in Modern Societies: Myths of Homeland and Return." *Diaspora* 1 (Spring): 83–99.

Said, Edward. 1978. *Orientalism*. London: Routledge and Kegan Paul.

–. (1981) 1997. *Covering Islam*. New York: Vintage.

–. 1998. "The Myth of 'The Clash of Civilizations.'" Transcript of video lecture. Executive produced and directed by Sut Jhally. Edited by Sanjay Talreja. University of Massachusetts Amherst: Media Education Foundation.

Salman, Ramazan. 1992. *AIDS-Prävention und migration: Sexuelle probleme von männlichen türkischen jugendlichen in der Bundesrepublik Deutschland*. Bd. 15. Hannover: Hrsg. vom Niedersächsischen Sozialministerium in der Edition AIDS.

Sanders, Leslie. 2001. "White Teacher, Black Literature." In *Talking about Identity: Encounters in Race, Ethnicity, and Language,* edited by Carl E. James and Adrienne Shadd, 168–76. Toronto: Between the Lines.

Sandoval, Chela. 2000. *Methodology of the Oppressed: Theory out of Bounds*. Minneapolis: University of Minnesota Press.

Sarrazin, Thilo. 2010. *Deutschland schafft sich ab* [Germany Is Abolishing Itself]. Stuttgart: Deutsche Verlagsanstalt.

–. 2016. "Introduction to 'Germany Abolishes Itself: How We Are Gambling with Our Country.'" *Occidental Observer: White Identity, Interests, and Culture* (blog), January 8, 2016. http://www.theoccidentalobserver.net/2016/01/08/introduction -to-germany-abolishes-itself-how-we-are-gambling-with-our-country/.

Sassen, Saskia. 2002. "The Repositioning of Citizenship: Emergent Subjects and Spaces for Politics." *Berkeley Journal of Sociology* 46: 41–66.

Schiller, Nina Glick, Linda Basch, and Cristina Szanton-Blanc. (1992) 1998. *Towards a Transnational Perspective on Migration: Race, Class, Ethnicity, and Nationalism Reconsidered*. New York: New York Academy of Sciences.

Schlagenwerth, Michaela. 2006. "Black Virgins: Islam and Sex. Five Muslim Women Tell All." *Signandsight.com: Let's Talk European,* March 20, 2006. http://print. signandsight.com/features/664.html.

Scott, James. 1986. "Everyday Forms of Peasant Resistance." In *Everyday Forms of Peasant Resistance in South-East Asia,* edited by James Scott and Benedickt Tria Kerkvliet, 5–35. London: Frank Cass.

Şeker, Nimet. 2008. "Director Neco Çelik: 'The Word Integration Is Like a Bar of Soap.'" *Babelmed,* October 8, 2006. https://www.babelmed.net/article/7108 -director-neco-celik-the-word-integration-is-like-a-bar-of-soapŞen, Faruk. 2003. "The Historical Situation of Turkish Migrants in Germany." *Immigrants and Minorities* 22, 2–3: 208–27.

Şen, Faruk, and Andreas Goldberg. 1994. *Türken in Deutschland: Leben zwischen zwei Kulturen*. Munich: Beck.

Şenocak, Zafer. 2000. *Atlas of a Tropical Germany: Essays on Political and Culture, 1990–1998*. London: University of Nebraska Press.

Sey, Cem Rifat. 2004. "When Turkish Men Love Men." Deutsche Welle, June 1, 2004. www.dw-world.de/dw/article/0,1564,1079381,00.html.

Seyhan, Azade. 2000. "Paranational Community/Hyphenated Identity: The Turks of Germany." Accessed November 11, 2006. http://jsis.artsci.washington.edu/programs/europe/wendep/SeyhanPaper.html.

–. 2001. *Writing outside the Nation*. Princeton, NJ: Princeton University Press.

Shafer, Susanne M. 1983. "Bilingual Education and Social Integration." Paper presented at The National Association for Bilingual Education (NABE) Convention, Washington, DC, February 17, 1983.

Sharma, Gouri. 2018. "#MeTwo: As Nationalist Anger Rises, Stories of Everyday Racism." *AlJazeera*, September 4, 2018. https://www.aljazeera.com/features/2018/9/4/metwo-as-nationalist-anger-rises-stories-of-everyday-racism.

Schiffauer, Werner. 2004. "Vom exil-zum diaspora-islam. muslimische identitäten in europa." *Soziale Welt* 55, 4: 347–68.

Shoshan, Nitzan. 2014. "Managing Hate: Political Delinquency and Affective Governance in Germany." *Cultural Anthropology* 29, 1: 150–72.

Simmel, Georg. (1908) 1971. "The Stranger." In *Georg Simmel on Individuality and Social Forms: Selected Writings*, edited by Donald N. Levine, 43–49. Chicago: University of Chicago Press.

Sirkeci, Ibrahim, Doğa Elçin, and Güven Şeker. 2015. "Chapter 10: Political Integration of the German-Turkish Youth in Berlin." In *Politics and Law in Turkish Migration*, 137–54. London: Transnational Press.

Smee, Jess. 2006. "Racist Attack Fuels Fear of Far Right." Inter Press Service: News Agency, April 24, 2006. http://www.ipsnews.net/2006/04/germany-racist-attack-fuels-fear-of-far-right/.

Smith, Anna Marie. 1998. *Laclau and Mouffe: The Radical Democratic Imaginary*. London: Routledge.

Smith, Jean Edward. 1969. *Germany beyond the Wall: People, Politics, and Prosperity*. Boston: Little, Brown.

Snelgrove, Corey, Rita Kaur Dhamoon, and Jeff Corntassel. 2014. "Unsettling Settler Colonialism: The Discourse and Politics of Settlers, and Solidarity with Indigenous Nations." *Decolonization: Indigeneity, Education & Society* 3, 2: 1–32.

Söhn, Janina, and Veysel Özcan. 2006. "The Educational Attainment of Turkish Migrants in Germany." *Turkish Studies* 7, 1: 101–24.

Soja, Edward W. 1996. *Thirdspace: Journeys to Los Angeles and Other Real-and-imagined Places*. Cambridge, MA: Blackwell.

Soloveitchik, Rina. 2016. "Interview with Judith Butler: Trump is Emancipating Unbridled Hatred." Zeit Online, October 28, 2016. http://www.zeit.de/kultur/2016-10/judith-butler-donald-trump-populism-interview.

Soysal Nuhoğlu, Yasemin. 1994. *Limits of Citizenship: Migrants and Postnational Membership in Europe*. Chicago: University of Chicago Press.

Spiegel International. 2011, April 22. "Firebrand Politician Can Remain a Social Democrat." http://www.spiegel.de/international/germany/victory-for-sarrazin -firebrand-politician-can-remain-a-social-democrat-a-758709.html.

Spivak, Gayatri C. 1993. "Can the Subaltern Speak?" In *Colonial Discourse and Postcolonial Theory: A Reader,* edited by Patrick Williams and Laura Chrisman, 66–111. London: Harvester Wheatsheaf.

Spohn, Margret. 1993. "Alles getürkt: 500 Jahre (Vor)Urteile der Deutschen über die Türken" [Everything faked: Germans' 500 years (mis) judgments of Turks]. Oldenburg: Bibliotheks- und Informationssystem der Universität. (Studien zur Soziologie und Politikwissenschaft) Zugl.: Oldenburg, Universität. Diplomarbeit [Sociology and Political Science, PhD diss., Universitat Oldenburg].

Stoler, Anna Laura. 1995. *Race and the Education of Desire: Foucault's History of Sexuality and the Colonial Order of Things.* Durham, NC: Duke University Press.

Suárez, Ramón Máiz, and Ferrán Requejo Coll. 2005. *Democracy, Nationalism and Multiculturalism.* London: Frank Cass.

Sullivan, Shannon. 2006. *Revealing Whiteness: The Unconscious Habits of Racial Privilege.* Indianapolis: Indiana University Press.

–. 2014. *Good White People: The Problem with Middle-class White Anti-racism.* Albany: SUNY Press.

SUSPECT. 2010. "Judith Butler Refuses Berlin Pride Civil Courage Prize 2010." *Nohomonationalism* (blog), June 21, 2010. http://nohomonationalism.blogspot. com/2010/06/judith-butler-refuses-berlin-pride.html.

Takle, Marianne. 2011. "(Spät)Aussiedler: From Germans to Immigrants." *Nationalism and Ethnic Politics* 17, 2: 161–81. doi:10.1080/13537113.2011.575312.

Taylor, Charles. 1994. "The Politics of Recognition." In *Multiculturalism: Examining the Politics of Recognition,* edited by Amy Gutmann, 25–73. Princeton, NJ: Princeton University Press.

Teraoka, Arlene Akiko. 1997. "Multiculturalism and the Study of German Literature." In *A User's Guide to German Cultural Studies,* edited by Scott Denham, Irene Kacandes, and Jonathan Petropoluos, 63–78. Ann Arbor: University of Michigan.

Thomas, William I., and Florian Znaniecki. 1927. *The Polish Peasant in Europe and America.* New York: Alfred Knopf.

Times (London). 1971. Educational Supplement. August 13, 1971: 8.

Toelken, Barre. 1985. "'Turkenrein' and 'Turken, Rausl' – Images of Fear and Aggression in German Gastarbeitterwitze." In *Turkish Workers in Europe: An Interdisciplinary Study,* edited by Norman Furniss and Ilhan Basgoz, 151–64. Bloomington: Indiana University Turkish Studies.

Tölölyan, Khachig. 1996. "Rethinking Diaspora(s): Stateless Power in the Transnational Moment." *Diaspora: A Journal of Transnational Studies* 5, 1: 3–36.

Travis, Alan. 2012. "Stark Choice under New Immigration Rules: Exile or Family Breakup." *Guardian,* June 8, 2012. https://www.theguardian.com/uk/2012/jun/ 08/immigration-rules-couples-stark-choice.

Tully, James. 1995. *Strange Multiplicity: Constitutionalism in an Age of Diversity.* Cambridge, UK: Cambridge University Press.

References

–. 2000. "Struggles over Recognition and Distribution." *Constellations*, 7 4: 469–82.

–. 2001. "Introduction." In *Multinational Democracies*, edited by Alain G. Gagnon and James Tully, 1–33. Cambridge, UK: Cambridge University Press.

–. 2002. "Reimagining Belonging in Circumstances of Cultural Diversity." In *The Postnational Self: Belonging and Identity*, edited by Ulf Hedetoft and Mette Hjort, 152–77. Minneapolis: University of Minnesota Press.

Turner, Henry Ashby. 1992. *Germany from Partition to Reunification: A Revised Edition of the Two Germanies since 1945*. New Haven, CT: Yale University Press.

Uçar, Ali. 1990. "Çok kültürlü toplum ve göçmen çocuklarının eğitim sorunları" [Multicultural Society and Education Problems of Immigrant Children]. *Yenidil*, Week 4, 14–16.

Vail, Tobi. 2010. "Judith Butler – I Must Distance Myself from This Complicity with Racism." *Jigsaw's Guide to Feminist Theory* (blog), June 23, 2010. https://jigsaw-feministtheoryguide.blogspot.com/2010/06/judith-butler-i-must-distance-my-self.html.

Veronika, Roses [@rosesveronika]. 2018. "My German teacher was guessing the future professions of pupils in the class (10th grade): 'Well ... Veronika, you are going to be a Russian porn actress ... ' No one was laughing. 'Joke' #MeTwo." Twitter, July 28, 2018, 2: 12 pm. (tweet deleted). https://twitter.com/rosesveronika/status/1023315301411303425.

Vertovec, Steven, ed. 2010. *Migration*. Critical Concepts in the Social Sciences. Abingdon, Oxon: Routledge.

–. 2018. "Religion and Diaspora." In *The Routledge Diaspora Studies Reader*, edited by Klaus Stierstorfer and Janet Wilson, 25–35. Abingdon, Oxon: Routledge.

Volkery, Carsten. 2011. "'Well, I Want You to Integrate': Germany's Integration Provocateur Goes English." *Spiegel International*, January 20, 2011. http://www.spiegel.de/international/germany/well-i-want-you-to-integrate-germany-s-integration-provocateur-goes-english-a-740524.html.

Weaver, Matthew. 2010. "Angela Merkel: German Multiculturalism Has 'Utterly Failed.'" *Guardian*, October 17, 2010. https://www.theguardian.com/world/2010/oct/17/angela-merkel-german-multiculturalism-failed.

Weber, Barbara. 1995. "Immigration and Politics in Germany." *Journal of the International Institute* 2, 3. https://quod.lib.umich.edu/j/jii/4750978.0002.306?view=text;rgn=main.

Weller, Susie. 2015. "The Potentials and Pitfalls of Using Skype for Qualitative (Longitudinal) Interviews." National Centre for Research Methods Working Paper 4/15. http://eprints.ncrm.ac.uk/3757/1/Susie%20Weller.pdf.

Wengeler, Martin. 1995. "Multikulturelle Gesellschaft 'oder, Ausländer raus'? Der sprachliche Umgang mit der Einwanderung seit 1945." In *Kontroverse Begriffe: Geschichte des Öffentlichen Sprachgebrauchs in der Bundesrepublik Deutschland*, edited by Georg Stötzel and Martin Wengeler, 711–49. Berlin: Walter de Gruyter.

Werbner, Pnina. 1997. "Afterword: Writing Multiculturalism and Politics in the New Europe." In *The Politics of Multiculturalism in the New Europe: Racism, Identity and Community,* edited by Tariq Modood and Pnina Werbner, 261–67. London: Zed Books.

–. 1998. "Diasporic Political Imaginaries: A Sphere of Freedom or a Sphere of Illusions." *Communal/Plural: Journal of Transnational and Crosscultural Studies* 6, 1: 11–31.

–. 2000. "Divided Loyalties, Empowered Citizenship? Muslims in Britain." *Citizenship Studies* 4, 3: 307–24.

–. 2002. "The Place Which Is Diaspora: Citizenship, Religion and Gender in the Making of Chaordic Transnationalism." *Journal of Ethnic and Migration Studies* 28, 1: 119–33.

Wertheim, David J. 2017. "The Price of an Entrance Ticket to Western Society: Ayaan Hirsi Ali, Heinrich Heine and the Double Standard of Emancipation." In *Anti-Semitism and Islamophobia in Europe: A Shared Story?*, edited by James Renton and Ben Gidney, 267–321. London: Palgrave Macmillan.

Wikipedia. "Christian Democratic Union of Germany." Last edited 27 January 2022. https://en.wikipedia.org/wiki/Christian_Democratic_Union_of_Germany.

–. "German Nationality Law." Last edited 27 January 2022. https://en.wikipedia.org/wiki/German_nationality_law.

–. "Kanak Sprak." Last edited 25 January 2022. https://en.wikipedia.org/wiki/Kanak_Sprak.

–. "Ladino." Last edited 8 March 2021. https://en.wikipedia.org/wiki/Ladino.

–. "LSVD." Last edited 21 February 2020. https://en.wikipedia.org/wiki/LSVD.

Wildcat. 2014. "The Deep State: Germany, Immigration, and the National Socialist Underground." *Viewpoint Magazine,* September 11, 2014. https://viewpoint mag.com/2014/09/11/the-deep-state-germany-immigration-and-the-national -socialist-underground/.

Wirth, Louis. 1945. "The Problem of the Minority Groups." In *The Science of Man in the World Crisis,* edited by Ralph Linton, 347–72. New York: Columbia University Press.

Worbs, Susanne. 2003. "The Second Generation in Germany: Between School and Labour Market." In "The Future of the Second Generation: The Integration of Migrant Youth in Six European Countries." Special Issue, *International Migration Review* 37, 4: 1011–38.

Wyatt, Caroline. 1998. "Anti-foreigner Campaigning in Bavaria." BBC News, September 13, 1998. http://news.bbc.co.uk/2/hi/special_report/1998/09/98/german _elections/169484.stm.

Yeğenoğlu, Meyda. 2002. "Sartorial Fabric-ations: Enlightenment and Western Feminism." In *Postcolonialism, Feminism and Religious Discourse,* edited by Laura E. Donaldson and Kwok Pui-Ian, 82–99. New York: Routledge.

Yorukoglu, Ilgin. 2010. "Marketing Diversity: Homonormativity and the Queer Turkish Organizations in Berlin." In *Islam and Homosexuality,* edited by Samar Habib, 419–44. Santa Barbara, CA: Praeger.

Young, Iris Marion. 2000. *Inclusion and Democracy.* New York: Oxford University Press.

References

Young, Robert J.C. 1995. *Colonial Desire: Hybridity in Theory, Culture and Race*. London: Routledge.

Yuval-Davis, Nira. 1997. *Gender and Nation*. London: Sage.

—. 2006. "Intersectionality and Feminist Politics." *European Journal of Women's Studies* 13, 3: 193–209.

—. 2013. "Citizenship, Territoriality and the Gendered Construction of Difference." In *Democracy, Citizenship and the Global City*, edited by Engin Isin, 171–88. New York: Routledge.

Zaimoğlu, Feridun. 1995. *Kanak sprak: 24 Mißtöne vom Rande der Gesellschaft*. Hamburg: Rotbuch.

Index

Notes: The following abbreviations are used in subheadings: "AfD" for Alternative for Germany, "CDU" for Christian Democratic Union, "CSU" for Christian Social Union, "FRG for Federal Republic of Germany, and "GDR" for German Democratic Republic. "(f)" after a page number indicates a figure. In endnote citations, "Ch" indicates the chapter number.

Abadan-Unat, Nermin, 53, 57
academic discourse. *See* social sciences research
accommodation: approach to, 16, 23–25; map of, 33(f); as problematic, 32; role in creating diasporic identity, 38. *See also* hostility–hospitality
accountability, 230–34
achievements, exceptional, 93
acknowledgment, reciprocal, 271–72
activism: anti-Islamoracism, 82, 261; anti-racist, 248, 261–62; about belonging, 171; importance of individual, 275; journalists and, 266; of LGBTI+ Turkish Ausländer, 260; marginalization within, 277; need for new ways of organizing, 284–85; participants', 208–9, 221–22, 227; participants' understanding of, 228;

self-reflexivity and, 230, 232, 286; solidarity as conditional, 47
acts, 239–48; and alliances to fight racism, 285; approach to, 6, 19, 22, 27; challenging ranking, 244–45; challenging stereotypes, 243–44; as contentious, 234; and contribution to citizenship studies, 280–82; decisiveness and assertiveness behind, 228–29; as dialogical, 265; diasporic citizens' aims served by, 263; as disruptive, 273–74; effectiveness of, 267; on hostility-hospitality axis, 86; influence of, 271, 273, 277, 278; intersectional approach in shaping, 275; #MeTwo, 246–48; passive resistance, 240–43; point-to-plural meanings, 284; as political and not political, 268; principles for inclusiveness

Index

317

suggested by, 276; provide understanding of differences, 283; and structures of difference, 269–70; use of media to publicize, 266; use of term, 239

adaptation, 164–65, 190, 275. *See also* integration

Adenauer, Konrad, 50

AfD. *See* Alternative for Germany (AfD)

Afghanistan, 139

African-American culture, 254

Agathangelou, Anna, 160, 262, 282

Ahmed, Fiaz, 143

Ahmed, Sara: on aliens and strangers, 145; and conceptual framework, 6; on hate and fear, 131, 139; on home, 36; on multiculturalism, 15; on people who have already taken shape, 86

Ahmet (Güler's husband), 203

Alamancı (German guest workers), 157–58, 208

Alamancı Festivali, 254

Alamanyalı (from Germany), 157–58, 162, 184–85

Alamanyalıyım, 184–85, 189; "I am from Germany," 210–11

Albrecht, Richard, 57

Alevis: association for, 227; *Cemevi's* importance to, 292*nn*2–3Ch4; classes, 164; converts to Islam, 159, 160; identity of, 161, 236–37; minority-majority relationship with Sunnis, 163

Alexanderplatz, 133

Ali (participant): on divisions in Berlin, 65–66; on East and West Berlin, 71; on going to war, 237, 239; on his identities, 236–37, 275; on self-perception, 104; on Turkishness, 101

alienation, 45–46

aliens, 145

Allain, Kristi, 91

Allen, Amy, 283

"Alles getürkt" (Spohn), 103

Allgemeine Gleichbehandlungsgesetz (AGG, General Act on Equal Treatment), 75–76

alliances. *See* solidarity

Allied Control Council, 50

Allied Kommandatura, 50

Allies, 50

Alltag (Everyday; film), 252–53, 254, 263, 268

Almanlaşmak (becoming like a German), 184–85

Alp (participant): on Germanness, 9, 82–83; on Germans' lack of life experience, 222; on Islamoracism, 8; on Kreuzberg, 176; on labour migration, 3; on people of colour, 119; on resistance to racism and discrimination, 284; on Sarrazin's book, 78; on second-generation immigrants, 98

Alternative for Germany (AfD), 78, 129–30, 131–32, 140, 289

ambivalence, 234–37

Anderson, Benedict, 163

Antalya, 127, 292*n*5

anti-discrimination law, 75–76, 232–33, 236, 275

anti-essentialism, 147–48

anti-racist activism, 248, 261–62

anti-Semitism, 131, 135, 143, 247, 261. *See also* Jews

Anzaldúa, Gloria: on borderlands, 17, 198, 199; and conceptual framework, 6; on conscious awareness, 223; on experiences of LGBTI+ community, 213, 215–16; on high expectations for mestiza women, 104; on internal and external struggle, 219; on stubbornness and malleability, 228

April 23 (Children's Day), 166

Arab culture, 214

Arabesk, 57; Gazino, 254; Turkish, 254

Arabic language, 256

Arabs, 8, 94, 105–6, 110, 161, 244

Arda (participant): experiences based on her skin tone, 116, 117, 118; on her educational experiences, 99–100; internalizes stereotypes, 240–41; on jokes about Turkish Ausländer, 57; on "Where do you come from?," 158–59

Arneil, Barbara, 25–26

art, 176, 221, 242, 253, 254, 261. *See also* films; literature; music

Arzu (participant): on *Almanlaşmak*, 184–85; on ambivalence, 234–35; on analyzing her earlier feelings, 225, 237–38; on belonging in Germany, 183; claims Germany, 186–87; on discourse of extraordinary achievements, 93; experience of Turkishness in her work, 104–5, 127; on her emotional connection with Turkish culture and Turks, 150, 153; on her multiple identities, 222; on increasing visibility of Turkish Ausländer, 191–92; on Islamoracism, 134–35; on learning Turkish in schools, 124, 165–66; on racism, 139; on ranking, 88–89; on right-wing groups, 131–32; on stereotypes, 122; struggles with her Turkishness, 207–8, 210–12, 213; on Turkishness, 3, 115–16, 218; Turkishness assigned to, 117

Asgharzadeh, Alireza, 108

Aslan, Emine, 8, 248

assertiveness, 226–30, 234

assimilation, 40–42, 143, 275. *See also* integration

asylum seekers. *See* refugees

Atatürk, 105, 161, 166

at-homeness, 169

attacks. *See* violence

Auschwitz jokes, 56

Ausländer (foreigners): approach to, 21, 49–50; category as important marker of recognition, 270; changes in citizenship laws affecting, 73; conditional acceptance in German society, 41; create something better than multiculturalism, 290; CSU's stance on, 72; defined, 11; diasporic citizenship and new ways of creating, 283; diasporic spaces of, 38, 39(f); discourses of, 154; as exceptional, 253–54; fears about, 130, 131, 132–33, 134 (*see also* racism); fears of, 66–67, 157; Germans' habits of ignorance and stereotyping of, 121–23; immigration and LGBTI+, 275; map of belonging, 33(f), 34; Muslims as, 3, 76–79, 131; 1980s–90s integration into German society, 58; politicians challenged to rethink policies on, 289; population statistics, 10, 52, 55, 59, 75, 82, 292n1Ch2; ranking of, 88–94, 120–21, 144–45, 159; right to make us-versus-them distinctions, 155; rights of, 142, 219; self-awareness and, 219–20, 227; as separate form of humanity, 277; survey of Germans' opinions on, 77, 80, 131; use of term, 12–13, 21, 56, 68, 69, 87–88, 188–89. *See also* German-born Turkish Ausländer; Germanness: Ausländer's challenge to; guest workers; immigrants; Turkish Ausländer

Ausländer children, 96, 97–100. *See also* education

Ausländerkriminalität (foreigner criminality), 67

Ausländerness: approach to, 30; of bodies, 41, 102, 115–19, 124; categorization of, 86; coexistence with queerness, 178–79; educational policies reinforce, 60–61; in homelessness and hospitality quadrant, 41–42; maintained in schools, 194; participants on, 92; participants internalize, 240–41; participants reclaim, 187–89, 190; serves to define Germanness, 87; as set of essential and exclusive characteristics,

Index

32, 34–35; supports proximation and estrangement, 145. *See also* Turkishness

Ausländerproblem (foreigner problem), 56–58, 66–67, 68

Ausländerzentralregister (AZR, Central Register of Foreigners), 82

Aussiedler (members of the German people), 12, 64

awareness: approach to, 280; born of struggle, 237; consciousness and, 200–6, 223, 230; dialogical alliances and need for, 275; in diasporicity vs nationality, 289; emerging from transgressions, 268; as motivating, 226, 238; as sensitivity to borderlands, 17; sources of, 282; as substitute for identity, 197. *See also* self-awareness

Ayda (participant), 178, 186, 207–10, 213, 244

Aygen (participant), 180, 205

Ayla (participant): on generational differences, 168, 192; on German privilege, 129; on headscarves, 111; on ignorance and insensitivity, 126, 241, 242; on Kreuzberg, 175; on Sarrazin's book, 78; on stereotypes, 121, 122; on young Turkish men, 109

Aynur (participant): on *Alamancı*, 158; on being a Berliner, 172; on Germans getting to know Turkish Ausländer, 124–25, 126; on her emotional connection with Türkiye and Turks, 152; on her Turkishness, 201, 206; on jokes about Turkish Ausländer, 57; on Kreuzberg, 174

Ayşe (participant): on *Alamancı*, 157; on Berlin Wall, 54, 66; challenges Turkish/German binary, 186, 201; on choosing Germany, 226; on her gender identity, 213; LGBTI+ community and, 209; on LGBTI+ sexuality in Turkish culture, 215,

216; on personal becoming political, 258–59; physical appearance of, 102–3; on stereotypes, 108; on suitcase children, 98–99; on Türkiyeli, 162, 163; on where she feels comfortable, 71

Ayten (participant), 114, 119, 132–33

Aziza A (participant): diasporic citizenship practices of, 255–57, 263, 268; on interviews about her, 128; on Kreuzberg, 176; on unveiling, 112

Aznar, Jose Maria, 79

backwardness, 92–93, 110, 111, 113, 158

Bakare-Yusuf, Bibi, 16

Bakhtin, Mikhail, 204, 205, 224

Ballard, Roger, 90

Barış (participant): on balance, 228; on double life of some LGBTI+ Turkish Ausländer, 216, 217; on his activism, 227; on his identity, 162–63, 213; on intersecting oppressions of LGBTI+ Turkish Ausländer, 218; on poster campaign's success, 260

Basch, Linda, 180

Bavarian election campaigns, 72

Bavarian model of education, 42, 59–60, 98

BBC, 77

Becker, Birgit, 195

Bektaşi people, 159, 160, 292n2Ch4

Belma (participant), 116, 117–18, 158, 201, 202, 207

belonging: activism about, 171; acts and, 248, 277; among "my own people," 152–56; approach to, 20, 22–23, 29, 31, 148, 169, 196–97, 198–99, 223; Ausländer assert, 87; cities and, 263–64; community provides sense of, 286; diasporic past shapes, 149–50; difficulty addressing contemporary dilemmas of, 279; dominant discourses challenged, 4–5; double consciousness as

320

awareness of, 200–6; of German-born Turkish Ausländer in Berlin, 95, 173, 182, 201; of Germans and Turkish Ausländer together, 32; to Germany vs Türkiye, 151–52; in Kreuzberg, 174–79, 182; of LGBTI+ Turkish Ausländer, 218; map of, 33(f), 34, 35; moral and performative dimensions of, 185; multiplicity of, 162–63; and myth of return, 157; participants on, 3, 5, 17, 181–84, 207; participants claim Germany, 186–87, 225; participants shape their own, 196; and politicization of struggle, 219, 222; in quadrants of diasporic spaces, 40, 42, 44, 45; ranking and, 119; spaces of, 38, 39(f), 86, 145; stereotypes internalized to achieve, 241; of suitcase children, 99; terms for claiming, 189, 190; third space and, 37, 206–13, 223; "Where do you come from?" and, 94–95; of younger generations, 193, 194. *See also* inclusion
Benhabib, Seyla, 25, 264, 272
Berger, John, 53
Berlin: associations representing Turkish Ausländer in, 260; becomes German capital, 62; belonging to, 95, 173, 182, 201; diversity of, 10–11; forging of participants' connections with, 149; German citizenship and participants' love for, 185; Germanness and, 172–73; political parties in, 285; as site for formation of diasporic citizens, 264; as site for transgressive encounters, 263; support for AfD in, 78; Turkish Ausländer ranked as Black in, 94; Turkishness in other German cities vs, 207–10, 211, 229; violence against Ausländer in, 70; vocabulary for participants' claim to, 189. *See also* East Berlin; Kreuzberg; West Berlin

Berlin model of education, 41, 59–60, 98
Berlin Pride, 137–38
Berlin Wall: building of, 52, 53–54; fall of, 62; invisible wall, 65, 71; participants on, 54, 66; poem about, 64–65; stereotypes and, 241; as symbol of unification, 169
Bernstein, Richard, 253
Bhabha, Homi, 40, 205, 207, 222
Bickford, Susan, 238
Bilateral Recruitment Agreement, 52
Bild Zeitung (newspaper), 67
binaries
— acts and practices destabilize, 277
— Ausländer/German and Turkish/German: assimilation based on, 46; collapse of, 102–3, 177–79, 183; creation of, 85–87; maintenance of, 126–27, 128, 145–46; masks differences, 106; participants on, 181; participants challenge, 184, 187, 201, 206, 212–13, 246; physical appearance and, 116; Wengeler articulates, 69
— children of immigrants deconstruct, 279
— diaspora studies and citizenship studies critique, 17
— homosexual/heterosexual, 215
— inclusion/exclusion, 280
Birgül (participant), 67, 245
Black civil rights movement, 27
Black people, 94, 119, 247
Black Virgins (Zaimoğlu), 254
Board on Children and Families, 96
bodies, 35, 101, 140. *See also* hair colour; headscarves; skin colour and tone
Bonn, 51
borderlands, 198–221; approach to, 36, 197, 223; defined, 198; diasporic awareness as sensitivity to, 17; diasporic citizenship and, 225; double consciousness and, 200–6; homophobia, 213–18; politicization

Index

of struggle, 219–23; third space, 206–13, 223; use of term, 196, 199
Borderlands (Anzaldúa), 6, 17
borders, 35–36
Bosphorus (police operation), 71
boundaries, 39, 40
boundary crossings, 4, 177–79, 180, 268–69
boundary-blurring. *See* binaries: Ausländer/German and Turkish/German
Bourdieu, Pierre, 221
Bouyeri, Mohammed, 76
box.de (magazine), 217
Boyarin, Daniel, 36
Boyarin, Jonathan, 35–36
Brah, Avtar, 38
Brandenburg, 260
Bremen, 209–10, 244
Brubaker, Rogers, 130
built environment, 172
Bülent (participant), 153
burkini, 8, 79–80
Butler, Judith, 138, 148

Çağlar, Ayşe, 58
Çalışkan, Gül, 11, 91, 140, 142, 180
Cameron, David, 79
Canada, 212, 243
Cannes, 8, 79
capital: education as, 60–61; hair colour produces cultural, 118; sources of cultural, 221; wisdom produces social, 228
Capulets (in *Romeo and Juliet*), 253
CDU. *See* Christian Democratic Union (CDU)
Çelik, Neco, 252–55, 257, 263, 268, 270
Cemevi (house of gathering), 164, 292*n*2Ch4
Ceyda (participant), 113–14, 152, 244
Checkpoint Charlie, 54
Chicago school of sociology, 40–41
Children's Day, 166

Cho, Lily, 6, 18
Christian civilization, 35, 130–31, 140, 143
Christian Democratic Union (CDU): changes from within, 229; desire to limit Turkish and Vietnamese populations, 67; forms FRG's first government, 50; meeting with CSU, 76; security measures introduced by, 80; Turkish Ausländer in, 190, 292*n*3Ch4
Christian Social Union (CSU), 72, 76, 80
Christianity, 115
Christians, 253, 261
Christopher Street Day (CSD), 178, 227, 259, 266–67
cities, 263–64. *See also* Berlin
citizenship: diasporicity and skepticism about, 19; dissonance with diasporas, 18–19; dual, 72, 73–74, 185–86; group-differentiated, 4, 18, 19, 47; juxtaposition with diasporicity, 17; in Kaya's work, 12; as matter of civic responsibility, 224; participants challenge conventional notion of, 173; *Türkiyelism*'s vision of, 159. *See also* diasporic citizenship; German citizenship; multicultural citizenship
citizenship studies, 16–18, 31, 280–82
citizenship tests, 41, 76, 135–36, 137
clash of civilizations, 35, 130–31, 140, 143
"Clash of Civilizations, The" (Huntington), 140
class status, 92–93, 158, 181–82
Clifford, James, 38, 156
clothing, Islamic, 8, 79–80. *See also* headscarves
Cogolin, 80
Cohen, Rina, 156
Cold War, 50
colonial mimicry, 40
colonialism, 8, 81, 107, 140, 141–42
coming out, 148, 215–17, 265

communities of struggle, 31, 280, 283–86

community: diasporic citizens and, 142–43; among LGBTI+ people, 259; among Othered people, 29; among Turks and Turkish Ausländer, 152–56

conditional hospitality, 90–91, 96, 124

Conference of Education Ministers, 59

Council Directive 2000/43/EC, 75

Council of German Chambers of Commerce, 97

Crath, Rory, 91

Crenshaw, Kimberlé, 24–25

Cresswell, Tim, 267–68

CSD. *See* Christopher Street Day (CSD)

CSU. *See* Christian Social Union (CSU)

cultural citizenship, 4

cultural identity, 15–16, 23–26. *See also* Germanness; Turkishness

Cultural Politics of Emotion, The (S. Ahmed), 131

cultures: accommodation extends beyond, 145; African American, 254; approach to, 19, 20, 23–26; created by new generation of Turkish Ausländer, 171; Dhamoon on multiculturalism and, 14; diversity, national identities, and, 142; as fiction, 160–61; interchange between, 141; Islamic, 213–14; language as inseparable from, 204; lost through assimilation, 40–41; multiculturalism and hierarchy of, 15; as only one mode of difference, 270; participants on, 85, 222, 252; of poverty, 92–93; and second-generation immigrants, 96; Western, 158, 287; younger generations and, 193–94. *See also* German culture; multiculturalism; Turkish culture

Dağtaş, Mahiye Seçil, 111

Dale, Gareth, 51, 53, 83, 92

Damla (participant), 105, 207, 241–42

dance parties, 217, 258, 268

dark-heads, 88, 94. *See also* hair colour

Das Geheimnis Meiner Türkischen Großmutter (*The Secret of My Turkish Grandmother;* Güngör), 251

Day, Richard, 42

deception, 103–4, 117

decisiveness, 226–30, 234

deliberation, 271–72

democracy, 43

deportation, 72

Derrida, Jacques, 90, 235

Deutschland schafft sich ab (*Germany Is Abolishing Itself;* Sarrazin), 77, 78–79, 130, 136

Dhamoon, Rita: on category of "the people" in political systems, 272; and conceptual framework, 6; on culture, 23, 24, 25, 26, 85; on discourse, 22; on ethical commitment, 274; on identity, 205, 270; on integration, 42–43; on Islamophobia, 110; on multiculturalism, 14–15, 16; on new forms of subjectivity, 284; and politics of diasporic citizenship, 286; on power, 20, 21; on system of stratification, 28–29

dialogical alliances, 274–76

dialogue, 16, 265, 271

diaspora studies, 16–18, 31, 280–82

diasporas: conditions creating, 179; dissonance with citizenship, 18–19; Germany as home to multiple, 287, 288; as non-places and multiple places, 38; span multiple borders, 35–36

diasporic citizenship

— aims of, 282, 283

— approach to, x–xi, 5–6, 10, 16, 18–20, 31, 224–25, 282

— attributes of diasporic citizens, 225–37: ambivalence and anti-labelling, 234–37; decisiveness and assertiveness, 226–30, 234; emotional and experiential signs, 237–39; self-

Index

reflexivity and accountability, 230–34, 237, 283, 286
— challenges German politicians, 289
— as epistemological and political project, 280
— essential difference with other forms of citizenship, 48
— vs multiculturalism, 14
— politics of, 262–76; being aware of vehicles of power, 270; being critical and deliberative, 271–72; being dialogical, vocal, and media savvy, 265–67; being out in public space, 263–65; being transgressive, 267–69; demanding dialogical alliances, 274–76; disruptive acts and practices, 273–74; uses, 286
—in quadrants of diasporic spaces, 46–47
—as responsive to disruption, 284
—tension within term, 18–19
—use of term, 18. *See also* acts; borderlands; German-born Turkish Ausländer; homesickness–homelessness; hostility–hospitality; practices
diasporic encounters: ambivalence in, 235; analyzing ranking in, 120–21; approach to, x, 6, 19, 21, 22, 26–27, 29; boundaries enacted in, 39; diasporic subjects become citizens through, 48; hostility–hospitality and, 34; map of relationships worked out in, 33; participants' media interviews, 128–29; social order maintained in, 145; stereotyping in, 122–23; strategies for dealing with different bodies in, 35; use of term, 16. *See also* acts; diasporic citizenship: politics of; practices
diasporic past, 149–51, 158, 159–61, 164–67, 173
diasporic spaces, 38–47; homelessness and hospitality, 40–42; homelessness and hostility, 45–47; homesickness and hospitality, 42–44;

homesickness and hostility, 44–45; types, 38, 39(f)
diasporicity: approach to, ix, 16–17, 20–23, 30, 169, 225–26, 280; awareness involved in nationality vs, 289; contradiction within, 37; defined, 5, 224; juxtaposition with citizenship, 17; and skepticism about citizenship, 19; source of, 149; tension between ethnocentric fear and, 285
dichotomies. *See* binaries
Die Tageszeitung (newspaper), 70
differences: acts, practices, and, 269–70, 283; approach to, 20, 22–23, 24, 25, 26, 28, 29; diasporic citizenship, binaries, and, 277; generational, 165, 167–68, 192–93; headscarves and, 115; homelessness emphasizes, 199; imagined unity and Ausländer's, 153, 154; minorities and, 265; multiculturalism and, 290; multiple manifestations of, 273; offer resistance to dominant contexts, 179; and openness to disruption, 284; policies favouring certain types of, 43; and politics of diasporic citizenship, 269; postmodern understanding of, 231–32; pre-formed identities erase, 106; purity and, 205; ranking of, 119; and us-versus-them distinctions, 155. *See also* diversity
differential consciousness, 230
differentiated citizenship, 4
Dilekçeli Alman (contract German), 186
disclosure, reciprocal, 272
discourses: of Ausländer, 154; Dhamoon on, 22; on estrangement and proximation, 126; of exceptionalism, 93, 144; hostility–hospitality and, 77; of integration, 192; on migrant generations, 97; minority, 105; on Othering, 47; on pluralism, 13; supranationalist, 130; on terrorism, 110; *Türkiyelism*, 159, 162–63. *See also* dominant discourses; social sciences research

discrimination: compounded (*see* intersectionality); exoticization as positive, 217–18; by intersectional activists, 275; laws against, 75–76, 232–33, 236, 275; Muslims expect, 144; perpetuated by habits of ignorance, 81; resistance to, 284; Sarrazin and, 77, 78; second-generation concept's role in, 98; skin colour and, 115, 119; against Turks by Turks, 162. *See also* racism; xenophobia

disease, 213, 214, 216

displacement: diasporic citizenship and, 225; diasporic mindset defined by, 37; identities of, 278; and map of belonging, 33; meaning of, 148; role in creating diasporic identity, 38. *See also* homesickness–homelessness

diversity: of Berlin, 10–11; as challenge to German citizenship, 63; of culture as threat to national identities, 142; discourses of integration destroy, 190–91; educational policies fail to account for, 60; of German culture, 288; Germany's need to embrace, 289; of groups, 43; identity politics offered by, 177; of Islam, 108; of Kreuzberg, 176; linguistic mixing as form of, 205; of minorities and majorities, 146; multiculturalism and, 14, 15; of Muslims, 111, 140; provides cultural capital, 221; Said on living in, 143; of Turkish Ausländer, 11, 158–59, 206; Turks' difficulty in accepting their, 162; of Western culture, 287. *See also* differences

documentaries, 254–55

dominant discourses: approach to, 4–5, 29; linguistic resistance to, 204, 205; open to divergent interpretations, 207; participants' capacity to recognize, 225; participants trespass into, 235

domination: and antagonistic resistance, 45; approach to, xi, 28; covers over

social change, 287; diasporic peoples' creative response to, 279–80; fluidity of, 231–33, 269, 274; multiculturalism fails to address, 14–15; need for resisting, 283; and participants' motivations for acts and practices, 277; racism as product of, 85; struggle for, 40. *See also* privilege

double consciousness, 200–6

double movement, 148

dual citizenship, 72, 73–74, 185–86

DuBois, W.E.B., 200

Dundes, Alan, 56

East Berlin: as capital of GDR, 51; communist regime in, 50; compared with Kreuzberg, 241; Germans getting to know Turkish Ausländer in, 124, 125; hair colour and cultural capital in, 118; participants on divide between West and, 71; participants' use of term, 65; travel to West Berlin from, 54

East Germans, 63, 65, 66, 89

East Germany, 65, 130, 191. *See also* German Democratic Republic (GDR)

Eastern Europe, 63–64

economic functionalism, 43. *See also* labour migration

economic miracle, 52, 53

economic recession, 54–55

economy, 141–42

education: Alamancı status and, 158; and conflicts among students from different parts of Türkiye, 159; connection with Türkiye produced through, 167; Germans' acquaintance with Turkish Ausländer through, 125; for guest workers' children, 59–62, 98–100; hair colour, cultural capital, and, 118; Koran school, 208; as meeting ground, 187; and open-minded people's racism, 139; stereotypes and, 243–44. *See also* Turkish language: in schools

Egorova, Yulia, 143
Eibach, Richard, 24
Ekşi, Mete, 227
Ela (participant): on belonging, 181; on connection with other Turkish Ausländer, 169–70; on Germanness, 181, 183; on home, 32; on living between two worlds, 200–1; on outsiderness, 95; politicization of struggle by, 221; on self-perception, 104; Turkishness of, 157, 207–8, 210, 229–30
Elke (Yıldız's German friend), 126–27
emancipation: female, 111–12
Emel (participant), 107
emotional signs, 237–39
emotions, 131, 140, 225, 278, 289. See also fear
England and UK, 79, 143, 210–11, 226, 251
Erdem, Esra, 139
Erdoğan, Recep Tayyip, 246
Erkan (participant): on alliances to fight racism, 285; on anti-discrimination law, 75–76; on changes wrought by LGBTI+ community, 260; on changes wrought by unification, 170; on changing CDU from within, 229; on exoticization, 217–18; on Germanness, 9, 120, 186, 220; on his family's displacements and identities, 159–61, 163; on homelessness for Germans vs Turks, 216, 218; on immigration as coming out, 148; on Islamoracism, 134–35, 136–37, 138; on making personal causes into public ones, 259; on the media, 266; on naming, 265–66; on people of colour, 119; on political leaking into private, 139; on politicization of struggle, 219–20; on resisting labelling, 235–36; on rhetoric of Christian vs Muslim, 130; on Sarrazin, 77; on self-reflexivity, 230–31, 232; on Turkish Ausländer's increasing presence, 189–90; on Turkish culture, 213–14,

221; on Turkishness, 105; on Turks as Muslim Ausländer, 3, 76; on uncertain times, 82
essentialism, 43, 147–48, 155, 240
"Est ist Zeit" ("It Is Time"; song), 255–56
estrangement: acts and, 239; challenging stereotypes leads to, 244; in diasporic spaces, 39(f), 85–86; dominant discourses and, 225; and map of belonging, 33, 34; participants' sense of belonging and, 181–84; as pole on hostility-hospitality axis, 35; politics of, 145; privilege maintained through discourses of, 126; shaped by race and class, 181
ethnic Germans, 12, 63–64, 75, 89
ethnocentrism, 89, 288
EU External Affairs, 164
Eurocentrism, 20, 79–81, 90
Europe, 8, 52, 287, 288, 289, 290
European Union (EU), 75, 113
Eurovision Song Contest, 250–51
exceptionalism: assimilation and, 41; Çelik on, 253–54; discourses of, 93, 144; individual Ausländer and, 128, 221; and internalization of stereotypes, 240, 241
exclusion: binary with inclusion, 280; felt by German-born Turkish Ausländer, 181; felt by Turkish Ausländer in aftermath of unification, 71; Germanness premised on, 23; language's role in, 202, 203; logic of, 86–87, 120, 123, 124; and participants' political aim, 277; of Turkish LGBTI+ community, 215–16, 218. See also marginalization; outsiders
exoticization, 217–18
experiential signs, 237–39
experts, 41, 126, 127

family reunification, 55, 79
Fanon, Frantz, 219, 231
fascism, 133

father-daughter relationships, 249–50, 255

Fatma (participant): on being a Berliner, 172, 201; on being at home in Germany, 181–82; on generational differences, 191; on German citizenship, 185; on German language, 165; on Germanness, 117, 201, 218; on her activism, 227; on her son, 193–96; on increasing visibility of Turkish Ausländer, 191; on integration, 187; on racism, 85, 133–34; on reactions to her mother's headscarf, 110–11; on rise of Islamoracism, 8–9, 130; on stereotypes, 108, 121; on Turkish language, 166, 202–3, 204; Turkishness of, 103; on Turkishness, 102, 201, 219; on uncertain times, 82

fear: about Ausländer, 130, 131, 132–33, 134; Ausländer's, 66–67, 157; and Europe and the West's current problems, 289; fear-mongering in media, 284; S. Ahmed on, 131, 140; tension between diasporicity and ethnocentric, 285; white Germans', 9. *See also* Islamoracism and Islamophobia; racism; xenophobia

Federal Republic of Germany (FRG): education for children of guest workers in, 59–62; founding, 50; immigration history, 51; recruits guest workers, 52–55. *See also* West Germany

Fellows, Mary Louise, 274

feminism, 221

feminists, 9, 137, 138

fetishization, 217

films, 76, 242, 252–53, 254, 263, 268

Final Settlement Treaty, 62

Fincher, Ruth, 176

first names, 195

First Reich, 49

first-generation immigrants, 96

foreign workers. *See* guest workers

foreigners. *See* Ausländer

foreignness, 252. *See also* Ausländerness

Foucault, Michel, 21, 45, 46, 267–68, 283, 284

France, 8, 73, 79–80, 134

Frankfurt, 68, 136

Frankfurter Allgemeine Zeitung (newspaper), 67, 227

French people, 80

French State Council, 80.

FRG. *See* Federal Republic of Germany (FRG)

Friedrich Ebert Foundation, 77

friendship, 126–27, 154

Frisch, Max, 49

Funda (participant), 116–17, 118, 125–26, 152, 158, 242

Galantino, Nunzio, 80

Ganz oben. Türkisch – Deutsch – Erfolgreich (documentary), 254–55

Ganz Schön Deutsch (*Very Nice German;* Güngör), 251

Gastarbeiter. See guest workers

Gayhane (gay house; dance party and nightclub), 217, 258, 268

Gays and Lesbians *aus der Türkei* (GLADT): on anti-discrimination law, 232–33; anti-racist activism of, 262; appointees and board members of, 213, 217; dance parties and, 258; and diasporic political activism, 260; founding, 259; mission, 292n1Ch5; provides platforms for diasporic citizenship, 263

Gaziantep, 211

GDR. *See* German Democratic Republic (GDR)

gender identities, 213–14

gender relations, 97, 108–9, 113, 214, 255

gender rights, 135

Geneva, 80

German for Beginners (book), 237

German citizenship: Ausländer's challenge to, 83–84; belonging does not result from, 181–82; Berliners' experience of, 11; complex relationship with Germanness, 49, 117; first names of Turkish Ausländer children and, 195; obstacles to obtaining, 62, 83; population statistics on, 73; postwall debates about, 71–76; Turkish Ausländer claim, 185–88, 189

German citizenship laws: CDU's position on, 229; citizenship tests, 41, 76, 135–36, 137; efforts to reform, 72–73; *jus sanguinis* and, 10, 63, 81, 83; 1913 ethnicity-based, 51

German culture: diversity of, 288; as flexible and soft, 229; vs Kreuzberg culture, 253; LGBTI+ sexuality and, 213, 215, 216–18; mixing with other cultures, 254; people comfortable with Turkish and, 211–12; Şenocak on growing up in, 200

German Democratic Republic (GDR), 50–51, 52, 53–54, 62, 293n2Ch5. *See also* East Germany

German Jews, 89, 292n1Ch3

German language: difficulty of learning, 164; earlier Turkish Ausländer's failure to learn, 188; Germanness and, 221; in Kreuzberg, 176; mixed with Turkish, 165, 204–5, 209, 255–56; new generation as closer to, 167; participants' changing relationship with, 226; participants' self-need to prove skills in, 237; rap in, 255–56, 257; role in belonging, 201–4; in schools, 59–60, 98–99, 165, 202–3, 243; Şenocak on learning, 200; TV shows in, 245–46

German men, 109

German women, 109, 110–11

German-born Turkish Ausländer
— approach to, x, 5, 6, 287
— conceptual frameworks for study of, 6, 13–26; accommodation, 23–25; diaspora studies and citizenship studies, 16–18; diasporic citizenship,

18–20; diasporicity, culture, and power, 20–23; multiculturalism, 13–16
— concern with German politics, 81–82
— maps of belonging, 33(f), 34
— methodology for study of, 7, 26–30, 291n1
— participants' educational backgrounds, 62
— 2003–16 changes in participants' lives, 7, 8–9
— use of pseudonyms vs real names for, 291
— use of term, 12, 155–56. *See also* Ausländer; borderlands; diasporic citizenship; homesickness–homelessness; hostility–hospitality; Turkish Ausländer

Germanness
— approach to, 30, 49–50, 83
— Ausländer's challenge to, 83–84, 93, 182, 183, 184
— body's role in determining, 41, 102, 115–19, 124
— complex relationship with German citizenship, 49, 117
— creation of, 50–51
— encourages new generation's Turkishness, 168
— English people's reaction to participants', 211
— as ethnic identity, 120
— German language and, 221
— German-born Turkish Ausländer as part of, 105
— Germans claim sole possession of, 129
— in homelessness and hospitality quadrant, 40
— incompleteness of, 288
— jokes about Turkish Ausländer, 56–57
— light skin represents, 117
— map of belonging, 33(f)
— mixing languages as mark of, 205

- multiculturalism and, 14
- new Germans, 41, 83, 142, 191–94
- 1980s–90s Ausländer integration into German society, 58
- as opportunity and threat, 146
- Oriental hip-hop ruptures, 256
- Özdemir, Cem: challenges, 245
- participants: challenge assumptions about, 5, 229; claims to, 37, 115, 123, 150, 183–85, 196, 262; disconnect and distance from, 154, 167; hope and pessimism about, 9; lifestyles subordinate to, 225
- politicians challenged to rethink definitions of, 289
- post-wall citizenship debates, 71–76
- premises of, 22, 23
- privilege of, 118–19, 120
- racial terms of, 247
- recent immigration trends and, 82
- recruitment of guest workers, 52–55, 64, 74
- as set of essential and exclusive characteristics, 32, 34–35, 120
- source of challenges for, 10, 11
- stereotypes' role in preserving, 87
- term Alamanyalı challenges, 162
- third space draws from, 207
- transforms Turkishness, 200
- of Turkish Ausländer, 169–98; in aftermath of unification, 169–72; Berliners, 172–73; challenging integration and Ausländerness, 187–92; claiming German citizenship, 185–88, 189; Kreuzberg and, 173–79; naming, 195–97; new Germans, 191–94; simultaneous belonging and estrangement, 181–84; translocal, 179–80
- Turkish gender relations reinforce, 109
- Turkishness as mode of confrontation with, 101

- unification, 62–71. See also binaries: Ausländer/German and Turkish/German
Germans: acquaintance with Turkish Ausländer, 123–29, 210; in Alltag, 253; belonging with Turkish Ausländer, 32; claim sole possession of Germanness, 129; desire to maintain privilege, 144; diasporicity can educate, 289; East, 63, 65, 66, 89; ethnic, 12, 63–64, 75, 89; journalists as bridge between Turkish Ausländer and, 251; lack ability to think globally, 266; lack life experiences, 222; men vs. Turkish men, 109; opinion polls and, 77, 80, 131; as Others, 288; as outsiders, 154; participants on ingratitude of, 181; in relationships with LGBTI+ Turkish Ausländer, 217; stereotyping and habits of ignorance of, 121–23; subcategories of, 89; use of term, 12; us-versus-them distinctions by Ausländer vs, 155; West, 65; women vs. Turkish women, 109; women's reactions to headscarves, 110–11. See also binaries: Ausländer/German and Turkish/German
Germany: approach to, 31, 280; colonialism of, 8; historical treatment of LGBTI+ community in, 136; increasing diversity in, 7; multiculturalism and, 13–14, 16; need to understand tension within, 285; participants' belonging to Türkiye vs, 151–52; participants claim, 95–96, 184–85, 186–87, 225; participants' re-migration to, 226; participants shape their own belonging in, 196; reimagining, 83, 84, 169, 287–90. See also Berlin
getürkt (trickery), 103–4
Gilroy, Paul, 149
Gitmez, Ali, 53

Index 329

GLADT. *See* Gays & Lesbians *aus der Türkei* (GLADT)
globalization, 8, 80–81
Gogh, Theo van, 3, 76
Gold, Gerald, 156
graffiti, 220, 253, 254
green card system, 74
Green party, 72, 192
group-differentiated citizenship, 4, 18, 19, 47. *See also* multicultural citizenship
Grundgesetz (constitution), 50, 51, 69
Gubrium, Jaber, 27
guest workers: Ausländer as children of, 96; descendants demand recognition for experiences of, 188; education for children of, 59–62, 98–100; *Gastarbeiter* and other names for, 53, 55, 91, 92; German, 157–58, 208; Germans "oppressed" by children of, 97; memory of experience of, 173; political reclaiming of identity of, 249–50; recruitment of, 52–55, 74; role in ranking, 88; Turkish Ausländer's ongoing identity as, 93. *See also* Ausländer; labour migration; worker exchanges
Güler (participant): on Berlin Wall, 54, 66; on decisions about acting, 240, 241; on ethnic separation in education, 60; on homeland, 95–96; on language, 203; on mispronunciations of Turkish names, 196–97; on stereotypes, 108–9; on Turkishness, 102; on us-versus-them distinctions, 155
Güngör, Dilek, 249–51, 257, 263, 268
Güvenç, Bozkurt, 161

Habbe, Christian, 57
habits of ignorance, 81. *See also* hostility–hospitality: stereotypes and habits of ignorance
hair colour: cultural capital gained through, 118; and Germans'

acquaintance with Turkish Ausländer, 125; passive resistance offered by, 243; role in passing for German, 116, 117; role in ranking, 88, 90, 94
Haiti, 18
Hall, Stuart, 25, 154, 197, 199, 239, 276
hamam (Turkish bath), 214, 293n3
Hanru, Hou, 174
harem, 214, 293n3
Haritaworn, Jin, 137, 138
hate, 131, 140, 289. *See also* Islamoracism and Islamophobia; racism; xenophobia
hate crime. *See* violence
Hauschild, Thomas, 56
headscarves, 8, 46, 77–78, 107–15, 127, 242
Hebdo, Charlie, 134
Heidelberger Manifest (Heidelberg Manifesto), 57
Heine, Heinrich, 143
Herising, Faith, 231
heterogeneity. *See* differences; diversity
heteronormativity, 236
heterosexism, 259
heterosexuals, 265
Hidalgo, Anne, 80
hierarchy. *See* ranking
Hignett, Kelly, 65
hijab. *See* headscarves
hip-hop, 254, 255–57
Hirsi Ali, Ayaan, 143
Hitler, Adolf, 78
Holland, 73, 76
Holocaust, 248
Holstein, James, 27
home, 32, 36
homeland: in diasporic spaces, 38, 39(f), 40, 42, 44; identity in foreign land vs, 147; participants claim Germany as their, 95–96, 184–85; participants' lack of, 207, 210; role in diasporic identity, 35. *See also* Türkiye

homesickness–homelessness, 147–98; acts and, 239, 273; *Alamancı*, 157–58; ambivalence and, 235; approach to, 30–31, 35–37, 47, 147–48, 168, 197; belonging among "my own people," 152–56; Berliners, 172–73; as concealed process of negotiation, 272; diasporic citizenship and, 225; diasporic spaces of, 38, 39(f); diversity of Turkishness, 158–64; homelessness for Germans vs Turks, 216, 218; homelessness and hospitality, 40–42; homelessness and hostility, 45–47; homesickness and hospitality, 42–44; homesickness and hostility, 44–45; integration and Ausländerness, 187–92; Kreuzberg, 173–79; living memory, 149–51; map of, 33(f), 34; myth of return, 149, 156–57; naming of Turkish Ausländer children, 195–97; new Germans, 191–94; and not choosing a home, 198; participants assumed to be homesick, 95–96; participants on choosing homelessness, 208; Peck on homelessness, 66; repeating diasporic experiences, 164–67; similarity vs difference emphasized in, 199; simultaneous belonging and estrangement, 181–84; translocality, 177, 179–80; Turkish Ausländer claim German citizenship, 185–88, 189; Turkishness of different generations, 167–68; unification's aftermath, 169–72; vacationing in Türkiye, 151–52, 183

homogeneity: colonialism and, 141; cultures' lack of, 287; desire for German nation's, 63, 66, 83; participants question Turkishness's, 159; of second-generation children, 98; Turkishness as project of, 153

homonationalism, 8, 136–39

homophobia, 213–18, 221, 259, 260–61, 262

host societies, 38, 40–41, 42, 44, 45–46, 58

hostility–hospitality. *See also* accommodation
— acquaintances, experts, and exceptions, 123–29
— acts and, 240, 273
— approach to, 22, 30, 34–35, 47, 86, 144–46
— children of suitcase children, 100–1
— as concealed process of negotiation, 272
— diasporic citizenship and, 225
— diasporic spaces of, 38, 39(f)
— disruption as response to, 283
— and dominant's group control and accommodation, 24
— hospitality as concept, 90
— hospitality and homelessness, 40–42
— hospitality and homesickness, 42–44
— hostility and homelessness, 45–47
— hostility and homesickness, 44–45
— insulation against hostility, 286
— Kreuzberg and challenges to, 37
— map of, 33(f)
— naming, 87–88
— opposition to homesickness–homelessness vs to, 154
— outsiders, 94–100
— in range of public discourse on Ausländer, 77
— stereotypes and habits of ignorance, 121–23, 125, 126, 127, 128, 129
— theories of accommodation, 85
— Turkishness and, 101–20; deception, 103–4, 117; general characteristics of, 101; headscarves, 46, 107–15, 127; meanings for Turkish Ausländer, 101–2; as obligation, 106; as opportunity and threat, 146; people of colour, 119–20; skin colour and tone and, 90, 102, 115–19, 124; sub-minorities within, 105–6, 292n4. *See also* Islamoracism and Islamophobia; racism; ranking

Index

House of Representatives (FRG), 50
Howard, John, 79
Howarth, David, 148, 227–29
Hoyerswerda, 68
Hunter, Margaret, 115
Huntington, Samuel P., 140
hybridity. *See* diversity

ibne (effeminate men), 214
identities: acts' revelation about, 239;
    alliances and mutation of, 286; ap-
    proach to, 20, 22–23, 31, 197, 281;
    in Çelik's art, 252, 254; and contra-
    diction in diasporic accountability,
    231; cultural, 15–16, 23–26; dias-
    poric, 35, 36, 38, 156, 222; diasporic
    citizenship and re-creating, 227–29;
    diasporic spaces and, 38, 39(f), 42,
    43, 44; difficulty addressing con-
    temporary dilemmas of, 279; of
    displacement, 276; dominant dis-
    courses challenged, 4–5; essential-
    ized and strategically essentialized,
    147–48, 155–56; as fiction, 160–61;
    in foreign land vs homeland, 147;
    gender, 213–18; homelessness's and
    homesickness's role in defining, 36–
    37; individual activism and, 275;
    map of, 33(f); multiplicity of, 28, 47,
    48, 198–99, 206, 222, 225, 235–37;
    Muslimness, 107, 112–14, 130–31;
    Oriental, 101; political reclaiming
    of guest-worker, 249–50; and polit-
    ical view of citizenship, 271; power,
    ranking, and, 277; and sensitivity to
    borderlands, 17; as source of pro-
    ductive power, 238; of "the people"
    in political systems, 272; *Türkiyelism*
    and, 163; and use of terms for for-
    eigners, 69–70; "Where do you
    come from?" and, 91. *See also*
    Ausländerness; Germanness; na-
    tional identities; Turkishness
identity politics, 154–56, 166, 176
Ilkay Leon (Fatma's son), 165, 193–96

illness, 213, 214, 216
immigrant politics, 81–82
immigrants: assimilation of, 40–41;
    Çelik on stories about, 252–53;
    children of immigrants as diasporic
    citizens, 279; citizenship tests for,
    41, 76, 135–36, 137; desire for be-
    longing, 4; ethnic German, 12, 63–
    64; first- and second-generation, 96–
    98; Germany's complex relationship
    with, 49; inter-ethnic alliances
    among, 285; vs race in construction
    of others, 119; translocality, 179–80.
    See also Ausländer; guest workers;
    refugees
immigration: as coming out, 148; hist-
    ory of, 51, 82; as issue in LGBTI+
    community, 275; laws on, 75; poli-
    cies on, 43, 72, 74, 79, 139. *See also*
    migrations
in-betweenness. *See* third space
inclusion, 232, 234, 276, 277, 280. *See
    also* belonging
Inclusive Mosque Initiative, 138
Independent Commission on Migration
    to Germany, 74
India, 168–69
Infratest dimap, 80
insiders, x, xi
integration: *Ausländerproblem* and,
    56; burkinis and, 80; citizenship
    laws and, 73–74, 75; dance parties
    as space for, 258; diasporic citizens
    argue for, 142; education's role in,
    41, 59–60, 61; of ethnic German
    immigrants, 63; of foreigners in
    Europe into host societies, 58;
    in homesickness and hospitality
    quadrant, 42–43; through language,
    202, 203; Mueller on Turkish Aus-
    länder's lack of, 97; multiculturalism
    hinders, 79; of new Germans, 194;
    participants claim, 187, 188–92,
    245–46; participants' definition of,
    41, 229; participants object to, 252;

Turkish women's unveiling as act of, 111–12. *See also* adaptation
intellect, Muslims', 77
Interior Ministry, 53
intersectionality: anti-discrimination law and, 232–33; Crenshaw's study of, 24–25; embraced by diasporic citizens, 277; LGBTI+ community and, 218, 262; narrative analysis exposes, 28; in participants' experiences, 236; in shaping acts and practices, 275; of Turkish Ausländer, 93
İpekçioğlu, İpek, 215, 216, 259
Iraq, 139
İrem (participant): on challenging stereotypes, 243–44; on claiming Turkish culture and language, 245–46; on German citizenship, 185; on *getürkt,* 103; on her activism, 227; on high expectations for foreigners, 104; on integration, 189; on Kreuzberg, 176; on ranking, 92; on silencing, 160–61; on Turkishness, 105–6, 162–63, 164, 212–13
Isin, Engin F., ix–xi; on cities, 173, 264; and conceptual framework, 6; on conflicting wills, 39; on drive toward identity, 42; on group encounters, 40
Islam: curiosity about, 3, 8–9, 76, 127; headscarf's role in creating image of, 107–8; homophobia in, 222, 261; participants on, 113–14. *See also* Alevis; Muslims
Islamic clothing, 8, 79–80. *See also* headscarves
Islamic culture, 213–14
Islamists, 114
Islamoracism and Islamophobia: activism against, 82, 261; burkini ban, 8, 79–80; citizenship tests as, 135–36, 137; functions and justifications for, 108, 109–10; groups promoting, 132; increase in, 7–9, 130–31, 135, 261;

in LGBTI+ community, 9, 136–38, 218, 261; vs mainstream racism, 138; and Muslims' self-consciousness, 134; as resurgence of ethnocentric values, 288; in Sarrazin's book, 78; understanding Germany's, 140–44. *See also* Orientalism; racism
Israel, 143
İstanbul, 159, 160, 255, 257
Italian language, 257
Italians, 242
Italy, 52, 55

Jacobs, Jane, 176
James, Carl E., 122
JAN Trust, 80
Jewish question, 143
Jews, 56, 89, 143–44, 292n1Ch3, 292n1Ch4. *See also* anti-Semitism
jokes, 56–57
Joppke, Christian, 4
journalists. *See* media
Judaism, 159, 160
judgment. *See* ranking
jus sanguinis (citizenship of the parents), 10, 63, 81, 83
jus soli (place of birth), 10, 63

Kanak Sprak (dialect used by Turkish Ausländer), 204
Kanake (derogatory term for foreigner), 187, 204
Katarina (participant), 203
Kaya, Ayhan, 11–12, 130, 198
Keith, Michael, 38
Kemal (participant), 203
"Kendi Yolum" ("My Own Way"; song), 256
Khan, Sadiq, 80
Kohl, Helmut, 70
Kolya Yunus Çetin (Leyla's son), 195–96
Koran school, 208
Kramer, Heinz, 164
Kreuzberg: art and music in, 177, 221, 256; in Çelik's work, 253, 254, 255;

culture shock of, 211; displacement transformed in, 264; East Berlin compared with, 241; focal point in struggle of homelessness and homesickness, 37; Germanness and, 173–79; lack of assigned identities in, 212; main street transformed in, 171; nightclubs in, 258; participants' experience covering news stories in, 250–51; poster campaign in, 260; project on immigrant women's lives in, 82; Turkish guest workers settle in, 55; Turkishness in, 102, 116; vocabulary for participants' claim to, 189

Kurdish people and identity, 105–6, 159, 227, 292n4

Kurt, Kemal, 64–65

Kymlicka, Will, 13–14, 24, 44

labelling. *See* naming and labelling

Labour Day, 193, 230, 232, 293n1Ch6

labour migration, 3, 52–55, 64, 74. *See also* economic functionalism; guest workers

Ladino, 159, 292n1Ch4

Laguerre, Michel, 18

language, 159, 252, 292n1Ch4. *See also* German language; Turkish language

laws: anti-discrimination, 75–76, 232–33, 236, 275; on asylum in Germany, 67, 69; on immigration, 75; prohibiting Islamic clothing, 8, 79–80. *See also* German citizenship laws

Le Figaro (newspaper), 80

left wing, 69, 112, 137, 138, 236

Lesben- und Schwulenverband in Deutschland (LSVD), 137, 213, 259, 293n2Ch5

Lesbenberatung Berlin (Berlin Lesbian Counselling Center), 262

LesMigraS (LGBTI+ organization), 262

Lewis, Bernard, 140–41

Lewis, Oscar, 92–93

Leyla (participant): on AfD, 132; on clash between Christendom and Muslimness, 130–31; on division among Muslims, 83; on generational differences, 165, 192; on German citizenship, 185; on her desire to contribute, 262; on her identity, 189; on her son's name, 195–96; on increasing visibility of Turkish Ausländer, 192; on Kreuzberg, 175; on Mehmet case, 172; on Muslims' need to explain themselves, 134; on people who don't belong, 3, 17; on ranking, 88, 89, 94; on West Berlin/ East Berlin divide, 71

LGBTI+ community: adaptation, immigration, and, 275; citizenship test questions about, 135; conference for Turkish background, 260; defined, 292n2Ch1; diasporic citizenship practices of, 258–62; differing priorities within, 236; go to war, 237; groups representing racialized minorities, 262 (*see also* Gays and Lesbians *aus der Türkei* [GLADT]); homelessness and homesickness feelings in Turkish background, 37; homelessness and hostility quadrant and, 46; homophobia in Islam, 222, 261; Islamoracism within, 9, 136–38, 218, 261; naming's importance in, 265; participants' desire to make visible, 227; and participants' struggles with Turkishness, 208, 209; pride parades, 137–38, 178, 259, 266–67; racism within, 217–18, 259; Turkish culture and, 213–17, 218, 259, 266

liberal multiculturalism, 13, 14

Ling, L.H.M., 160, 262, 282

Linke, Uli, 6, 11–12

Lintner, Herr (German MP), 245

Lisnard, David, 79

listening, 238–39

literature, 55, 58–59, 251–52, 261. *See also* social sciences research
living memory, 149–51
Lorde, Audre, 239
Lowe, Lisa, 156, 233
Lower Saxony, 292n3Ch4
LSVD. *See Lesben- und Schwulenverband in Deutschland* (LSVD)
Lübeck, 68
Ludwigshafen, 70
Lynch, Sandra, 154

Maizière, Thomas de, 80
Mandel, Ruth: on *Ausländer* as term, 87; on the Berlin Wall, 54; and conceptual framework, 6; on diversity of Turkish population, 11; on guests, 91; on participants in her study, 67; on Turkish Ausländer, 76
Mannheim, 60
marginalization: within activist work, 276; justifications for, 93–94; of LGBTI+ community, 213; multiculturalism fails to address, 14; paradoxical, 48; role of second-generation concept in, 98; of Turks by Turks, 208; undoing one's own, 235. *See also* exclusion; outsiders
Markell, Patchen, 24
marriage, 164
May, Theresa, 79
May 1 (Labour Day), 193, 230, 232, 293n1Ch6
Mayer, Frederick, 27
McQueen, Fraser, 80
meat, 193–94
media: on Ausländer children, 97; citizenship tests and, 136; diasporic citizens' use of, 266–67; future work by, 285; hire Turkish Ausländer, 191; participants' experience working in, 104–5, 127, 249–51, 257, 263, 268; portrayals of Turkish Ausländer in, 58–59, 66–67, 68, 70, 92, 128–29, 249–51; racist fear-mongering in,

284; on unveiling and emancipation, 112
Mehmet (young man threatened with deportation), 46, 72, 172–73
Melda (participant), 246
Melissa (participant), 242–43
memory, 149–51, 160, 163, 164, 173, 188
Merkel, Angela, 45, 76–77, 79, 82, 132
mestiza women, 104, 228
Mesut (participant), 57
#MeTwo, 246–48
Michaels, Walter Benn, 15
Migration (Vertovec), 96
migrations: approach to, x–xi; history of, ix–x; labour, 3, 52–55, 64, 74; reasons for twentieth and twenty-first century, 4; reconstitution involved in, 149. *See also* immigration
Milczarek-Desai, Shefali, 184, 222
MILES (Centre for Immigrants, Lesbians and Gays), 259–60, 263
military service, 214
mimicry, 205
Minh-ha, Trinh, 231, 287, 290
Ministry of the Interior and Home Affairs, 74
minorities: characteristics and treatment of, 44; differences and, 265; as political forces, 45
minority discourses, 105
minority identities, 46
Mocan, Naci, 142
modernization, 111, 112, 114
Moghissi, Haideh, 111
Mohr, Jean, 53
Mölln, 56, 68, 70
monologism, 288
Montagues (in *Romeo and Juliet*), 253
moral panics, 137
Mueller, Claus, 97–98
Müge (participant), 178, 213
multicultural (as term), 88
multicultural citizenship, 4, 13, 15, 18, 290
multicultural hybridity, 15–16

Index

multiculturalism: approach to, 13–16; critique of, 290; economic functionalism of, 43; European leaders on failure of, 45, 76–77, 79, 82; in homesickness and hospitality quadrant, 42. *See also* cultures

multi-layered citizenship, 4

Mummery, Jane, 168

music, 112, 254, 255–57, 258, 263, 268

Muslim civilization, 35, 130–31, 140

Muslim women: preoccupation with bodies of, 107; self-image of, 113; stereotypes about, 108, 109, 110–11, 113, 114; theatrical plays about, 254; unveiling of, 111–12

Muslimness, 107, 112–14, 130–31

Muslims: as Ausländer, 3, 76–79, 131; in Ausländer's own ranking, 159; diet of, 193–95; experiences of Jews vs, 143–44; in German version of *Romeo and Juliet*, 253; greater opportunities for, 191–92; participants struggle to be proper, 208; religious identity conflicts among, 237; Sarrazin's views on, 77–78; self-consciousness of, 134. *See also* Alevis; Islam; Islamoracism and Islamophobia; Turkish Ausländer: labelled as Muslims

Muslims in Europe: A Report on 11 EU Cities, 76

Muslims under the Rainbow (book), 260

myth, 152

myth of return, 149, 156–57

naming and labelling: approach to, 12–13; of Ausländer, 67, 69, 90, 93–94; diasporic citizens resist, 234–37; of guest workers, 53, 55, 91, 92; need for new, 5; of new Germans, 191; by participants, 12, 88, 187–88, 189, 195–97, 250, 265; participants as Alamancı, 157–58; passive resistance and, 242; replacing "ethnic" names with German, 247; stereo-types of Turkish names, 121; of Turkish Ausländer children, 195–97

narratives: approach to, 6, 27–30; on guest workers, 92; methodology for obtaining, 7, 291*n*1; participants' several layers of, 222; S. Ahmed on hate and fear in, 131

national identities: crisis in Western nations, 142; in diaspora and citizenship studies, 17–18; diasporicity and, 20; monologist awareness of, 289; as pre-given, 26; questions of what defines, 161; Türkiye's, 111, 114, 162. *See also* Germanness

nationalism, 53, 64, 131, 140, 158

National-Sozialistischer Untergrund (NSU), 71

nationhood, 11, 17–18

nation-state: approach to, x, 31, 280; building of modern Türkiye, 161; creation of, x, 19; difficulty addressing contemporary dilemmas of, 279; exclusion's role in building, 23; and Germany's self-understanding, 288; identity and nature questioned, 287; role in defining cultural groups, 24; Turkishness as homogenizing project of, 153; *Türkiyelism* challenges, 163

naturalization, 72, 73–74, 83

nature vs urban environment, 151–52

Naunyn Ritze Youth and Cultural Centre, 252

Nazis and Nazism, 53, 57, 135, 141, 247

neo-Nazis: in AfD, 131; attacks against Ausländer, 67–68, 71, 227, 234; groups outlawed, 69; racism extends beyond, 139; rallies, 134. *See also* right wing; white supremacy

Neukölln, 260

new Germans, 41, 83, 142, 191–94

Nike, 178

9/11, 8–9, 76, 110, 135, 140, 144

noble foreigners, 89–90, 94

normality, 254

North Americans, 90
Not an Oriental (Fairy) Tale (Kurt), 64–65
not-at-homeness, 169
NSU. *See National-Sozialistischer Untergrund* (NSU)

Open Society Institute, 76
opinion polls, 77, 80, 131
oppression: competition and, 28; oppressed as oppressors, 231–33, 269, 274
Oranienstrasse, 171, 175, 177, 178, 179, 258
Oriental: identity, 101; music, 255–57, 258; women, 111–12
Orientalism: Ausländer's lifestyles as "Oriental," 56; *getürkt* as type of, 103; as publicity tool, 266–67; Said on, 25, 107, 140, 141; use of term, 107. *See also* Islamoracism and Islamophobia; racism
Other. *See* Ausländer; German-born Turkish Ausländer; Muslims; Turkish Ausländer
Othering, 28, 47, 275
Otherness, 29, 34, 161–62, 163. *See also* Ausländerness; Turkishness
Ottoman Empire, 161, 163
outsiders, 94–100; approach to, x, xi; cultural capital and, 61; Germans as, 154; in Germany and Türkiye, 206; in Türkiye, 46. *See also* exclusion; marginalization
Özcan, Veysel, 74–75
Özdamar, Emine Sevgi, 147
Özdemir, Cem, 69, 72, 192, 244–45
Özil, Mesut, 246
Özkan, Aygül, 292n3Ch4

Parekh, Bhikhu, 16, 43
passing for German, 116–17, 118
passive resistance, 240–43
passports. *See* German citizenship
patriarchy, 109, 112

Patriotic Europeans Against the Islamization of the West (PEGIDA), 78, 129–30, 132, 140, 289
Peck, Jeff, 6, 64, 66, 69–70, 89–90, 181
Pécoud, Antoine, 11
PEGIDA. *See* Patriotic Europeans Against the Islamization of the West (PEGIDA)
people of colour, 119–20
perpetual arrivants, 91
person-centred inquiries, 273
Petzen, Jen, 137, 139
Phelan, Shane, 286
Phillips, Anne, 24
Pile, Steve, 38
platforms, 257, 259, 263, 264, 268
pluralism, 13, 42
Poland, 157, 210
police, 71, 191
policies: affirming homesickness and hospitality, 42–43; on assimilation, 41; on guest workers, 52–53; intersectionality needed in, 236; Islamophobia shapes, 141; policy makers on migrant generations, 97; politicians challenged to rethink, 289. *See also* education; immigration: policies on; laws; multiculturalism
political: change, 22, 29; membership, 5–6; space, 38, 40, 139; systems, 272
political subjects, 37, 45, 48. *See also* diasporic citizenship
politicization of struggle, 219–23
politics: accommodation involves, 145; of defining cultures, 24, 26; and emotional signs, 238–39; identity, 154–55, 166, 177; immigrant, 81–82; mixing languages as form of diasporic, 204–5; Turkish Ausländer's increasing presence in, 190. *See also* diasporic citizenship: politics of
Politics of Aesthetics, The (Rancière), 263
Polletta, Francesca, 27
Porter, John, 15
postcolonial space, 197

poster campaign, 260
post-migration, 82–83
Potsdam, 70
poverty, culture of, 92–93
power: accountability exposes dynamics of, 234; approach to, 16, 20–21, 22, 282; Ausländer discourses lack, 154; being aware of vehicles of, 270; diasporic accountability and, 233; diasporic citizenship centres on issues of, 273; diasporic citizenship disrupts relations of, 284; fluidity of relations of, 197; of Germanness vs Turkishness, 201; identity, ranking, and, 277; identity as source of productive, 238; inequalities within groups, 43; in Kreuzberg, 176–77; marginalized people's risks in challenging, 283; multiculturalism fails to address, 14–15, 290; role in determining acts and practices' effectiveness, 267; role in determining transgressions' effectiveness, 268; subject formation process conditioned by, 274; terms of reasonable deliberation shaped by, 271; third space as source of, 207; in "Where do you come from?," 91
practices, 248–62; and alliances to fight racism, 285; approach to, 6, 19, 22–23, 27, 248–49, 257–58; Aziza A's, 255–57, 263, 268; Çelik's, 252–55, 257, 263, 268; as contentious, 234; and contribution to citizenship studies, 280–82; decisiveness and assertiveness behind, 228; as dialogical, 265; diasporic citizen attributes applied through, 239; as disruptive, 273–74; effectiveness of, 267; Güngör's, 249–52, 257, 263, 268; on hostility-hospitality axis, 86; influence of, 271, 273, 277, 278; intersectional approach in shaping, 275; LGBTI+ community's, 258–62; point-to-plural meanings, 284; as

political and not political, 268; principles for inclusiveness suggested by, 276; provide platforms, 263; provide understanding of differences, 283; and structures of difference, 269–70; use of term, 248
Precious Big Sister, 256. See also Aziza A (participant)
Preston, Kayla, 140, 142
pride parades, 137–38, 178, 259, 266–67
private space, 139, 221, 272
privilege, 120–29; acquaintances, experts, and exceptions, 123–29; differing types and degrees of, 273; functioning of, 233; of Germanness, 118–19, 120; Germans desire to maintain, 144; of heterosexuals, 265; participants on difficult experiences as, 219–20; and principles for inclusiveness, 276; white people deny their, 142. See also domination
proximation: acts and, 239; and Ausländer as exceptions, 128; in diasporic spaces, 39(f), 85–86; dominant discourses and, 225; in friendships between Germans and Turkish Ausländer, 127; and map of belonging, 33; as pole on hostility-hospitality axis, 35; politics of, 145; privilege maintained through discourses of, 126
Puar, Jasbir, 139
public space, 221, 227, 263–65, 271–72
Purdie-Vaughns, Valerie, 24

race, 66, 88, 94, 181
racism: activism against, 248, 261–62; addressed in media portrayals of Turkish Ausländer, 58–59; alliances against, 284–85; toward Ausländer post-unification, 64, 68, 70, 227; elimination of, 125; increase in, 129–30, 284; institutional and structural, 135–36, 137, 247; vs Islamoracism, 138; within LGBTI+ community,

217–18, 259; #MeTwo stories, 246–48; and need for new forms of understanding, 280; participants on, 85, 129, 133–34, 139; toward people of colour, 119–20; and political space, 139; as product of domination, 85; in Sarrazin's book, 78–79; University of Leipzig study on, 131; white people's, 125, 129, 138. *See also* anti-Semiticism; discrimination; Islamoracism and Islamophobia; Orientalism; xenophobia

Rancière, Jacques, 263

ranking, 88–94; among Ausländer, 159; approach to, 120–21, 144–45; as biased process, 277; bodies and, 88, 90, 94, 101, 118–19; in colonialism, 141; and Germans' acquaintance with Turkish Ausländer, 126; Özdemir challenges, 244–45; participants challenge, 256–57; passive resistance and, 242–43; self-internalization of, 145; among Turks in Berlin, 210

Raschke, Christian, 142

Razack, Sherene, 107, 231–32, 235, 270, 274

ReachOut (counselling centre), 262

Rech, Heribert, 135

recruitment of guest workers, 52–55, 64, 74

reflexivity. *See* self-reflexivity

refugees: Eastern European, 63; laws on asylum, 67, 69; sexual orientation and, 266–67; Syrian, 82, 130, 131; violence against, 68. *See also* immigrants

resilience, 262

resistance: to assimilation, 41; disruption as, 283; German citizenship and, 186; goal of everyday antagonistic, 45; in homelessness and hostility quadrant, 46–47; mixing languages as act of, 204, 205; participants' understanding of, 228; to

racism and discrimination, 284–85; role in cultivating diasporicity, 20; role in move from homesickness to homelessness, 36; younger generation and, 192–93. *See also* acts; diasporic citizenship; practices

responsibility, 231, 233

right wing: "clash of civilizations" rhetoric used by, 130; CSU, 72, 76, 80; extremism of, 288; on headscarves, 112; Islamophobia promoted by, 80; jokes as fantasies of, 57; violence by, 70, 109, 132; vocabulary used by, 69. *See also* Alternative for Germany (AfD); neo-Nazis; Patriotic Europeans Against the Islamization of the West (PEGIDA)

rights: of Ausländer, 142, 219; of Black people, 27; participants demand, 189–90; sexual orientation, 135–36, 138–39; of Turkish Ausländer, 71–72, 82, 185–87

Roma, 119

Romeo and Juliet, 253

"Roots of Muslim Rage, The" (Lewis), 140–41

Rostock-Lichtenhagen, 68

rotation, 42, 59–60

ruptures. *See* acts; practices

Rushdie, Salman, 168

Russians, 247

Rygiel, Kim, 18

Safran, William, 156

Said, Edward: on civilizations, 142; on cooperation, 285; on culture, 25, 141; on living in diversity, 142–43; on Orientalism, 25, 107, 140, 141

Sanders, Leslie, 231

Sandoval, Chela, 230

Sarkozy, Nicolas, 79

Sarrazin, Thilo, 77–79, 130, 136, 140, 141, 142

Sassen, Saskia, 18

Saygılı, Bali, 213, 215, 216, 217–18, 265, 266–67
Schengen Area, 79
Schiffauer, Werner, 62
Schiller, Nina, 180
Schmalz-Jacobsen, Cornelia, 67
schooling. *See* education
Schroeder, Gerhard, 72, 182
Scott, James, 45, 46, 267
second-generation immigrants, 96–98
Seda (participant): on *Alamancı*, 158; as expert on Islam, 127; on her headscarf, 110, 242; Kurdish identity of, 105–6; on third space, 207; on World Cup, 177
segregation, 60, 61, 124
self-awareness: Ausländer and, 219–20, 227; as catalyst in becoming diasporic citizens, 224; external gaze implicated in, 113; generational differences in, 193; shifts after unification, 171; of Turkishness, 104, 105–6, 115–16, 128, 212–13. *See also* awareness
self-reflexivity, 230–34, 237, 283, 286
Selim (participant): on avoiding generalizations, 284; on children of suitcase children, 100; on generational differences, 167–68, 192–93; on his identity, 184; on his son's belonging, 194; on new Germans, 191; on racism, 129; on ranking, 94; on Sarrazin's book, 78
Selin (participant): on *Alamancı*, 157; on being a Turkish Berliner, 173; on estrangement, 181–82; on German citizenship, 186; on Germanness, 183; on Germans' acquaintance with Turkish Ausländer, 123, 125, 126; on headscarves, 113–14; on her educational experiences, 99–100; on her emotional connection with Türkiye and Turks, 152; on her family's mobility, 179; on mixing languages, 204–5; passive resistance

of, 241–43; on teenagers' defiance, 219; on use of *Ausländer*, 188; on World Cup, 177
Senkel, Günter, 253
Şenocak, Zafer, 169, 172, 190–91, 198, 200
7/7 terrorist attacks, 144
Sevgi (participant), 67
sexual orientation rights, 135–36, 138–39
Sey, Cem Rifat, 215
Seyhan, Azade, 6, 43, 148, 161–62, 163
shared citizenship, 271–73
silences, 240, 241, 242–43
silencing, 160, 161, 240
Simmel, Georg, 39
skin colour and tone: and internalization of stereotypes, 241; passive resistance offered by, 242–43; role in determining Germanness and Ausländerness, 41, 102, 115–19, 124; role in ranking, 90, 118–19
Skype, 7, 291n1
sly civility, 205
Smith, Anna Marie, 233
SO-36 (nightclub), 258, 268
soccer, 177–78, 192
Social Democratic–Green (SPD) government, 72, 73
social encounters. *See* diasporic encounters
social group (as term), 15
social media, 246–48
social sciences research: concept of first- and second-generation immigrants, 96; future work by, 285; on German education system, 62; 1960s writing on migration, 53; 1970s and 1980s writing on guest workers, 58; 1990s writing on Germanness vs non-Germanness, 69; portrayal of Turkish Ausländer in, 93, 97–98. *See also* discourses
Socialist Unity Party (SED), 50

solidarity: among communities of struggle, 280, 283–86; dialogical, 274–76; diasporic activists' view of, 47; for diasporic causes, 260; diasporic citizens seek, 263; dissolution of, 137; among German-born Turkish Ausländer and supporters, 221; against Islamoracism, 82; lack of feminist, 109; among light- and dark-skinned Turkish Ausländer, 118; across multiple lines, 233; among Othered people, 29; participants on, 9; among people of different diasporas, 120; among Turkish Ausländer and LGBTI+ community, 178–79; against xenophobia, 69

Solingen, 56, 68, 69, 70

Soviet Union, 50

Soysal, Levant, 58

spaces: of competing narratives of identity and belonging, 182; constituted by Germans and Ausländer, 40; of not belonging, 145; personal affiliation and, 201; political, 38, 40, 139; postcolonial, 197; public, 221, 227, 263–65, 271–72; role in interpreting bodies, 102; Turkish Ausländer and LGBTI+ community share, 179. See also diasporic spaces; third space

Spanish: language, 159–60, 257; people, 242–43

Spätaussiedler (ethnic German immigrants), 12, 63–64

Spivak, Gayatri Chakravorty, 156

splitting, 222

Spohn, Margret, 103

Statistisches Bundesamt (Federal Statistical Office), 82

Stavrakakis, Yannis, 148, 227

stereotypes: diasporic citizens' reluctance to impose, 274; in German literature, 55; Germanness preserved by, 87; getürkt, 103; about headscarves, 107; justify marginalization, 94; news writing perpetuates, 250;

participants challenge, 243–44, 253, 256, 262; participants internalize, 240–41; reinforced by researchers and policy makers, 97–98; about skin tone, 116, 119; Turkish Ausländer overcome, 192; about Turkish guest workers, 68; Turkish men, gay sexuality, and, 214. See also hostility–hospitality: stereotypes and habits of ignorance; media: portrayals of Turkish Ausländer in; Muslim women: stereotypes about; Turkish women: stereotypes about

stories. See narratives

strangers, 145

strategic essentialism, 147–48, 155–56

Structuring Immigration, Fostering Integration (report), 74

Suat (participant), 217

Submission (film), 76

subordination, 231–33, 269, 274

Suedeutsche Zeitung (newspaper), 227

suffering, 238–39

suitcase: children, 98–101; incident, 133, 134

Sullivan, Shannon, 48, 125, 129

Sunnis, 163, 237

supranationalist discourse, 130

SUSPECT (LGBTI+ organization), 138, 262

Sweden, 74

Syrian refugees, 82, 130, 131

Szanton-Blanc, Cristina, 180

Tandoğan, Hakan, 217, 258

Tarkan (participant), 217

Tauqir, Tamsila, 138

Taylor, Charles, 13–14, 24

TBB. See Turkish Organization of Berlin-Brandenburg (TBB)

Tecmen, Ayşe, 130

Temiz, Erkan, 65

terminology. See naming and labelling

terrorism, 80, 110, 133, 135, 144. See also 9/11

Index 341

theatrical plays, 253, 254–55
Therese (İrem's German neighbour), 243–44, 245–46
third space, 37, 187, 206–13, 222, 258
3Sat (TV network), 254
Toelken, Barre, 56
transgression, 268–69
translocality, 37, 177, 179–80
transmigrants, 179
transnationalism, 179
trickery, 103–4, 117
Trump, Donald, 131
Tully, James, 25
Tunç (participant): on Berlin Wall, 54; on challenging social norms, 242; on divisions in Berlin, 71; on first encounter with East Germans, 66; on German-born Turkish Ausländer, 228; on his journey to political activism, 220; on his relationships with Türkiye and Germany, 150, 151–52; on journalists, 266; on Kreuzberg, 171–72, 174–75, 176–77; on new Germans, 192; Şenocak, Zafer, 169–70, 171, 190–91, 198, 200; shows attributes of diasporic citizenship, 279, 280; on white Germans, 9
Turk (as term), 68
Turkish Ausländer: anniversary celebration of arrival of, 181; approach to, 50; arrival as guest workers in FRG, 52, 54; as "barbaric," 111; belonging with Germans, 32; characteristics passed down through generations, 93–94, 97, 99, 100; and criticism of Turkish culture, 221; discrimination at work, 76; diversity of, 11, 158–59, 206; education for Turkish Ausländer children, 60, 61–62, 98–100; first encounters with East Germans, 66; Germans' acquaintance with, 123–29, 210; hired for their knowledge of Turkish language, 191, 251; homeland concept questioned by, 96; image of guest workers, 53;

increase in hatred against, 157; jokes about, 56–57; in Kaya's work, 11–12; labelled as Muslims, 3, 7–8, 76, 83, 107, 131; legal rights of, 71–72, 82, 185–86; meanings of Turkishness for, 101–2; need for self-deprecation, 251; population statistics in Germany, 11, 55, 75, 292n1Ch2; portrayals in artistic works, 55, 58–59, 251–52, 253; portrayals in social research, 93, 97–98; ranking of, 94; reaction to changes in citizenship law, 73; response to light-skinned Turkish Ausländer, 117; sub-minorities within, 163. *See also* Ausländer; German-born Turkish Ausländer; Germanness: of Turkish Ausländer; media: portrayals of Turkish Ausländer in
Turkish Berliners (as term), 173
Turkish culture: as "defective," 189–90; gay-lesbian and, 258; Kreuzberg's, 174; LGBTI+ sexuality in, 213–17, 218, 259, 266; mixing with other cultures, 254; participants claim, 245–46; participants' emotional connection with, 150; people comfortable with German and, 211–12; at schools, 194; Şenocak on growing up in, 200; Turkish Ausländer hired for their knowledge of, 191; Turkish Ausländer's criticism of, 222–23
Turkish dance parties, 217, 258, 268
Turkish government, 52
Turkish language: desire to keep alive, 36, 167, 203; Germanness and, 182; in homesickness and hostility quadrant, 45; in Kreuzberg, 176; mixed with German, 165, 204–5, 209, 255–56; as motivating force for participants, 210, 229–30; participants claim, 245–46; participants' emotional connection with, 150–51, 152;

participants on lack of "sexiness" in, 257; and participants' struggle with Turkishness, 208; role in belonging among "my own people," 153; role in ranking among Turks in Berlin, 210; in schools, 124, 165–66, 167, 194, 202–3; Şenocak on learning, 200; Turkish Ausländer hired for their knowledge of, 191, 251

Turkish men: LGBTI+ sexuality and, 214–15, 217; stereotypes about, 108–9, 214; as threats, 109–10

Turkish Organization of Berlin-Brandenburg (TBB), 232, 260, 274

Turkish Parents' Association, 227

Turkish shops, 174

Turkish women: in participants' music, 255, 256; stereotypes about, 102, 108–9, 110–11, 114, 121, 127; unveiling of, 111–12

Turkishness
— Alamancı status and, 158
— in diasporic spaces, 45, 46
— diversity of, 158–64
— emotional aspects of, 149–50
— generational differences in, 167–68, 193
— as homogenizing project of nation-state, 153
— language classes foster, 166, 167
— participants on: desire to experience, 258; desire not to be reduced to, 270; and different treatment in housing market, 102; hopes for normalization of, 3, 134; injustice and, 219; minority discourse and, 105; physical and behavioural characteristics of, 101; pride in, 100, 177–78; question homogeneity of, 159; reject Turkishness, 207; skin colour and, 115–17; unclear relationship with, 201; vocabulary and, 189, 250
— passive resistance and, 242–43
— and politicization of struggle, 219
— as set of essential characteristics, 120

— speaking good Turkish as mark of, 205
— third space and, 207–13
— transforms Germanness, 200. See also Ausländerness; binaries: Ausländer/German and Turkish/German; hostility–hospitality: Turkishness and; self-awareness: of Turkishness

Türkiye
— education policies of, 99
— headscarves and identity of modern, 111, 114
— minority outsiders within, 46
— mixing languages in, 204–5
— myth of return to, 149, 156–57
— names given to children in, 195
— Otherness of the past in, 161–62, 163
— participants and: dubbed Alamancı in, 157–58; dubbed Almanlaşmak in, 184–85; emotional connection with place and people in, 150–51, 152–53, 154, 167–68, 206; feeling of Germanness when in, 183; fellow students and colleagues from, 211–12; forging of connections with, 149; internalize stereotypes about, 241; question connection with, 37; shape their own belonging in, 196
— ranking among Turks in Berlin and knowledge of, 210
— Turkish Ausländer living part time in, 179, 257
— vacationing in, 127, 151–52, 183
— in World Cup, 177–78
— younger generation's feelings toward, 193

Türkiyelism (type of discourse), 159, 162–63

tweets, 247

UK. See England and UK

unemployment rates, 74, 76

unification, German, 62–71; anti-Ausländer violence in aftermath of,

56, 64, 67–69, 70, 71, 109, 227; Berlin Wall and, 62, 64–66, 71; and Germanness of Turkish Ausländer, 169–72
unintegrated ethnic minorities, 44
University of Leipzig, 77, 131
Unter Uns (Among Us; newspaper column), 249–50, 263, 268
unveiling, 111–12
Ünzile (participant), 111
urban environments, 151
United States, 18, 140, 162

vacationing, 127, 151–52, 183, 292n5
Vallaud-Belkacem, Najat, 80
veils, 8, 80. *See also* headscarves
Veli (participant), 191, 203
Veronika (Russian tweeter), 247
Vertovec, Steven, 96, 149
Vertriebene (the expelled ones), 51
Vietnamese Ausländer, 67, 68
violence: anti-Ausländer, 132, 182, 233, 241, 288 (*see also* unification, German: anti-Ausländer violence in aftermath of); in dominant systems, 238; groups promoting anti-, 262
vocabulary. *See* naming and labelling
Volk, das (the people), 62–64, 83–84, 169

war, 237, 239
Wengeler, Martin, 69, 97
Werbner, Pnina, 38, 265
Wertheim, David J., 143
West, 288, 289
West Berlin, 50–51, 54, 66, 71, 118
West Berlin senate, 50
West Europeans, 90
West Germans, 65
West Germany, 66. *See also* Federal Republic of Germany (FRG)
Westdeutscher Rundfunk (TV network), 55
Western civilization, 140; culture, 158, 287

Westerners, 222
"Where do you come from?" (question asked of Ausländer): Ausländer never ask, 152; in Canada, 212; as challenge, 149; in England vs Germany, 210–11; German privilege and, 120; identity tension in, 184; implied in term *Ausländer*, 87; outsiderness and, 94–95; and reclaiming integration, 189; role in ranking, 91, 94, 159; younger generation's response to, 193
white Germans, 9, 78, 247
white people, 125, 129, 142
white supremacy, 115, 118, 138. *See also* neo-Nazis
whiteness, 233, 248
Wirth, Louis, 44
Worbs, Susanne, 96
work force, 202
worker exchanges, 52, 64. *See also* guest workers
World Cup, 177–78
World Have Your Say (TV program), 77–78
worldism, 160, 282

xenophobia: in aftermath of unification, 64, 67–69, 70; CSU's, 72; guest worker system promotes, 53; toward guest workers, 54–55; increase in, 157; jokes as, 56–57; in reaction to *Black Virgins*, 254; in survey of German residents, 77. *See also* anti-Semiticism; discrimination; Islamoracism and Islamophobia; Orientalism; racism

yabancı (foreigner), 12, 181
yabancı kökenli (foreigner origin), 88
Yeğenoğlu, Meyda, 107, 111
Yeliz (participant), 113–14, 156–57, 177
Yener (participant), 203
Yeşim (participant), 113–14

Yıldız (participant): on Ausländerness, 92, 102; on belonging, 207; on Germans' acquaintance with Turkish Ausländer, 126–27; on her emotional connection with Türkiye, 150–51, 206; on jokes about Turkish Ausländer, 57; on mixing languages, 204; passive resistance of, 242–43; on ranking, 88, 89; Turkishness of, 103
Yılmaz-Günay, Koray, 261

Yorukoglu, Ilgin, 135, 138–39
Young, Robert, 205
Yuval-Davis, Nira, 221

Zaimoğlu, Feridun, 204, 253, 254
Zehra (participant), 87, 206
Zeynep (participant), 117
Zinn, Alexander, 137
Zionism, 143
Zivilcourage Prize, 137–38

Basic Cinematography